More Praise for This Book

"*ATD's Handbook for Consultants* is another winner! Packed with guidance from more than 35 renowned experts, this book is full of brilliance and inspiration. Read it!"
—Ken Blanchard, Co-Author, *The New One Minute Manager* and *Simple Truths of Leadership*

"I remember my move from graduate school to working in a consultancy. I had academic expertise but needed a guide to help me unlock the consulting relationships in front of me. This handbook would have been a lifesaver! The content and tools meet you where you are on your growth continuum. You will speed your productivity as you access the world's leading advisors in our field and amplify your career."
—Tacy M. Byham, PhD, CEO, Development Dimensions International (DDI)

"What a compendium of consulting information. With the level of detail for those that are starting out in this business, there is no more authoritative source. This handbook nails down all the essential elements of the consulting business."
—RADM (ret.) JB Godwin III, President and CEO, Mercy Medical Angels

"The consulting experts who contributed the tips and tools to these chapters make it an invaluable resource for anyone at any stage in their consulting career. It is the ultimate guide to helping you be the best consultant you can be for yourself and your clients."
—Jeff Hayes, President and CEO, The Myers-Briggs Company

"This book is an absolute treasure for any experienced consultant, brand-new consultant, and anyone in between. Elaine has used the power of her own established consulting career to gain real gems from her wide circle of colleagues. A must-have for your bookshelf."
—Bev Kaye, Author, Keynote Speaker, and Recipient, ATD Lifetime Achievement Award

"Elaine Biech expertly navigates the complexities of consulting, offering insights and strategies that are both innovative and grounded in theory and real-world experience. This book will equip you with the tools and knowledge to make your practice successful."
—Kimo Kippen, Aloha Learning Advisors; former CLO, Hilton Hotels and Resorts

T0291410

"Looking for a rehash of traditional consulting best practices? You've come to the wrong place. Instead, Elaine and her cadre of performance and mission-based contributors offer powerful new consulting methods that promise to keep up with a rapidly changing world."
—Jim Kirkpatrick, Co-Author, *Kirkpatrick's Four Levels of Training Evaluation*; Senior Consultant, Kirkpatrick Partners

"*ATD's Handbook for Consultants* brings together experienced consultants and luminaries in the field, offering both a long-term perspective and a present-day look at the business of consulting. Whether you're new to the business or an old-timer like me, this is a book you'll want to keep within arm's reach for years to come. I know that I will."
—Jim Kouzes, Co-Author, *The Leadership Challenge*; Fellow of the Doerr Institute for New Leaders, Rice University.

"In today's complex and competitive environment, it is essential for consultants to be successful and deliver the results desired by clients. This book will show you how."
—Patti and Jack Phillips, CEO and Chair, ROI Institute; Co-Authors, *Maximizing the Value of Consulting* and *The Consultant's Scorecard*, 2nd Ed.

"Become a trusted advisor, shape business strategy, or even hang out your shingle as an independent consultant with the *ATD's Handbook for Consultants* as your go-to guide. This compilation of insights from consulting trailblazers will help you find your niche, your network, and your income as a TD consultant."
—Becky Pike Pluth, CEO, The Bob Pike Group

"Elaine has been an invaluable asset to AGI as we have scaled our business and invested in the development of our leadership team of over 100 managers and executives. Her deep knowledge, extensive consulting experience, and vast network of talented experts make her an unparalleled authority on leadership in the corporate world."
—Craig Rohde, President and CEO, Architectural Graphics

"This is the ultimate road map for navigating the exciting world of consulting! Whether you're a fresh-faced newcomer or a seasoned pro, this handbook sheds light on the hidden secrets that make consultants truly shine. Prepare to unlock doors to success, boost your confidence, and dominate the growing gig economy—one insightful page at a time."
—Martin Schneider, President and CEO, Center for Creative Leadership

"This book will supersize your consulting, intellectual capital, extend your career, and grow your business for years to come. All you need to know about being a results-focused, successful consultant is in this gem of a book. Thank you, Elaine!"
—James Smith Jr., CSP, CEO and President, Dr. James Smith Jr.

"You've got smarts and ambitions: That's a great start, but it's not enough. This book offers many insights and tools to better serve your clients, amplify your impact, and keep your humanity."
—Michael Bungay Stanier, Author, *The Coaching Habit*

"This book is the one I wish I had before I started my consulting business, and it will make a remarkable difference in how others start, run, and thrive in their business in the future."
—Eddie Turner, Leadership Consultant, EDDIE TURNER

"From my experience in the military working with consultants, I find this handbook highly valuable. It covers all the key issues to take you to consulting success."
—Karlheinz Viereck, Lieutenant General (Ret.), Germany, Head NATO's Joint Forces Education, Training, and Exercises

"If there was ever a 'can't miss' book, this is it. Elaine Biech has picked the most profound topics for aspiring novices and seasoned practitioners and enlisted the most acclaimed experts to reveal their wisdom on the key elements. That recipe will greatly benefit anyone aspiring to be a more successful consultant, regardless of where they are in that journey."
—Jack Zenger, CEO, Zenger|Folkman

Elaine Biech, Editor

ATD's Handbook for Consultants

PRESS
Alexandria, VA

ATD Press is an internationally renowned source of insightful and practical information on talent development, training, and professional development.

ATD Press
1640 King Street
Alexandria, VA 22314 USA

Ordering information: Books published by ATD Press can be purchased by visiting ATD's website at td.org/books or by calling 800.628.2783 or 703.683.8100.

Library of Congress Control Number: 2023952415

ISBN-10: 1-957157-34-8
ISBN-13: 978-1-957157-34-4
e-ISBN: 978-1-957157-35-1

ATD Press Editorial Staff
Director: Sarah Halgas
Manager: Melissa Jones
Content Manager, Learning & Development: Jes Thompson
Developmental Editor: Jack Harlow
Production Editor: Katy Wiley Stewts
Cover Designer: Shirley Raybuck

Text Design: PerfecType, Nashville, TN
Printed by BR Printers, San Jose, CA

This handbook is dedicated to Edgar H. Schein, whose perception and insight continue to shape the world of OD and TD today.

1999 Recipient of ATD's Lifetime Achievement Award
March 5, 1928–January 26, 2023

Contents

Section III. Delivering Results: The Work of a Consultant

Section IV. Developing Business: Finding and Keeping Clients

Foreword
DANA ALAN KOCH AND ELLIOTT MASIE

Any handbook for talent development consultants would be incomplete without a discussion about generative artificial intelligence (AI) tools. On the other hand, such a discussion also runs the risk of quickly becoming obsolete, simply because the technology is advancing so rapidly. So, what is an author to do?

As we pondered how to approach AI in this handbook, we decided to think outside the box. That's when inspiration struck. What would happen if we, the authors, came up with some prompts that you, the reader, could put into the AI system of your choice (OpenAI's ChatGPT, Microsoft Copilot, Google Gemini, or any of the new tools or technologies coming to the field monthly)? And what if those prompts were designed to help you understand the impact of generative AI on TD consultants? Well, if we did that, the content would be fresh and current each time you entered a prompt. What better way to get your creative juices flowing?

Every chapter and topic in this handbook could stimulate a prompt for you to enter into a generative AI tool to gain deeper insight. We invite you to actively use these tools to continue learning about the implications of this evolving technology on your work.

An Experiment

Before we go any further, let's conduct an experiment. Ready? Open your favorite generative AI tool and enter the following prompt:

> List at least three ways in which AI would enhance and three ways in which AI might decrease the revenue streams for consultants in the learning and development world.

Now compare your answer to the one we received from ChatGPT:

AI has the potential to significantly transform the landscape for consultants in the learning and development (L&D) sector. Here are three ways AI could enhance revenue streams, followed by three ways it might decrease them:

Ways AI Could Enhance Revenue Streams for L&D Consultants

1. **Personalized learning solutions:** AI can analyze individual learning needs, allowing consultants to offer highly personalized and effective learning solutions. This can lead to higher client satisfaction and retention.
2. **Efficiency and scalability:** AI-driven tools can automate routine tasks, analyze data quickly, and handle large volumes of learners simultaneously. This can open up new markets and reduce costs, increasing profitability.
3. **Data-driven insights:** AI can provide deep insights into learning effectiveness, helping consultants optimize their programs and demonstrate their value to clients, potentially leading to higher demand and pricing power.

Ways AI Might Decrease Revenue Streams for L&D Consultants

1. **Market saturation with automated solutions:** As AI-driven L&D solutions become more prevalent, the market may become saturated, making it harder for consultants to compete without significant differentiation.
2. **Reduced need for customized training:** With the rise of sophisticated, off-the-shelf AI learning platforms, there might be a decreased demand for customized training solutions typically offered by consultants.
3. **Depersonalization of learning:** Over-reliance on AI could lead to a perception of depersonalization in learning experiences. This might reduce the appeal of AI-based solutions when the human element is crucial.

In summary, while AI presents significant opportunities for growth and innovation in the L&D consulting sector, it also brings challenges and the potential for market disruption. Consultants will need to adapt to these changes, leveraging the benefits of AI while also addressing its limitations and the evolving needs of their clients.

The AI-generated response you received will be different from ours, and it will be different if you ask the same question in a few weeks or in a few years. Why? Because the technology is advancing and learning all the time. This example shows why most content describing how to use generative AI (or any type of AI) could quickly become obsolete with the next leap in the technology.

Prompts for You

To gain fresh thinking on the benefits, impact, and potential of AI in the world of talent development consulting, we've crafted a list of prompts for you to ask. As you review the responses generated, keep in mind that they may contain bias and made-up content (hallucinations). Also, consider any legal implications of using AI-generated content.

With these warnings, try a few of these prompts or come up with your own:

- How can AI help me grow my L&D consultancy business?
- How do I know if I am ready to become an independent consultant in the area of talent development?
- How can I best harness the power of AI technologies to serve my TD clients?
- What are five practical ways I could use AI to increase my customer base as a talent development consultant?
- What are the potential challenges and ethical considerations that talent development consultants might face in incorporating AI into training methodologies? Suggest strategies to address these challenges.
- How might the demand for specific skill sets change in the workforce due to the integration of generative AI, and how can consultants help organizations address these evolving skills requirements?
- How might generative AI influence the measurement of training effectiveness? Suggest measurement considerations that TD consultants should focus on in an AI-driven landscape.
- Write a chapter on the future role of generative AI in the work of consultants in the learning and leadership development fields. Include a vision for the future, benefits, words of caution, case studies, and practical examples, along with a list of ways L&D consultants will need to adjust their mindset.

If that list does not satisfy your curiosity, give this prompt a try:

> As a consultant in talent development and learning, I want to understand the implications of ChatGPT on my role. What insightful questions would you pose to ChatGPT?

Going Beyond AI

Despite the powerful, and yes, ever-growing, capacity of generative AI, it is just one of several tools and resources that consultants can (and should) turn to for guidance on how to run a successful consulting business. In the end, there's nothing like the real-world experience of an effective consultant—the know-how gleaned from years of helping clients solve their L&D and business needs while putting their heart, sweat, and tears into turning their business into a thriving enterprise. That's what this handbook brings to the table, and it's something that generative AI alone cannot.

Once again, by tapping her network of consulting superheroes, Elaine Biech has set a new standard for excellence for a book on what it takes to flourish as a consultant. What sets this handbook apart is its meticulous organization, thoughtful structure, clarity, and comprehensiveness. The helpful section overviews and anchoring luminary chapters set the stage for a wellspring of deep insights, practical approaches, and invaluable advice from consultants actively navigating the trenches. Whether you're a seasoned consultant seeking to build your business, increase your revenue, or refine your craft in other ways—or if you're a newcomer eager to build a strong foundation—this book is not just a guide; it's a road map to success in the dynamic world of consulting.

By picking up this book, you're equipping yourself to learn from some of the most masterful consultants our industry has ever seen. And that's what we hope you do—absorb the expert advice, put it into action, and watch your business bloom.

Dana Alan Koch is a co-host of the *Learning Geeks* podcast and director of Accenture's Institute for the Applied Learning Sciences. **Elliott Masie** is chair of the MASIE Learning Foundation.

Acknowledgments

It is an honor to edit *ATD's Handbook for Consultants*. Creating a handbook requires a team of dedicated and talented professionals who are willing to work long hours and meet outrageously short timelines with incredibly high-quality standards. Fortunately, our brilliant team produced a premier product that is practical and provocative, challenging and inspiring. Without these dedicated people, this book would not be in your hands today.

- First and most important, thanks to the almost four dozen chapter and sidebar authors who responded to our call for content. We appreciate your expertise. You each accepted the topic we needed, conducted your research, and created content that enhances the overall purpose of the handbook and meets the needs of our readers. Lead authors are listed in the table of contents, but you will also find sidebar authors and contributing authors throughout.

- Thank you to the five luminary guest authors—Peter Block, Marshall Goldsmith, Ann Herrmann-Nehdi, Peter Schein, and Michael Zipursky—whose chapters set the tone for each section. You are busy, and that's an understatement. Yet you took the time to share your consulting wisdom with our readers. A huge thank you to each of you.

- A special thank you to Peter Schein, whose father, Edgar, passed away just as we started the handbook. You stepped in and wrote an inspiring and personal tribute to your father that will encourage consultants—especially experienced consultants—to align their professional and personal lives.

- Thank you to the ATD staff who recommended timely topics and awesome authors. A special shout out to Justin Brusino who was our greatest backer for this handbook. He values all the ATD members who are consultants as well as those who are contemplating a consulting career. Woohoo, Justin!

- We are grateful to everyone who helped ensure that this handbook represented a diverse audience. Our diversity reaches all attributes. We are excited to debut a number of first-time authors.

- Writing content is the first big task, but honing it into a clear, concise, coherent, consistent, and grammatically correct message is the critical second task. It is an honor to work with a talented editorial staff that includes Jack Harlow, Melissa Jones, and Katy Wiley Stewts. You are the heart of the project that makes all of us look good!
- Of course, you can't tell a book by its cover—but a great cover grabs your attention. Thank you, Shirley Raybuck, for grabbing our attention with an exciting and expressive cover.
- Finally, thanks to Dan Greene for your encouragement as I take on these exciting projects.

And of course, thank you to ATD, Tony, Justin, Jennifer, and Courtney, who continue to offer me projects that allow me to grow, develop, and be a lifelong ATD volunteer.

Introduction

ELAINE BIECH

Are you thinking about starting your own consulting practice? Well, your timing couldn't be better. The gig economy is in full swing, and it has forever changed the world of work as we know it. Many people are leaving traditional nine-to-five jobs for more agile roles. The shift away from the full-time employment model toward contract, freelance, and other nontraditional arrangements has made it easier for those who prefer a more flexible, self-directed work life. Consulting is at the top of the list of career paths for talent development professionals and others who have unique skill sets and expertise—like you.

In addition, it's becoming easier to get consulting work. Many companies can't fill their hiring needs, and they embrace the experience and flexibility that consultants bring. As the workplace continues to change, talented consultants are increasingly in demand because companies can't do everything in-house. In our fast-paced world, companies lack the specialized skills and expertise to handle their growing needs, and they often don't have the staffing flexibility to complete special projects that require more employee hours. They appreciate the value of the consultant's fresh new ideas and outside opinions, as well as the speed and efficiency that comes with bringing in an expert. No wonder the Bureau of Labor Statistics cites consulting as one of the fastest growing industries of this decade at $320+ billion and growing! Consulting is more respected than ever.

While the decision to become a consultant may seem easy, the tricky part is knowing how to become a *successful* consultant. It isn't the right choice for everyone. Yes, consulting can be incredibly rewarding and lucrative, but new consultants need to understand its enigmas to truly be successful. This handbook unveils a few of the mysteries that separate successful consultants from mediocre ones. Whether you're just starting out or celebrating a decade or more in the business, you'll find something in this handbook to empower and inspire. Those new to the industry will gain clarity about consulting and insights to help them understand what they're getting into. Experienced consultants will find different ways to view what they do and how they can be more effective at growing their businesses.

What Can You Expect From This Handbook?

ATD's Handbook for Consultants is a definitive guide that strives to answer all your burning questions. We have worked hard to make this publication:

- **Authoritative.** Most of our authors have been in the consulting field for decades. We are honored that Peter Block—who wrote the seminal guide to consulting, *Flawless Consulting*, more than 40 years ago, now in its fourth edition—contributed the opening chapter. You'll also hear from experts such as Rita Bailey, Holly Burkett, Wendy Gates Corbett, Jonathan Halls, Cindy Huggett, Bill Treasurer, Sharon Wingron—well, check out the table of contents for yourself. I think you'll be impressed with the author lineup.
- **Broad.** A handbook must be expansive enough to appeal to people at different stages of their career. For example, new consultants will want answers to basic questions (such as, what unique skills will I need, how should I name my business, and why should I select consulting as a profession?). Consultants who have been in the business for a while, on the other hand, may want to peruse some stretch topics (such as the challenge of working in and on your business at the same time).
- **Complete.** This may be the biggest challenge when you think about a handbook and the breadth of the consulting field. Consultants need to know a lot about their area of expertise, but it gets complicated. To be successful, you also need to know about running a business, what's required to be an entrepreneur, and how to market and sell your consulting services. We've got you covered with several business topics, ranging from how to establish a 21st-century consultant's office to creating a business strategy.
- **Practical.** Between its two covers, this handbook provides new tools and more efficient practices, such as how to write a winning proposal or develop passive income. It is also supported by more than four dozen additional tools from the chapter authors, which you can download for free from the ATD website. Free tools—now that's exciting! In addition, our authors have also provided more than 100 consulting tips, which are embedded throughout the chapters.
- **Implementable.** To ensure you can immediately put these ideas to the test, each chapter ends with a section titled "Actions You Can Take Now" to give you a quick start in the right direction.

- **Informative.** This handbook explores a variety of career options beyond being an independent consultant. There's a chapter on joining a boutique consulting practice and another on what you'll learn working for a large consulting company.

Starting a new career or growing your business can seem daunting, but this handbook provides quick access to the information you need without searching through multiple books, articles, and online sources. I believe this handbook is a great place to start, with its collection of topics, the content in each chapter, and the ease with which you will be able to find what you need. It will take you along your journey to becoming the most successful consultant you can be.

What Content Will Support Your Consulting Plans?

The 35 chapters in this book hold a vast amount of knowledge no matter where you are in your career. And if something sparks your curiosity, you'll find contact information for each author so you can network with them to explore their topics in more depth.

We've divided this handbook into five sections: exploring consulting, getting started, delivering results, developing business, and focusing on your future. Each section introduction includes commentary about key upcoming themes and some "ebbvice" (four to seven actions you can take to address the topics). Much like the consulting tips and activities you will find in each chapter, these actions are easily implementable.

The chapter following each section introduction was written by a consulting luminary. Together, Peter Block, Marshall Goldsmith, Ann Herrmann-Nehdi, Peter Schein, and Michael Zipursky have more than 200 years of consulting experience. Their chapters provide a valuable personal perspective about what's most important for you to know.

Where Should You Start in the Handbook?

With so many good topics, how do you know where to begin? Start by determining where you are in your consulting career. Are you still toying with the idea of becoming a consultant? If so, turn to section I. The authors here provide much to think about before you make the move. If you've decided to move into consulting, peruse sections II and III for ideas about breaking into the profession, what you might offer your clients, and how to name your business. If you've been consulting for a few years but want to achieve more, check out section IV for tips on attracting more clients through marketing, networking, sales, and even volunteering. If you've been a consultant for a while, turn to section V, which challenges you to view your business differently.

Remember to check the list of resources in the back, which were all recommended by our authors. Many are directly related to consulting, but I urge you to move beyond that to other topics. For example, if you are feeling uncertain or fearful about moving into consulting, consider reading Bill Treasurer's book about taking risks. Other books may seem like a stretch but explore the skills and attitude you'll need as a consultant. For example, Paulo Coelho's *The Alchemist* explores themes of personal growth, destiny, and the journey toward one's dreams. Although it's a work of fiction and not explicitly about consulting, *The Alchemist*'s themes and lessons—such as uncertainty, learning from experience, navigating challenges, persistence, and resilience—encompass much of what you'll require to be successful in the consulting world.

Another option is to review and download the online tools, which may help you work through some of your questions. You will find checklists, assessments, templates, planning forms, and other tools to help you make decisions and create your next steps.

Ready for Answers?

No matter what stage of your consulting career you're in today or how or where you start in *ATD's Handbook for Consultants*, you're sure to find practical actions you can implement and thought-provoking concepts you can mull over before you make your next move. If you want to become the best consultant you can be, the centuries of expertise found in this handbook provide an invaluable investment in your professional development and your future.

I'll close out this section with some food for thought. Have you ever wondered what other consultants think is critical to being an excellent consultant? I've been collecting responses to this question for years. Here's what's currently in the top 10:

1. Knows how to methodically diagnose any problem, structure, organization, or even a person
2. Creates and nurtures a personal and professional bond with all clients
3. Is constantly learning, growing, and developing; is well-read
4. Never misses a deadline
5. Can prepare a compelling report with clear, helpful graphics

6. Understands and practices entrepreneurial skills
7. Admires the client and becomes a true friend
8. Is ethical above all else
9. Is technologically competent
10. Knows how to run or participate in a meeting with equal effectiveness

SECTION I

Exploring Consulting
So, You Want to Be a Consultant?

Thinking about moving into consulting? This section delivers a wealth of knowledge from experts who have experienced the switch. If you are still in the training field, Rita Bailey identifies the consulting skills that every trainer should have, making you a better trainer as well as preparing you for a consulting profession. Then, three of our consulting authors—Sarah Cannistra, Maurine Kwende, and Bill Treasurer—share what you need to know before making the transition into consulting. Cindy Huggett rounds out the section by reminding you to clarify your why—why do you want to be a consultant?

As Peter Block, this section's luminary consulting author, points out in his *block*buster (I had to do that) book, *Flawless Consulting*, a consultant's success requires concentration on two processes:

- Being as authentic as you can be at all times with the client
- Attending directly (with words and actions) to the business of each stage of the consulting process

Block believes that consulting is a human endeavor about building relationships that matter, and for the past 40 years, his book has been the go-to guide to building trusting and meaningful partnerships between consultants and their clients. In his luminary chapter, he states that, "The consulting process begins with four questions: What matters to you? What are you concerned about? What outcomes are you after? What did you try that didn't work?"

5 Methods to Guide Your Decision

Now it's time for you to be a consultant to yourself. Before you jump into consulting, you'll need to answer Block's four questions about your professional situation. But how can you gain that insight? Try these five methods to help guide your decision about becoming a consultant.

1. Interview a Consultant

To learn more about what you are getting yourself into, interview a consultant. Consider it your take-a-consultant-to-lunch assignment. Gain as much information as you can about what it's like to be in their shoes by asking questions like:

- How did you get started?
- Why did you decide to become a consultant?
- What do you do for clients? What problems do you solve?
- What's a typical project like? A typical client?
- What's the biggest lesson you've learned as a consultant?
- What's a typical day or week like for you?
- What are the work-life balance issues for a consultant, and how do you address them?
- What's the greatest challenge for you as a consultant? The most frustrating?
- What would you do differently if you could start your consulting practice over again?
- How can I best prepare myself to become a consultant?
- What would you miss the most if you quit consulting?
- What should I have asked about that I didn't?

You will not be able to ask every question listed here, so make sure you're asking those that are most important to you. And I'm sure you will think of others too!

2. Assess Your Skills

You are skilled and knowledgeable about the area you will consult in. To be a successful consultant, you'll also need to know the consulting process (reading *Flawless Consulting* and chapter 15 of this book will help) and become an expert in communication, problem solving, managing meetings, designing surveys and materials, team building, and facilitating.

Remember that you are in charge of a business, so you need to be skilled in business development (sales, marketing, and niche identification) and business management. Among myriad other details, you'll need to determine a business structure, understand office technology, track expenses, project income, understand your financial data, develop contracts, and select a banker, an accountant, and an attorney.

Probably the most important is to check your mindset. What kind of self-talk are you practicing? Carol Dweck has given credence to the concept of a growth mindset. Her research supports the idea that what we think becomes reality—especially when it comes to our talents and abilities. Your mindset about consulting will permeate everything you do.

3. Talk to Your Family

Sit down and have a frank discussion with your spouse, significant other, roommate, or family. Block out enough time to present your idea, your thoughts about the transition, your vision, and any possible concerns. Ask them to think beyond everything going smoothly—what if things go wrong? Having a home office sounds great, but will they accept you being underfoot all day? How supportive will they be if the big deal doesn't come through and you need to dig into the family savings to stay afloat? How supportive will they be after you skip yet another family outing because you have to work on Saturday. You need your family's support—100 percent of it.

4. Establish a Startup Budget

Determine your financial requirements, including your startup costs, your annual expenses, and your income. Begin by identifying everything you need to open your consulting practice—equipment, furniture, an office, supplies, legal support, and so on. Then determine what your costs will be for one year.

Next think about your revenue and what income you will require. Calculate your salary, taxes, benefits, and business expenses for one year. Be thorough! Although it's time-consuming this will give you an accurate picture of what you'll need to earn to break even.

You can also use what I call the "3x rule" (pronounced "three times rule"), which provides a fast and relatively accurate estimate of what you should be aiming to make in a year. For example, if you want a salary of $90,000, you will need to bill three times that amount, or $270,000. Why is it that high? Well, you'll pay yourself $90,000 in salary, but you'll use the rest to cover:

- **Fringe benefits,** such as insurance, FICA, unemployment taxes, workers' compensation, and vacation time
- **Overhead,** such as advertising, rent, professional development, telephone, supplies, clerical support, and management
- **Down time,** including days when you are traveling, on vacation, or in training development; you'll also require time to prepare for your clients

In addition, any good business should be looking for a profit. As a startup company working out of your home, you may be able to follow something closer to a 2x or 2.5x rule. However, while it may seem tempting, I caution you not to cut your budget too closely. If it's too tight, you may experience cash-flow problems.

Finally, I recommend having at least six months of living expenses set aside that you can tap into as you start.

5. Share Your Plans

Begin networking with others to gain their insight. You likely don't have to have a business plan yet. But even if you do, it may be informed by what you learn from your discussions with others. Who should you talk to? I recommend:

- People you know who work inside organizations that hire consultants. Learn how the consulting relationship is perceived from the employees' perspective.
- People who know what you do and what skills you possess. Determine if they think you could consult with what you know.
- Friends and relatives who know you personally. Learn what they think you are good at and what you need to hone.
- Your professional association network. Discover who is consulting or who needs a consultant. Learn more about the trends in your specific industry.

Hopefully these five methods will provide you with the insight you need to make the decision about becoming a consultant. In the end, however, I believe that the most important reason to become a consultant is because you want to.

CHAPTER 1

What Is Still True

PETER BLOCK, *LUMINARY CONSULTING AUTHOR*

It began with the director of an IT department back in 1976. I was working in the training and development department of Esso Research and Engineering before it became Exxon.

At the time, Esso was starting to build out its organization development (OD) function. It was exciting because we were at the forefront of the OD movement. The company had consultants, National Training Lab involvement, and even decided to train internal people to run T-groups—and I was a part of it.

Then, the IT director came to me with a problem. His organization was making recommendations to line managers, but the managers weren't doing anything with them. By then, he'd gotten acquainted with our work, so he came to us and said, "Could you put together a workshop for our people? We know our recommendations are good, but nobody's acting on them." We created a workshop for his team around having impact when you don't have control. We ran it for IT for a few years, and they seemed to like it. So, we decided that maybe we should offer it more broadly. We did, and we've been running it ever since.

A Flawless Start

Somewhere along the way, I gave a talk, and a publisher came up to me and said, "Peter, that was a nice talk. Have you ever thought of writing a book?" And I said, "No, I don't even believe in ideas. I don't have a brain; I have a mouth. I can talk and break people into small groups. Leave me alone." He came back six months later, "Peter, would you like to write a book?" "No."

Six months after that he came back and said, "Peter, I'll guarantee you $20,000 if you write the book and at the end of two years, if you don't have royalties in that amount, I'll make up the difference." I said, "You got yourself an author."

I wrote the book, and it was fun. Those days, it was a typewriter, whiteout, and carbon copies. I had to have a hard copy done by a typist and it cost me, I don't know, $500 or so. I sent the publisher the book and then he went bankrupt. So, it sat on a shelf for a couple of years until Pfeiffer and Jones bought it.

I was embarrassed by the book because it was so practical. I was doing organization development at the time, and my partners were very conceptual. But I wrote it with a cookbook in mind. I didn't know if what I was doing as a consultant was relevant to staff, but I had a suspicion it was. So, we published the book.

And that's how *Flawless Consulting* came into being.

What Is Consulting?

Consulting is a human endeavor about building relationships that matter. In *Flawless Consulting*, I found a way to give a concrete, tactile structure to building relationships in a form that is accessible to technical people, marketing people, those in HR, and anyone else doing relationship-based work. (Maybe even bosses.) Consulting has everything to do with leadership. You can call it relational or participative leadership, but leadership has the core elements of needing a relationship, needing to deal with resistance, and needing to communicate what's working instead of what's not working. I go through the same basic process in *Flawless Consulting* and our workshops, and it's what leaders must do well every day.

Ultimately, consulting skills are not just for consultants. They are for everyone who must cultivate relationships at work. Consulting is about being willing to focus on relationships and realize that people make decisions based on what it's like to be with you, not on your background, your credentials, your history, or who you've worked with. Everybody's introduced as if their resume means something. In reality, it means nothing. What matters is what it's like to be with you as a consultant in this moment.

In most workplaces, the business perspective and organizational life treats relationships as a means to an end. In consulting, relationships are the point: They are the way to have influence and see the world change. Workplaces are human systems—no matter how many innovations occur, relationships are essential for having impact. Today's digital world is seen as a miracle, but the printing press was also a miracle. The telephone was a miracle. Our humanity is still at stake, and the *Flawless Consulting* process gives consultants a structured way to build relationships without demanding discomfort.

There are ways we show up that have little impact—like when we show up to work as a pair of hands, there for the sake of the client. We acquiesce too easily. We seek to be helpful, not impactful. However, we're not serving the client if we don't meet them as an equal. I recall one occasion when I went to meet a client at his office. The assistant greeted me and said, "Ed is in there waiting for you." I walk in, the room is empty, and I'm thinking, "Whoops, I'm losing it. He's not behind the desk." Suddenly, the wall opens, and he has his own bedroom and bathroom built into his office. And I think "Wow, I'm with somebody important." Even in the face of that, I still showed up as an equal.

The Steps

The consulting process begins with four questions:
- What matters to you?
- What are you concerned about?
- What outcomes are you after?
- What did you try that didn't work?

After listening and restating what I've heard, I ask, "Not only do I want to know what you want for this project, but what do you want from me in terms of how I work with you?"

It's not always an easy question, but once you hear the answer, you have the right to say, "Well, I'm unable to fill some of those expectations. And if I did, it would not serve you in the way you want."

Finally, you can say, "Now, here's what I want from you." In asking for what you want, whether you're talking to the company president, the CEO, or a first-line manager, you've treated them as a human, and they can say yes or no. The radical thing about this thinking is that you're recognizing that your wants matter and you can show up as a collaborator and partner with the client. You're not simply a pair of hands or an expert.

As you reach an agreement, ask yourself, "Will it work the way it's set up now?" If you don't think it will, but you can't say no, minimize the risk or exposure. In the exchange of wants, the capacity to express doubts, and to say, "I don't think that's going to serve you," or "I don't think that will work," is what partners do for each other. I've never seen a client who wanted something done who wouldn't be responsive to that moment if I didn't preface it by saying, "I hope you don't mind but there's some things that I want from you under certain conditions." Or sometimes I just say, "Well, I got it. Here's what you want. Let me tell you what I want to make this successful."

Consulting Tip

Know what you want before meeting with a new client. This may be difficult to express if you are new to consulting. If that's the case, plan time immediately after every first client encounter to reflect on what happened. Note your responses so your learning can continue:

- What does my client want?
- How will I deliver it?
- What do I want?
- How clear was I?

The words here matter. You are talking about a want, not a need. There's a prayer and a pleading in saying, "I need" because someone can't say no to a need. Asking for what you want is what adults do with each other. It can be softened in your own way, but the point is that you have a right to ask for it. At the same time, ask the client, "How is this going? Are you getting what you want out of this conversation?"

If you get resistance, ask, "What are you concerned about?" but don't argue with them. Resistance means you are getting somewhere because they're taking you seriously by arguing with you. This is what partners do. And if you ever find yourself explaining the same thing for the third time, call for a break because you're starting to argue and there's nothing to argue about. If clients give you a hard time, take their side. Anger, overconfidence, leaning on your resume and what you did elsewhere, trying to talk people out of their position instead of helping them elaborate on their doubts, and not asking them about their role in having created this thing are all ways of disempowering yourself. I can confront and support all in the same moment. And, of course, I'm afraid of people with power, but I don't have to act like it.

Flawless Consulting: A Guide to Getting Your Expertise Used, 4th Edition

For more than 40 years, *Flawless Consulting* has been the go-to guide to building trust and structuring meaningful partnerships with others for greater influence and impact. The book is an intuitive and insightful distillation of research and more than 50 years of firsthand experience, walking readers through the skills, tools, and behaviors needed to find success in the consulting world.

Key topics covered include:

- The five phases of consulting: entry and contracting, discovery, feedback and recommendations, implementation, and evaluation and termination
- The roles consultants play
- How to deal with client resistance
- The contracting meeting
- The difference between internal and external consultants
- The importance of collaborative relationships
- Consulting in the virtual world

Flawless Consulting also shares a series of helpful checklists and worksheets to help you use this proven and flawless approach with your clients.

Being Flawlessly Authentic

Most of what we do as consultants is putting into words what we see happening. It's very simple. If it's not going well, you say, "This isn't going well." If the client seems angry, you say, "You are raising your voice." If they think they don't have time and keep looking at their watch and picking up calls, you say, "You're looking at your watch." That's being authentic. It's also expressing your own doubts and saying, "Here are my concerns about this project." Consultants are not cheerleaders. Clients don't need a cheerleader and we should not want to become one.

Being authentic is mostly expressing what you see happening, putting it into nonpunishing words, being curious, and asking questions they wouldn't normally hear such as, "You're telling me what's wrong with middle management and top management and this program and that program. So, what's your contribution to its failure?" Your ability to authentically help clients with their problem hinges on that question. Because if they can't answer it, then their stance is one of helplessness. Most of what flawless consultants do is confront people with their chosen helplessness, meaning helplessness is not the natural state.

Clients have a choice as to whether to be an agent and an activist no matter what the world is doing. Anybody that's waiting for someone else's transformation is doomed. You give people a path in which they have choices they couldn't see before you arrived. Period. And you should always treat them as if they're making a choice, even if they tell you they can't. That's the ultimate gift. Everybody complains about their boss's boss and the top management, or those people in that department, but all those complaints are a waste of breath, even though you must listen to them. So, leave a place for silence. Take a break and check out. Listen, and see if what you're hearing is what they're saying. That's what clients buy from you: to be heard and seen. They don't buy expertise. They have expertise inside their own building, but for some reason, it's not working and that's why you're there.

What's New

While so much remains the same since I first rolled out *Flawless Consulting*, one change is that the world has become even less focused on relationships, which are now more commodified thanks to all the digital and remote ways of relating. But we don't care how remote we are; the relationship is what matters. We have to keep inventing ways for people to connect to one another, but it's harder from a distance because video conferences and long-distance communication make spending casual time together obsolete. We used to be able to walk in a room, chat a little bit, take a break, and then chat a little bit more. Then we might leave for a while and come back and chat again. Those chats were the norm. I learned more and got more connected by asking, "What's going on here? What are we really doing here?" than I did after I said, "OK, let's start the meeting."

Consulting Tip

Identify your unique way of authentically humanizing every client contact. It could be simply asking how the person is feeling. It could be referring to a personal item that your client mentioned in the last meeting. It could be having a special opening line such as, "How goes it?" Or it could be consciously using their names and remembering their spouse's or children's names. Write them down if you must.

As consultants, we must humanize every moment as best we can, and there are 1,000 ways to do it once we have that in mind. I worry that in a world of increasing control and consistency and financial measures, we've forgotten how to connect. However, I don't want to buy that as a version of what makes a difference in the world or how work gets done. It's still done partly through knowing and knowledge and competence, but it's always about who's speaking and to what extent they are in touch with the people being spoken to. And, I still think there's a place for mystery; a place where, as consultants, we don't have to figure out where we're going. There are so many ways we can create a place for not knowing, a place for mystery and ambiguity. We can create a customized response for this moment in this situation for our clients. That's what they want, but it's not what they ask for.

Good and Not So Good Consulting

You can be an internal consultant, influencing for change where you have no direct authority or control, or you could be an external consultant hired by an organization. What makes for good consulting, assuming you know your business, is the deep belief that you're not right. Nothing is more destructive to consultation than certainty—thinking you're the expert. Expertise and authority alone don't make things happen. The darkest side of consulting occurs when you think you're right and know what's best for an organization or another person. Instead, all you can do is confront your clients with the choices they have and know that they're the ones accountable for their actions if they choose one way or another. You're not.

Consulting Tip

Never believe you have the only right answer. You don't.

Good consultants also don't claim victory. Some might say, "Well, because we worked with that group, they saved $400,000. They got rid of 35 people. And their response time decreased." But you didn't do that. You may not have talked to customers—the client did. Instead, say, "Our success has been supporting people who knew they wanted to make real change and had the courage to do it." It's tricky work and you must be willing to live through other people's success. If you credit yourself with the world they made a difference in, you'll become a surrogate manager. If you can't live with that, get a job as a line manager or contract as a surrogate manager.

Consultants who try to manage get a bad rap. You shouldn't try to take over, control things, or make recommendations to pursue one path. If you are critical and judgmental, and participate in judging the competence of your clients, you've taken on a managerial role, not a consultant role. If somebody brings you in and says, "Would you evaluate my key people?" don't call yourself a consultant. Just call yourself a surrogate manager. Instead, ask why they're outsourcing the hard parts of their job? Better yet, ask the client, "Why would you ask me to evaluate somebody that you see twice a week? What don't you trust about yourself?"

In this situation, you're not being asked to evaluate their top performers—you're being asked to evaluate the ones they've lost faith in. They're hoping you can give them a reason to say, "I'm sorry, I think you're great, but the consultant told us you're out of here." Too many consulting engagements fall under change management when they're really about risk management, staff reduction, and shutting things down. That's not change management; that's coercion. And when others feel vulnerable or like they're losing control, they shut down. Maybe the consultant's job is to put what they thought was bad news into words in a way that doesn't make their clients feel judged or forced.

Summary

I've shared here what I've learned after more than 40 years in consulting. Some things have changed, but a lot of what I do is still true. We are welcoming a new era of consultants. If you are new to consulting, here's what I say to you: Stop saying how inexperienced you are. Stop making excuses for yourself. Stop exaggerating what you don't know. Make eye contact and act as if age and experience are nonissues because you are experienced—you survived childhood and the school system. Also, somebody let you into the room. As soon as I'm allowed in the room, I leave all my doubts at the door.

But don't overcompensate with overconfidence. If I say, "I've been doing this for years," it doesn't mean I've been doing it well. If I say, "When I was your age, here's what I did," that implies I turned out OK. I didn't. None of us turned out OK. Age is irrelevant.

Young people have a freshness, a curiosity, a not-knowing attitude, and an energy that's useful. And if you're wrong, just say, "I'm wrong." You have nothing to prove. Your family may be the only people in the world to whom you have something to prove—that's why you got the advanced degrees. I got a master's degree because I knew it would make my mother happy. Once I graduated, nobody in the world was interested. So let go of all that stuff because you are very experienced. If you're 24 years old—that means you have 24 years of experience dealing with the world.

And if you're an experienced consultant, stop turning things over to the next generation. That does not let you off the hook. You didn't create this mess, but you tried to fix it. Instead say, "Welcome," and imagine a world you help make better together.

Actions You Can Take Now

- **Understand your gifts.** Ask two people you work with to tell you two things you do uniquely well. Be sure to ask for abilities and something more specific than "liking people, being a good problem solver, and meeting deadlines."
- **Identify what matters.** Ask yourself what special and unique gifts you bring to your work. Write down why the work you do matters to you.
- **Plan your contracting meeting.** Use the checklist that accompanies this chapter to plan your next contracting meeting. You'll find it online at td.org/handbook -for-consultants.

About the Author

Peter Block is an author and citizen of Cincinnati, Ohio. He is the owner of Designed Learning, a training company that offers workshops designed to build the skills outlined in his books, including *Flawless Consulting, Stewardship, The Answer to How Is Yes, Community: The Structure of Belonging, The Abundant Community, Confronting Our Freedom, An Other Kingdom,* and *Activating the Common Good.* Peter is a founder of the Common Good Collective and part of the Common Good Alliance of Greater Cincinnati. Today his work focuses on the restoration of the common good and creating a world that reclaims our humanity from the onslaught of modernism and development. Learn more at designedlearning.com.

Essential Consulting Skills for Trainers

RITA BAILEY

When I was entrusted with leading the corporate university at Southwest Airlines, my vision was clear: Make it the go-to destination for all training needs. However, the initial curriculum was based on topical interest and customer requests rather than data-driven assessments. While we proudly presented a catalog filled with diverse offerings, many of the courses, such as "Accounting for Non-Accountants," were never fully developed. In the beginning, we were content with responding to training requests as they came, inadvertently becoming mere order takers. But as the demand grew, we found ourselves supplementing with off-the-shelf products and external trainers, sometimes resulting in irrelevant content and questionable relevancy.

A turning point came when I saw a new IT team prioritize five projects out of more than 30 that were submitted by various departments. This experience opened my eyes to the importance of aligning training initiatives with the company's overarching goals and specific department objectives. We realized the importance of forming closer relationships with our internal customers to better understand their true needs and tailor our offerings accordingly.

To prepare for this transformation, I invested considerable time and effort in developing a diverse skill set. I honed my expertise in project management, data analysis, business strategy, leadership, and communication effectiveness. Seeking personal coaching and mentorship from seasoned consultants provided me invaluable insights from their wealth of experience.

My background in training and internal consulting proved to be valuable assets when I took the leap to pursue a new path as an international speaker, facilitator, and strategic coach. Today, as a seasoned consultant, I derive immense fulfillment from guiding organizations and leaders through transformative journeys, offering strategic direction, and fostering positive change. This journey has reinforced the power of aligning training with company objectives and underscored the importance of continuously evolving my skills to stay ahead in the dynamic world of corporate consulting.

What Trainers Can Learn From Consultants

Trainers and consultants share some overlapping skills—both require strong communication, interpersonal, and project management skills. Consulting requires deeper content expertise, analytical skills, and business acumen, including sales and marketing skills. However, I contend that every trainer should be adept in several consulting skills. In fact, practicing consulting skills while you're still a corporate trainer can set you up for greater success whenever you're ready for the transition to consulting.

Let's explore the benefits of using consulting skills in training to drive a holistic, comprehensive view of business and client goals. Table 2-1 compares the difference between how trainers and consultants approach their work.

Table 2-1. Differences in Approach Between Trainers and Consultants

	Trainer	Consultant
Goals	Enhances knowledge, skills, and performance of learners, while ensuring that training is engaging, relevant, and effective	Analyzes business problems and provides objective and practical advice and solutions to help clients achieve their desired outcomes
Approach	Follows a structured approach—creating a training plan and delivering training through various modes, such as facilitating, workshops, or online modules	Follows a more collaborative approach—gathering data, conducting analysis, and providing tailored recommendations to address problems
Expertise	Expected to be an expert in the subject matter they are teaching, with a focus on delivering a specific set of skills or knowledge	Expected to be an expert in problem solving, with a focus on analyzing complex business problems and providing tailored solutions
Interaction	More hands-on, structured, and standardized training methods in terms of leading exercises, facilitating discussions, and providing feedback	One-on-one with clients, interacting closely over a longer period to observe, gather information, analyze data, and provide recommendations
Outcome	Measured in terms of the trainees' improved performance or productivity in specific areas	Measured in terms of the client's improved business performance or profitability, whether in specific departments or the overall organization

By adapting a consulting approach, you can shift your mindset from problem-based to solution-based and position yourself as a valued resource. You can show that you are aware of the key business drivers and key performance indicators (KPIs) affecting the organization, such as revenue growth, cost management, customer satisfaction, culture, market influences, and industry trends.

Consulting Tip

Learn how to read the organization's financial statements including its income statement, balance sheet, and cash flow statement. Understand how the organization generates revenue, manages expenses, and invests in growth opportunities.

Consider a few specific examples of how trainers can use consulting skills:

- A company hires a new team of sales representatives and wants to improve their performance. As a trainer using consulting skills, you might conduct an analysis of their current sales process, identify areas for improvement, and then, understanding the problem from a more in-depth perspective, provide tailored training and coaching to help the team reach their goals.
- A nonprofit organization wants to develop a new fundraising strategy. As a trainer using consulting skills, you might lead a group brainstorming session to gather ideas and insights from stakeholders, conduct research on successful fundraising strategies in the nonprofit sector, and develop a customized plan that meets the organization's unique needs.
- A healthcare organization is implementing a new electronic medical record system and needs to train staff on its use. As a trainer using consulting skills, you might conduct a needs assessment to identify the specific skills and knowledge they need to effectively use the new system, develop training materials tailored to their needs, and provide ongoing support, coaching, and metric tools to ensure a successful transition.
- A manufacturing company wants to improve its production efficiency. As a trainer using consulting skills, you might conduct an analysis of their current production process, identify bottlenecks and areas for improvement, and develop and deliver

training programs that help employees develop the skills and knowledge needed to work more efficiently and effectively.

In the rest of this chapter, we'll further explore the topics outlined in Table 2-2 and how they help to enhance your consulting abilities. While the focus will be on trainers who want to become consultants, if you have already turned consultant, you should still make sure these skills are in your repertoire.

Table 2-2. Key Consulting Skills for Trainers

Topic	Consulting Skills
Having a solution-oriented mindset	Focusing on proactively finding solutions rather than dwelling on the problems; understanding the root cause of problems to determine potential solutions
Listening and analyzing	Listening to understand the client's perspective and underlying concerns and then synthesizing the information to draw conclusions or identify patterns
Asking the right questions	Asking thoughtful and relevant questions that elicit useful information, insights, and perspectives
Getting to the root causes	Asking why multiple times to peel back the layers of the problem and get to the underlying issue
Establishing credibility	Gaining trust and respect from others by demonstrating your expertise, reliability, candor, and integrity
Showing the value	Demonstrating the benefits you can provide by highlighting how your skills, knowledge, and experience contribute to the success of the organization, a project, or a relationship
Managing the data	Organizing, storing, protecting, and maintaining data throughout a project's life cycle
Strategizing	Developing a plan or strategy for achieving specific goals or actions and selecting the best approach based on the available resources and constraints
Thinking creatively	Approaching problems and challenges in new and innovative ways that go beyond traditional patterns and conventional thinking
Setting clear expectations	Communicating clearly and specifically what you want, need, and expect from others
Establishing client connections	Building and maintaining relationships with clients based on trust, respect, and effective communication
Being a change management expert	Navigating changes in strategy, structure, processes, and culture to ensure they are managed effectively

Having a Solution-Oriented Mindset

Having a solution-oriented mindset starts by identifying the problems and working collaboratively with stakeholders to find a solution. This approach involves looking at the bigger picture and considering all factors that may be contributing to the problem. As a trainer, you are then able to determine the appropriate solution to address the specific needs of the learners and organization.

When it comes to addressing issues or challenges in the workplace, using a consulting approach will reveal a variety of nontraining solutions. Here are some possible examples:

- **Improving processes.** Issues can arise due to inefficiencies in processes or procedures. By reviewing and finding ways to optimize these processes, organizations can reduce errors, improve quality, and increase productivity without the need for additional training.
- **Redesigning job roles.** Poorly defined job roles and responsibilities lead to confusion and inefficiencies. By redesigning them, organizations can clarify expectations and improve performance.
- **Implementing technology.** Technology can help automate tasks, improve communication, and provide access to data and information. By implementing new tools and systems, organizations can improve efficiency and reduce errors.
- **Improving communication.** Organizations can reduce errors and improve performance by improving communication channels and providing clearer instructions.
- **Providing additional resources.** Employees may be struggling due to a lack of resources or support. By providing additional resources, such as staffing or equipment, organizations can help them perform their jobs more effectively.
- **Reducing workload.** Overloading employees with too much work can lead to burnout and mistakes. By reducing workload and providing additional support, organizations can improve performance and reduce errors.
- **Improving work environment.** A positive work environment can lead to increased motivation, engagement, and productivity. By improving the work environment, organizations can create a culture of excellence and improve performance.

These nontraining solutions may be more appropriate and effective than training solutions in some situations, depending on the root cause of the issue and the specific needs of the organization.

Consulting Tip

Learn as much as you can about your organization's industry. Read the strategic plan, identify trends and challenges, and learn more about its competitors. Subscribe to and read industry journals and newsletters.

Listening and Analyzing

Before you start asking all kinds of questions, you need to be able to do one thing well—*listen*. Listening intently to what stakeholders and clients are saying is the starting point to understanding the real need and making any project a success. It also helps establish rapport. If you don't listen carefully to what stakeholders are telling you about their business and current situation, you'll have no way of understanding what solutions will give them the result they want to achieve. As Simon Sinek (2010) says, "There is a difference between listening and waiting for your turn to speak."

One of the best ways trainers can adopt a consulting approach is to go from know-it-all to learn-it-all. Let go of the belief that you know all the answers and challenge your own ideas by asking yourself the hard questions, embracing collaboration, and seeking input from others who think differently.

Even if you believe you know the answer, a good consultant listens more than they talk. Check your attitude, be fully present and attentive, and be willing to adjust when you hear things that may trigger certain emotions. Think of a time you strongly disagreed with something a client said. How did you react? If it was negatively, you likely shut the conversation down—game over. If, on the other hand, you asked questions for clarity and put your own emotions aside, this likely gave you a true understanding of where the client was coming from.

Analytical listening involves using active listening skills while processing and analyzing the information being communicated. Here are some tips:

- Listening for patterns in the information being communicated, such as recurring themes or issues, can help you gain a deeper understanding of the client's concerns and needs.
- Asking open-ended and follow-up questions can help clarify and expand on the information being communicated, leading to a more detailed understanding of the situation.
- Identifying the key points and main ideas being communicated by the client helps to organize the conversation.
- Listening for emotions and reactions helps you understand the client's perspective and how they feel about the situation.
- Synthesize and validate the information being communicated to gain a comprehensive understanding of the situation.
- Consider alternative perspectives and solutions, which can help lead to creative and innovative solutions to the challenges you're addressing.

Asking the Right Questions

Deep, thorough questions can be your best friend if you want to uncover the most important underlying issues. Asking good questions benefits both you and the client because it shows that you have the expertise and knowledge to help them. It also helps you build or strengthen your relationship and establish trust.

To ask the right questions, it is important to have a clear understanding of the conversation or interaction's purpose. This will help you frame the questions so they're relevant to the topic. It also helps uncover any underlying assumptions, biases, or motivations. By asking thoughtful and relevant questions, you can gain valuable insights, identify potential solutions, and make more informed decisions.

The following prompts will help position you as the expert by asking questions that align training to your client's business goals.

- **What is the number 1 priority or goal for your business, department, or team during this fiscal year?** Determine their priority based on the organizational needs. You can then decide how best to help them achieve the most important goals.

- **What other stakeholders need to be involved in the decision process or project implementation?** Ask this question early in the process to ensure that you're working with the appropriate person or people responsible for outcomes.
- **Are there any obstacles that may get in the way of making progress or achieving the desired result? or What do you believe needs to be strengthened to support achieving this goal?** These questions help you identify weaknesses. Getting clients to speak openly can help them deal with their issues, remove the roadblocks, and open the path for smooth execution.
- **What other options have you considered or looked at to achieve this?** This question helps you better understand what they have done up to this point or are thinking about.
- **What is the value of this to you (or the company)?** When you agree about what's at stake and the value of what you're creating, you are better able to position your offering in a way that aligns with the value proposition.
- **What problem do you want to address or solve? What's not happening that you want to happen? What is the desired outcome? What if your client has already determined that training is the solution without fully assessing the problem or need?** These questions are great starters to help overcome the tendency to always offer training as a solution. In this situation, be prepared to address resistance from challenging clients. Be sure to react in an unemotional manner.

Getting to the Root Cause

Seeking to understand root causes of problems rather than just treating symptoms is an important consulting skill that can serve trainers well. When you respond to a request by giving the client what they asked for rather than what they need, the problem likely won't be solved in the long term. If the client comes back and says the training didn't work, it's likely that you did not get to the root cause before delivering a training solution.

If you view training as an ecosystem, it allows you to consider everything that might be contributing to the problem. For instance, if invoices are not being paid in a timely manner, should you immediately schedule a four-hour training session for the accounting staff? Or, do you conduct a needs assessment to determine the root cause of the problem? A need assessment might reveal a bottleneck in the process, bad job fit, or leadership issues that need to be addressed.

Here are a few scenarios when failing to identify the root cause led to delivering training for problems that were not training issues:

- **Lack of clear goals or direction.** If employees are unsure of their goals or the direction the organization is headed, they may underperform, waste time on unneeded initiatives, or make mistakes. In this case, providing training on a specific task or skill may not be helpful. Instead, the organization may need to clarify its goals and provide direction and guidance.
- **Poor work environment.** If employees are working in an environment that is not conducive to productivity or well-being, training on a specific task or skill may not be effective. In this case, the organization may need to address the work environment—such as improving lighting or air quality—to improve employee performance.
- **Inadequate resources.** If employees do not have the necessary resources, such as equipment or staffing, they may struggle to perform their jobs effectively. Training on a specific task or skill won't address this issue. Instead, the organization may need to provide additional resources to support employee performance.
- **Poor leadership.** If employees are not receiving clear guidance and support from their leaders, they may struggle to perform their jobs effectively. Rather than training on a specific task or skill, the organization may need to provide leadership training or address issues with the current leadership.
- **Lack of motivation or engagement.** If employees are not motivated or engaged in their work, they may underperform or make mistakes. The organization may need to address employee motivation and engagement through strategies such as recognition or incentives.

Root cause analysis is a popular structured technique that helps answer why the problem happened in the first place. Determine what happened, why it happened, and what needs to be done to reduce the likelihood that it will happen again.

Consultants can use different processes and tools to perform a root cause analysis, such as problem analysis, gap analysis, performance metrics, benchmarking, process mapping, and brainstorming. The key is to take a structured, analytical approach that allows for a comprehensive understanding of the problem and systematic approach to determining a solution.

Establishing Credibility

Trainers who have a good understanding of how the business operates and generates revenue make better decisions and have strong credibility with stakeholders, including business leaders, managers, and employees. This can help establish trust and ensure that training is viewed as a valuable investment.

By demonstrating honesty, integrity, and transparency, you continue to increase your credibility account. When you are seen as believable, competent, and trustworthy, clients will respect your expertise, take you more seriously, and be open to your ideas. The most valuable compliment a client can pay you is to consider you part of their corporate family.

In his book *The Speed of Trust*, business expert Steven M.R. Covey describes four core principles of credibility:

- **Integrity** means being honest, adhering to your values and principles, and being consistent in your actions. When you have integrity, you walk your talk and people can rely on you.
- **Intent** refers to your motives and sincerity. It's about genuinely caring about the well-being of others and seeking mutual benefit in your interactions. When people perceive that you are not self-serving, they are more likely to trust you.
- **Capability** involves your competence, skills, and proven track record. You consistently demonstrate your expertise and deliver on your promises.
- **Results** show that you consistently deliver on expectations. Meeting or exceeding expectations builds trust and reinforces the belief that you are dependable.

Showing the Value

Trainers often struggle to show and communicate the value of what they do. As a consultant, one of the first questions to ask when starting a partnership with a new client is, "Who determines the value of training?" Multiple key stakeholders typically help determine the value of training; for example:

- **The organization** determines the value of training based on the impact on employee performance, productivity, engagement, and overall business outcomes. The organization may also assess the cost of training in relation to the benefits it provides.

- **The employees** who receive the training may determine its value based on how it helps them improve their skills, job performance, and career development. They may also consider the relevance and usefulness of the training program to their job roles.
- **The client's customers** may determine the value of training based on their experience with the trained employees if the training is focused on customer service or other customer-facing roles. This may include factors such as responsiveness, quality of service, and satisfaction with the overall experience.
- **Regulatory bodies** may determine the value of training in some industries based on compliance requirements and the impact on public safety, health, or other factors.

It is important to consider the perspectives of different stakeholders and assess the impact of training from multiple angles to determine the overall value. You must be able to demonstrate how your services can help them achieve their goals and objectives and that your services are worth the investment.

Managing the Data

Why is data so important?

Data and analytics are vital tools for consultants. We rely on the information they provide to gain valuable insights, improve decision making, enhance client understanding, measure success, identify opportunities and risks, and deliver better results.

Most trainers have no formal background in evaluation, measurement, analytics, or return on investment (ROI), and it's easy to focus on other things when they're not a full-time priority. However, this area offers several benefits that can make a significant, positive impact on training programs and your own professional growth. Executives want to see the business connection from learning, and data is the bridge that aligns training to the business or organization. For example:

- **Evidence-based training.** Data and analytics provide the evidence to support decisions and strategies. You should start by establishing why you are implementing a solution and the appropriate measurement to determine the success.
- **Improved training outcomes.** Consider process improvement versus performance evaluation. If you approach evaluation from the perspective of improving the program rather than the individual, you are better able to collect credible data and minimize the fears associated with negative results.

- **Efficient resource allocation.** When you understand which aspects of training are most effective, you can allocate more time, effort, and budget into solutions that will yield the best results.
- **Continuous professional development.** When trainers become more data-savvy professionals, it opens more opportunities to stay current with industry trends and communicate with management, clients, and other stakeholders.

Strategizing

Executives are not the only ones who need to think about strategy. Strategic thinking skills enable trainers and consultants to use critical thinking to solve complex problems and plan for the future.

However, developing strategizing skills doesn't happen overnight. First, allow yourself time to think strategically. Get a clear understanding of the industry, trends, and business drivers. Pay attention to issues that get raised on a recurring basis and common obstacles employees are experiencing. Ask others for their opinions and thoughts to develop your inquiry skills.

An aspect of strategic thinking is anticipating problems before they happen. It's usually not a matter of if something will happen or change, but *when*. Do scenario planning to proactively plan for the unknown.

Challenge the status quo by becoming more curious and aware of internal and external trends, practices, and challenges. When you let go of assumptions and question everything, you look at information from different points of view, approaches, and potential outcomes.

As a consultant, you may be brought on with a specific emphasis on strategizing, but regardless of the scope of your engagement, your client will appreciate and benefit from your skills in this area. You'll be able to anticipate when planned initiatives might go off the rails or be better able to push back on assumptions your client is making.

The process of strategizing typically involves several steps:

- Define specific objectives that align with the overall mission and vision of the organization.
- Analyze the current state of business by conducting a SWOT analysis or similar assessment to identify internal strengths and weaknesses as well as external opportunities and threats.

- Based on the analysis of the current situation, identify potential strategies for achieving the defined objectives.
- Consider different scenarios and evaluate the potential impact of each strategy on the organization's goals and objectives.
- Develop an action plan that outlines the steps for implementing the strategy.
- Track progress against the action plan and adjust as needed to ensure that the organization stays on track to achieve its goals.

Thinking Creatively

Once you're thinking bigger, your ability to think more creatively also expands. If your typical preference is reading, consider listening to podcasts or watching different genres of movies or documentaries. If you have certain go-to hobbies or sports, try something new. Establishing new rituals will help stimulate more creative, innovative thinking. As an example, instead of watching the news, I started spending an hour each day using my Oculus, a virtual reality (VR) headset, to visit a different country. Journaling is also a great way to capture creative thoughts.

When you think creatively, your capacity for innovation expands and helps you:

- Approach problems in new and innovative ways, leading to more effective, efficient solutions.
- Brainstorm new groundbreaking ideas, products, and services that can revolutionize or change how your clients work.
- Be more flexible and adaptable as you consider alternative solutions and ideas.
- Express yourself in new ways, helping you communicate ideas more effectively.
- Build confidence, solve problems, and come up with innovative ideas.
- Learn and retain new information as you make connections and see patterns that were not as obvious before.

Setting Clear Expectations

At the start of the process, trainers and consultants must be clear about their goals and objectives and ensure that all stakeholders are aligned and understand these expectations.

Develop a clear scope of work, including activities, deliverables, and timelines. Communicate regularly to keep all stakeholders informed of progress, issues, or changes.

Identify and manage risks early on and communicate any potential impacts to the timeline or deliverables. Being transparent about your approach and methods and sharing your reasoning with stakeholders builds trust and manages expected outcomes. It can also reduce confusion and frustration. If circumstances require, be prepared to redefine or renegotiate project goals, scope, timeline, or deliverables. Measure and report on progress against the goals and objectives defined at the start of the project.

Good consultants are experts in giving tough feedback to the client, but when things are not working, you must learn to give the information to the client in a timely manner so changes can be made quickly. Good trainers must do the same.

Establishing Client Connections

As you become a more self-aware trainer and adopt a consultant's strategic and creative thinking skills, you will feel more confident when connecting with your clients. Even though we all communicate in our own way, there are a few foundational skills that help you connect with clients:

- Put yourself in their position so you can communicate from their perspective.
- Communicate clearly and learn as much about them as possible.
- Be responsive.
- Build rapport.
- Provide value.
- Use technology—e-mail, social media, and messaging platforms—to streamline communication.
- Maintain a professional demeanor, establish credibility, and hold a positive reputation.
- Don't promise things you can't deliver.
- Keep in touch to make sure your clients are satisfied and find out if their needs are changing.
- Respect their time.
- Express your appreciation.

Establishing a connection with your internal clients is critical to building a relationship with them and truly understanding how you can help find their best solution. As Peter Block states in his chapter in this handbook, "Ultimately consulting skills are not just for consultants. They are for everyone who must cultivate relationships at work." And that includes trainers.

Being a Change Management Expert

Becoming a change management expert is critical for trainers and consultants. Change management enables you to design and implement effective training and other OD programs that not only teach new skills, but also help employees adapt to changes in the organization, such as new products, processes, procedures, and policies.

Here are some of the key skills necessary to becoming a change management expert:

- Have a deep understanding of the change management process, including the different stages and types of change and the impact of change on employees and the organization.
- Effectively communicate with stakeholders about the changes that are taking place and articulate the reasons for the change, the benefits, and what employees can expect during the process.
- Develop and deliver training programs that help employees understand and adapt to the changes that are taking place. This includes creating training materials, delivering presentations, and providing coaching and support.
- Lead and influence others to ensure that the change process is successful. This includes building key relationships, gaining buy-in, and inspiring all stakeholders to embrace the change.
- Have strong analytical skills to evaluate the impact of the changes on the organization and make data-driven decisions.
- Have a basic understanding of project management principles and manage the change process effectively.
- Use change readiness assessments to identify potential obstacles or challenges that may arise during the change process and develop strategies to mitigate them.
- Practice continuous improvement thinking, always looking for ways to improve and incorporate feedback from employees to ensure that the change process is successful and sustainable.

By developing these skills and expertise, you can become an effective change management expert and help your organization successfully navigate through change initiatives.

Summary

Trainers who use consulting skills to link their training programs to the business can enjoy a range of benefits, including increased relevance, greater alignment, improved ROI, and better feedback. By showcasing the impact that training programs have on business outcomes, trainers can build their reputation as strategic partners.

Actions You Can Take Now

- **Practice strategic thinking.** Block weekly time on your calendar to think about big picture strategy without getting bogged down. Focus on how to make things better and build on the things that are good instead of just what needs to be fixed.
- **Seek a mentor.** Identify a mentor who is outside your reporting structure. Look to someone who can help you learn more about your organization's business perspective.

About the Author

Rita Bailey is an independent consultant, facilitator, author, and executive coach. She is the founder and CEO of Up to Something, a consulting firm that helps organizations develop their leadership capacity through immersive leadership programs. Her experience spans more than 40 years in a variety of leadership roles, including head of Southwest Airlines University for People, past ATD chair, and CEO of Boxages (a family gift box company). Rita has worked with a wide range of global organizations across industries, including healthcare, manufacturing, energy, technology, hospitality, government, and nonprofits. She is a frequent speaker at conferences and events. Learn more about Rita's work at uptosomething.com.

CHAPTER 3

From TD to Consulting
Transition Success
SARAH CANNISTRA

When it comes to trying something new—a hobby, a workout regiment, a business—the hardest part is actually getting started.

It was 2019 and I was unfulfilled and burnt out working as the director of learning program development for an organization that was misaligned with my core values. I was desperate to make a change, but wasn't sure what to do next, so I started reading Julia Cameron's bestselling book, *The Artist's Way*.

In her book, Cameron suggests doing a daily activity called Morning Pages, where you write three pages about whatever comes to mind, *by hand*, first thing in the morning. I did this exercise for months, taking the opportunity to write whatever random thoughts came to mind. Some days, the pages of my tie-dyed notebook were filled with snapshots of career moments that made me most proud and energized. Other days revealed a series of vignettes imagining my future if I really lived my life on my own terms, doing what I loved to do. The challenge was, I had no idea what that actually looked like. I knew I loved talent development and was energized by helping other L&D practitioners grow in their careers. I had an innate ability to quickly develop practical and modern L&D strategies, but didn't know how to bring those ideas together into my next career move.

Then, one August morning, the words just came to me—The Overnight Trainer. I didn't know what it was or what it meant, but I knew it represented the start of something new.

In this chapter, we'll explore steps you can take that will help you transition from thinking-about-it to starting your own consulting business.

From Scary to Success

If you've been feeling the itch to start something of your own, you may also be asking yourself these questions: *How do I figure out where to start? What does that look like for me? How do I find my starting point in the wide field of consulting? How will I stand out among the competition? Aren't there already people doing this? What will everyone think of me for going out on my own?*

I call these thoughts the "starting scaries." They're like the Sunday scaries—you know, those feelings of anxiety or dread that happen the day before you have to head back to work (in fact, those feelings may be the reason you've decided you need a change)—but they're focused on starting a new venture.

The starting scaries caused me to sit on the idea of The Overnight Trainer for 10 months before I dared to explore how it could work as a business. However, when I finally asked myself the following six questions, I was able to move from *scaries* to *success*:

1. What parts of my current and past roles have given me energy?
2. What moments in my career have I been most proud of? Why?
3. What am I known for that I enjoy doing?
4. What are my inherent skills and strengths I want to leverage and share with others?
5. What legacy do I want to leave behind? What impact can I have now that brings me one step closer to that legacy?
6. What could it look like to share my skills, strengths, experiences, and expertise with others?

Answering these questions led me to the first iteration of my business—consulting with L&D leaders on high-level learning strategy, and an online course for new L&D professionals to learn the industry ropes. What ideas are they bringing up for you?

Consulting Tip

Reflect on the six questions and start to envision how you can move from scaries to success.

Staying Committed

If the hardest part of launching a business is getting started, the second hardest part is sticking to it.

Before I started The Overnight Trainer, I'd already been through several failed entrepreneurial journeys. A few blog sites, an online fitness company with a friend, a health and life coaching practice—they all dwindled within months (or for some, weeks) of launching. I had the passion and was enthusiastic about what I was offering, so what happened?

The truth is that I bailed. When I didn't see success overnight (no pun intended)—when no one read my blog, bought my fitness program, or hired me as their coach—I took it as an immediate sign that it wasn't working. My businesses failed not because of what I had to offer, but because they were fueled by reasons rather than purpose.

If you're reading this handbook, you're likely either thinking about starting a consulting business or already have one. So, what are your reasons? Here's a few I hear most often:

- I want to be my own boss.
- I want more freedom and flexibility.
- I'm looking for more financial opportunities.
- I want to choose who I get to work with.
- I only want to do the things I am good at or enjoy doing.

Do these sound familiar? I'm sure they do. They were my reasons for starting many of my businesses. But they are also to blame for my failures.

Unfortunately, relying on reasons to fuel your business can turn against you when it gets tough or feels slow. For example, when I launched my health and life coaching practice in 2016, I was still working full time as a director of corporate training for a large real estate organization. While I had a passion for health and fitness at the time, my desire to start a business was rooted in three other reasons:

- Make enough money to leave my full-time role.
- Have flexibility and freedom to work when and where I wanted.
- Focus only on what I'm really good at and passionate about.

I did all the things you're supposed to do to start a business. I identified my ideal client, created an offering, built a website, and put myself out there on social media. But I didn't have true time flexibility and freedom because I was still working full time (like you may be), so

I had to work on my business when I could before or after work. While I was able to focus on what I was passionate about, I also had to spend time and energy on things I didn't enjoy, like social media, marketing, accounting, and web design. These normal business activities took time and energy away from my reason of focusing on what I was good at. And when the money didn't start rolling in as quickly as I expected, the last of my reason fuel burned out.

Flash forward three years (to the month). This time I was working as an L&D director for a different real estate company. I was ready to restart my entrepreneurial journey. And while I had the same reasons for doing so, this time I took a different approach: getting a clear picture of my "why."

You'll learn more about finding your "why" in other chapters, but here's how I look at it: Your reasons are typically what you're running from and what you'd like to change. Your why should be what you're running toward—the impact you wish to have through your business. This is what will ultimately help you stay committed to the bigger picture of the impact you want your business to have.

My why has evolved over time, but today it is "to help purpose-driven people find, land, create, grow, and love the L&D career of their dreams so they can live a life of fulfillment, inspiration, and freedom."

Whenever things feel hard—when I'm in a tight time crunch to get something back to a client or have an unexpectedly slow month—and my reasons are telling me that nothing is working, I can look to my why. That's what brings me back and keeps me committed to my path.

> **Consulting Tip**
>
> Create a list of all your reasons for starting your consulting business. Even though these won't fuel your business, they will help you make a decision about consulting.

Preparing for Change

There's one thing that most entrepreneurs aren't quite prepared for when they leave their full-time job: loneliness. Creating a supportive community you can rely on is essential.

When you work full time at a company, you are constantly connected with people. Whether you're remote, hybrid, or in-office, you're surrounded by other people (virtually or in person) who are working toward the same business goals in one way or another. While you will be working with clients and companies as a consultant, at the end of the day, when you work for yourself, the only person working toward your company goals is you.

One way to recreate this sense of community is to form a board of directors for yourself. I was introduced to this concept by a former client of mine, who casually mentioned that I was on his board of directors. When I asked what that meant, he shared that his board was made up of coaches, mentors, peers, cheerleaders, and ideators who were there to bounce ideas off of, leverage and lean on when needed, and learn from. I immediately put together my own board of directors for my new business.

Susan Stelter (2022) recommends asking these questions when putting together your own personal board:

- "Have I chosen a couple of people who already reached a goal that I have for myself, who have inspired me, or helped others realize their potential?"
- "Have I chosen people from diverse backgrounds?"
- "Have I chosen people who will challenge me to think and act critically? Have they been supportive of me and my goals in the past?"
- "Have I chosen people who will benefit from this relationship too?"

I once heard a coach say that "starting a business is the deepest inner work a person could ever do because it fundamentally changes who you have to show up as." This still rings true for me. Starting a consulting business will change how you communicate, what you prioritize, and the boundaries you set. It will quickly show you where (and with whom) you need to spend more time, and it will give you a lens into what (and who) may be holding you back.

It's also important to remember that not everyone will understand what you're doing, and that's OK. Think about applying the talent development principle "if we design with everyone in mind, we essentially design for no one" to your consulting business. If you try to make everyone understand what you're doing, you risk no one understanding.

To simplify, think of the people in your world—your board of directors, family, friends, co-workers, and so on. Now, sort them into your inner circle and your outer circle:

- The **inner circle** consists of your board of directors, as well as those you trust, who share your vision and won't judge you. They may not be on your board, but these people offer support and unbiased thoughts and feedback. You want them to understand why you're starting and building your own business.

- The **outer circle** consists of the people close to you who just don't get it. They most likely care deeply about you, but their values may not align with yours or they are very judgmental or they don't line up with your ideal business customer, client, or partner. Maybe they had a bad experience with starting a business and that's the only lens they can see through. You may want to be more selective about sharing information and new ideas with the people in your outer circle.

When I started The Overnight Trainer, I never imagined how much it would change my life. Not just the impact I've had on my clients or the financial freedom I've created for my family, but the relationships I would form and the boundaries I would need to set. Finding my personal board and understanding who fit into my inner and outer circles allowed me to sort out which people I could bounce ideas off of and who would give me honest, judgment-free feedback. This exercise not only strengthened my relationships with others, but ultimately led me to build trust in myself, my abilities, and what I had to offer.

Making the Transition

We've already explored what getting started looked like, but you might still be wondering how to take the first step. Now that you have a better idea of what you'd like to do in your consulting business, including the impact you'll have, let's look at a handful of different ways to break into the consulting business, as well as a few of the pros and cons for each.

Side Hustle

The side hustle is one of the most common ways to begin the transition from full-time employment to owning a consulting business. By definition, a side hustle is a job or occupation that brings in extra money beyond your regular job and main source of income.

- Pros: Conceive of and play around with your business, build a brand, and create awareness while still having a full-time income to lean on.
- Cons: Because you're working fulltime, you'll have a limited number of hours to spend dedicated to growing your business. This is typically referred to as "working the 5-to-9 after your 9-to-5."

Contracting

If you're still wondering whether a full-fledged consulting business is right for you, picking up a contract could be a great way to test the waters. To explore available talent development contracts, use LinkedIn's "contract" filter under "job type."

- Pros: Try consulting without having to spend time building brand awareness.
- Cons: Many contracts are for short-term, full-time consulting work, which may interfere with full-time employment.

Partnerships and Apprenticeships

Do you know someone who is already doing something similar to what you would like to do in your consulting business? Reach out to them and ask if they would be willing to let you partner with or shadow them. This is the route I took when starting the L&D strategy piece of my consulting business. I partnered with another strategic L&D consulting firm and helped on the backend with business content development before they gave me the opportunity to be a contract consultant. This gave me a glimpse into the inner workings of a consulting firm.

- Pros: Learning from someone who is already doing the work you want to do gives you a unique perspective and peek behind the curtains to validate your desire for owning your own consulting business.
- Cons: Some people may be hesitant to have you join their team, knowing you want to start your own business. I suggest being upfront about your intentions; you may be surprised by how many people are willing to help.

All In

If you feel clear on your why, your impact, your offers, and your marketing and brand awareness, and you've already experienced proof of concept, you may be ready to go all in and take your business full time.

- Pros: With no time constraints from working another full-time job, you can focus 100 percent of your working time toward growing and marketing your brand and business.
- Cons: With no full-time income backing your consulting business, it could place pressure on you to achieve a certain revenue amount each month.

Within Your Current Organization

This is one of the most underrated ways to get started, but it's a very significant (and potentially fruitful) one. Depending on the type of relationship you have with your leader and organization, you could share what you are passionate about and the goals you have for starting your own business. Then you could ask if there are any available consulting opportunities inside your organization. I recently had a client decide, after nine years at her organization, to start her own TD consulting firm. Her first official client was her previous company!

- Pros: Because you already have name recognition and expertise inside your organization, this could be an easy transition into contracting or consulting.
- Cons: Usually requires a strong, trusting relationship with your employer and the backing of the company. Otherwise, they could think that you are planning an exit.

A note on moonlighting policies: While we have certainly seen a shift in the acceptance of side hustles, part-time contracts, and after-hours consulting work, many companies still have policies in place regarding *moonlighting*—or having a second job in addition to your regular employment. Understand your company's policies and procedures, and check with HR to make sure you are not at any legal risk. Always be upfront and honest about your intent or you may be perceived as being unethical.

Consulting Tip

If you're currently employed, review your company's moonlighting policies and proceed accordingly.

Putting Yourself Out There

If the hardest part of starting a consulting business is getting started, and the second hardest part is staying consistent, a very close third is putting yourself out there online.

We've all heard the saying "content is king," but what does that mean for someone who is just starting a new business journey?

When I officially launched The Overnight Trainer in May 2020, I'd done the work. I decided the impact I wanted to have, what that looked like, and chose to create a side hustle.

Then, like many other early entrepreneurs before me, I started to sell. Unfortunately, no one knew who I was. I hadn't built any connections or trust with my desired audience. My first course was a total flop.

If I could go back and do it over again, I would have read *Content Inc.* by Joe Pulizzi before launching that first course. Why? Because once I started incorporating his model, I saw my success quantum leap. According to Pulizzi (2015), "The absolute best way to start and grow a business today is not by launching or pushing products, but by creating a system to attract, build, and retain an audience. Once you've built a loyal audience, one that loves you and the information you send, you can most likely sell the audience anything you want. This model is called Content Inc."

The problem is many new entrepreneurs freeze at the idea of creating content and putting themselves out there. For example, have you ever had these thoughts?

- Other people are already talking about this. . . .
- Who would want to hear from me?
- What more do I have to add to this conversation?
- I haven't done this long enough to add value. . . .

If you have, know that you are not alone. In fact, when it comes to social media in general, there's the unspoken 99 percent rule, which says that 99 percent of people observe and 1 percent share their thoughts and ideas.

To be successful, you'll need to shift your mindset and move into the 1 percent. I call this the guru fallacy. When it comes to putting ourselves out there as business owners and creating content, most people become consumed with self-doubt. Deep down, we believe we are not expert enough to share our thought leadership because that right is reserved for the so-called "gurus."

But here's the most important thing to remember—there's a difference between being an *expert* and having *expertise*. Those gurus are considered experts because they've been doing whatever it is they've been doing for a long time. They have spent years, if not decades, perfecting their craft and they share from an expert lens. But there's a big delta between what they've become a thought leader in and their day-to-day expertise and experiences. While the guru can provide valuable insight, they may not be able to share how to practically apply their thought leadership.

People want to learn from and work with someone who can help them get from point A to point B—that's where you come in. Your thought leadership can provide actionable insights that feel attainable to your audience (and prospective clients). Your ideal client is looking for someone a few steps ahead of them on the path, not someone who's already reached the top of the mountain (Figure 3-1).

Figure 3-1. The Guru Fallacy

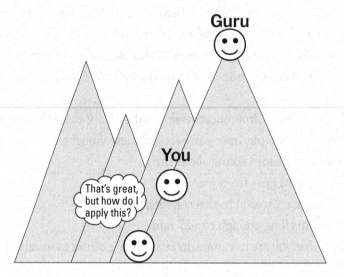

So, the next time you start to wonder, "Who am I to put this out there?" try reframing that thought as "Who out there will be helped by this?"

Piloting and Proof of Concept

As TD professionals, we know the importance of piloting a learning solution before implementing it across the organization. We do this because it allows us to get feedback from users and stakeholders, which will make the end product more meaningful and successful. Yet, for some reason, when it comes to starting a consulting business, we often forget this important step in the launch process.

To figure out where to start piloting in your consulting business, I encourage you to try the hamburger test: Imagine you're eating a big, juicy hamburger with all your favorite toppings. Do you eat it bite-by-bite or do you shove the whole hamburger in your mouth? I'm assuming that because you are alive and reading this book, you probably took a few bites.

Imagine your consulting offering as the whole hamburger. Maybe you are envisioning a certain length of time you'd like to work with a client, or a particular scope of project you'd like to attract. What would it look like to take just one bite of this consulting offering and pilot it to your audience?

For example, when I began the L&D career coaching arm of my business, I figured I'd work with L&D career transitioners for six months, during which I'd help them identify their next target role, refine their resume, and meet weekly to discuss challenges and breakthroughs. But, rather than going all in with that hamburger of an offer, I asked myself the following questions:

- What part of my offer seems most fun to play with?
- What would it look like to offer that one part?
- What do I want someone to get out of this pilot?
- How will I know this pilot is a success?

In the end, I decided to offer one-off 1:1 coaching sessions to help people identify their next target role. It was a small bite out of my big offer and it allowed me to test my offer in a noncommittal way so I could ensure it was aligned with my overall purpose.

After conducting a few complimentary sessions, I realized that six months was too long for both me and my clients because the people I was interested in working with were eager to be in their new roles in three months. The pilot test also highlighted the power of asynchronous communication and coaching. So, I shortened my offering to match the market and offered bi-weekly sessions.

In his 2009 book, *The Power of Less*, Leo Babauta encourages readers to abide by the principle of "starting small" by choosing "something so small that success is almost guaranteed." He goes on to say that "a small success is not as satisfying as a big success, but it's only small in the short term. If you start out with a small success, and build upon that, and so on—until you have a series of small successes that add up to a very large success."

Without that pilot test, I would have been offering a package my clients most likely would not have found as valuable, and I may not have been very successful in selling it. I was able to take the feedback from my aligned pilot clients and make tweaks. This also gave me the proof of concept and testimonials I needed to successfully take my larger offer to the market.

Summary

In the other chapters of this book, you'll be introduced to models and concepts that will bring the ideas discussed here to life. As you read, I encourage you to remember that you've already made the most important decision in starting your consulting business—picking up this book.

Actions You Can Take Now

- **Try Morning Pages.** Spend each morning for the next week writing (by hand!) three pages of whatever comes to your mind. Ask yourself, "What am I learning about me with this process?"
- **Identify your starting scaries.** Think about what may be holding you back from taking the leap in your own business. Once you identify these barriers, meet with someone who will be candid and honest with you about the reality of your concerns.

About the Author

Sarah Cannistra is an L&D career, executive, and business coach, and founder of The Overnight Trainer, a coaching practice that helps purpose-driven people find, land, create, grow, and love the L&D career of their dreams so they can live a life of fulfillment, inspiration, and freedom. With more than a decade of experience in the L&D field and a degree in organizational leadership and learning, Sarah has held roles such as corporate trainer, instructional designer, director of training, and head of learning. She uses her past experience as a modern learning business leader and hiring manager to coach and consult her clients to ultimate career and business success. Learn more by visiting TheOvernightTrainer.com or connect directly at hello@theovernighttrainer.com.

CHAPTER 4

The Business Side of Consulting

What I Wish I Knew Before Starting Out

MAURINE KWENDE

Stephanie Smith was known at her organization for her excellent work ethic and dedication. She also had a great attitude and was fun to be around. Unfortunately, Stephanie and her boss didn't get along, and the work environment became toxic. Stephanie decided to quit and start her own business where she would be her own boss. Once it was up and running, Stephanie realized entrepreneurship wasn't a bed of roses—she had to deal with demanding clients and stress over how to keep the lights on. Stephanie was at a crossroads, not sure if she had made the right decision to start a business or if she should return to working for someone else.

Like Stephanie, many people start a business because they don't feel valued at work, do not get along with their boss, or receive low pay. And while these are valid reasons for quitting a job, they are not good enough reasons to start a business.

When I started my company, I had been working in the industry for more than 20 years. I had expertise in my field and had worked with many internal customers solving their TD problems. You probably have some experience in your specific field, which is a good start. However, becoming a successful entrepreneur requires a different skill set. In this chapter, I'll explore a few of the business fundamentals I wish I had known before I went out on my own as a consultant.

Keeping an Eye on Finances

I wish I'd known how important it was to learn how to manage your business with an eye on finances. You need to set the stage for your business financially. You need to start by asking yourself, what is the dollar amount you need to make this year? I have met many business owners who plan their year by setting a goal for the dollar amount they want to reach for the year and then breaking it down to monthly. And it doesn't have to be complicated—a simple Excel template can be used as your financial system.

I like to use a mind mapping tool called MindMeister to create my financial system. This program allows me to put things in buckets, which is how my brain likes to map out plans, and it provides a link I can share for feedback and accountability. MindMeister is very similar to Miro and Canva, which I have also used, but I prefer the central nexus template in Mind-Meister. I suggest including two key categories when building the central nexus template: markets relative to your consulting and planning for funds management.

You'll need to answer lots of questions:

- How do you track your expenses versus income?
- Do you need to invest in your business?
- Where do you save your money?
- Do you have business accounts set up?
- How do you document all your financial interactions?

This information will not only set you up for success, but it will also keep you compliant with the IRS. Understanding how to do your accounting and financial reporting is also very important. The most common tool for documenting and managing finances online is QuickBooks.

Consulting Tip

Open business checking and savings accounts. You should never pay for business expenses from your personal accounts.

Managing the Financial Highs and Lows

My first consulting project came through a referral, and I continue to receive referrals. But I still vividly recall the times when I didn't have any projects coming my way for months despite actively searching for opportunities. My friend Linda did not have any business for nine months; when she finally found a coaching client, they only met twice a month for an hour each time. Linda couldn't pay her bills and had to rely on her husband's income. Another friend, Marcus, consistently made seven figures in the same year. The only difference between our experiences was who had a plan for times when we didn't have a client and a plan for the cash overflow period. The common saying, "Failing to plan is planning to fail" applies here—without a plan, I would have failed in my first year of business.

About 10 percent of businesses fail in their first year, and up to 50 percent fail in the first five years. Do not become part of that statistic.

Financial expert Dave Ramsey (2003) lays out six steps to find financial peace. Step 3 is focused on planning for the future by creating an emergency fund and safety net. You need to figure out what you can do to ensure that you can still live comfortably and pay your bills if there are financial gaps while in business.

Complete a plan for your first six months. Here's a six-step guide to financial planning before you start your consulting business:

1. List your monthly expenses, including all bills, mortgage, insurance, shopping, health, family, and investments.
2. Multiply that amount by six to determine your expenses for six months.
3. Set aside savings for six months.
4. Plan for an additional emergency fund of at least $1,000.
5. Decide on the type of business you want and make a list of the expenses it will incur during the first six months. Some things to think about include:
   - Will you rent office space?
   - What does it cost to register the business?
   - Will you hire employees?
   - Will you need health or life insurance, and if yes, what will it cost?
   - Will you set up a 401(k)?
6. Total all your expenses and work toward putting this money aside before you start your business.

In addition, consider that a full-time job typically includes not only a paycheck, but also other costs such as health insurance, income taxes, a retirement investment, and life insurance. These are paid on a monthly basis and some are covered by your employer. And you may not realize who else is relying on your income, such as your immediate family or monthly charity and faith-based commitments. Being intentional helps develop a mindset of planning for these commitments to ensure continuity.

Devising a Transition Strategy

Having a transition strategy should be your next step. Complete an environmental scan of the service you want to offer, the problems you are trying to solve, whom the solution is for, and whether it's a viable solution. Inform your family and friends of your decision. This is important because your family and inner circle will be your support system. You might experience some schedule changes; for example, attending business meetings and scheduling time to work on the business and in the business. This might make you late for picking up kids from school or other important personal commitments, so having support from your friends and family is crucial to your peace of mind.

Now that you've figured all these things out, it's time to start setting up your business. Critical steps include registering your business, obtaining a business license, and performing all legal aspects of the business. You'll also want to speak to your employer about your decision. If you care about your work family, you owe them respect, and being honest and open about leaving to pursue your business dream is worth sharing with them. Several of my close friends were able to transition from full-time employees to consultants with the same employer. It's worth having that discussion with your employer, asking them if it's possible to work with them as a consultant. They may want to work with you.

Another thing to consider is remaining employed in your full-time role and working on your consulting business after office hours and on weekends. Then you can move to working part time until you are ready to go out on your own. If you have been a good employee, many employers will be flexible and supportive of your goals.

Promoting and Pricing Your Consulting Services

As a child, I dreamed of becoming a business owner and I always had an entrepreneurial mindset. I was always trying to sell something, whether it was an idea or a product like candy to my peers. In the summer, I'm always excited to see young children selling lemonade in the neighborhood—they are business owners in the making. Having sales skills is one of the most important skills in business. As an independent consultant, how do you rate? Are you good at selling? Are you good at negotiating? For example, there are so many graphic designers out there—why should a customer pick you over other options? What is your unique value proposition? Why should clients do business with you? Afterall, they don't know you or your business yet. Katrina Sawa, in her book *Jumpstart Your Business*, says that as a business owner, you are selling outcomes. You are also selling yourself so that clients do business with you.

I worked full-time for more than 20 years on different continents. As a full-time employee, you have co-workers and stakeholders who know you and your work. As an independent consultant, you are now a business owner—your network needs to know this too. How can you get the word out, and where can you find the people who need to know you are in business? Do you have a social media account? If yes, great! If not, you will need to create one and indicate in your profile that you are in business. This sets the stage for you to keep having contracts and projects to work on. For example, you can create a header on your LinkedIn profile, include a blurb about what you do in the about me section, and link to your business website and portfolio, which should include work samples potential clients can see before deciding to hire you for a contract.

Know that you cannot sell to everyone. Not everyone likes pizza, for example, and even among those who do, some just like cheese pizza or vegetarian pizza. Maybe they only like a specific brand of cheese pizza that uses a specific type of cheese only found in a specific store. It's the same for independent consultants. Who are you selling to and what is the outcome they need? What can you do so they will trust you and do business with you? Can you provide a free sample of the product you offer? If you do this strategically, you can also collect their email address and start a mailing list to send information and share resources. If they find your sample compelling or useful, you will build trust and connections with potential clients.

How do you price your products and services? When I started in business, I was told I should charge less than everyone else to start making money. I was told to provide everything free for a year. I was told many things, but in the end, I had to go with my gut and offered a price I was comfortable with. I made a few mistakes and learned from them. If you make mistakes, learn from them and move on. Keep trying different ideas until you get to what really works for you.

Whatever you decide to do, remember that you are in business and the price you charge must cover your insurance, 401(k), and other benefits you no longer receive from an employer. For example, if you are charging $150 per hour, decide how much is your real pay and what amount goes to the other expenses. Have a dollar amount for each and when you eventually get paid be sure to include savings and put your money in different accounting categories.

Consulting Tip

Pay yourself first. Too many consultants take what's left over after everything else is paid. That is no way to run a business. Set a salary for yourself, and then commit to writing the check.

Leaning On Your Network

I attribute my success to having a great network of independent consultants who share ideas and sometimes partner and work with one another. You must make yourself visible in your community so clients can find you. Try joining the chamber of commerce and attending business networking events or conferences in your area of expertise. Be selective when choosing these networking opportunities. Ask what you need to achieve from them—for example, growing your sales and marketing skills—and be sure to focus on reaching those goals.

Finding a networking group in your community is crucial to your growth as a business owner. I wish I had known how important they were when I was starting out. Through my networking group I've learned various skills such as elevator pitches, business planning, how to write a winning proposal, and how to negotiate rates. During one event, I asked if anyone was willing to share templates, and I'm so glad I did. I received templates for business plans, elevator pitches, written proposals, financial spreadsheets, and marketing samples. Local business bureaus and advisors in the US can also provide templates and help you set them up.

Knowing Your Worth

I really wish I had known about the consulting income rollercoaster. Starting a business is hard, and not knowing when the next paycheck will come is even harder. During the many years I have been in business, there have been times when, despite doing all I could, the universe wasn't sending me the contracts I was looking for. What are the options? One option is to go back to working full time. Some go that route, but it also takes a while to find a good job. A second option—and a common mistake made by new consultants is to settle for less than what you are worth. For example, don't accept an offer from a client that pays a lower rate than your price point simply because you are worried another opportunity won't come. Why? Unfortunately, the client might come to you with another contract because you offer cheap services. And they also have a network they'll tell about this consultant who does great quality work at a cheap price. Word goes around and you gain referrals, but you are being noticed for the wrong reason. I did this several times, and each time, I wrongly convinced myself that it was worth it. Don't—it is not worth it.

John Maxwell's law of the mirror says, "You must see value in yourself to add value to yourself." He explains this further by saying that the value we place in ourselves is usually the value others place in us, and I believe it also reflects in our services (Maxwell 2022). Do you value yourself? Do you value your time? Do you value your services? Do you value your skills? Value, value, value. If you keep settling for less, I challenge you to do some self-reflection and invest in coaching so you can see the value in yourself and what you offer. I encourage you to tell yourself that you deserve to be paid what you are worth. If you decrease your value, you are setting the stage for how you want your services to be valued by your clients. I went into it thinking that I could raise my rate later, but I couldn't. In fact, some clients asked for additional discounts, thereby making it worse. In the end, I had to let go of those clients and start over to receive the rates I deserved. When you start thinking of giving your services away, reflect on the law of the mirror and do not settle.

Dealing With Impostor Syndrome

As I've mentioned before, I've gone through periods when I had no work despite all the effort I was exerting. Whenever this happened, I had to deal with many thoughts—whether to quit, if business was right for me, or if I knew what I was doing. I had moments when I second-guessed myself and felt like an impostor. I experienced many limiting beliefs that held me back from moving forward. Many others have experienced these feelings too.

Telling yourself you will never make it as a business owner is a *limiting belief*—a thought, idea, or opinion that one believes to be true even when it is not. My book *Dream Big and Live Your Dreams Boldly* discusses limiting beliefs as little voices that show up every time we embark on a new project, challenge, or goal. Those thoughts will always be there; however, to deal with them, we need to reframe our mindset, have a positive attitude, pay attention to our self-talk, and stay away from self-sabotage. Your support system will help you remember that you are not what you are telling yourself. But, ultimately, it starts with you. You need to love yourself first and coach yourself on why you are experiencing the limiting beliefs, what your best possible future self looks like, and what you can do to get there. As a new business owner, you'll face challenges but you'll also need to remind yourself of why you are in business in the first place.

If you're experiencing impostor syndrome you must manage it. As you grow your business, it will occur less frequently. Michelle Obama, former first lady of the United States, put it nicely when she said, "I still have a little impostor syndrome, it never goes away, that you are actually listening to me" (BBC 2018). Impostor syndrome is normal, but you shouldn't let it stop you from doing business. You have the power to overcome it by reminding yourself that while you might be new in business, you have unique gifts, talents, and abilities. You have the right to sit at the table as a new business owner because you have so much to offer.

Summary

My goal as a consultant is not only to solve customer problems using my gifts and talents; I want to make a difference in the community. In his book *Put Your Dreams to the Test*, John Maxwell asks, "What use are your dreams if they do not benefit others?" I believe this to be true. Sharing my dreams with others and inspiring them to take action and live their dreams is what I believe will be my legacy. If you are just getting started, you need to create a picture of what the end looks like—what you want your legacy to be. This will help you determine the right goals and plan to get there.

Having a strategy in place helped me stay focused and my mindset ensured that I did everything it took to succeed in business. Going back to being employed was not an option. Challenges will come, but the decision to work hard and stay in business is driven by your why. I hope this chapter has inspired you to start your business, stay in business, and live out your why. I wish I had known how valuable this was to being a successful consultant.

Actions You Can Take Now

- **Put a price on your head.** As a consultant, you need to get paid for the work you do. Take time to develop your pricing strategy.
- **Name your network.** Who do you want in your network? How can you tap into their expertise? What steps can you take to create a supportive network?
- **Reflect.** Review the Reflection Questions for New Consultants tool online at td.org/handbook-for-consultants. This will help you figure out what you need to learn before starting a consulting business.

About the Author

Maurine Kwende, PhD, is the CEO and founder of EMK Learning Solutions, a company that provides training, instructional design, coaching, leadership, and professional development services to individuals and organizations. Maurine's purpose is to empower others to dream big, act, and reach their full potential through her company, as well as her Dream Big and Boldly Academy (DBBA) for aspiring and emerging leaders, her nonprofit for women and girls, her books, her research, her YouTube channel, and her *Empowerment Minutes* podcast. Prior to becoming an entrepreneur, she spent 20 years in the L&D field. Maurine holds a doctorate in learning technologies design research from George Mason University, with research interests in decision making, artificial intelligence, and emerging technologies. She believes you can be anything you want to be if you take action.

Taking the Plunge
Making the Big Leap Into Consulting

BILL TREASURER

It usually starts with a low-volume curiosity. Maybe you know someone who surprised you by successfully striking out on their own. That sparked a question you hadn't considered before: "I wonder if I could start my own business too?" The more you contemplate the question, the louder the curiosity volume gets.

Or maybe your interest has more to do with suffocation. You're tired of the office drama, dealing with endless volumes of paperwork, attending meeting after boring meeting, suffering through bad bosses, and generally feeling like a cog in a broken machine. That big company you're working for seems smaller and more confining every day. You're done doling out little portions of your soul for an uninspiring job.

Although millions of people have had to make the decision to stay or go, their reasons for standing on the edge of that career leap in the first place often come down to an intense dissatisfaction with the present and a strong desire for a more fulfilling future.

The purpose of this chapter is to help you decide whether you should take the plunge into the world of consulting. You'll learn some key questions to help make a careful and thoughtful decision. You'll also be introduced to two quick but effective frameworks for evaluating whether to make the big career leap.

It's worth noting that I took the plunge you're considering. My interest in striking out on my own grew over the course of a handful of years. I had worked for two small boutique consulting companies—one provided leadership development services and another conducted experiential team building programs. Both companies were led by owners who themselves had struck out on their own; one after a distinguished military career, and the other after a successful career as an insurance agent. After working for those two small companies, I got a job with Accenture as a manager in its change management and human performance practice.

During my time at Accenture, one of the world's largest management and technology consulting firms, I soaked up everything I could learn about organization development. I was fulfilling my educational passion through my professional discipline and things were good. I was assigned to interesting client engagements, I had a great boss, and I was paid very well. When I pitched the idea of becoming an internal executive coach dedicated to helping the company partners become more effective leaders, my boss signed off on the idea. I was able to develop the role, eventually coaching 35 executives—all of whom outranked me—on a regular basis. I became a consultant to the consultants.

Seems like a great situation, right? So, why did I leave? A few things started turning up the volume of my internal voice. First, although I loved working with internal clients, I had become entirely removed from the interesting business challenges that came with being in a client-facing role. I enjoyed coaching, but not enough to do it full time every single day. Second, as I coached executives on the importance of living and leading in alignment with their deepest values, I started to realize I was slowly becoming out of step with my own. I have a strong need for independence, creativity, variety, and frankly, risk taking. My coaching role didn't fully satisfy those needs. I stayed because I enjoyed the work, had a supportive boss, and was treated well by the company. But in the back of my mind, there was a gnawing sense that something was missing.

Then something happened that shifted everything for me—September 11, 2001. I had grown up in New York, and seeing those towers fall had a profound impact on me. It felt like someone had ripped open the curtain and revealed a dark secret: No one is safe. Life is precious, fleeting, and should be lived to the fullest because it can be over in an instant. For me, 9/11 was like a giant domino block that fell in an inevitable direction. Living life to its fullest meant living life courageously now.

My epiphany on 9/11 was the catalyst for a lot of soulsearching, fact finding, and calculation. I started my company—Giant Leap Consulting—in August 2002, and I left Accenture about a month later. My company's goal was to help people and organizations build the courage to take whatever big leaps they might be facing. After all, I had just taken my own.

Should You Take the Plunge?

I can't decide for you whether you should take the big leap or not. But I can help you make the decision. And make no mistake, it's a big decision. If you get it right, it could lead to a meaningful and fulfilling career. But if you get it wrong, you could wipe out hard. The question you'll need to answer is, "Is this the right career risk for me?"

A career risk that's right for you may be wildly absurd for someone else; to that person, you'll be viewed as crazy for taking it. But when faced with a career risk that's the right one for your life, you'd be crazy not to take it. The question becomes, what's the right risk? In my view, right is not a function of safety; it's a function of compatibility. Is the career risk your considering compatible with your values, interests, talents, and vision of your future self?

While I can't guarantee that following my suggestions will result in the successful launch of a lucrative consulting business, I can guarantee that you'll be free of regrets however your decision pans out. Why? Because you'll know you made the decision thoughtfully and in a clear-headed, eyes-wide-open kind of way. If you apply and follow my guidance, the risk you take will be the right one for you.

The Holy Question

In my book, *Right Risk: 10 Powerful Principles for Taking Giant Leaps With Your Life*, I introduce what I call the "Holy Question." I describe it as the four most important words you'll ever learn: What do you want?

The Holy Question holds you accountable to yourself while helping you understand the future you want to create. This is your life we're talking about. No one else can answer the Holy Question for you. You have a responsibility to answer the question truthfully and carefully because a lot is at stake. It can also take you a while—it's not uncommon to start with a clearer idea of what you don't want than what you do. You may already know, for example, that you're done working for bad bosses or obnoxious hours (especially nights and weekends). You're tired of doing the menial tasks that you outgrew years ago. Knowing what you don't want is the first step toward pinpointing what you want, but it works on the dissatisfaction side of the equation—what you're hoping to move away from.

Now give yourself permission to think on the dream side of the equation—the place you want to move toward. What would your career look like if you were inspired to go to work? What would you be doing if you applied yourself to make a bigger and more lasting impact? What would your career look like if you were surrounded by people you admired and enjoyed working with? What would a fulfilling day at work look like? You want that, right?

The point of the Holy Question is to help you paint a vision of the future you hope to advance toward by taking your big leap. It's holy because its sacred. You don't want to be schlepping to work each day slugging it out in an unfulfilling and uninspiring job. You want to be living your career calling, passionately applying your creativity, surrounded by amazing colleagues, and doing meaningful work that matters. A job can be hell. A vocation feels divine.

As you think about the Holy Question, make sure to focus on the impact you hope to have on the other side of the risk. One of the most fulfilling parts about being a consultant is co-creating with your clients to help them face challenges, solve hard problems, and build great companies full of great people. Your aim should always be to add value for whomever you work with, and in whatever situation you're brought into. Your answer to the Holy Question should factor in the value you hope to add on the other side of the leap.

The 5Ps

At this point, you may be thinking, "Wouldn't it be easier if I just made a quick pros and cons list?" Yes, it would be easier. And far more dangerous too. A pros and cons list limits your evaluation to what you might gain and lose. However, big career decisions are too important and nuanced to be made solely on the grounds of gains and losses. As you evaluate your big leap, I suggest instead considering the 5Ps: passion, purpose, principle, prerogative, and profits. While they require more in-depth thinking than a simple pros and cons list, they will help you more accurately decide whether the career you're considering is right for you. If you end up with a strong degree of alignment between each of the 5Ps, there's a very good chance that you should be taking the risk.

Passion

When you think about this risk, does it give you positive energy and excitement or does it make you tired? Does it feel like a burden or fortify you with energy? By arousing the strongest, most untamed parts of your nature, and stirring up the wild mustangs in your soul, your passion can provide the raw energy and wherewithal to suffer through the anguishing moments that often accompany a career risk. The first P asks, "Are you passionate about what you might be leaping toward?"

Purpose

Passion is great, but it works best when it's harnessed in the right direction. Ask yourself, "How will this risk make me a more complete person? How will this risk further my life's purpose? How will it help me get to where I want to go? If I take this risk, will it uphold what I'm all about?" Risk should be about the destination, not compensation. So, ask, "Where will this career risk take me?" not "What will this career risk get me?"

Principle

The right career risks are governed by a set of values that are both essential and virtuous. Like all big risks, career risks are essentially decisions; when facing a decision of consequences, principles form a set of criteria against which you can judge the risk. Ask yourself, "By taking this risk, will I be embodying a value system that I believe in? Will taking this career risk be a concrete way of living my values more fully?"

Prerogative

The power to choose a career of your own making is your right and privilege. Ask yourself, "Am I taking this risk as an exercise of my own free will, choice, and agency? Or will I be taking it because someone else is pushing me in that direction? Am I being pushed off the ledge, or am I leaping because I choose to?" When the decision about whether to take the career risk is an exercise of your own choice, you'll be better able to live with whatever outcomes the decision results in. It's your career and the decision to leap should be your call.

Profit

Yes, you absolutely should gain something by taking the career risk. But profit doesn't just equate to making more money. You profit, too, by doing inspiring and meaningful work, collaborating with talented colleagues, working on interesting assignments, and making a true and lasting impact. So, your career risk should come with a real potential for gain. However, this should be the last criteria that you evaluate, because your judgment can get clouded by the pot of gold on the other side of the rainbow. Many smart people have made dumb career choices because they were chasing a buck.

The 5Ps are powerful criteria with which to consider whether to take your big career jump. They are certainly more comprehensive than a basic pros and cons list. They also help you answer a key question that is sometimes referred to as the Theory of Least Regrets: "What will I regret *the least*? Taking this career risk and possibly failing, or not taking the risk and never knowing if I could have been successful?"

Here are a few more key questions to consider as you stand at the edge of a career risk:

- **Upsides and downsides.** What could go right and how likely is it that it will? What could go wrong and how likely is it that it will?
- **Controllables and uncontrollables.** What important factors can you control? What important factors are beyond your control?
- **Contingency plans and red flags.** If you take the career leap and it starts to go bad, how reversible is it? What plans can you put in place upfront so you can act quickly if the decision goes south? What are some early red flag indicators that you should reconsider your decision?
- **Training and support.** What training do you need to close whatever skill or competency gaps you may have? Whose support and encouragement will help fortify you when the going gets tough?

Staying Resilient In Your Start-Up Business

By Dean Becker, Founder and CEO, Adaptiv Learning

You worked many years in a traditional corporate environment, always exceeding your performance objectives and rising to increasing levels of responsibility and authority. But you craved a level of independence and creativity that could never exist in an inside position. So, you ventured out on your own, full of optimism and certainty that you would succeed.

Six months in, after contacting all your friends and former colleagues who promised to send business your way, you've come up dry. What seemed like a great idea at the time is starting to feel like a huge mistake.

If it's any consolation, you're in very good company. Anyone who's left a corporate job for a startup business has had their resilience tested many times, especially in the early days of their new venture. Here are a few tips to help you manage and even avoid some of the inevitable pitfalls of solopreneurship:

- **Check your thinking.** You are resilient. You've always been optimistic and confident that you can overcome any adversity and succeed. You've seen your way over, around, or through just about every difficulty. But the stress of starting a business from scratch can interfere with your resilient thinking, making the new, unfamiliar challenges you're facing seem bigger and worse than they really are. You might feel helpless and unsure how to proceed. Just take a breath, think about how you've worked through similar issues successfully in the past, and come up with one thing you can do right now to solve the problem. Chances are that this will help you get back on track.
- **Check your perfectionism.** You set high standards for yourself. You might be driven by an internal iceberg belief like "If it's not done perfectly, it's a failure" or "I must get everything right." Because you may be the only human resource in your new company, you need to be ruthless about where you spend your time and energy. This is easier said than done, but self-awareness is a good place to start melting the perfectionism iceberg.
- **Get some help.** It's possible that you have always done well by going it alone. However, in this new role, you don't have time to figure everything out on your own. Fortunately, there are people who will be pleased to help you if you just ask. Create an informal board of directors by making a list of colleagues, friends, and even family, who can help you navigate the road ahead. You will be surprised by how many will be eager to help.
- **Get some sales training.** If you are trading on your subject matter expertise in the new business, you probably need to sharpen your sales skills. Effective business development is crucial to your success and is largely a learned capability. Online resources like LinkedIn offer an array of e-learning content and other materials that you can tap into. Seek out a proven sales professional in your network and get some recommendations.
- **Be realistic.** Most startups take years, not months, to achieve a stable, predictable level of revenues and profits. If solopreneurship is truly for you, you'll need to be focused, persistent, and resilient over the long term. This may be the biggest challenge of all.

How can you stay resilient in your startup business?

The Worst-Case Grid

The 5Ps reflect a qualitative way of assessing your career risk. For those who prefer a more quantitative approach, the Worst-Case Grid (WCG) offers a way of objectifying the subjective experience of a big risk into a single numeric value (Figure 5-1). It's really easy to

Figure 5-1. The Worst-Case Grid

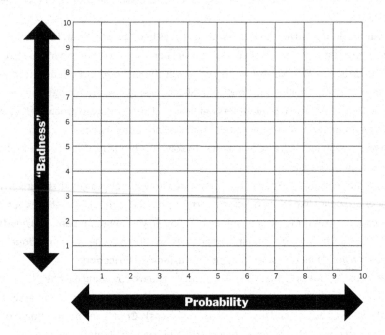

use—just create an x and y axis and divide each into a 1 to 10 scale. Put the word "badness" on the y axis and "probability" on the x axis.

Think of badness as the worst possible outcome if your career risk crashed. When I was considering leaving Accenture, for example, the worst outcome would have been destroying my financial situation. That outcome would have resulted in me and my wife moving in with her parents. While not a 10, let's call it an eight. Once I landed on that number, I could move to the x axis and consider the probability of that bad outcome occurring. While a lot of new businesses fail—some estimates suggest at least 50 percent fail within five years—I had done some things to mitigate that likelihood. I had a graduate degree, more than 15 years of consulting experience, and had taken some night classes about how to start a business. So, I figured that the probability of a catastrophic outcome was about a two. To figure out my WCG total, I multiplied the numbers from my x and y axis (8 x 2) to get 16. That number wasn't threatening enough to stop me from taking the big leap.

The WCG is a simple tool for quickly and objectively evaluating a risk. However, you'll need to decide what risk number you can live with. For me a 16 was a low number. Even 25 wouldn't have stopped me. But for someone else, 25 might be too high a threshold.

You can (and should) also create a Best-Case Grid (BCG), in which the y axis envisions the best-case outcome. That is, if the career risk works out even better than you could have imagined, what great outcomes might you gain, and what's the likelihood of those things happening?

Consulting Tip

Make a list of the worst things that could happen if you start a consulting practice. Also make a list of the best things that could happen.

Beyond Evaluation

Let's assume that after carefully evaluating your big career risk, you decide to take the plunge. The next thing you have to figure out is how. You'll need to do a lot more planning and take action. You'll need to set up a business entity, get business insurance, set up a place to work, buy office equipment, write a business plan, create or buy marketing material, possibly secure funding, and figure out a million other details. So, for goodness' sake, don't quit your job the same day you decide to take the big leap!

Take solace in knowing that things don't have to happen in one gigantic lunge. Big leaps should start with and be built upon little leaps. I call it "weight shifting." Start shifting your energy and attention slowly into your new career while still working in your current one. Do the things you need to do to launch your business one thing at a time, on your own time. You might have to get up a little earlier each day or devote some of your lunch hour to knocking out some of the items, but you'll get there.

I'd also recommend talking to other people who have made the leap and gotten to the other side successfully. Consider asking:

- What details would they advise you to attend to?
- What unforeseen challenges did they face?
- What unexpected hardships did they endure?
- Having been through it, what advice do they have for you as you strike out on your own?
- What resources do they suggest you tap into?
- Who else would they recommend you speak with?

The purpose of the conversation isn't to quell your enthusiasm for starting your own business. It's to get a clear and realistic understanding of what challenges you'll face as you progress. It's a reality-check conversation.

One thing that you'll likely hear from each successful person you talk to is that, looking back, they wish they had taken the plunge years before they did.

Consulting Tip

Examine a calendar and pick a date to start your consulting practice. Share that date with someone who can give you candid feedback, and ask them how realistic this date is. Enjoy the conversation.

Summary

One thing you'll mostly likely ask people who have jumped into the world of consulting is, "Is it worth it?" I can only speak from my own experience, but my answer is a resounding, "Yes, yes, YES!"

Today I live a life of my own design. My consulting business provides opportunities that fully engage my creative energies, allow me to spend my time on tasks that captivate my attention, and experience the tight link between the work I put in and the results I get. Yes, some of those outcomes are financial. More importantly, Giant Leap Consulting reflects my own value system and its mission aligns with my own: to help people and organizations get superior results by being more courageous.

Don't get me wrong, I definitely have hard days and so will you. While most clients are overwhelmingly decent and good, some are persnickety and temperamental. Travel is a grind. Managing the financial and accounting stuff can be drudgery. I still have to occasionally work late at night or on the weekend. But those downers are far outweighed by the upsides. The most rewarding aspect is seeing the positive difference that my company makes with clients. I draw such pride from watching clients muster up the courage to take on challenges or pursue ambitious opportunities that they otherwise would have avoided. I love helping them take giant leaps.

Actions You Can Take Now

- **Plan ahead.** Thoughtfully answer the questions in this chapter, evaluate your big decision using the 5Ps, sketch out worst-case and best-case grids, and identify the likelihood of each scenario materializing.
- **Gather more information.** Read *The New Consultant's Quick Start Guide: An Action Plan for Your First Year in Business* by Elaine Biech.
- **Build up your savings account.** The more money you can save before launching your business, the better you'll feel knowing that you've got some financial breathing room. I recommend saving a minimum of six-months' worth of income.
- **Have a heart-to-heart.** If you have a significant other, plan dedicated time to discuss your plan with them. Let them know how much their support means to you as you transition through this journey.
- **Get healthy.** Start exercising, eating right, and meditating. You're going to need to be in good shape for the hard work ahead.

About the Author

Bill Treasurer is the founder of Giant Leap Consulting, a courage-building company that has worked with renowned clients such as NASA, eBay, UBS Bank, Spanx, Lenovo, Saks Fifth Avenue, Southern Company, and the US Social Security Administration and Department of Veterans Affairs. Bill is the author of six books, including the international bestseller, *Courage Goes to Work: How to Build Backbone, Boost Performance, and Get Results*. He is also a former captain of the US high diving team, and has performed more than 1,500 dives from heights that scaled to over 100 feet. Hence the name of his company, Giant Leap! You can connect with Bill at btreasurer@giantleapconsulting.com.

Clarify Your Why

CINDY HUGGETT

A consultant's journey begins when they start providing client solutions and generating revenue. Or does it? Some would say the journey begins well before then during the business planning phase. Others would say it begins when they get a business license or set up their website. No matter when or how a consultant begins, these first steps determine their initial direction and ultimately their path to success. For some, this may be smooth and easy, but for most, the path is likely to be rocky, bumpy, and full of twists and turns.

My consulting business began accidentally almost 20 years ago when I was caught in a large organizational layoff. My boss quietly asked if I would stay on as a contractor, doing essentially the same training manager job, just as an external consultant. What was initially bad news turned out to be one of the best things that ever happened to me. My former employer became my first client, and many of the other laid off employees went to other organizations, who in turn called me to do work for them too. It was an unusual but ideal start.

It took me a few years to figure out that virtual training was my consulting niche. I started as a training generalist—facilitating leadership programs, creating performance management systems, and offering course design services—but I kept getting asked about the virtual technologies I infused into most of my recommended solutions.

After taking on some focused consulting projects, I discovered my passion for virtual training. Despite its rocky reputation for boring online lectures, I found it was possible to create engaging online experiences. With three components—an interactive design, a skilled facilitator, and prepared participants—virtual training could be both appealing and effective. My business focus became helping others learn how to do those three things well. I saw organizations struggling with it and wanted to help.

As I transitioned my services from general to specific, I intentionally invested time both privately and with others to help me gain clarity on my business direction. Why was I going to go all-in on virtual training? If I was going to dedicate a significant amount of time to helping organizations move to the virtual classroom, what would ring true for me in that? By asking these questions, surveying my skills, looking at the marketplace, and recognizing my lifelong love of teaching, I clarified my why as a deep desire to enable others to create engaging virtual training that translates to meaningful business results. I wanted to empower others to see the positive possibilities that virtual training could offer, and to have practical tools to create it. I was already passionate about the topic; getting clear on the why and the what helped solidify my services.

Looking back over the last 15 years of my journey, any time the work became challenging or monotonous, when it seemed difficult or I was stretched to my limits, returning to my roots always helped me mentally get back on track. When I've been asked to take on projects that weren't quite the right fit for my core offerings, I've been able to consider whether to make an exception by looking at it from my primary point of view. I've also returned to it when thinking through business expansions and updates. Knowing not just what I do but why I do it has resulted in tremendous benefits, time and time again.

So why do some consultants have an easier journey than others? And more importantly, how do they make it happen? The difference is having a crystal-clear direction. The successful consultants have taken the time to clarify what they do and why they do it, and then use that information to guide them along the way. Understanding their why helps them make daily decisions and careful choices. One step at a time, they forge forward on a clear-cut path to success. In this chapter, we'll tackle common challenges new, and experienced, consultants face, and how clarifying your why can help you sidestep them yourself.

Consulting Challenges

Imagine the consultant's business journey—from its starting place to its end point—as a road trip across the expanse of time. Along the way, most consultants encounter three common obstacles. Consultants who have successfully clarified their why are able to either overcome these challenges or quickly sidestep them. Let's look at these obstacles to see if you recognize them:

- **Scope creep.** Consultants typically have a niche product or service that makes up the primary focus of their business. But over time, these offerings can veer away from center. It may start as a simple client request in the middle of a project—"While you're at it, could you also help us with this other thing?" Or it might be a gradual addition of new but unrelated services over time. Consultants who freelance may have a hard time turning away from a money-making opportunity, so they say yes despite the risk of losing focus on their core offerings.

- **Slogging through challenges.** Sometimes the drudgery of day-to-day hurdles can steal the joy of working. Most consultants love what they do and find passion in their service to others. Yet difficult clients, tough circumstances, and unexpected problems can quickly creep into the mix. Consultants who get bogged down into the minutiae of cumbersome challenges can lose their motivation, risk burnout, or worse. Just going through the motions may work for a short while but sustained stress usually leads to catastrophe in the long run.

- **Stale consulting services.** While on the surface this may seem like a confusing challenge, it's actually more of a problem than most people realize. The crux of the issue is that a consultant's primary solution will eventually become obsolete if it stays exactly the same over a long period of time without adapting or responding to current business realities. For example, think of a consultant who facilitates time management workshops without adjusting the content to recognize digital calendars. Or a consultant who only takes appointments by telephone when the rest of the world is expecting video conferencing. Less extreme examples include consultants who use the same proposal template for more than 10 years or have the same exact blueprint approach for every client request. For sure, there's value in time-tested solutions, but too much complacency can lead to less than desirable outcomes. Good enough doesn't lead to great results.

A Strategic Solution

The primary answer to these challenges, either as a preventative tool or as a fix-it solution, is to clarify your why. Whether you are just getting started as a consultant, or you've been one for a while, it's never too late to go through this process. Ideally consultants clarify their why when they start their business, and then revisit it periodically to renew and refresh. But investing in the process anytime will yield fruitful results.

Once you determine the reasons for your consulting practice—not just what you do but why you do it—you will be able to stay focused on what matters most. Clarifying your why helps you create a solid pathway for navigating your consulting journey. This knowledge serves as a guidepost for difficult decisions and helps keep you motivated even when times get tough. You'll also identify your unique skill set so that you're better equipped to recognize and avoid bad business decisions when appealing but incorrect choices come your way. And with a clear purpose, your desire to stay current and continually improve will strengthen.

Various analogies exist to describe the process of clarifying your why. Some call it finding your true north or discovering your guiding star. Others refer to it as writing your mission statement or catching your vision. While these are all valid options and could add value to your consultancy, I believe that clarifying your why has a distinct purpose and process.

Years ago, I had the privilege of attending one of Steven Covey's leadership train-the-trainer programs. During that program, Covey shared a story that still sticks with me. He talked about a medieval construction site with dozens of bricklayers at work. When the first mason was asked about his job, he said he was laying bricks and mortar to make a wall. The second and third masons responded the same. But the fourth mason joyfully said, "I'm building a cathedral!" He looked beyond the individual bricks to the inspirational building—the big picture and the end result. By keeping the end goal in mind, he had the motivation to complete his repetitive tasks.

This simple story encapsulates what it means to clarify your why: recognizing the underlying reasons behind what you do, envisioning the big picture of success, and using that information as motivation for moving forward. And keeping this behind-the-scenes truth at the forefront of your mind so that you have extreme clarity to use as both a filter and a guidepost.

How to Clarify

Despite the title of this section, which implies there is one way to clarify your why, there are many methods you can use. You can choose just one or a combination of these approaches. Some require resources while others just need your commitment. What they all have in common is dedicated reflection time to help reveal your core purpose. Some consultants find the discovery process quick and easy; others need an unhurried pace for contemplation. By slowing down to determine what's important to you, and why it's significant, you can then speed up to provide value in the places that matter most.

Consulting Tip

Schedule a specific day and time with yourself to clarify your why. Plan which technique you will use and protect your time. Keep your date with yourself—don't cancel!

Review the following techniques, making note of the ones that most appeal to you:

- **Create a vision board.** For consultants who benefit from seeing pictures and graphics, a vision board delivers results. Start by looking for inspirational quotes, notes, and images. As you notice ones that spark your interest and imagination, use them to form a collage. You can use printed materials and physical supplies or collect digital resources on an electronic whiteboard. Either way, your visual imagery should reveal patterns and themes, which you can use to discover your key motivations. For example, your curated collection may revolve around the idea of "helping others start something new so they can go and grow," which you could then use as the foundation for your business.

- **Go on a silent retreat.** A silent retreat is exactly what it sounds like—time and space filled with nothing but mindfulness. It's a set duration on the clock, in a distraction-free zone, where you can sit with your thoughts. To embark on this quiet adventure, leave your mobile devices behind, find a comfortable spot, and just breathe. If staying relatively still feels stressful to you, make it a moving meditation—walk, hike, or bike. Just make sure the motion doesn't become your focus. The point of a silent retreat is to find a peaceful place in your mind so you have adequate thinking space. In the midst of the silence often comes clarity. If you're used to a fast-paced, always-on, noisy environment, then the first part of the experience may just be a stepping stone to stillness. Once you can quietly settle in with your thoughts, you can reflect on people, places, feelings, and things that bring you true joy. Extended periods of silence help most people think deeply. Use the inward reflection time to help you find the authentic meaning behind your work.

- **Join a business mastermind group.** For some, internal thoughts are best processed out loud in the company of others. External thinkers benefit from conversation. And what better place to have this dialogue than with other like-minded consultants? Whether you call this group your mastermind crew, your personal board of directors, or your advisory team, the point is to bring together a diverse squad with dedicated time for brainstorming and feedback that everyone can benefit from. Make use of this opportunity to talk through your consultancy's mission, vision, purpose, and values. Gather external input to help you gain clarity on your work. Combine the wisdom into a conversation that works for you, but remember that you alone make the final determination on what matters most in your journey. About a decade ago, I used this technique during a pivotal time in my business, sharing aloud my thoughts during a weekend retreat. My trusted advisor network listened and offered feedback, and the results turned into the unique underlying principles that form my why.

- **Work with a mentor or coach.** Connecting with an experienced mentor or business coach may be the best option for those who need individualized assistance to identify their main purpose. One-on-one time with a formal mentor or qualified coach provides a focused space to clarify business goals. More specifically, a skilled mentor or coach can help you discover hidden gems and buried thoughts that could lead to better perspectives. Competent coaches actively listen, ask pointed questions, observe patterns, and give personalized guidance. They can provide tailored insights that may otherwise go unnoticed and add perspective from their own treasure trove of experience. Think of this person as a guide who can help you see things that wouldn't otherwise rise to the surface in your own self-exploration.

- **Complete a personal audit.** Audits involve a thorough search through records to look for congruence or challenges. A personal audit, in the context of clarifying your why, includes a thoughtful reflection of where you spend your time and resources. Review your calendar, your finances, your inbox, and your experiences, making note of what energizes you and what drains you. Beyond the potential personal benefits, a personal audit can reveal what's below the surface of your consulting practice. In other words, it looks for actual patterns of behavior so that you can use that data to make observations and conclusions. For example, you may reluctantly spend time on the administrative aspects of your business, preferring to use that calendar space for client interaction. But a deeper dive into the types of client interactions that bring joy and satisfaction may expose a common thread that unwraps your why. For me, during an informal personal audit early in my career, I realized there was a certain type of client that I was drawn to like a magnet. Discovering this pattern helped me recognize how much I enjoyed it, which led me to crystallize my focus on that type of project work.

Connecting Your Why to a Business Need

Discovering your why might actually be the easy part. Fitting that into what clients need and will pay for can be more challenging. The process of clarifying your why should also include a survey of the business environment and potential client requirements. Then ask yourself, "How do my personal values align with my potential client's needs?"

You've probably heard the saying, do what you love, the money will follow. It's one thing to love what you do, but it's another to make money doing it. As you clarify your why, connect it to relevant business needs in the marketplace. Try creating a Venn diagram with three overlapping circles labeled: What I am passionate about, what I am good at, and what someone would pay me to do. Any items that fit under all three headings provide a clue about what part of consulting would make you happy as well as connect your why to a business need. This is where you can apply your passion and strengths in the context of what your clients need.

Finding your why is important, but also remember that it may evolve and change over time. Many consultants discover that their why develops an altruistic bent beyond making money to more meaningful parts of life. These elements might include relationships, investing in people, spreading kindness, or adding positive value to the world around you—the things that make a difference and create lasting impact. It's nearly impossible to place a monetary value on these sentiments, but the investments can return dividends in ways that are more personally valuable and meaningful. Keep reflecting on your why as you gain more clarity about your purpose and how it aligns with consulting. As you do so, you will likely experience a greater sense of fulfillment and motivation in your personal and professional life.

Consulting Tip

Looking for another view of the importance of clarifying your why? Check out Simon Sinek's "Start With Why" TED Talk.

Summary

Your consulting journey may be just starting or you may be well into years of service. Either way, it's always a good time to clarify your why. If it's your first time thinking about it, then review the techniques listed in this chapter. If you are revisiting it, consider what methods have worked for you in the past and return to them.

There are specific times in a consultant's journey when it's prudent to revisit your foundation. For example, personal changes may require a recalibration of what's most important to you. Or you may need to re-establish your purpose after significant industry or environmental changes. For example, the COVID-19 pandemic forced many consultants to reflect on and even pivot their businesses. A periodic review helps you stay true to your foundation and relevant in the marketplace.

I personally take annual self-reflection time to review and revisit all aspects of my business. Some years this takes the form of a weekend retreat, while other years it's a short visit to a local coffee shop. Regardless of the location or amount of time, it always includes reassessing my why.

Actions You Can Take Now

- **Remind yourself.** Once you take the first step to clarify what you do and why you do it, you'll want to keep that information in the forefront of your mind. This can be a surprisingly simple thing to do—write it on a strategically placed sticky note on your desk; create a wallpaper for your smartphone so you see it every time the screen lights up; or create daily (or weekly) calendar notifications for a recurring reminder to revisit your why.
- **Share with others.** Share your why with others. Tell a trusted advisor who can help you stay accountable to it. Use it to motivate you and spur you along each step of the way.

About the Author

Cindy Huggett, CPTD, has vast experience delivering engaging learning solutions. She's the author of six acclaimed books on the subject, including *Virtual Training Tools and*

Templates: An Action Guide to Live Online Learning and *The Facilitator's Guide to Immersive, Blended, and Hybrid Learning.* As a 20-year pioneer of virtual training, Cindy upskills trainers and designers to help them create actionable virtual training and hybrid learning. She has taught thousands of people to leverage live-online training through her cutting-edge workshops and presentations on topics related to leadership, learning, and technology. Based in Raleigh, North Carolina, Cindy serves clients globally. To learn more, visit cindyhuggett.com.

SECTION II

Getting Started
Your Plan for Success

You've weighed the pros and cons and made the decision to try consulting. Now, it's time to determine the best path for you. That's what this section is all about.

Our luminary consulting author Ann Herrmann-Nehdi has more than 35 years of experience running a family business. In her chapter, she shares her secret for success: her 5 Ps of business strategy (payoff, process, people, possibilities, and pivot). Ann's 5 Ps detail the things you need to consider as you begin your consulting quest and continue your success. She advises you to "create your future plan by imagining where you want to be at a specific time in the future, and then capture the details on paper." Ann offers some high-level thinking that's appropriate for a "luminary" contribution, but she also mixes in some practical and actionable advice. The best news? She takes you through the process of creating your plan and then shares it as a downloadable tool.

If you are at the planning stage, remember to clarify your role with ideas from Sharon Wingron, tap into Maureen Orey's ideas for naming your business, and identify all the details of setting up your consulting office with Jonathan Halls. Then, Jacob Kuczmanski, Sy Islam, and Mike Chetta will introduce you to working as a consultant on the inside, while Brian Washburn overviews your role as an entrepreneur.

5 Paths to Break Into Consulting

If you've decided consulting is right for you, what opportunities exist to get started? Think about your ultimate goal. Do you want to be a partner in one of the Big Four accounting firms? Will you eventually own your own firm? Do you think you will always want to consult as a sole practitioner? Or do you want to teach part time at a small university and consult on the side? There are many ways to enter the field. I'll review five here.

1. Large Firm Employee

If you have just graduated from college, working for a large firm is your best bet to experience the consulting profession. As an employee in a large firm, you will be an extra pair of hands assisting with large projects, which is a great way to get experience. Consulting is typically listed as one of the top paying jobs. If you have a bachelor's degree and land a gig at a major firm, you can typically expect to earn between $60,000 and $80,000; for some, the salary can even approach $100,000. These figures typically include base salary, a signing bonus, and relocation expenses. However, keep in mind that first-year consultants may work up to 14-hour days and travel most weeks. If you stay in school longer, the rewards are greater. MBAs from top schools can expect to be offered a base salary hovering around $150,000 as new consultants with firms such as Deloitte, Accenture, McKinsey, Bain, or the Boston Consulting Group. These jobs generally come with a great deal of pressure because you're expected to generate (sell) a certain amount of consulting services. Travel is another drawback. If you're thinking about choosing this route, make sure to read chapter 8—Jacob Kuczmanski shares more about these large firms, including who they are and what they do.

2. Small Firm Employee

As a consultant in a small, local firm, you would experience similar advantages to those working for a large, national firm. You'll probably be able to experience a wider variety of tasks and be given more responsibility sooner. However, if traveling is one of your goals, keep in mind that working for a small firm often means you'll be limited to working with businesses in your locality. Your salary may be half what it could be with a large firm, but you typically have less pressure, more opportunity for a variety of projects, and more involvement in the entire consulting process. Find small consulting companies by checking with your local, industry-specific association chapters. Many small firms do not find value in advertising, so a local librarian or chamber of commerce can help you. Read more about what to expect in a boutique consulting practice in chapter 9 by Sy Islam and Mike Chetta.

3. Subcontractor

Rather than becoming an employee, you could subcontract with a firm. Many businesses and consulting firms are looking for subcontractors who can fill in the gaps left by downsizing or launching new initiatives. As a subcontractor, your position may be less secure, but you will have the flexibility to grow while gaining a rich experience and developing a sense of the market. The work probably won't be full time, but this gives you time to develop your own business.

Who might hire you? You could consider looking at the larger companies previously listed. Or, if you like the idea of being a training consultant, consider reaching out to some of the leading training suppliers, such as American Management Association (AMA), DDI, Franklin Covey, Herrmann International, and The Ken Blanchard Companies. In addition, there are new consulting matchups, such as PwC's Talent Exchange, which connects independent consultants with PwC opportunities.

4. Side Hustle

If you're not ready to take the plunge, you could consult part time while keeping your current job. Some people use their vacation time and weekends to work on small projects—with their employer's approval, of course. For example, if your specialty is team building or facilitating decision-making meetings, you might be able to lead weekend retreats for boards of nonprofit organizations. Part-time work won't give you the full flavor of what it is like to solely depend on consulting as a career; however, it will give you an idea of whether you like the profession. But remember, always inform your manager of your plans.

5. Self-Employed Independent Consultant

And of course, there's the ultimate choice—starting your own consulting practice. If you've developed expertise in an area, you might choose to build and run your own business around that niche. You can specialize in virtually anything, including management, IT, marketing, finance, healthcare, the environment, and social media. Today's gig economy is encouraging many people to start their own businesses. A consultant is generally thought of as being in the highest skill end of the gig economy spectrum.

As an independent consultant, you can make all the decisions, do what you want when you want, and receive all the recognition. The drawback, of course, is that you also have to assume all the risk, be responsible for all the expenses, and potentially lack someone at your level who is readily available for discussing business plans and concerns. According to Consulting.com, the average annual revenue of an independent consultant is $97,000, but your revenue potential is wide open and completely uncapped. With a good plan you can break through to a seven-figure income. If this is the path you imagine, you'll want to focus on Brian Washburn's chapter, which overviews a consultant's critical role as an entrepreneur.

There are other ways to break into consulting, but these are the most common. Which one appeals most to you?

The 5 Ps of Business Strategy

Possibilities, People, Payoff, Process, and Pivots

ANN HERRMANN-NEHDI, *LUMINARY CONSULTING AUTHOR*

The pungent smell of the smoke overwhelmed me. My eyes watering, I saw in the near distance—a distance that kept drawing closer—the mountain was burning. My company's headquarters for 35 years stood right in the path of growing flames. There was a very good chance we could lose everything! At that moment, in the midst of it all, I wondered, what now?

But I am getting ahead of myself! More on that story later. We all face critical times when we need to stop and think about where we are, how we are progressing, and where we want to be. Whether you're wondering what the next big step will be for your business or dealing with a surprise recession, an unforeseen pandemic, or a dramatic change in your marketplace or even facing an impending fire, we all reach moments when we need to take a minute to think beyond today and focus on the future.

Thousands of books, articles, and blog posts have been authored about business strategy. They all seem to talk about dreaming up the possibilities and charting the future story of your business. And then you need to pull together the people to make it happen, ensure you can make it all pay off, and put in place the right processes for success. But sometimes, even with the best laid plans and strategy, you'll realize that it's time to pivot.

The basis of the 5 Ps (possibilities, people, payoff, process, and pivots) comes from my experience running a business for more than 35 years. My family's business is now in its third generation, and it's gone through all five Ps several times. Along with a lot of great advisors, sweat, stress, and luck, I have a secret weapon that I've used as a guiding principle to navigate the twists and turns of ongoing success: Whole Brain Thinking.

A metaphor for how we think, the Whole Brain Thinking Model is based on brain research conducted and developed at GE's Management Development Institute, which highlighted the areas of cognitive diversity that exist within each of us (Figure 7-1). A wide array of workplace applications in management and leadership development, innovation, and strategic thinking models has emerged as a result. For example, every business has competing priorities that it must pay attention to when growing in order to be successful.

Figure 7-1. The Whole Brain Business Model

Used with permission from Herrmann Global.

Possibilities

Susan had been dreaming for more than a year about an exciting idea she had for her consulting company. "So how do I know?" she asked when she reached out to me for advice. "Does this idea make sense? Should I go for it?" When I asked her why this had been going on for so long, she said, "I'm stuck. I can't seem to figure out how to focus on strategy and long-term goals when I feel like the day-to-day is eating me alive."

This situation is all too common and I've heard it from many business leaders. They know how important strategy is, and might even enjoy strategic thinking, but they find themselves constantly dealing with day-to-day noise that only seems to get louder. As I listened to Susan, I thought back to the many times I had found myself in that situation, and I recalled some advice I'd gotten from my father years earlier: "Create your plan by imagining where you want to be at a specific time in the future. Then capture the details on paper." Deceivingly simple yet powerful!

One of the reasons so many people struggle with strategic thinking is because it can seem complex and overwhelming. It's easy to get wrapped up in all the obstacles and micro decisions you need to make along the way. So, what can you do? Use the one page future plan to stop, dream about where you want to be, and capture that vision in a non over-whelming way.

To create your own one page future plan, start with a blank piece of paper or digital document. Then follow these steps:

1. Select a point in time you feel comfortable with, whether that's two, three, five, or even 10 years in the future. (Note: Many people have told me that in today's quickly changing world, 10 years feels completely out of reach, and that's OK. The important thing is to step out of today and imagine yourself in whatever timeframe you have planned.)

2. Put today's date on the left side of the page, and then list your chosen future date on the right side.

3. Draw a line across the page. (I like to use a diagonal line heading upward because that mentally implies positive progress and growth, but you can divide your page however you want.)

4. Now, step away from your day-to-day environment to refresh your thinking and open your brain to possibilities. Be intentional about this! Try leaving your normal workspace, whatever that means for you (even if it is at home), and taking a walk to clear your thinking. See what bubbles up—this is a useful form of intentional daydreaming!

5. Imagine yourself being very successful doing what you described in your future state. As you think about it, your first reaction might be, "That's impossible. How

in the world can I ever do that?" But you can't let these thoughts stop your process. If you are struggling, try one of these techniques:

- ° Think of someone else creating this future. What would that person be doing? Removing yourself from the picture neutralizes your self-limiting beliefs.
- ° Try placing yourself at that point in the future and then analyze how you got there.

6. Once you've put the dates in place and imagined what that world looks like, describe your future state in as much detail as possible, answering the following questions:
   - ° What are you doing?
   - ° What are you selling? What aren't you selling?
   - ° What are you paying attention to?
   - ° What have you stopped doing?
   - ° Who are your customers?
   - ° Did you leave any customers behind?
   - ° How are you making money?
   - ° Who's helping you?

7. Bridge the gap between today's state and your desired future state. In essence, write a story about your future. (Technically, this part is called *scenario planning*, and it's a basic tenet of strategy building.)

8. Share your ideas with others to get reactions and build excitement. Bring together people who are willing to ask you thoughtful or provocative questions to help you gain greater clarity. Use these insights to begin forming the vision of your future state.

9. Test the reality of your vision by exploring the steps required to reach this desired future state.

A note on writing your future story: Linear thinkers (those in the B quadrant of the Whole Brain Thinking model) find it much easier to start with today and progressively move toward the future. Big picture thinkers (D quadrant) like working backward from the future state to the present. More relational thinkers (C quadrant) love to think of this as a story they are telling and may prefer working with others to develop it. Analytical thinkers (A quadrant) typically want to be as goal and measurement focused as possible. Your preference doesn't matter. What's important is that you start writing your story. Capture the things that seem most obvious to you first. You can fill in the blanks later.

When I went through this exercise some years ago, I realized my story had a big gaping hole—funding. I didn't have the necessary funding to bring on the talent and people necessary to accomplish my future vision. And I wasn't sure where to go from there. So I started having conversations with my trusted advisors, and through those conversations, several available options became obvious. Make sure that you look at any gaps and ask yourself, "In what way might I _____, in order to _____?" For example, "How might I find $10 million in immediate funding to build the platform I need to hire the talent required for my targeted growth?"

Consulting Tip

The possibilities planning process often reveals more than one possible future. In that case, use what you learn to create additional one page future plans as needed.

If, after going through all these steps, you find that the timeline you selected was too short, don't worry. Your future state may well be on point, but if your ability to accomplish it in the designated timeframe was overly optimistic or ambitious, simply push your timeframe— perhaps by adding an additional three to five years.

People

The people strategy warrants attention because people are the engine that makes things happen. Let's start with customers! Getting upfront and personal with your customer targets (or personas) and their needs is essential in any business. Start by answering these questions:

- Who are they?
- Why do they care?
- Will your product or service provide a solution to their problems?
- How many potential customers are there?
- Is there already an available solution they are happy with?

Building a clear and solid understanding of and empathy for your future customers is essential. The renowned Stanford School of Design suggests starting with empathy when developing any new offering. But watch out! Don't fall into the trap of thinking you know what your customers want and need. Reach out beyond the confines of your own brain and get real insights and data to really understand the problem you're solving.

If you are looking at a strategic change in your existing customer base, one somewhat painful lesson I've learned is that your existing customers may not want a new and different offering if what you're currently providing suits their needs. (Remember New Coke?) If they don't understand why they need to change, you may need to educate them. You'll also need to recognize that it is sometimes easier to get new customers on board than to re-educate existing customers.

Beyond your customers, your people strategy also includes your team. Whether you're a three-person venture or a 10,000-person organization, the people who are actually going to translate your future state into reality are key to your strategy's success. My research for the past 40 years has shown that successful businesses need a cognitively diverse team, and this is particularly important for CEOs and entrepreneurs. Your unique thinking preferences make you brilliant at what you do, but they can also represent your greatest challenge.

Years ago, as part of a CEO group, I worked with Angela. She was one of the savviest businesspeople I knew at the time, especially when it came to her ability to negotiate fantastic prices and find terrific distribution resources. She was incredibly organized, practical, and good at execution, but when it came to change, she really struggled. If the situation didn't have an immediate next step attached to it, she would freeze up and put it off. She might make incremental improvements, but they were rarely innovative. When changes in the global supply chain caught up with her business, Angela was so unprepared that the whole system just stopped working. Without a Plan B, she ultimately ended up losing the business.

Because Angela had surrounded herself with people who thought in very similar ways, her team was often able to quickly make decisions and reach consensus. This was exacerbated by cultural norms that discouraged conflict, which meant that even if her team had other ideas, they weren't bringing them up. What made Angela so incredibly good was also her greatest downfall. So, make sure you are surrounded by a group of people who not only think differently than you, but are also willing to challenge your thinking.

It's critical to understand your customers and how they think and what they need, but also how your team thinks and what they bring to the table. They are a critical part of the next P—payoff.

Payoff

Payoff seems like such an obvious thing to discuss in any business context, so I'm amazed at how often it gets overlooked. Sometimes this is because the business leader isn't inclined to think in terms of this perspective, or they don't have the right team member to help them quantify it. Perhaps they are missing processes that allow them to track the payoff or their vision just didn't include any thinking in that direction.

Nevertheless, the payoff may be the place to start if it's not part of your natural thinking. I think Marjorie Blanchard, the leader of the office of the future for the Blanchard companies, said it best during a conference panel: "Your first priority should be to understand whether you have customers that will pay for what you want to sell and deliver to them." Again, without seeming too basic, not only do you need customers, but you need to make money! The return on investment, the cash flow, managing payables, and so on are critical. The nuts and bolts of good business is dependent on finances.

Unfortunately, I've seen too many companies fold because they were not on top of their core numbers. Their lack of understanding meant they didn't have a financial plan in place to address major changes in the marketplace, leading to the rapid demise of their business.

Get real with your numbers. Understand them! If you don't understand them, make sure someone on your team can help you. Put it at the top of your review list, and pay attention to any patterns or trends that may indicate something is going off the rails. Even the best business leaders I know have been caught off guard by changes in the economy or the environment. Don't let that happen to you. In addition, get advice on your pricing. You may find that you're under charging!

Process

Process is actually my favorite P even though it's not my preferred thinking style. I've learned the hard way just how critical processes are to helping your business grow and execute against a strategy. There's a saying, "Every organization is perfectly designed for the results that it gets." If you are not getting the results that you want, what processes do you need to develop to ensure you can get them?

Michael Wilkinson, who owns the Atlanta-based consulting and training company Leadership Strategies, realized after a recession that the company didn't have a process for adjusting the budget when unexpected downturns occurred. So he invented the envelope process to address it. Whenever things get financially tight (and Michael knows his numbers well enough to see that coming), the company puts certain expenditures aside or in an envelope until cash flow or revenue could support them.

Processes are so essential that people may find it hard to do their job effectively without them. Imagine how frustrating it would be if someone had a job to do but wasn't sure how to do it because the processes were not clear, not documented, or kept changing. This slows them down and may endanger a client relationship or create a problematic quality control situation. Confusion and misfires are often a sign that processes need clarification.

When you're in a small team, you can get away with figuring out the processes or inventing them as you go, but that isn't scalable if you want to grow your business. I know some leaders who are determinedly process phobic, believing that processes are overly controlling and create complexity (especially if they also have to follow them!). However, if this describes you, I encourage you to talk with people who are doing process work—ask them what processes they need and then give them the resources to put those processes in place.

Pivots

Pivoting is something that I find myself talking about almost every day to both my internal and external partners because today's environment requires constant pivots to stay relevant.

As Rory McDonald and Robert Bremner (2020) wrote in *Harvard Business Review*, "Changing direction is, in theory, a good thing for a business. The path to enduring success is rarely a straight line. Cornelius Vanderbilt switched from steamships to railroads, William Wrigley from baking powder to gum. Twitter launched as a podcast directory, Yelp began as an automated email service, and YouTube was once a dating site. Research shows that new ventures that reinvent their businesses—even multiple times—cut their chances of failure by conserving resources while continuing to learn more about customers, business partners, and new technologies."

Pivots require you step back and evaluate where you are headed by focusing on the first p—possibilities. They're typically prompted by a business context that requires you to change to stay alive, thrive, or grow. And it can be scary to pivot, especially if all seems to be going well in the short term but looks ominous or uncertain in the longer term.

One of my favorite examples comes from my own company and the significant pivots we took to scale to the next level when my son, Karim Nehdi, took over the leadership position. We were having a hard time attracting talent because our location was very remote. In addition, our business was changing dramatically, which meant we needed a new type of talent. My son had encouraged me to consider going 100 percent remote as a company or to at least try a hybrid model, but I was resistant to the idea because it created several unknowns and would have a big impact on our culture. (Keep in mind that this was long before the COVID-19 pandemic, so remote work was still a pretty radical idea.)

Then, out of nowhere, a rapidly moving fire threatened our corporate building and came close enough to require a complete evacuation. (See, I told you we'd circle back to that opening story!) The fire never reached our building, but due to smoke damage and other issues, everyone in the company effectively had to go 100 percent remote. (Sound familiar to recent pandemic-related implications?)

We continued to pilot the remote work model for the next nine months, discovering several very big advantages along the way. Most importantly, working remotely changed our mindset about pivoting by demonstrating our ability to make bold changes. It was the beginning of a reinvention process that has totally transformed our organization and culture. We've been fully remote for eight years now, and our growth has been unparalleled, even during the COVID-19 pandemic.

Pivoting is a critical part of strategy for every business. Countless organizations (maybe even yours) found themselves required to pivot as a result of an economic downturn, a major change in the industry, a supply chain issue, a merger and acquisition, or even a pandemic. You fill in the blank.

So, how do I deal with pivots? Just like many of you, pivots make me uneasy. In fact, I've rarely faced a pivot I was comfortable with. Discomfort aside, there are steps you can take to make the transition easier:

- **Pay attention to warning signs.** If your team, peers, or customers are saying that changes are happening—listen to them! If a change happens and you get caught off guard, it may be too late to pivot by the time you realize what is going on.

- **Use the possibilities exercise outlined in this chapter.** Anticipate a pivot, then work through the 5 Ps to think through everything it may entail.
- **Be ready to shift as needed.** Just like a tennis player waiting for a serve, you need to be flexible enough to shift. It may help to consider a temporary change to assuage your anxiety.
- **Include your team.** Bring your team together to get engagement and alignment. They may be feeling just as much discomfort as you are, and they may be relieved to hear that you're paying attention to the issue.
- **Consider this a creative challenge!** Pivots are often caused by experiencing a new situation that may require a new solution. Let your brain play around with some ideas. Bring your most creative thinkers to the table and see what they can add.

4 Qs Whole Brain Walkaround

One last tool for you to consider as you work through your strategy and business growth is the 4 Qs walkaround. This very simple tool can help you expand and best leverage Whole Brain Thinking in your daily workflow. They're so simple that you might overlook them, but asking these four questions is profoundly clarifying and provides a great development tool for your team:

- What is the problem?
- Why is it important?
- Who is most affected or involved?
- How do I recommend we take action and get started?

Start by having your team members work through the 4 Qs before they come to discuss a potential idea or problem.

- **"What is the problem?"** will appeal to the A (analytical) quadrant—the logical, fact-based thinkers. You want them to very clearly define what the problem to solve is. It helps to frame it as "How might we _____ in order to _____?"
- **"Why is this important?"** will appeal to the D (innovative) quadrant—the big picture, long-term thinkers. The goal is to see how the solution to the problem supports the long-term vision.

- **"Who is most affected or involved?"** will appeal to the C (relational) quadrant—those on your team who are more focused on relationships, customers, and community and are great at intuitively picking up the clues around what's going on in the culture, either internally or externally.
- **"How do I recommend we take action and get started?"** will appeal to the B (practical) quadrant—those focused on plans, process, structure, timing, and execution.

Using this approach guarantees a Whole Brain Thinking mindset regardless of the cognitive diversity of your team. By design, it broadens the conversation beyond a singular perspective to stretch the thinking of the team member you're interacting with, which saves you tremendous time. Your entire team can focus on what they know the best in a whole brain discussion.

Summary

Ultimately, using the 5 Ps (possibilities, people, payoff, process, and pivots) will accelerate your business efforts at all times, not just when you seek to develop a strategy. The more you use the 5 Ps, the greater your abilities will be when navigating competing priorities, dealing with change, and setting your company up for continued growth.

Actions You Can Take Now

- **Create your one page future plan.** If you think you have already thought through your future, do this exercise anyway! As you challenge your own thinking, you will find that new insights and ideas emerge. Share these with your closest advisors, and prepare to work through the other Ps.
- **Block 60 minutes weekly on your calendar for 5 P thinking time.** If possible, spending 30 minutes a day is even better. Make sure to honor this time—turn off notifications and work on a P, even if it is only to do a brief mental check in.

About the Author

Ann Herrmann-Nehdi is chief thought leader and chair of Herrmann International, the originators of Whole Brain Thinking and the HBDI assessment. Author of the *Whole Brain Business Book*, Ann is a researcher and C-suite advisor who focuses on the practical application of neuroscience and cognitive diversity to human and organization development. Her TedX talks have more than 500,000 views, and her research has influenced the way people around the globe approach their work. She is now researching the future of work and learning in the flow of work. Learn more about Ann's research and tools at thinkherrmann.com.

— CHAPTER 8 —

Consulting in a Large Company

JACOB KUCZMANSKI

When graduating college or starting your career, you have many options if you want to begin consulting. You can work for a midsize or large firm or start at a small boutique. Some people even choose to work independently. All options have their pros and cons, but you need to find the option that works best for you.

After graduating with a master's in organizational psychology and completing several internships, I began working at a midsize consulting firm. As one of around 4,000 employees, I was able to get in front of clients on day one and access many opportunities and have great exposure. I felt the culture of the company fit what I was looking for. However, after working there for three years, I decided it was time to move on to a large consulting firm. My decision was driven by the fact that my learning had somewhat plateaued, and I wanted exposure and access to new and different client experiences, more learning opportunities, and a wider network of experts in my practice area.

Now that I have worked at the large firm for five years, I've formed an interesting perspective on the best and worst parts of the job. In this chapter, we will explore large consulting firms, how consulting is different in a large company, what it's like to work for a large consulting company (the good and the bad), and how to get started and grow your career (including practical and actionable advice to help you decide if this career path is right for you).

How Do Large Consulting Firms Differ From Other Consulting Experiences?

What is a large consulting firm? There is no ideal answer, but large consulting companies offer a lot of services to multiple industries and employ thousands of consultants, often across many locations or countries. Some firms may offer their clients end-to-end solutions, while others specialize in certain capabilities, like business strategy or technology implementation. These companies—such as Accenture, Bain, Boston Consulting Group, Booz Allen Hamilton, Capgemini, Cognizant, Deloitte, Ernst & Young, KPMG, McKinsey & Company, and PricewaterhouseCoopers—generally have strong brand recognition in the market, are recognized for their innovation and thought leadership, and have a proven track record for tackling complex client challenges.

When you look inside most large consulting firms, you will see a few things in common:

- They all have well-designed processes in place and an abundance of resources and systems at their disposal. These processes and resources span onboarding, sales, delivery methodologies, engagement, financial management, and even career progression.
- The project work is complex and the solutions are often end-to-end, multiservice, or integrated. These projects may require large teams of cross functional consultants and a lot of coordination and project management.
- They have large, established clients, which often include Fortune 500 companies, government agencies, and nonprofit organizations.

There are also some distinct differences between large consulting companies and small or independent consulting firms (Table 8-1).

What Is It Like to Work in a Large Consulting Firm?

Many factors will influence your overall experience when you work within a large consulting firm, such as your organizational alignment and network, access to resources, internal firm contributions, clients, project team, and project role.

Table 8-1. The Differences Between Small and Large Consulting Firms

	Small or Independent Consulting Firms	Large Consulting Firms
Number of clients	Low	High
Number of services and offerings	Low and specialized	High and diverse
Level of resources, systems, and processes available to consultants	Low	High
Who is responsible for sales?	All employees	Most senior employees
Compensation structure	Varied based on sold work: • Hourly or daily fees • Project-based fees • Retainer fees	Consistent: • Base salary • Individual bonuses based on performance • Individual and global bonuses based on sales (for most senior employees)
Reporting structures	Primarily reports to a client lead	Reports to several people based on matrixed organizational structure and complex project teams; for example: • Project manager (internal or client) • Project lead (internal) • Workstream lead (internal) • Practice lead (internal) • Internal supervisor (internal) • Subject matter experts (internal) • Client project lead (client) • Client sponsor (client)
Additional responsibilities	• Business development • Offering development	• Business development (senior employees) • Offering development (mid-level to senior employees) • Practice development • Internal employee experience or culture initiatives (such as employee resource groups, local office engagement teams, and internal programs)

Working in a Matrixed Organization

When working for a large company you will be aligned within a matrix, which is often organized by functional practice (such as change management), industry, or location (such as the Midwest or the United States). This alignment gives you a starting point to establish and grow your network and is often the best place to look for guidance and mentorship because others in your matrix are familiar with your work and have often already dealt with the same challenges you are facing. It is also important to focus on building your personal brand within a matrixed organization so you are able to stand out from your peers, who probably have similar skills and experience.

Wealth of Resources

An advantage of working for a large company is the number of resources available to you. Most large consulting companies have robust internal onboarding, training, and development programs that provide the skills and knowledge you need to quickly become productive. They often have dedicated development teams that create consulting-specific learning content and programs, as well as tools and processes that are designed to help you with all facets of staffing, project management, expense management, and governance. You'll be able to leverage on-demand learning content to develop your skills and peer learning opportunities like communities of practice and employee resource groups.

You also will have access to a larger knowledge repository—which provides sample deliverables and templates, previous client project stories, and other sales materials to inspire starting points—so you never have to start from scratch.

Supporting Internal Initiatives

When working for a large consulting firm, you will likely be expected to work on internal initiatives to support the company, including research, developing learning content, organizing internal events, or working on pitch presentations. These activities give insight into different parts of the company, are a great way to meet and network with people from across the organization, and may provide you with new experiences, resources, and skills.

Clients and Mastering the Project Assignment Process

Although your company experience is certainly important, you must also consider your client experience, which may vary greatly depending on the size of the client, the scope of the work you are responsible for, and your project team. In a large consulting firm, it is common to be assigned to one project at a time, although some consultants work across multiple projects depending on the scope of the project or their functional practice.

Getting assigned, or staffed, to a project is much like a job search. You can either rely on your professional network or go through the formal staffing channels. If you choose to go through the formal staffing channels, you'll typically review a list of available positions (like an online job board). If you find an interesting position that you have the right skills to accomplish, you can reach out to the person designated with filling the position. The two of you will set up a short informal interview so you can learn more about the project and the role and they can learn about your experience. If both sides agree you would be a good fit, you will be assigned to the role.

The alternative approach is to work with your network to find a role. Your network may know about newly available roles before they are posted, which means you may have a better chance of becoming staffed to better projects because you can express interest before anyone else has a chance. This approach is often best for more experienced consultants who already have a network of contacts across the company.

Consulting Tip

Set up informational interviews with current and past employees who have worked with a large consulting firm. Ask questions to help you understand what it is really like to work there and determine if it is a good fit for you.

Complex Projects and Diverse Teams

Once assigned to your project and role, you will be introduced to your project team, which can be as small as one other person or as large as 100 or more other consultants. Generally, consulting at a large firm means that you can expect to work on complex projects that require a combination of different services and an in-depth understanding of the industry and the internal client organization. Therefore, your team may be made up of only employees from your company, some from your company and some from the client, or even employees from multiple consulting firms.

Large consulting companies have the capacity take on complex projects that may be beyond that of small or independent consulting firms, such as:

- **Digital transformation of large organizations.** These projects require significant expertise in digital strategy, data analytics, and technology implementation. They may involve working with multiple departments and stakeholders and require extensive change management and employee training.

- **Large-scale merger and acquisition integration.** These projects involve complex operational, financial, and cultural integration. They require deep expertise in postmerger integration and transformation, as well as extensive experience working with both the acquiring and target companies.
- **Organizational restructuring and optimization.** Helping large organizations optimize their operations—including streamlining processes, improving efficiency, and reducing costs—requires expertise in areas such as process improvement, change management, and performance measurement.

Navigating Project Roles

Your role in any project will vary depending on the size of the project team, the type of engagement, and your functional practice. For instance, you may find yourself in a business analyst role, working closely with the client to gather requirements and design solutions, or you may be working on the delivery of a project or a specific solution with a team of consultants. The length of time you spend on a project or in a particular role also varies greatly and can be as short as a few weeks or as long as a few years. There are some consultants who have worked with the same client for their entire careers!

Overall, when working in a large consulting firm, you will often have to do a mix of company-specific and client-specific work to be successful. It is important to understand this complex matrix, be open to learning and networking, stay up to date on changes within the industry and functional practice, and build your network and experience. This ensures that you can work, learn, and grow on the job.

Day in the Life of a Consultant at a Large Consulting Firm

Your day-to-day life as a consultant at a large consulting firm is greatly dictated by your level of experience, but it may not be all that different than working in a small or independent firm. More junior consultants (with one to three years of experience) typically spend their days working closely with colleagues on their projects and attending internal meetings to develop frameworks, analyze data, design solutions, and review deliverables.

More experienced consultants (with four to eight years of experience) may find themselves taking on more leadership roles, such as leading project teams, running client workshops, and overseeing the delivery of complex projects. They may also be asked to provide coaching and mentorship to more junior consultants, work with clients on strategic decisions, and manage engagements from start to finish.

To help paint the picture of a typical day at a large company, let's look at the schedules of two different consultants: Jordan is a junior-level consultant who recently joined the company, six months after graduating from college. Sam is a senior-level consultant with seven years of consulting experience.

Jordan's Typical Day

- 8 a.m.: As a new joiner at the company, Jordan knows that building strong relationships with colleagues and clients is the key to success. He starts his day by logging on to his computer and catching up on emails, ensuring that he responds promptly to his client and project team messages.
- 8:30 a.m.: He attends an internal company meeting, where he introduces himself to his colleagues and actively participates in the discussion. This begins to establish his personal brand as a reliable and engaged team member.
- 9 a.m.: Jordan joins his team's daily meeting to review progress on project deliverables and discuss priorities for the day. By working closely with his team, Jordan builds relationships and establishes trust, which ultimately helps produce successful outcomes for the client.
- 10:30 a.m.: Jordan actively participates in a client workshop, where he takes detailed notes, summarizes key takeaways, and assigns owners for any action items. He demonstrates his commitment to delivering high-quality work and building strong relationships with the client.
- 12 p.m.: During his lunch break, Jordan takes the opportunity to catch up with his colleagues, asking about their interests and getting to know them better.
- 1 p.m.: Jordan takes on the task of analyzing data and preparing slides for an upcoming client meeting; he pays close attention to details and asks his project lead clarifying questions.

- 3 p.m.: Jordan meets with the client to present his analysis and answer any questions they may have. He focuses on demonstrating his knowledge and expertise and building trust and credibility with the client.
- 5 p.m.: Jordan wraps up any loose ends and prepares for the next day.

Sam's Typical Day

- 8 a.m.: Sam starts her day by logging on to the computer and catching up on emails. Because she has been with the company for seven years, she presents at an internal company meeting, where she shares expertise and insights with her colleagues, demonstrating how she is providing value to her client, and establishing herself as a leader within the organization.
- 9 a.m.: Sam leads her team's daily meeting, where she reviews progress on project deliverables, delegates new tasks, and sets priorities for the day. As a leader, she focuses on communicating and collaborating effectively and building strong relationships to ensure her team is aligned and working toward their shared goals.
- 10:30 a.m.: Sam leads a client workshop to collect feedback and address any issues they may have, demonstrating her expertise and building trust with the client.
- 12 p.m.: During her lunch break, Sam has a one-on-one conversation with a member of her team and shares some advice about how to handle a difficult situation.
- 1 p.m.: Sam assists a junior consultant with data analysis and presentation prep.
- 2:30 p.m.: Sam meets with a mentee to provide career advice and guidance, showing her commitment to developing her colleagues' careers and building relationships with future leaders within the organization.
- 3 p.m.: Sam meets with a client to discuss project strategy.
- 5 p.m.: Sam reviews her team's work and provides feedback, ensuring that they are producing high-quality work that meets the client's needs.
- 5:30 p.m.: Sam ends her day by catching up with her team, addressing any last-minute tasks, and building relationships within the organization. She knows that by consistently delivering high-quality work, building strong relationships, and establishing a personal brand, she will continue to succeed and make a positive impact on the company and its clients.

What Should You Consider Before Working for a Large Consulting Company?

Think about where you are in your consulting career journey. What do you still want to learn? What experiences will be helpful to your development? What kind of client do you want to serve? What kind of atmosphere do you want to experience? Let's look at some of the pros and cons I've found based on my experience working for a large consulting company.

The Pros

One of the best parts of working at a large consulting company is the ability to access highly experienced colleagues and interesting and challenging projects. You are exposed to many different people, companies, and company cultures, and you get to help your clients do things they never thought possible. You are given the opportunity to own your career and progress when you are ready. Large companies also provide extensive support and resources to conquer any challenges you may face. You also have the flexibility to work on internal initiatives that you are personally interested in or passionate about and you are supported and encouraged to do so. And, thanks to the range and complexity of the projects you work on, you get to be an expert in many different fields.

The Cons

The worst parts of working at a large consulting company are the pressure to perform and the frequent company changes. You are always competing against your peers, and the pressure to stay ahead of the curve can be daunting. Additionally, the frequent reorganizations and priority changes can be confusing and difficult to keep up with. Another challenge is finding your place within a matrixed organization. This can be difficult for new joiners, especially when starting out, and can lead to feelings of disconnection from the company until you find your place. Lastly, work-life balance can be difficult. You must often work long hours to get the job done, and you're expected to work on internal initiatives in addition to any client work. Finding the right balance can be challenging.

Additional Considerations

While not inherently positive or negative, there are also workplace politics to consider when working for a large consulting company. How you play the game can certainly make a difference in your success within a firm, and it is important to be aware of the politics at work and how you are perceived. For example, your network often has a direct influence on the projects you are offered and the opportunities presented to you. Knowing and impressing the right people at the right time can go a long way. The politics often vary from company to company, region to region, practice to practice, and team to team, so it is important to understand the environment you are in and be aware of its nuances.

Ultimately, however, it is a personal choice—you need to decide how involved in workplace politics you want to be. You should always focus on doing good work for your clients and the company and being easy to work with. This is often enough to progress and navigate the political landscape.

Working at a large consulting company can be incredibly rewarding and provide access to many opportunities and projects. It can also be challenging, so it is important to make sure you are comfortable with the environment and that it is the best fit for your career goals and aspirations.

Career Development and Growth

You will find that there is a somewhat prescriptive career path to follow when working for a large consulting firm. To be successful and progress quickly, it is important to understand how the firm operates, its expectations for growth, and what you need to do to move forward in your career. To do this, many consultants find it beneficial to focus on establishing their network, finding mentors and leaders who can guide them, building their personal brand in the company, leveraging the training resources available to them, and working productively and in a sustainable way to avoid burnout.

Traditional vs. Alternative Paths for Career Advancement

Consultants at large firms typically start out as an entry-level associate or analyst and work their way up to a manager, then a senior manager or director, and eventually a partner or managing director. To move along the path, there are certain tasks and milestones you need to complete. For example, you may need to successfully demonstrate specific skills within a certain amount of time, develop certain technical competencies, or display expertise before moving up to the next level.

The metrics by which you are evaluated also change as you take on more senior roles. As a junior consultant, your primary performance metric is *utilization*, or the amount of your time that you are charging to a client. As you become more experienced, your utilization matters less because in addition to delivering work for your client, you are expected to contribute to the success of the firm in other ways, such as developing new tools or approaches or leading internal initiatives. Finally, as you move into more senior roles, you are primarily evaluated by the number of sales and new work that you bring into the firm. You should always be aware of how you are being evaluated and what the expectation is for your career level.

However, this is not the only consulting career path. Many large firms also offer an alternative career track that focuses on building your expertise and becoming a thought leader, rather than focusing heavily on sales. This track is usually taken by individuals with a strong interest in a certain area who are looking to develop and deepen their professional knowledge and specialized skills. This track is great for those seeking career satisfaction in a specialized field, as well as those looking to become collaborators and advisors to their clients.

Strategies for Advancing Your Career

Regardless of which career track you select, there are several practical strategies and approaches you can take within your company to progress your career.

The first is to work closely with your mentors and formal supervisors to understand your options, get exposure to people and opportunities, and make the right decisions for your career growth. It is important to also be vocal about what you want so your mentors and leadership can provide the best advice and become advocates for you across the firm.

You should also cultivate relationships with other consultants and build a strong network of key contacts within your organization. Not only can this make it easier to be exposed to projects and resources, but you'll also demonstrate that you can work well with others and can develop a strong team dynamic.

Always focus on establishing and growing your own personal brand. Whether through the type of projects you work on, presenting at internal events, attending conferences, or publishing articles—these activities will help you gain visibility and establish yourself as an expert in a particular area. Being known for something is an important part of being successful in the consulting industry and can lead to many opportunities in the long run.

Maximizing the Benefits of Formal Training

One of the most valuable benefits of working for a large consulting company is the formal training opportunities offered to employees. These firms provide a vast array of training programs, both in-person and online, covering a range of topics relevant to the consulting industry.

As I mentioned earlier, large consulting companies typically have dedicated teams of learning designers, developers, and faculty who create and deliver high-quality training content. As a result, employees can learn from the best in the industry and access a wide range of resources that would not be available elsewhere. These firms also offer the chance to attend and present at large conferences, which can help employees stay up to date on the latest trends and best practices in their field. Some large consulting companies also partner with top universities to offer executive education programs, which employees can use to earn advanced degrees or certifications. By taking advantage of these resources, employees can continue to grow and develop their skills, which is essential to advancing their careers in this fast-paced and dynamic industry.

Working Productively and Sustainably

In addition to working with mentors, developing your network, building your personal brand, and tapping into training resources, it is also important to consider the way you work. Working productively and sustainably in a large consulting firm can seem overwhelming, but it is possible if you use all your available resources.

For example, large consulting firms typically have a knowledge management system for consultants to save previous project deliverables, sales materials, and client stories (in an anonymized form). Leveraging these examples and resources can provide a great starting point for any new project; it's also a great way to learn who has completed similar work so you can talk to and learn from them.

With so many tasks and activities to organize, it is also important that you become disciplined in time and task management. Many consultants find it helpful to use a physical or digital notebook and a personal task management app. Others use more sophisticated project management software to manage their tasks, as well as their team's tasks, status, dependencies, and deadlines.

Furthermore, it is important to set boundaries between your work life and your personal life, communicate those expectations with your clients and teammates, and take care of yourself to avoid burnout. Setting guiding principles can also help you stay focused and ensure you are focusing on the right priorities—for example, "I build trust-based relationships by demonstrating my abilities, being transparent, and consistently delivering on my promises." These guiding principles provide direction and help you determine what work to focus on, how you work with others, and how you lead.

You should also consider using your company's wellness resources, like health counseling services and your paid time off (PTO). I took advantage of my company's eight-week paternity leave when my daughter was born. It's important to prioritize self-care and make use of these resources to manage stress and improve your overall well-being. With a range of wellness resources available and a commitment from leadership to prioritize employee health, employees in large consulting companies can find the support they need to thrive in both their personal and professional lives and work productively and sustainably.

How to Get Started With a Career in Consulting at a Large Company

Working for a large consulting firm is a great opportunity for consultants at any point in their career—whether they've just graduated from college or are later in their career or want to experience something different from being an independent consultant (solopreneur) or have been working for a medium-sized firm.

The process and strategies for getting a job at a large consulting firm are not much different than many other corporate jobs. However, there are a few distinct differences depending on your entry point. There are five primary entry points to joining a large consulting company:

- **Intern.** It's possible to convert from an intern to a full-time employee. Interning with a company is a great way for a student (or recent graduate) to see if they fit within the company and for the company to see if they fit into the organization.

- **College graduate.** These people are typically going through the hiring process for the first time. They need to start by researching different firms and then make sure that their college experience and professional background line up with the criteria for the interview process.
- **Early career transition.** Individuals looking for a career change, typically from a similar corporate environment, usually have at least three to five years of experience. They need to make sure that their background is in line with the job requirements and then focus on selling themselves as a good fit for the job. They need to know how to articulate their experiences and create an application that stands out.
- **Experienced hire.** Experienced consultants who have already progressed in their careers or have worked in the industry before need to focus on networking, securing references and referrals, and building a solid reputation.
- **Acquisition.** Entering a large consulting firm through the acquisition of a smaller consulting firm is also possible. Large consulting firms often acquire smaller firms for their expertise, proprietary methodologies, or intellectual property. This could present some unique challenges for the new consultants because of differences in corporate culture and working styles. But, if they can find their place in the new firm, it is a great opportunity to expand their experience, work on new and different kinds of projects, and explore alternative career paths.

Regardless of your entry point, you'll find that the interview process is largely the same as any other corporate job. Everyone's journey to working for a large consulting firm is unique and requires hard work, dedication, and research. You need to understand the specific requirements for becoming employed and make sure that you can demonstrate how your skills and capabilities meet the criteria. Most importantly, develop relationships and use your network to get the job you want. With the right skill set and a focused strategy, you can be well on your way to a successful career in consulting.

Exit Opportunities

As you become more experienced, there will come a time when you have to decide whether to go for the next promotion or leave the company and try something new. Becoming a managing director or partner is not a goal for every consultant, so it's important to explore the different exit opportunities available after working for a large consulting company.

While it is common for consultants to leave one large firm for another one, there are several other possible exit opportunities. When consultants exit depends largely on how much experience they have, their long-term career goals, how old they are, and their lives outside work. Many people leave large consulting firms for a slower pace of work, fewer hours, more flexibility, and sometimes higher pay. Some leave the firm only to return years or even months later; this is commonly referred to as a boomerang employee.

Considering these factors, there are three common exit points:

- **Two years and out.** This scenario typically applies to people who join a large consulting firm right out of college. There is large variability in where they go next; for example, they may join a startup, work for a large corporation (often referred to as working an industry job), work for a smaller consulting firm, or go back to school to earn an MBA.
- **Mid-career transition.** Someone who has spent several years at a large consulting firm may be looking for a change. Their next move is often to a large corporation or smaller consulting firm.
- **Senior exit.** In this scenario, an experienced managing director or partner leaves the company. Often, they join an industry client as a director or take a role in the C-suite, but they may also retire.

While these three scenarios may not cover every option, they are the most common.

Summary

Working in a large consulting firm offers a unique experience that differs from other consulting endeavors. Your organizational alignment, availability of resources, internal contributions, clients, projects, and teams are all important factors that make up your day-to-day work life. Although there are pros and cons to working in such an environment, career development and growth opportunities are vast, and there are multiple career paths to explore. Building your network, cultivating relationships, and establishing a personal brand are key strategies for advancing your career in consulting, as is maximizing the benefits of formal training and working sustainably. Getting started with a career in consulting at a large company requires a clear understanding of the industry and a commitment to ongoing professional development. Ultimately, working in a large consulting firm can be a rewarding and challenging career choice for those who are willing to put in the time and effort to succeed.

Actions You Can Take Now

- **Determine your entry strategy.** Use the Responsibilities by Level at a Large Consulting Firm exercise, which can be found online at td.org/handbook-for -consultants, to identify where you would enter based on your years of experience and level of responsibilities.
- **Where do you fit?** Research different large consulting firms and identify where you would fit into an organization's matrix based on your ideal practice, location, and industry.

About the Author

Jacob Kuczmanski is a senior manager with Accenture's talent and organization consulting practice. He specializes in talent strategy, talent development, skills-driven organizations, and learning programs and solutions. He works primarily with clients in the banking, fintech, utilities, and energy industries. Jacob holds a master's degree in industrial-organizational psychology from Xavier University and a bachelor's degree in psychology from Indiana University. He lives in Chicago, Illinois, with his family. Contact him at jacobkuczmanski@gmail.com.

CHAPTER 9

Is a Boutique Consulting Practice Right for You?

SY ISLAM AND MIKE CHETTA

When you imagine a consulting firm, who do you think of first? If you're like most people, you think of companies like Accenture, PricewaterhouseCoopers, Deloitte, Ernst & Young, KPMG, Boston Consulting Group, Aon, or Mercer—massive organizations offering a wide variety of consulting services from accounting to human capital. But small organizations also offer specialized consulting services; in fact, many companies work with these boutique consulting firms.

According to the US Bureau of Labor Statistics, consulting is one of the fastest growing industries of this decade, with a market size of $329 billion (Statista 2022). Despite what you might imagine, those consultants don't all work for big consulting firms. Many work on their own or in a boutique consulting firm.

For example, when we began our consulting practice, TalentMetrics, we surveyed the market to see which companies were offering the outsourced people analytics, survey creation, facilitation, and training design that we planned to offer. After our initial review, we found that this was a unique combination of services, especially in the boutique consulting space.

We knew that our firm needed to sit within the context of the industry and determined that our skill set around analytics and program evaluation would serve as the source of our competitive advantage. We also knew that we had relatively expansive professional networks through which to build a boutique business that centered around those practice areas. This process took rigorous self-examination on our part to determine where our company would fit into the large market of consulting firms and where to best focus our energy. Because our specialty was particularly niche and only a few places would consider purchasing from us, we decided to lean heavily on our personal networks and individual promotion to grow rather than invest in a sales force. In addition, because our work does not require much physical space, we opted to forgo purchasing an office space in exchange for working as a fully remote company. This allowed us to attract talent from all over the United States and is a considerable advantage regarding overhead.

In this chapter, we'll cover a range of boutique consulting questions, such as whether to start your own practice or join someone else (small or large), who you might need to partner with, whether you need a physical location, and how to market and sell your products and services.

What Is a Boutique Consulting Firm?

While there's no single way to define a boutique consulting firm, you can consider two criteria: size and specialization. Boutique consulting firms usually have fewer than 500 employees and their specializations may take the form of product offerings.

Typically, larger consulting firms offer major talent development services and may provide a one-size-fits-all experience for their clients. Boutique consulting firms, on the other hand, are more likely to offer personalized and tailored solutions, possibly in only a few specialized areas of human resources or talent management, such as surveys, training, or assessment. Boutique firms may be more flexible with their product and service offerings. Because they don't have an entire library of predesigned inventories, assessments, training content, or platforms to immediately provide to clients, their business model is often more consultative and less about selling products.

Another form of specialization may be in the form of industry or area. Some boutique firms focus on a specific market or business type, such as healthcare, while others might focus on a specific geographic location due to their staffing and resources.

Figure 9-1 illustrates the unique position that boutique firms hold between solo practices and large consulting firms. Boutique firms certainly can tackle the smaller work that a solo practitioner may take on, such as individual coaching projects and small-scale facilitation. However, they may also be big enough to develop a proposal and deliver results on the same projects as a larger firm. The limit depends on the skill sets of the firm's employees. As the complexity of the work increases, there is a requisite increase in the skills a consulting firm needs to meet client expectations and work goals.

Figure 9-1. Project Complexity and Firm Size

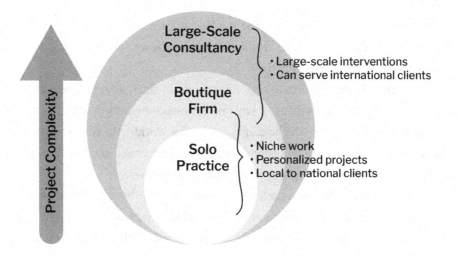

Boutique firms typically operate in a more entrepreneurial fashion that's closer to a startup, especially if there are only a few principal owners. However, as they add more employees, these firms often adopt a more streamlined variation of the typical consulting firm hierarchy, which includes more overlap between employees' roles. While a larger firm has clear role designations (leading to much larger workforces), boutique firms often rely on consultants serving in multiple roles (whether as a facilitator, content creator, or salesperson). Much of what a boutique firm does is influenced by the expectations of the leadership and the employees.

Consulting Tip

There are several benefits and considerations for starting or joining a boutique firm, whether it works on custom projects or broader initiatives like a larger consulting organization. Use the Boutique Consulting Self-Reflection Worksheet located at td.org/handbook-for-consultants to help determine the next step in your consulting journey.

To Start or Join a Firm

Due to some of the broad constraints (or considerations, depending on your point of view) described thus far, you may be wondering about the advantages and disadvantages of working for or starting a boutique firm.

Starting a boutique firm requires a large investment in time, energy, and capital. While there are many factors to that decision, a key one to consider is whether you have partners who are willing to strike out into the boutique consulting world with you. You need a group of trusted potential partners who will support you on your journey and potentially help you get through the initial lean times of your new consulting business.

Working for an established boutique consulting firm can be advantageous if you like working on projects from beginning to end. You're able to gain valuable client experience while still working directly with those who are creating materials and managing the larger project. Due to their size and relationships with their clients, boutique firms also have more flexibility in the solutions they offer. Thus, they also require employees who have a wide range of skills and are ready to use them at any time. Larger firms, on the other hand, often have well-developed systems and structures in place. When a client works with them, they may have an expectation of how that organization will implement their solutions. Thus, your role within a larger consulting firm may be more specialized.

Why Not Just Apply to a Large Consulting Firm?

In this postpandemic world, attitudes about work have changed and many people are focused on increased flexibility and less stress (Parker, Horowitz, Minken 2022). The last few years have highlighted the trials and tribulations that come with being employed at a large, traditional organization—including large consulting practices. Principles, culture, co-workers, management, expectations (or lack of clarity related to them), and even environmental factors can influence the employment value proposition and how you view a more structured employment situation.

However, even though attitudes are changing, we must acknowledge some commonly held beliefs about working at a large consulting firm. Traditionally, benefits of working at a large consulting firm include:

- **More resources.** Established consulting firms have more resources and (potentially) greater support for professional development, training, and other career advancement opportunities.
- **Prestige.** Large consulting firms often have a well-known reputation in the industry, which can be helpful if you are still building your own professional brand and network.
- **Larger network.** These well-known firms typically have a long list of established clients and a team of salespeople; they can provide more opportunities for exposure to different industries and types of projects.
- **Greater stability.** The big consultancies often have a more stable client base (recurring projects and deliverables) and more financial resources, which can provide greater job security and stability over time. You would probably work in a reasonably well-defined role with a focus on one aspect of the business.

With those benefits come some caveats. You should consider what you are currently looking for in your career and what skills you are looking to acquire and hone. These points highlight some of the positives of working in a small or boutique firm:

- **Greater opportunities to influence.** Boutique consultancies typically have a flat organizational chart, which means individual employees have a greater ability to directly influence projects and outcomes. Large consulting firms may have more rigid and complex structures and processes, making it harder to have a direct impact.
- **Less bureaucracy.** Small consulting firms may have less bureaucracy than large consulting firms, which can make it easier for you and your team members to navigate internal processes and make decisions. In contrast, large consulting firms may have more matrixed and bureaucratic internal systems, which can slow down decision making and even limit the autonomy of individual team members.
- **More flexibility.** Boutique firms often work with a smaller range of clients or industries, which can give employees exposure to a greater variety of projects and challenges. In contrast, large consulting firms may have more specialized practices or industry focuses, which can limit the types of projects and clients that you and your colleagues will work on.
- **More personalized attention.** Boutique consulting firms often have a more close-knit and collaborative culture, which means team members can receive

more personalized attention and support from their colleagues and managers. In contrast, large consulting firms may have a more impersonal or competitive culture, which can make it harder for team members to receive individualized attention and feedback.

- **Greater entrepreneurial opportunities.** Typically, small consulting firms offer team members greater opportunities to take on entrepreneurial roles (such as business development or thought leadership) or handle more than a few aspects of an ongoing project (such as scheduling, client relations, deliverables, and communication). The more structured sales, business development, marketing, and analytics functions at large consulting firms can limit your opportunity to influence and work on these aspects of projects.

As we previously discussed, the opportunities to make changes, work across teams, or even create new business may be limited at a large consulting firm. Thus, working at a small boutique human resources management or talent management organization may be a better fit if you are more self-motivated and energetic.

Stephen Cohen (2017) describes the importance of having some of the entrepreneurial qualities that employees of a startup display:

- **Self-starters.** You need to be self-motivated and able to take initiative, as there may not always be clear instructions or established processes.
- **Flexibility.** Small consulting firms are often characterized by smaller projects, frequent change (in deliverables or expectations) from clients, and unexpected challenges. Being able to adapt quickly and remain flexible through uncertainty is a great trait for you to possess in such a setting.
- **Creativity.** Boutique firms typically require consultants to be creative problem solvers because they may need to come up with innovative solutions to complex problems with limited resources and no previous deliverables or documentation available.
- **Entrepreneurial mindset.** Focusing on growth, innovation, and even some risk taking, while you continue to meet other more administrative tasks, may help you to excel.
- **Team players.** Small firms require employees to work collaboratively and fulfill multiple roles much more frequently than large, more established firms.

Those who can work well in a team, communicate effectively, and support their colleagues are best suited for these companies.

- **Resilience.** With fewer employees and resources comes the possibility of long hours, tight deadlines, and high stress levels. If you can get your work finished with a high level of precision and maintain a positive attitude when facing adversity, then a boutique firm is a good choice.

One thing to consider is that it's not an either-or proposition. If you start at a boutique firm, you can always move to a larger firm, and if you are currently at a large firm, you can always transition to a smaller boutique consultancy. Many of our former colleagues have gone on to work for large consultancies while others have made the shift to boutique consulting. In your career, you may end up enjoying both sides of the consultancy coin.

Consulting Tip

Learn more about what you want by creating a personal list of pros and cons for working as a solo consultant, being employed by a large consulting firm, or launching a boutique consulting organization.

Working on Your Own—or With Help

You may be wondering how many people a boutique firm typically employs. The answer is one that is rooted in the work of consulting—a boutique firm doesn't require a specific number of people. The question you should be asking is how many people you need for each project. Boutique consulting firms often run lean in terms of resources, which means you don't have much wiggle room to bring on extra people. Clients expect boutique firms to manage costs, which often requires managing the time charged by consultants on each project.

So, rather than theoretically considering the number of consultants needed, you should understand the product and service offerings of your boutique consulting firm well enough to establish how many hours of work are needed. For example, if your team is working on an instructional design project, how much time is required to design the program and implement the training? From there you can identify how many consultants, and perhaps contractors, you'll need to fulfill the roles and complete the work. Working with contractors is essential for boutique firms because they bring unique talents that are necessary for short-term aspects of a project. For example, in an instructional design project, you may need someone to do voiceover work or character design. Because a boutique firm wouldn't want to invest in a full-time employee for either of those roles, employing a contractor is necessary for that project.

> **Consulting Tip**
>
> Recruit the best consultants you can. Identify what skills you will need, but remember that you also want consultants on staff who can help build your business by creating excellent client relationships.

The nature of your work is key to developing a sense of who you wish to partner with. Some work lends itself to a solo business. But one of the key differences between a boutique consulting firm and a solo practitioner is the desire to work with others in delivering each initiative. Coaching and e-learning design can be completed by a solo practitioner, but more complex work requiring a variety of skills is better suited to a boutique consulting firm fulfilling a specific niche. Even as a solo practitioner, however, there are times when you will have to work with other contractors. The difference is that a boutique firm allows the people you work with to remain consistent and relieves some of the pressure to find talent to fulfill certain roles.

As the owners of a boutique firm, we have found it easier to have a staff of consultants along with a group of contractors whom we can depend on. This allows us to create the flexibility necessary to run a firm that is not looking for the largest projects but may need specialized skills. We often look for people with technical skills in learning and people analytics.

Does Physical Space Matter?

In the consulting world, it is common for consultants to visit clients directly. Speaking to clients at their convenience and on their home turf allows consultants to facilitate meetings and easily access materials. So, there are many small and midsized consultancies (or divisions of large consulting firms) that operate with a predominantly remote, geographically dispersed workforce.

Furthermore, when it comes to physical space, many businesses have seen a shift toward reducing office space. This is due to a variety of factors related to economic conditions and the growth of technology, but was also influenced by the COVID-19 pandemic and Great Resignation that followed (Sull, Sull, and Zweig 2022). Potential drawbacks to having a physical office include the cost of rent and utilities, commute times for employees, and the need for maintenance and upkeep.

It's important to carefully weigh the pros and cons and determine if having a physical office is the right choice for your business. Table 9-1 presents several points and counterpoints for whether you should want or need a physical location.

Table 9-1. Do You Need a Physical Location?

	Physical Location	Remote Office
Professional image	Physical office space can help establish a professional image for any business. It can create a sense of legitimacy and credibility that can help attract customers and clients to your firm.	As office space is not necessary to provide excellent consulting services, perhaps devoting financial resources to enabling employees to work remotely can help create a more professional image. Providing your employees with better laptops, as well as cameras, lights, monitors, desks, chairs, or greenscreens can prepare them to work effectively and represent a professional image.
Teamwork	A physical office can facilitate collaboration and communication among team members. Being in the same space can allow for spontaneous whiteboarding sessions, quick meetings, and more efficient decision making.	With the veritable explosion of virtual meeting platforms and productivity and collaboration tools, teams can communicate quickly and efficiently, as well as generate content simultaneously on the same documents. This allows work to be done by geographically dispersed workforces.
Productivity	A physical office provides a structured environment that can help increase productivity. With fewer distractions and a dedicated workspace, employees may be able to focus more on their work and thus be more productive.	With a reduction in many types of distractions (especially for those who set up dedicated office space) and the elimination of commuting, many remote employees can better structure their work and schedule. This may make them more productive than in an office environment.

Table 9-1. (cont.)

	Physical Location	Remote Office
Client interactions	A physical office can provide opportunities for face-to-face interactions with clients and partners. This can help build relationships and establish trust, which can be difficult to do over remote communication channels.	Most employees spend at least some of their time interacting with others through meeting software. Although this may have been an issue in the past, it is now the standard of communication. It's possible to build trusting relationships without being in the same room.
Access to resources	A physical office not only allows for face-to-face communication, but also provides better access to resources (including office equipment, steady internet, meeting rooms, and administrative support).	Technology platforms and productivity tools available as cloud-based solutions or downloaded locally encourage seamless collaboration and data access, which makes remote work successful.
Work-life balance	Having a physical office can help create a clear separation between work and personal life. You can leave work at the office and enjoy personal time without the distraction of work-related tasks.	Working remotely can allow for a better balance when it comes to an employee's professional life and their personal needs. Limited commuting can help improve their mental health and reduce stress, allowing them to be more energized and less distracted at work.

Marketing a Boutique Firm

With the different challenges that you might face in the boutique consulting world, one of the major concerns is marketing. Building and maintaining a recognizable brand can be quite difficult. The process of branding in a boutique firm is a unique prospect, and whether you start a boutique firm or work for one, you'll have the opportunity to influence the firm's brand in ways you may not realize.

Large consulting firms usually have a dedicated marketing team and a sales force that assesses what products and services will scale across a large global client base. Boutique consulting often begins with a thought process around what products and services can be sold or marketed effectively. While a large firm can invest money and time to brand specific products and offerings, boutique consulting firms must be more mindful of their time and energy spent on branding.

Boutique firms may use some traditional marketing techniques, such as direct mail, email marketing, or social media marketing. But these choices will be influenced by a budget and the firm's reach. Unlike traditional retail businesses, consulting firms do not sell to the frontline worker—the focus is from a business to business (B2B) perspective. Those who work at a boutique firm may have a bigger impact on branding and marketing through their client work and network.

When we began our boutique consulting journey, we narrowed our product and service offerings based on an analysis of the consulting market. When you look at the potential products and services you can offer, you should consider the following:

- **Service or product specialization.** What service or product can you offer that's better than others in the market?
- **Market size.** Is the market large enough for your specific service? Is there enough space for you to sell within this product or service market? If the market is large, it may be able to sustain an additional entrant. However, a market that is too small may require you to expand your range of services.
- **Network.** Also consider whether you have the right network to facilitate potential marketing leads. This is one of the most important methods for building your business. In B2B sales, your network may prove invaluable to the survival of your boutique consulting firm.
- **Client.** In the marketing process, you should determine what your ideal client looks like. Try to imagine what companies you would best provide services for. This may be based around a particular industry or on company or organization size. Determining who your ideal client is will help you to determine where to focus your marketing efforts.
- **Marketing methods.** Consider your marketing budget and how you can best get the word out about your business. Have you already started a blog? Do you have a podcast you can use? How can your network help get the word out about your services?

Consulting Tip

List everyone in your network. Include current and former business contacts, people you know from volunteer work, individuals you have met at civic meetings, colleagues, relatives, your college friends, social contacts, and others. Then think about who they could connect you with. Who can lead you to your next clients?

Once you have determined what your market position is and where you can fit within the context of a boutique consulting firm, you and your partners can plan for selling.

Who Sells?

Selling is the key to any consulting firm regardless of size or specialization. If you are thinking about starting your own firm, it is extremely important to decide where you want to spend your resources and to thoughtfully consider a few things related to networking, proposing services, signing contracts, receiving work authorizations, and developing statements of work. All of these depend on sales.

Titus Maccius Plautus, a Roman playwright from 200 BC, is credited with saying, "You have to spend money to make money" (Blackbean 2022). In general, this is sound business advice—and it may be applicable to your boutique firm, depending on the products and services you plan to offer. Before you completely reject the idea of hiring skilled salespeople, consider some of the broad benefits of investing in a sales force (Fields 2022):

- **Increased revenue.** A dedicated sales force can generate more leads and potential revenue by reaching out to new or existing clients, sharing information with them, and closing contracts with minimal involvement from the firm's principals or owners.
- **Improved customer service.** Salespeople can provide more constant and personalized attention to clients, which can lead to stronger relationships and increased loyalty. Being top of mind is paramount in consulting.
- **Competitive advantage.** Having dedicated salespeople can give a small business a competitive advantage over others who do not have such employees or contractors.
- **Market insights.** Salespeople can provide valuable insights into client behavior, preferences, and market trends, which can help small firms make informed business decisions.
- **Flexibility.** A sales force is not something you need to have all the time; you can use contractors and scale the sales team up or down depending on your business needs.

Whether or not a small business should spend money on salespeople depends on a variety of factors, including the type of business, the size of the company, and its existing (not necessarily projected) financial resources. In addition to what we've already outlined, you should consider the following:

- The cost of hiring and training salespeople can be a significant expense that may not be justified by the potential return on investment. If you do hire salespeople, make sure you have an established evaluation system. Use understood and agreed upon metrics to measure the effectiveness of the salesperson or team to ensure that your investment is paying off in the form of increased revenue and profits.
- Investing in marketing and advertising may be a better use of your resources, especially if you can market to many potential clients at one time through professional meetings or existing social media and contact lists. These methods, along with simple word-of-mouth, are effective ways to help a sole proprietorship or boutique firm land projects.

In the TD or OD space, spending money to make money may not always lead to success. Consulting firms and thought leadership services are commonly referred to as transactional costs within business (which are defined as the cost of any transaction or exchange; CFI 2022). Thus, if you are a sole proprietor or small partnership and do not have established material or products ready to sell, you may want to avoid hiring salespeople, at least initially.

Consulting Tip

Consider joining ISA, the Association of Learning Providers, which is the only association completely dedicated to helping training consulting firms make the right decisions to grow their businesses. It's where you will find answers to all your questions about hiring a sales force, how to market, and how to become a thought leader in your specialty.

Summary

As a consultant you have many choices—from being a solopreneur to joining a large world-wide consulting firm to starting a boutique business. Remember that there are benefits to something in the middle that leverages advantages from both ends of the spectrum. As you consider the suggestions and concepts in this chapter, and use them to inform your next steps, know that we also used this information when going through our boutique consulting journey. The considerations and steps we have outlined here will help you decide whether a boutique consulting practice is right for you.

Actions You Can Take Now

- **Identify your uniqueness.** Review the work you have already done. What are the key things you know you have to offer? Whether it is instructional design, facilitation, coaching, or something else, identify what makes your work unique.
- **Assess your skills.** What products or services could you offer? What are you best at? What key capabilities make you a unique consultant? Create an all-inclusive list.
- **Is a boutique consulting firm in your future?** Look at the consulting marketplace. What do the large firms offer? Are there services or products that you would like to offer in a boutique consulting practice? How would what you offer be unique to what currently exists in the marketplace? List those services and products that would substantiate creating a boutique practice.

About the Authors

Sy Islam is co-founder and vice president of consulting with Talent Metrics. He has more than 15 years of experience providing data analytics and talent development support to organizations. He has consulted with Fortune 100 companies like IBM and professional sports teams like the Florida Panthers. Sy was awarded the Scientist-Practitioner Presidential Recognition Award by the Society for Industrial-Organizational Psychology for his science-driven practices in talent development. He is the author of the book *Leaders Assemble! Leadership Lessons From the Marvel Cinematic Universe*. He can be reached by email at sy@talentmetrics.io or online talentmetrics.io.

Michael Chetta is co-founder and managing partner at Talent Metrics. He has worked for and consulted with Fortune 500 organizations, public clients, and nonprofits; providing thought leadership and actionable analytics; and also influenced the design of global surveys, creating custom assessment and selection tools and crafting bespoke performance management processes. Mike is the director of the University of Central Florida's master's in industrial-organizational psychology program and runs a research lab focused on artificial intelligence (AI) and its utility for selection and assessment. He can be reached by email at mike@talentmetrics.io or online at talentmetrics.io.

The Independent Consultant
What's Your Role?

SHARON WINGRON

When you think of consulting in the talent development world, you probably think of the application of professional expertise—such as instructional design, training design and delivery, performance improvement, and other capabilities—that build professional and organizational success. While these may be the client engagement offerings or solutions, there is so much more to what a consultant does! And that's why I love what I do. As a consultant, I get to partner with my clients to move their organizations forward. Sometimes I'm simply an extra pair of hands, but if I do it right, I get to be a valued business partner who crafts solutions and executes projects to enable my clients' success for many years.

After more than 20 years as a consultant, however, I can confirm that what consultants do daily involves even more. I get to be a thinking partner, a resource provider, a solution architect, relationship builder, and valued business partner. The ultimate reward for a consultant is to be recognized as a trusted advisor. In this chapter, let's delve a bit deeper into these aspects of consulting. Think about the roles you play, what you are doing well, and how you might evolve into an even stronger consulting partner.

Thinking Partner

I'm an avid whiteboard fan—there's a 6-foot by 6-foot magnetic whiteboard leaning against the wall in my office (it was too heavy to hang). I love picking up dry erase markers, writing out ideas, drawing flowcharts and diagrams, and mind mapping, and then stepping back to take it all in. I get especially tingly when I jot down my thoughts on sticky notes and then create an affinity diagram by grouping them into categories on my whiteboard! (I also use digital tools like Miro or MindMeister to do this online.)

Yet, as much as I love using these tools, I've learned that they typically aren't as effective when I use them by myself. I need a thinking partner—someone to use the tool with me, to talk things through, to ask questions to gain clarity about what I'm saying, or to challenge me if I go on a tangent that doesn't make sense.

Being a thinking partner is one of the key roles consultants play. We challenge, clarify, prod, analyze, troubleshoot, and offer fresh perspective. We help our clients make sense of a vague idea in their head. We help them get clarity when they know they need to act, but aren't sure what to do. We challenge them when they are going down an unsuccessful path.

Recently, I was virtually facilitating an Everything DiSC train-the-trainer program for a group of airline pilots. While flying was their day job, the pilots were also tasked with building a leadership program for other pilots. My role wasn't just to facilitate learning; strategizing on the program and consulting on their approach was also part of the project scope. As I reviewed their slides, I found an issue.

They had taken liberties with the Everything DiSC Productive Conflict model to make it more about leadership and streamline for the sake of time. In essence, they adapted the model but sacrificed effectiveness for efficiency. So, I told them so! I advised them about why they needed to present the model the original way, what they were missing by presenting it the way they did, and how they could rework their material to accomplish their goals in a similar timeframe. I also informed them of copyright concerns.

It could have been tempting to think, "Well, they're the client and it's their program, so I guess they can do it their way." But that would have been a cop-out. I served them better by raising my concerns and helping them think about a more effective approach. They expressed gratitude and said that one reason they chose to work with me was because they knew I would keep them honest and they'd have a better program as a result of incorporating my input.

Resource Provider

Consultants act as resource providers to clients by bringing their specialized knowledge, skills, and experience to the table. In talent development, we have specialized expertise in how people learn, develop skills, get along better, and build organizational cultures in which leaders are inspiring, employees are engaged, people thrive, and results are achieved.

We focus on the people side as well as the technical and structural sides. What you know and can do forms the basis of the multitude of resources you'll provide.

TD consultants may deliver a two-hour virtual training session, craft a strategy with talent and learning as key business drivers, or design the organizational structure for a new customer success division. The scope of our projects varies widely, and so do the skills we provide as resources for our clients. Sometimes we'll be a small cog in the wheel of our client's operations. Other times we might be designing the system or acting as an extension of their leadership team.

Your network is another resource you bring to your clients. As you grow as a talent professional, so will your network of colleagues. These seasoned professionals are people you can call to help you think through your client's situation, or you can bring into the project as a subcontractor. You may refer your client to your colleagues if the work would be a better fit for them or if they have expertise you don't. You may help your clients source new hires if you know the right person for a role that just opened in their organization. The relationships you build greatly influence the range and depth of resources you can offer.

Along with providing yourself and your network to your clients, you bring a world of resources that are central to the work you do but not necessarily in the purview of your clients. One example from my world is the interactive agenda planning tool SessionLab. I first learned of SessionLab years ago and began using it to design the workshops and meetings I facilitate. Recently, I was working with a new client who sent me an Excel spreadsheet with topics for a leadership program I was designing; then, they sent me a Word document with the agenda for the first session. It quickly got ugly because I was updating the agenda, rearranging topics, changing speakers, and reworking the session's flow. So, I introduced my clients to Session-Lab, explaining what an invaluable resource it was to me and how it streamlined the design process while saving time and enhancing collaboration. They were so excited about it they immediately bought their own subscription! I saved them money, time, and frustration by sharing this one simple resource. And now they're likely clients for life.

Consulting Tip

SessionLab (sessionlab.com) is a program that automatically calculates timing as you make changes to your agenda, provides a library of 1,000 workshop activities and tools, and allows for collaboration with your team.

Solution Architect

The last job I had before spreading my wings as an independent consultant was as a senior business consultant in Arthur Andersen Business Consulting's change enablement practice. Our focus was to provide accompanying support, training, and resources for large-scale change initiatives, such as enterprise requirements planning (ERP) implementations or mergers and acquisitions. My last project was as the EMEIA region change manager for the implementation of Andersen's new consulting methodology, Architected Solutions. The framework was intended to be applied to any consulting project across the firm (Figure 10-1).

Figure 10-1. The Arthur Andersen Business Consulting Architected Solutions Methodology

Manage			
Change Enablement			
Program Management			
Project Management			
Strategy · Business diagnosis · Strategic direction · Operating strategy	**Business Architecture** · Organization design · Leadership · Process management	**Solution Delivery** · Solution scoping · Design · Build · Deploy	**Operate** · Application management · Service operations

While Architected Solutions is more often related to information technology these days, I really loved using that concept and framework for our business solutions. The Andersen framework considered that solutions need to start with strategy; have supporting business structures; be carefully scoped, designed, developed, and deployed; and then be supported while transitioning into operations. Throughout the process, change enablement, program management, and project management also need to occur.

This framework encapsulates what consultants do to reach solutions. Not every consultant will be involved in every aspect of this methodology, but every consultant is involved in some stage of it. Typically, TD consultants have specific areas of expertise, such as instructional design or coaching, through which the bulk of their work is done. For example, my background and focus started in training delivery and facilitation. Over time, I deepened my experience and expertise in other areas such as performance improvement and coaching. As a consultant, however, I apply a systems thinking approach to look across all aspects of a project. I consider the business structure and strategy and carefully craft solutions that reinforce and further that strategy.

As consultants, unless we're specifically hired as a pair of hands (in which case, we're typically considered contractors and not consultants), we build solutions for our clients. We don't just deliver a service—our job is to pay attention to initiatives and strategies the client is already pursuing. We employ root cause analysis, appreciative inquiry, and other thinking tools and processes to determine which solutions will meet their needs.

Relationship Builder

Consultants aren't lone wolves; at least, the successful ones aren't. You have a multitude of relationships to build and maintain to better serve your clients. While building relationships with your clients is key, other important relationships include (but aren't limited to):

- Colleagues you collaborate and commiserate with
- Colleagues who provide expertise you don't have
- Mentors who challenge and guide you
- Vendors who supply you with the tools of the trade
- Prospects you hope to transform into clients
- Teams that support and enable you to provide your services
- Contractors who help keep your business running
- Family and friends who ground you and help you avoid becoming a workaholic

So how do you build relationships? You do it by employing people skills (also known as human or soft skills) and living the best practices the TD profession espouses. Let's explore some of them:

- **Listen.** It begins with the first time you meet someone and start getting to know them—through the prospecting, contracting, and work phases and all the time in between. Tuning in to what's said and unsaid is a key skill for being a consultant. While it's important to share your thoughts and expertise at times, it's more important to listen carefully and thoroughly to understand your client, the situation, and their needs. Ask open-ended questions, clarify statements, check in on priorities, and gauge their reactions to your work. As you do this, your clients come to trust you and believe you have their best interests in mind.

- **Communicate.** Build relationships by presenting and sharing your thoughts and suggestions effectively. Be clear, confident, and concise, while staying open to feedback and recommendations from your client or other key stakeholders. Tailor your messages to your client's style. Pay attention to whether they start talking business or begin with personal connections, and respond accordingly. Note the pace and fervor with which they speak and match it appropriately.
- **Anticipate.** Your clients are often so buried in their day-to-day and immediate responsibilities that they can't see past next week. The more you can provide a longer view toward the horizon of the work you're doing (or can do) and the impact it will have, the more they'll value your perspective and trust you. Whether it is being available for future meetings, thinking through the next stages of project work, or suggesting other projects that may be useful, you deepen your relationships with your clients when you help them plan and prepare.
- **Respond.** People trust people they can count on. And one of the best ways to demonstrate that people can count on you is by being responsive to their requests and needs. Whether it is responding to their emails in a timely fashion, returning their calls, or providing the resources they requested, you need to be responsive.
- **Flex.** Sometimes, you need to adjust how you respond based on the client's needs. Recently, I was working with a new client to arrange some workshop dates. She missed a couple meetings and wasn't responding to my emails in a timely manner. So I did something I don't typically do with clients: I texted her. Yes! She responded within minutes, and we quickly set the dates and determined next steps. I had to get out of my standard email and phone call mode to use the communication approach that worked best for her.
- **Deliver value.** By demonstrating your expertise, providing solutions, following through, and executing, you can meet your client's needs and become a person they want to do business with again and again.

Business Partner

At the end of the day, consulting is a little strange because you aren't always responsible for the success of something. You are certainly a contributor, but you are rarely the person who is ultimately responsible for the project or initiative's success or failure. However, what you do as a valued business partner is to act as if you are that person ultimately responsible for success.

As business partners, you collaborate closely with your clients, work toward shared goals, and demonstrate that their business is as important to you as yours is. Excellent consultants don't just show up and do the same old, same old. First, research and get to know your client's business. Not just their company, but their business. Ask about their competitors. Pay attention to the business environment they operate in. Learn about their strategies, goals, challenges, and opportunities. And review their organization structure, culture, and human dynamics.

Then, customize your work to meet the client where they are and take them where they want to go (or perhaps where they need to go). In the last 20 years, I've facilitated several hundred DiSC workshops. I've never done the same one twice! Because I approach my work as a consultant, I dig into the organization and customize every single workshop for that client and what's important to them.

After the project is done, don't just ride off into the sunset or move on to your next client. Instead, stay in touch. Check in. Ask how the organization is doing—how have they improved, what have they accomplished since you last talked, and what new challenges are they facing? Offer some thoughts and recommend a book, an article, or a podcast that relates to what they've shared. This demonstrates you care about their success, and it positions you for future work. It shows that you want to be a business partner.

Consulting Tip

You can stay in touch with your clients in many ways. Think of five dormant clients (people you haven't spoken with in more than a year) and find a way to reach out. You could send them a book or journal with a note that says, "Saw this and thought of you." Or you could text them a picture with a message that you were wondering how their project is advancing. Or you could just pick up the phone, give them a call, and ask how they are!

The Trusted Advisor: What Consultants Really Do

As you've likely noticed, these aspects of consulting don't operate in isolation—they are intertwined, supporting and building on one another. So, what do consultants really do?

Whatever it takes to make the client successful! In training, a master trainer cares about the participants and their success; in consulting, a master consultant cares about the clients and their success. It's not about you! It's not about "Look what I did!" or "Well, I did my part. . . ." Your job is to enable your clients to shine.

When you consistently act with your clients' best interests in mind, you become a trusted advisor—someone your clients can count on, the first person they think of when they have a talent development challenge or need. You can accomplish this by acting in the roles described in this chapter and showing your value. Your clients should know that you'll help them think through their challenges, brainstorm ideas, provide resources, and point them in the right direction, all while keeping them and their business in mind. They know that you are there for them.

Here are a few examples from my work with a VP of human resources at a rapidly growing transportation company that demonstrate how she thinks of me as a trusted advisor:

- While we were designing a leadership development program for high-potential employees, she asked me for performance management resources. She knew she could count on me to help her find proven models that integrated into their overall talent system.
- She once texted me around 8 p.m. pondering a question the CEO had asked her about selecting the next cohort for a leadership development program. She couldn't get it out of her mind and wanted to bounce some thoughts off me. We set up time to talk first thing the next morning.
- When contemplating a recent struggle between an executive and senior manager, she called me to ask for coaching on how to handle the situation. I was her go-to person to help her think through how to handle it diplomatically.
- While preparing feedback for her training manager, she asked if I could share my observations and suggest resources for his development. She knew I would maintain confidentiality and provide the objectivity needed to point them both in the right direction.

Some may call these examples of scope creep, but I consider them evidence that I am a trusted advisor. I was initially hired by the company to supply DiSC assessments and facilitate training on interpersonal skills as part of their emerging leaders program. As I did my needs assessment, I discovered that although the program was delivering in three weeks, it was still being conceptualized and designed. I quickly started learning about their industry, researching their CEO, digging into their goals for the program, asking about current internal leadership frameworks, making suggestions, and adding value. As our partnership grew over time, we moved to a retainer agreement and I became an integral part of their talent solutions team. They knew they could count on me to be a resource and get the job done.

Summary

Want additional thoughts about what consultants do? Check out this book's resources section, where you'll find authors you know and books you should read. No matter what your area of expertise, you need to think beyond the products and services you deliver as a consultant. Your job is much greater and much more exciting! Check out the Consultant's Role Tip Sheet at td.org/handbook-for-consultants to learn how to make all five of these roles more exciting. Most consultants say they want to make a difference. But if you truly want to make a difference, you need to consider your extended role: How can you be a better thinking partner? What can you share with your clients as a resource provider that goes beyond what you were hired to do? Do you have all the skills required to be a solution architect? What can you do today to enhance your role as a relationship builder?

All these add up to being the best darn business partner. How might you add value and evolve into the strongest consulting partner possible?

Actions You Can Take Now

- **Contemplating consulting?** Most organizations use consultants in some capacity. Find out what services consultants are providing for your company, how they are contracted, how they are evaluated, and any other information you can gain about the consulting relationship.
- **Meet a consultant.** Interview three to five consultants you know. Ask them about what they do, what they love, and what they see as the benefits and pitfalls of being a consultant. Use this information to develop a well-balanced understanding of what consulting is all about.
- **Try a side gig!** If you are thinking about making the switch to consulting, consider taking on a consulting project to test the waters before you leave your day job. Use your vacation, weekends, or other off hours to complete a project similar to the

work you'd be doing if you were a full-time consultant. This will give you a feel for not only the work but the freedom and constraints of the role.

About the Author

Sharon Wingron, CPTD, has been enabling clients to connect, adapt, and thrive in the workplace with assessment-based solutions that develop PEOPLE (personal excellence–organizational performance–leadership effectiveness) since 2002. She is an award-winning Everything DiSC by Wiley Authorized Partner and a leader in the application of psychometric assessments. Sharon was the first member of the ATD International board of directors to achieve the Certified Professional in Talent Development (previously CPLP) designation and is an expert facilitator for the ATD Master Trainer program. She travels widely and supports clients around the world. Contact Sharon via developpeople.com or disclearningsolutions.com.

CHAPTER 11

Naming Your Business

MAUREEN OREY

Coming up with a name is one of the most exciting and nerve-wracking things you'll experience as you begin to create your consulting business. There are so many things to think about! According to Al Reis, author of the *22 Immutable Laws of Branding*, "One of the most important branding decisions you will ever make is what to name your product or service because, in the long run, a brand is nothing more than a name."

Nothing more than a name. . . . And as I've learned over time, that name will signify much about who you are, what you offer, and how you want the world to see you.

One of the first lessons I learned when I launched my business as an independent consultant centered around my business name. At the time, I had a personal bias against naming my business after myself (and I still do). So, in an attempt to avoid naming my business with my personal name, I called it Shane and Associates after my child. After all, I hoped my business would support the family. However, after I had a few more children, I realized that someday they would grow up and wonder why my business was only named after one of them! Around this time, my business was shifting from a side gig to my main gig, so I decided to rebrand when I launched the business full time. I began researching ideas and options for the new name, but it wasn't any easier the second time. I came up with a new name that served me well for the next dozen years or so, but I still had more lessons to learn.

As I began exploring ideas, some of my first thoughts centered around the industry I worked in—corporate training and development. I wanted a name that explained the focus of my business and gave some runway to grow my team and expand my areas of expertise. Some business advisors tell you to focus on a unique niche and others tell you to keep your options open. This was January 2009—the height of the Great Recession. I was afraid of pigeonholing myself and losing opportunities as a result, so I chose the latter approach of being a bit broader in my business focus.

My research for keywords, phrases, and concepts within the industry began with my professional association the American Society for Training & Development (ASTD). I read and reviewed everything from their annual *State of the Industry* report to newly released books; I also paid attention to the language they used for their professional certifications. Interestingly, my profession was also going through a transition—moving away from training and development to learning and performance. (ASTD also did a full rebranding a few years later, which is relevant to this chapter, so more on that later.) As I continued to explore options, I met with my coach to discuss potential client needs and identify market trends.

Ultimately, I landed on Workplace Learning and Performance Group for my new business name. I was pleased that it not only communicated what I did, but it aligned with the new verbiage of the industry and allowed for room to grow. One challenge I ran into was the name's length—I had to shorten the URL to WLPGroup.com (not very catchy). This led to a second challenge: Part of branding is ensuring we can be found online. While I thought the name was clear, my business somehow got labeled as a childcare company in a Google algorithm or online marketing database somewhere along the way. I still get telemarketing calls for playground equipment!

As I reflect upon the branding (and rebranding) process, I've found five core ideas to be helpful for naming a business. I use the acronym GAINS to remember them:

- Growable
- Available
- Image
- Notable
- Shelf life

In this chapter, I'll walk you through each of these ideas and offer some advice for naming your business.

Growable

When you start your business, you may be focused on a niche that is popular, trendy, or currently relevant in your industry. However, keep in mind that eventually you may want to diversify the work you do, the products you offer, or the markets you serve. It's not uncommon for your business to grow beyond just you.

So, consider a name that lends itself to future growth. For example, you could use "and associates," "group," "consultants," "institute," or "partners." If you are launching as an independent consultant, you might think you'll always be a solopreneur—but even if you do, you may want it to look like your business employs more than just you. Perhaps you don't use any of the previous qualifiers but instead opt for a name that takes a different approach.

A few years ago, my friend and colleague, Sharon Wingron, began to struggle with the image and identity of her business's name. When we first met many years ago, her, very successful, business was called Wings of Success and it focused on people development within corporations. However, Sharon had a vision to expand and grow her business beyond where it was at the time. I remember having long conversations discussing her vision and the marketing strategies she would need to grow the business. Sharon increasingly thought Wings of Success was not a strong enough name and that it did not promote the focus of her business. After much soul searching and long conversations with friends, family, and colleagues (and perhaps a few glasses of wine), Sharon rebranded as DevelopPEOPLE.

Since the name change, Sharon has significantly grown her business and received several industry awards for her success and achievements. Sharon's chapter in this handbook, "The Independent Consultant," discusses what consultants do. She believes that rebranding her business provided greater focus, made it more scalable, and positioned it for long-term success! Whether she hands it off to her successor or sells it to another company, DevelopPEOPLE will still be developing people for many years to come!

One of the main benefits of the growth step is that you can create a name that won't box you in but will provide clarity and focus for your business.

Available

This core idea is like the chicken or the egg paradox. I have met business owners who were so passionate and confident about their business's name that they failed to complete the due diligence when it came to getting the URL. If the URL is not available or it's too expensive, you need to go back to the drawing board. Be sure to research URL domains that are both available and relevant. Business (or product) names are typically used as the URL for your website, so you may need to hold a creative brainstorming session with friends, family, or colleagues to explore and test all your options.

In addition, check for common names that could be confused with others or may have very different meanings in other industries, countries, languages, or cultures. Perhaps you have heard about the Chevy Nova—this car's name was a failure in Spanish speaking countries because people heard "Nova" as "No Va," which roughly translates to "won't go." That is certainly not a great name for a car!

There are several online business name generators you can use if you hit a creative roadblock. All startup companies face challenges, including limited naming options, expensive domains for short names, and lackluster multiword names. It's an annoying reality that can hinder your progress if you're sitting on an excellent product or service that's ready to go to market. Strong and memorable brand names leave a lasting impression on customers. It's what makes them choose your brand over others without question. Brandable names also improve search engine optimization (SEO), making it easier for customers to find your business online.

With the advent of social media, you'll want to check multiple platforms for your business name's availability or for handles that sound like or relate to your business. Consider which platforms you plan to use (based on where your clients are likely to engage), and search for the handles you desire. Consider creating multiple social media accounts, even if you aren't ready to start using the platforms, just to lock in the names for your business.

One of the main benefits of this step is that with thorough research and due diligence, you can be confident about proceeding to the next step.

Consulting Tip

As you do your research, check domain availability through providers such as GoDaddy to see if your preferred name is available. You may also want to ensure that it is not trademarked by another company. The federal database of the US Patent and Trademark Office, Trademark Electronic Search System (TESS), will be helpful. And of course, try a Google search.

Image

It's important to consider the image you want your business to convey. Do you want to portray a business that's fun and innovative, traditional and reliable, or edgy and trendsetting? Will your business have a social purpose, such as giving back to the community or donating to children in need? Consider the words and related imagery your name may evoke. It is increasingly important that your brand makes an emotional connection, and an evocative name can do just that. Once you've decided on the name, you'll start making choices about the font, colors, and other aspects of your brand. Is your company's name and branding message clear? Does it communicate your intentions and resonate with not only you but also, and possibly more importantly, your target audience?

Ultimately, when it comes to naming and marketing your business, it is crucial that you own it. That is, you must be comfortable with the name and the resulting image. If you are not 100 percent confident in your business's name, people will know! It will be obvious in how you communicate and portray your business. Starting a business is hard enough, so it's important to choose a name you will love and embrace.

A good business idea can only go so far. Finding the right business name is vital for building a successful brand because it helps with recognition, creates a strong first impression, and differentiates your business from competitors. Ask yourself these questions when brainstorming company name ideas:

- What are your core values?
- What is your vision for the business?
- What is your mission statement?
- What does your business offer?

Use your answers to come up with a keyword list and business names that reflect the essence of your new business.

Consulting Tip

A part of your image is to consider where you will do business, so don't box yourself into a location. "Midwest Marketing" may have a certain ring to it in Madison, Wisconsin, but when you gain a reputation, will the name encourage a company on Madison Avenue to hire you?

Consider Accenture, the IT services and consulting company. After its contentious separation from Arthur Andersen in January 2001, Andersen Consulting ran an internal competition to determine its new name. The winning name, Accenture, was derived from the phrase "accent on the future." Kim Petersen, a Danish employee from the company's office in Oslo,

Norway, submitted the name, which she thought would represent the firm's intention to be a global consulting leader and high performer while also ensuring it was not offensive in any country in which Accenture operated.

One of the main benefits of this step is that not only will your clients have clarity about what you do—so will you!

Notable

Your business's name should be easy to remember. If it is provocative, it could be a catalyst for conversation; however, it may not serve you well if you have to explain what the name means. Picture yourself at a chamber of commerce event, an industry conference, or meeting a client for the first time—how do you want to start a conversation with a person you have never met?

Don't be too clever when you create a brand and company name. Stick to words that already have a meaning, rather than trying to make up words you'll just have to explain later. A well-chosen name can be a launch pad for further positive conversations, or it may simply be the start of a longwinded explanation of who you are and what you do. I once coached an accountant who hated networking or marketing herself. After some research and exploration, she opted for a pithy and lighthearted business name: The Bean Counter. This lighthearted approach became a humorous way to engage in conversation with potential clients.

Consulting Tip

If you are not satisfied with your company's name, begin the process of changing it now. If you put it off, another year may pass and you'll be wishing you'd started already. If it doesn't feel right now, it won't get better with time.

If you are reading this book, you might worry that it's already too late for you to take advantage of this advice. Perhaps you have already chosen and registered a business name. Don't stress or worry! You can always keep your legal business name after the rebrand. Sharon's legal business name is still Wings of Success, but her go-to market brand and DBA (doing business as) is DevelopPEOPLE.

Finally, consider how your name will fit or look on promotional items. Depending on your marketing strategy, you may want to have a booth at a trade show or local chamber of commerce event. Long names can make this challenging—trust me, I know.

One of the main benefits of a notable brand is that your colleagues and customers can easily remember and associate you (and your team) with the products and services you offer.

How I Named My Consulting Business

By Dave Dec, LiveToSpeak

The number 1 fear many people have in their life is public speaking. (Their number 2 fear is death.) There is an old joke that goes something to the effect of, "This means that at a funeral, most people would rather be the one in the casket than the one giving the eulogy." I wanted to start my own business to help people get rid of their fear of public speaking and being in the spotlight.

I thought my business's name should quickly reference this idea. I wanted people to see it and know exactly what I did. I showed people how to live and not die from the fear of speaking—how to feel the fear and do it anyway.

I thought about showing myself jumping out of a casket to give a presentation. Tacky, right? I wasn't about to do that, but what words could I use to get to the point of what I was offering?

The name soon came to me; I wanted people to LiveToSpeak. What a perfect name for my consulting practice! I shared it with a close circle of family, friends, and fellow consultants and LiveToSpeak passed the naming test.

Now I help people who are too afraid to speak in front of others move that fear down to the bottom of their list of fears. LiveToSpeak helps clients thrive, live, and speak.

Shelf Life

Change happens. This category can be a tough one. As technology continues to evolve, we gain new words and behaviors in connection with the new technology. Phonograph records became albums, which then gave way (oh so briefly) to eight-track tapes, which were followed by cassette tapes, CDs, MP3s, and now streaming music. Think about how we've moved from books on tape to audiobooks. It's rare to find someone who still pops a tape into their car or cassette player—we're now able to use our smartphones and e-readers to consume books in an audio format.

When thinking about your business's name, here are some considerations:
- Will it sustain the winds of change in the world?
- Will technological changes affect it?
- Will it still be relevant as the language of your industry changes?
- Will it still be relevant when you're ready to exit and sell the business?

My industry moved from training and development to learning and performance; it's now shifted to talent development. In 2015, ASTD rebranded from the American Society for Training & Development to the Association for Talent Development (ATD). While they toyed with names related to workplace learning and performance, their research showed that phrase never really took off with most of their member organizations or industry sectors. So they redefined their scope to talent development to stay current with the evolving world of work.

One of the main benefits for considering the shelf life of a business name is that you can prevent or reduce the need to rename or rebrand your business later.

Summary

Use the Business Naming Worksheet at td.org/handbook-for-consultants to help you remember what to consider when selecting a name for your consulting business. In addition, pay close attention to the business names of consulting companies you notice and find intriguing, and then contact the owner and ask for the story behind their company's name. You are likely to be inspired by some interesting stories.

Actions You Can Take Now

- **Claim your URL.** Research the availability of URLs, website names, and social media handles.
- **Have a contest.** Consider conducting a contest, much like Accenture did. Invite your colleagues, friends, and family to participate in your naming game.

About the Author

Maureen Orey, CPTD, is a skilled coach, facilitator, and innovative leader. Her mission is simple: to help organizations develop strong, resilient leaders and employees. She has worked with Fortune 50 corporations and professional associations to help them build their leadership capacity through high-impact consulting for more than 30 years. An author of five books, Maureen was recognized in 2017 by ATD when she received the Dissertation of the Year award for her doctoral study on the career benefits and return on investment (ROI) of volunteer leadership. She is passionate about leadership development, diversity, and inclusion in the workplace. Contact Maureen at maureen@wlpgroup.com or learn more about her work at wlpgroup.com.

Establishing the 21st-Century Consultant's Office

JONATHAN HALLS

The typical 21st-century consultant's office is virtual. This probably doesn't surprise you, given how the COVID-19 pandemic taught the world that folks could get as much, if not more, work done at home as in the office. But it's important because we're working with incredible technology in different ways and across boundaries we wouldn't have dreamed of 30 years ago.

I've led consulting practices in two countries: the United Kingdom and the United States. Like many consultants, I left the corporate world (where I led a large training department with a large budget and expansive faculty of 250 trainers) to build a small practice in London with five or six training consultants. I went from aligning learning strategy to corporate goals, managing resources and operations, leading change, and building relationships through the organization, to helping others do it.

My first year in consulting was exhilarating. We had many clients across Europe and an Oxford Street address in London, and I had a very healthy balance sheet. I opened a physical office in Alexandria, Virginia, in 2009 during the Great Recession. I continued working with my European clients through this new American entity while also looking for clients on this side of the pond. My new workspace had offices, a training room, a media production studio, reception space, a kitchen, and restroom. It was nice. I leased that space for three years, and since then, I have run my practice from many different places—commercial offices, home offices, and virtual spaces—depending on the season.

These experiences led me to see that the 21st-century virtual office is as much a mindset as it is a set of equipment and a space to work. In this chapter, we'll explore the gear you need to get started and the elements for developing the right mindset.

The New Workplace

Most consultants work on the run. They find a spare desk at a client's office, power up their laptop, and tap into the guest Wi-Fi network. Or they pound their laptop's keyboard at an airport departure gate, tuning out kids nearby watching Nickelodeon shows on their iPads. Consultants write proposals from home, with the dog scratching at the door, and they write follow-up emails on their smartphone while pushing a shopping cart around Costco.

The new workplace is also global. Consultants collaborate across time zones with teams from India, the UK, Latin America, and the US. You may be eating a sandwich at midday in New York while folks on the call in India are eating dinner. Adding to the dynamics are the different accents and how different cultures use the same words for different things.

As much as the new workplace for consultants is both virtual and global, the office mindset also means consultants are Jacks and Jackies of all trades. If you're in a solo practice, you are the IT and finance departments. You do the marketing and social media. And you take care of business development—the most important task. That means you are responsible for software upgrades, data security, and customer care. Your office is both a location and a mindset governed by what and how you work. So, for new or solo consultants, what does it look like in practice?

The New Office Gear

Every consultant needs to leverage technology, software, and space. While I don't profess to be an expert on how to open a consulting practice, I've learned a lot from the school of hard knocks. Of course, every consultant is different, as is their practice and the people they serve. No one software solution will work for every consultant. The key to finding the most appropriate solutions is first figuring out what you need.

Technology

One of the biggest decisions is what kind of computer to use. For many, it will be a choice between a Mac and one than runs Microsoft Windows. Some might opt for a Google Chromebook or a computer with an open-source system like Ubuntu, but unless you're an IT geek, and your clients are on Linux, I'd stick to Mac or Windows. Mac is universally considered easier to use, but if you're used to using a Windows computer, it's worth weighing the learning curve of adjusting to a Mac. I've attempted this twice in the last 15 years and found myself going back to Windows each time. Not because the Mac was bad, but learning how to use it takes considerable time.

Laptops offer the ultimate flexibility, but not all are created equal. Buy a laptop with a lot of RAM and solid-state storage. My preference is always to get the smallest one I can find because lugging heavy laptops with big screens around airports gets old very quickly. ·

Your phone will be your number 1 companion. You'll use it to take calls, share text messages, check your email, and surf the internet. You'll use it to file expense receipts, record ideas, and capture videos. It doesn't matter if you opt for an Android, Google, or Apple system, so go with what you know. I'd recommend ordering the model with the highest specs so it's ready for new apps. You'll want it to have loads of memory so you can store important data and apps. Also, consider a phone plan that allows for hot spotting so you can use it to connect your laptop to the internet.

Your phone will be your best friend on the road. Buy a case to protect it if you drop it. Also, save your files in the cloud to ensure you won't lose them. To increase battery performance, turn off any unnecessary background apps and turn off location services. If you've downloaded apps that you don't actually need, remove them from the phone.

Software and Apps

Once you've chosen a computer and phone, consider a software suite. A lot of consultants use the programs in the Microsoft Office suite. It's affordable, offers many choices, and works across Macs and PCs. But, just as some folks will never drive a Ford and always buy a Chevy, some refuse to use Microsoft products. They instead opt for the Google Workspace's suite or Apple's applications. The key to using these suites effectively is having a consistent workflow for everything from folder management to file naming conventions.

Google and Microsoft offer the ability to work in the cloud, but again consider your clients. Can you access the internet at their location or during travel? This leads to a conversation about cloud computing, which was all the rage five years ago and is now being challenged by edge computing.

In addition to the software you'll use on a daily basis, make sure you have communication, business, and productivity applications.

Apps for Business

There are many apps and software applications that can help you manage your consulting practice. The key to choosing the most appropriate is first asking what you need then looking for software that offers those functions. Here are some common apps and products that small business professionals and consultants use.

Accounting and Bookkeeping
QuickBooks, Zoho Books, and Sage Accounting are tools to help you manage your books, issue invoices, manage expenses, and run reports.

Office Productivity Suites
Microsoft 365 and Google Workspace provide a suite of tools from word processing and spreadsheets to scheduling and virtual meeting platforms.

Scheduling and Calendars
Calendly, Zoho Meetings, and MS Bookings are apps that enable clients to schedule meetings with you from their computers or smartphones.

Project Management
Monday, Smartsheet, and Asana allow you and your teams to plan projects and post accountabilities; some apps also offer support for both waterfall and agile project management.

Writing Tools
Grammarly and Hemingway are tools to help you sharpen your writing, avoid typos, and keep your grammar on track.

Customer Relations Management
HubSpot CRM, Zoho CRM, and Freesales help you stay on top of customer relations management.

Publishing Tools
Canva, Visme, and Adobe Spark help you design smart looking slide decks, brochures, and other publishable products.

Communication applications include Zoom, Webex, GoToMeeting, Skype, Teams, and Google Meet. It's best to register an account, even a free one, with each of these platforms. Spend time getting to know each unique interface so you won't waste time trying to figure out how to turn the camera on or adjust the microphone settings. Different clients will have their own platform. As soon as your budget allows, buy a subscription to that platform so you don't have to end a client call after 90 minutes and then log back in 30 minutes later because you have a free account.

Business applications include bookkeeping apps such as QuickBooks and FreshBooks. Consider the complexity of your revenue and expenses and discuss with your accountant which system will be easiest to use. You want to focus on consulting, not having to learn which buttons to click every time you log on. At a minimum, you'll need software that creates invoices, processes receipts, and reconciles bank statements. Products like QuickBooks will automatically file images of receipts. It's a terrific tool for road warriors sick of carrying paper receipts in their wallets. Look at the reports the program offers and be sure it produces a profit and loss (P&L) statement with the ability to drill into income and expense reports to track how the business is performing.

For productivity applications, consider project management software like Asana, Trello, or MS Project. If you have a large client base, a customer relationship management app could help keep things on track (consider HubSpot, Monday, Zoho, and Freshsales). If you want clients and potential clients to schedule meetings with you, consider using the Calendly app or Microsoft Calendar, which is part of the MS Office Suite. And if you want to back up your files as well as share them, consider using Dropbox or the file storage options embedded into Google and MS Office 365.

Home Base

Every consultant needs somewhere to drop their briefcase, keep the books they're reading, store swag from clients, and work on their laptop. We all live in different circumstances; however, while someone living in Tampa, Florida, may have a spare room to ring-fence as their homebase, someone in Manhattan may need to carve out an alcove off the living room.

Think carefully about how you arrange your desk and what's on the wall behind you. Keep whatever you'll need close at hand, and then file or store everything else. If possible, choose a space with sunlight and a window that opens for fresh air when weather permits. And avoid noise from kids, pets, the kitchen, or a workshop. If you are going to be at your desk for long periods of time, buy an ergonomic chair and make sure you position the monitor correctly. Consider a footrest to improve your posture. Keeping your space clutter free with few distractions is key.

You'll likely find yourself doing video conferences from your home office. Think about what your clients will see behind you when you appear on camera. While programs like Zoom and Teams can impose a virtual backdrop, keep in mind that the resulting fuzzy edges around your head may be distracting. Instead of relying on this feature, decorate the wall behind you. Consider adding a bookcase. Or add a textured backdrop using affordable peel and stick wallpaper with simple designs like bricks or shiplap. The camera won't be focused on the backdrop, so minor imperfections won't appear.

Consulting Tip

The next time you are on a Zoom call, examine each participant's background. What do you like and what don't you like? How can you use what you learn to create the best background for you?

If your office is in your home, don't publicize the address on your website or in your contracts. You don't want clients knocking on your front door during your son's birthday party. So, consider investing in a PO Box and list that address on your website. Or, for a nominal fee, you could buy a virtual address from a company like Regus or DaVinci, which provides a business address, collects your mail, and even answers your phone. These companies also rent physical offices that, while sparsely furnished, offer a professional place to meet clients or work away from home. Sometimes a client requires their vendors to have a physical street address; for example, contractors working with the federal government. I know consultants who rent a desk with lockable filing cabinets through a virtual office company like Regus— they never go into the office; they simply need to have that physical address.

The New Office Mindset

Life for consultants after the COVID-19 pandemic is different, but also remarkably similar. Yes, we're working differently—there's an increase in remote work and we seem to trust technology more. But we're still helping people solve problems. We're still building relationships. We're still doing research into how people work. We're still writing proposals. We're still helping people do change management. And we're still sending invoices. So, what does this mean for the 21st-century consultant?

Develop Networks

When I worked in the corporate world, I'd often have authors and famous speakers visit to talk about business trends and new ideas. When you work for yourself, you probably don't have access to those people. So, to stay on top of new and emerging trends, it's important to attend industry conferences like ATD's International Conference & EXPO and the Learning Guild's Learning and HR Tech Solutions. Not only will you stay up to date, but conversations with other practitioners will recharge your energy.

LinkedIn is a critical resource because people from outside our field use it to share the different ways in which they achieve similar goals. It's easy to get into a rut, so seeing how other professionals tackle problems can give you that spark to truly make a difference for your clients. Engaging in regular educational opportunities is also good—for example, you could watch a TED Talk or subscribe to podcasts by thought leaders.

Solo consultants need support. I recommend hiring a reliable bookkeeper to keep your financial records straight. Consider having a text editor or graphic designer on speed dial to check that your proposals are well written and not bursting with fonts and color schemes from the 1990s. As your administrative tasks increase, consider hiring a virtual assistant. I've worked with virtual assistants on many occasions, both offshore and in the same country. At first, I thought they'd solve all my problems, but then I realized they would still need good guidance. A social media specialist can implement a social media account if given clear instructions, but you need to develop the messaging and strategy because they don't know your market. Your bookkeeper might be the best in town, but they may also work with 40 other clients—don't expect them to remember every nuance about your business and guess how you want to itemize an expense.

Form Good Habits

Consultants juggle multiple activities—travel routines, administration practices, and self-care—that are easier to manage once you develop good habits. I wrote about travel in my book *Confessions of a Corporate Trainer*, so I don't want to bang on too much here. However, I urge you to join a frequent flyer program, if you haven't already, which will get you preferred treatment when flights are delayed, as well as early boarding and easy upgrades. Signing up for hotel loyalty programs also allows you to save your preferences so you can stop noting that you don't want the room across from the ice machine every time you make a reservation. Use credit cards that give you benefits like free airport lounge access or extra airline miles for every dollar spent so you can upgrade into first class. Learn how to take advantage of every perk in available loyalty programs.

Another essential habit for the 21st-century consultant is record keeping. This is a big topic and touches on how you manage correspondence, financial data, proposals, contracts, templates for proposals, and commercially sensitive information you're using for clients. The key to good records is twofold. First, you need a good system. Then, you need to follow it. In my experience, people are either good at creating systems or good at following them. You need to be good at both. Create a document folder structure that reflects your business and work style, and follow it until it becomes automatic.

Burnout is a chronic problem, so make sure to prioritize appropriate self-care. That means avoiding excessively long hours at the office, getting enough sleep, eating well, exercising, and carving out space for personal time. While these priorities may seem countercultural in a world that often values overtime as a badge of honor, studies show that working more than 55 hours a week increases your risk of stroke or heart attack and working more than 45 hours a week can increase the risk of diabetes (Pega et al. 2021; Gilbert-Ouimet et al. 2018). Working long hours increases your risk of an on-the-job injury, leads to lower work performance and affects mental health and sleep (Torres 2022). Lack of sleep itself is a chronic problem in society. If you want to be sharp in your work, you need sleep. In fact, one study showed that living on only four hours of sleep, over four days, produced the same level of cognitive function as someone who had consumed more than the legal limit of alcohol (Fryer 2006). Yes, there are some notable exceptions to these findings, but those exceptions are not the norm. The point is that if you want to be an effective consultant, you need to exercise sensible self-care.

Set Boundaries

Boundaries are important for staying sharp and fresh. The most important boundary is your personal life. In the old days, people used to pack their briefcases and leave the office at 5 p.m. Time in the evening was reserved for family and social activity. Now, people leave the office and check emails until 10 p.m.

Don't do it. Tell your clients upfront when they can expect a response from you and that your hours fall within certain times. Make sure clients know you'll send them to voicemail if they call after 6 p.m. Tell them that going to the hockey game with your daughter or granddaughter is the priority, but you'll manage around that to meet their deadlines. Make sure you don't work too many hours. If you're not making enough money, don't take on more clients—raise your fees.

> **Consulting Tip**
>
> If you are currently consulting, review your calendar to determine how you spend your time. Separate your time into categories—for example, design, delivery, marketing, billing, time with friends, family time, and hobbies—that are important to you. Are you satisfied with how you are spending your time?

Summary

The consultant's office needs to meet many demands. It must be accessible and able to reach across time zones and cultures. It should support efficient work while also protecting you from burnout. And as much as it's about equipment and software, it's also about mindset.

Starting a business as a consultant is exhilarating. You have more control and room to be creative than many corporate executives ever hope for. But it also carries many responsibilities. However, think of the impact you can have when you help others be better at what they do and help organizations perform better for their customers, clients, and owners. It's worth setting up your office—your gear and your operating mindset—so you can focus on helping clients.

Actions You Can Take Now

- **Review the apps on your smartphone.** Which ones do you hardly use? Make sure they are turned off and not operating in the background. Are there any apps you never use or need? Remove them from your phone. Routinely back up your data to the cloud in case your phone is lost, stolen, or damaged.
- **Smarten your meeting image.** Review the space you conduct video conferences in. What is in your background? Instead of using virtual backgrounds that give your head a fuzzy outline, change the background by adding a bookcase that holds a few books and some interesting objects. Look at where you've set up your webcam. If you're using your laptop's webcam, use something to lift

your laptop and raise the camera to eye-level—this will make you look like a television presenter.

- **Join a network.** Join a few professional associations so you can network with people in your field. There are thousands of associations focused on on many different interests, including the Association for Talent Development and the Association of Change Management Professionals. Look at your options and think about whether participating at the local chapter or national association level makes more sense. Consider where your clients are and what your business plan is. Then, ask yourself what you can bring to the association—the best way to network is through contribution.
- **Take an inventory.** If you are still in a 9-to-5 job, identify what equipment and tools you currently own versus what's owned by the company you are working for. It's easy to take for granted your current conveniences and forget what you'll need to buy, subscribe to, or sign up for.

About the Author

Jonathan Halls helps learning and talent leaders reinvigorate their training and talent departments with a focus on boosting credibility with stakeholders. He specializes in supporting learning science and digital media content. A former BBC learning executive, Jonathan has worked with clients in 25 countries for more than 30 years and was a member of the advisory panel for ATD's new Talent Development Capability Model. He has a master's and bachelor's degree in adult education and is an adjunct professor at George Washington University. Jonathan runs professional development workshops for learning and talent professionals and has written a number of books including *Confessions of a Corporate Trainer*. Learn more about his work at jonathanhalls.com.

CHAPTER 13

The Consultant as Entrepreneur

BRIAN WASHBURN

"Your business idea is great. Where's your first customer going to come from?"

My friend, Tim, was telling me about a conversation he'd had with his father. Tim had decided to leave his well-paying job (and benefits) to start a training and e-learning design business.

I thought about the question, but I wasn't sure about the answer. It was unsettling because Tim and I were co-founders. I was living in Seattle, Washington, and had several connections at Microsoft, Amazon, Starbucks, Boeing, Expedia, and T-Mobile. But while my contacts were enthusiastic that I had decided to start my own business, they politely let me know, one after the other, that they didn't need training support.

Where was our first customer going to come from indeed?

According to the e-commerce platform Shopify, "Entrepreneurship is the pursuit of creating, managing, and scaling a business by taking calculated risks and being innovative. Entrepreneurship involves combining resources, skills, and vision to bring forth new products, services, or solutions that meet market demands and create value" (Winter 2023).

Tim and I felt good about our area of expertise—how to design training programs. However, when it came to the business side of things, no matter how much we read and how many business plans we wrote, it was clear that we needed to learn a lot more about being entrepreneurs.

We'd never have guessed that our first customer would be AAA. No, not the automobile association—the small, academic-focused nonprofit, the American Anthropological Association. AAA was led by an executive director who wrote a thoughtful rejection in response to a cold email about our business idea. After meeting for coffee to talk about that feedback, however, we had our first paying customer. Take note if you're a budding entrepreneur—it's possible to turn a rejection into a paying client. It's amazing what a follow-up, face-to-face interaction can do.

It definitely went against Tim's nature to meet with this person who had just rejected our idea, but our experience provided an early lesson about entrepreneurship. Sometimes you must be uncomfortable to be successful. And by sometimes, I actually mean more often than not.

Now that we'd answered Tim's dad's question about our first customer, we had to figure out how to find our second customer.

Perhaps you are already working with a client, maybe even a handful of them. Or perhaps thinking about finding your first customer just made your anxiety shoot through the roof. Maybe you're somewhere in the middle. This chapter will help you zoom out and take a big picture look at some of the most important things you'll need to consider. Yes, you need more than just the skills you deliver—being a top-notch trainer, facilitator, speaker, coach, strategic planner, organization development expert, or e-learning designer will not help you to build a successful business.

> **Consulting Tip**
>
> It's important to be honest and candid with your manager. If you have a good reputation with your employer, they will often be your first client. If you're working on projects that your organization needs to finish, they may hire you as a 1099 employee (or an independent contractor).

What Got You Here Won't Necessarily Get You There

With a nod to Marshall Goldsmith's book of of a similar name, there's much more to consider than what made you successful today. For 15 years prior to starting my own business, I worked to hone my craft as an instructional designer and facilitator. I joined ATD, read books, attended conferences, presented at conferences, and built a network of like-minded individuals through local peer groups and social media contacts. At work, I was promoted from training manager to training director. I earned a master's in OD so that I could better understand how organizational systems contributed to the success (or failure) of training initiatives. I led a team, and people across the organization sought my counsel for making their own training programs better. Then, people from outside the organization started looking to me for help with training projects, and several even offered me positions in their companies.

The idea of going off on my own to launch a business, leaving the safety and security of a steady, guaranteed paycheck with benefits, was scary. According to a LendingTree analysis of data from the US Bureau of Labor Statistics, about one out of every five small US businesses fail within their first year and almost half fail within their first five years (Delfino 2023). But I was a person in demand! I was certain someone would be willing to throw a contract training project my way. Besides, I was working alongside a friend, in a partnership. He had a similar path of promotions, a master's degree, and had successfully helped his organization grow.

Once we were on our own, however, we quickly realized that just being good at instructional design and training facilitation wouldn't be enough to keep a steady stream of work coming our way.

Whether you're contemplating your own one-person consultancy or a partnership, or you're looking to grow a company and lead a team that sets the world on fire (in a good way, of course), your subject matter expertise might help attract your first client or two, but it probably won't lead to steady employment. Nor will it guarantee that every project will go smoothly or even make money.

What are some things that successful businesses have beyond deep, world-class subject matter expertise? Whether it's a successful sole proprietorship or Fortune 500 company, they all have someone (or a team of *someones*) who can focus on marketing, business development, sales, finance, customer service, and, of course, the actual business operations. Plus, they have a clear vision for what they want to achieve and how they plan to achieve it.

In his book *Good to Great,* Jim Collins introduces "the hedgehog concept," which is identifying what you do well and focusing on that. He says the thing you should really focus on falls at the confluence of three factors: what you are deeply passionate about, what you can be the best in the world at, and what can drive your economic engine.

Home In On Your Passion

Here's something to ask yourself as you set off on your entrepreneurship journey: Are you in it to make money, or are you in it because you think there's a way to make money doing something you love (and that also happens to be something that other people need)?

After I earned my master's in OD, I was hoping to land a nice OD position in a big company where I could make a lot of money; I also thought about become a consultant in the industry (so I could charge $350 an hour for my expertise). As I began reaching out to set up informational interviews, the head of OD at T-Mobile gave me a piece of advice that I carry with me to this day: "A lot of people can do OD work. Not a lot of people can do it well. If it's not something you're passionate about, I'd suggest you steer clear of applying for an OD job."

That hit hard because, truthfully, I wasn't passionate about OD. I may have liked it for a while, but what I truly loved was training and instructional design. I'm glad I was able to talk with people, and I'm even more pleased that I chose to pursue my passion. Pursuing a career in OD may have led to short-term gains, but I never would have been great at it.

Have you heard of Tope Awotona? He's a Nigerian immigrant to the US who set out to be a tech entrepreneur. Speaking on the *How I Built This* podcast, he told the story about how he just wanted to build and run a business. He noticed that grilling enthusiasts loved cooking on the Big Green Egg grill and thought he could quickly turn a profit by setting up a website selling Big Green Eggs to people who were passionate about grilling but lived too far away from larger cities where they were more readily available. While he did make some sales, this (and two of his prior entrepreneurial ventures) fizzled out. His major problem, he realized, was that he didn't care about grills or grilling.

So, Tope went in search of a problem he was extremely passionate about. He was tired and frustrated by the amount of back and forth involved in finding meeting times that worked for everyone. His solution? He built the Calendly app, which now generates many millions of dollars in revenue each year.

If you are going off on your own to start a coaching business or an OD consultancy, but aren't deeply passionate about those areas, I'd advise against it. In fact, there is an entire graveyard of failed small businesses that would suggest this is a very bad idea.

Think through your business idea and use these prompts to determine whether it is something you're truly passionate about:

- What are five things you like about this idea?
- Name at least three ways others might benefit from you and your idea.
- Can you create a vision statement for how your idea will make the world (or at least your small part of it) a better place?
- Have you ever lost sleep because you couldn't stop thinking about this idea?
- How do you know that this idea isn't a passing whim?

Consulting Tip

Consulting can be a lucrative business, but if you are only in it for the money, you will likely fail.

Where Subject Matter Expertise and Business Acumen Meet

Once you've found an area you're passionate about, there is still no guarantee that you'll be successful. Remember that stat about half of small businesses failing within the first five years? Entrepreneurship is hard. On the other hand, half of all small businesses are still going after five years, so there's hope!

What factors can best position you to land with the other small businesses still afloat (and perhaps thriving) after five years? Let's spend the remainder of this chapter thinking about the other two aspects of Collins's hedgehog concept (I've modified them slightly):

- How much of a subject matter expert are you?
- How much do you know about the other aspects of building and growing a business?

People typically have a whole range of experiences, talent, and abilities when they choose to go into business. Some have deep subject matter expertise; others have only recently been called to their area of expertise and think it'll be a good area to make a living but still have plenty to learn. Some people can transfer past experiences or education into the array of responsibilities they need to run all aspects of a business. Others start their companies with a vision for their passion and expertise, hoping they'll be able to figure out the business side as they go.

How Prepared Are You to Become an Entrepreneur?

One way to envision your proficiency on these two very important aspects of entrepreneurship—business acumen and subject matter expertise—is to look at the Entrepreneur Readiness Matrix (Figure 13-1). Each quadrant on the matrix offers an idea of where you might find yourself at any given point in your own entrepreneurship journey.

Figure 13-1. Entrepreneur Readiness Matrix

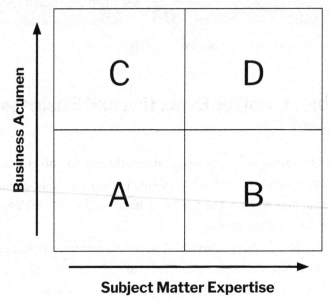

Quadrant A

Quadrant A represents individuals who have minimal expertise and limited experience in running a business. Individuals who fall into this quadrant:

- Recently graduated college
- Have only been in the field for a handful of years
- Have limited followership and interactions on professional social media platforms
- Are sought out by relatively few people for help or advice
- Are uncomfortable speaking as an authority on a topic in front of individuals or groups
- Hate having to sell themselves
- Have a passion but struggle to translate it into solving a problem for others
- Struggle to understand principles of finance or interpret basic financial and business documents
- Are prohibitively uncomfortable with not knowing where their next paycheck will come from

If you currently fall into in Quadrant A, you're right where tens of millions of other people find themselves today. You may want to spend more time preparing for your entrepreneurial venture before you take the leap. Potential entrepreneurs in this quadrant generally lack the deep subject matter expertise and the business and organizational skills to be immediately successful.

The good news is that you have options for the direction in which you'd like to grow. You can spend some time developing deeper subject matter expertise in the area where you have found a calling and a passion by continuing to work in that area, finding a mentor, or obtaining professional credentials. You can also put in some time researching what it really means to run a business, from sales to marketing to executing projects to budgeting and paying your taxes.

Quadrant B

Quadrant B includes individuals who are considered experts in their field but have little knowledge of what it takes to make a business successful. People who fall into this quadrant:

- Have been in the field for a number of years
- Hold an advanced degree or professional credentials in a specific field
- Are regularly sought out for help or advice in their area of expertise
- Are seen as an authority to speak on topics in front of individuals or groups
- Contribute to the field through networking, publications, or mentoring others
- Have limited followership and interactions on professional social media platforms
- Hate having to sell themselves
- Are extremely knowledgeable but struggle to distill that knowledge into an elevator pitch
- Struggle with or are ambivalent toward understanding the principles of finance and interpreting basic financial and business documents
- Struggle with or are ambivalent toward basic project management
- Are prohibitively uncomfortable with not knowing where their next paycheck will come from

If you find yourself in Quadrant B, your experience and expertise can help you establish a profitable consultancy or business. The further toward the right side of this matrix you find yourself, the more tempting it may be to believe that people will be willing to pay you (and handsomely) for your services. However, do you know where to find the people who want to pay for your services? And do you know how to sell them your services or how to run projects you can adapt with their evolving needs? Here's an eye popping statistic to keep in mind: According to a CBInsights 2021 study, about 35 percent of the small businesses that fail within their first five years do so because of a lack of market demand. Just because you decide to build a business based on your expertise, it does not mean that people will come to you. Knowing who your customers will be, how you'll find them, and why they'd want to pay you for your services will be extremely important.

Can you do all this and stay out of trouble with cash flow to ensure you're ready for tax season? (Remember, in the US, this will come around quarterly for businesses.) About 80 percent of small businesses have no employees, but if you find that you need help, will you bring on an independent contractor or hire a full- or part-time employee? If they'll be your employee, are you familiar with state and federal labor laws?

When it comes to making a living through your business, your expertise and experience is just half the equation. You may not need to develop expertise in all aspects of running a business, but you should learn a little bit about a lot of different key aspects of your operation's business side.

Consulting Tip

You don't have to cover every business aspect by yourself. Some people choose to pay for a coach; others find what they need through a volunteer business mentor. Organizations like SCORE offer free business advice for people who are just starting their entrepreneurial journey.

Depending on your situation, you can always find others to help with various aspects of the business—for a price. Instead of growing a deep expertise in the different business operations, you can fast track the progression of the vertical axis (business acumen) of the Entrepreneur Readiness Matrix by paying for certain services including:

- **Business coaching services.** A coach can be extremely helpful if you have an idea for a consultancy or service, but you don't know where to begin. A good business coach can help you clarify your vision and the problem you think you can solve while also identifying specific steps to move forward and challenging some of the assumptions you've made. A good business coach can also help guide you if that little voice inside your head begins to say that you can't do it.

- **Legal services.** A lawyer can assist with the initial paperwork for setting up a business and ensure the contract you use for client engagements mitigates your risks.
- **Accounting or tax services.** An accountant can help you monitor your profits, expenses, cashflow, billing, and taxes.
- **Marketing and lead generation services.** These can help you build your brand through a website or a social media presence (or campaign) while also identifying potential audiences to target for outreach and sales.

Of course, if cash flow is an issue and you don't have money for all (or even some) of these services, there is cost-effective software that you can leverage to help with key activities, such as accounting, project management, and automating marketing campaigns.

Quadrant C

Quadrant C focuses on people who have limited expertise in their chosen field and ample experience in the business world. Individuals who might fall into this quadrant:

- Recently graduated college or are relatively new to the field (midcareer change in their area of expertise)
- Are sought out by relatively few people for help or advice
- Are uncomfortable speaking as authorities on topics in front of individuals or groups
- Embrace and excel at selling themselves
- Can listen to potential customers and offer a custom elevator pitch based on their problems or needs
- Understand and make business decisions based on metrics and the business venture's financial health
- Have a system for project management and executing on deliverables
- Have a sense of cash flow and income projections

Quadrant C is an interesting place to be. You have the business skills necessary to make a consultancy successful, and you've probably identified a challenge to address, but how are you going to demonstrate your credibility on that topic and be taken seriously as someone who can solve that challenge? As you get started, you may wish to consider several paths.

You could work on developing your own skill set and subject matter expertise. Perhaps you've taken business classes, you've managed a business or a team, or you've run another business and seen the opportunity to approach a problem through your own business and expert e-learning designer or change management consultant lens. There is no quick fix to establishing your own expertise, but you can take a course and earn a certificate, read more research relevant to the area you want to specialize in, begin posting about it on social media, engage with thought leaders and practitioners on social media, and begin building a portfolio that shows potential clients what you're capable of.

On the other hand, if you want to fast track the expertise your company has about a specific area or capability, you may want to seek out a partner who can fill specific subject matter expertise gaps. If you choose this route, I'll offer the same warning that my attorney offered me: "Be careful—having a business partner is like a marriage. You need to find the right person and have hard conversations early on about your vision and expectations." Divorce for a business, like a marriage, can be painful and messy.

Consulting Tip

Join a professional association, which will typically offer research, newsletters, publications, and learning opportunities on a variety of topics for your field. Furthermore, associations generally offer networking opportunities, which are a good way to connect with and learn from others in the field; they're also good practice opportunities to network with a friendly audience.

Quadrant D

Quadrant D includes individuals who are considered experts in their field and have adequate knowledge to run a successful business. Individuals who fall into this quadrant on the matrix:

- Have been in the field for a number of years
- Hold advanced degrees or professional credentials in specific fields
- Have a sense for the pulse of the field and can see the origin of minor or major shifts
- Are regularly sought out for help or advice in their areas of expertise

- Are seen as authorities to speak on a topic in front of individuals or groups
- Contribute to the field through networking, publications, or mentoring others
- Have substantial, regular followership and interactions on professional social media platforms
- Embrace and excel at selling themselves
- Can listen to potential customers and offer a custom elevator pitch based on their problems or needs
- Understand and make business decisions based on metrics and the financial health of the business venture
- Have a system for project management and executing on deliverables
- Have a sense of cash flow and income projections

When a 2x2 matrix is introduced, the best place to be is often the upper right quadrant. While best is in the eye of the beholder, if you find yourself in Quadrant D, you're probably in good shape as you look to launch your consultancy or business.

The danger of Quadrant D is becoming complacent. My business partner Tim likes to say that if we're not growing our business, we're dying. Growth can mean many things, including bringing on more customers, more employees, more revenue, and more know-how.

It's important to recognize that change is the only constant. When it comes to subject matter expertise, you'll still need to stay on top of new trends, the latest research, and how advances in technology are influencing your field. Otherwise, the information you share with clients will get stale or out of date. When it comes to your business acumen, changes in laws, technology, accepted business practices, and your financial goals can all influence the business decisions you'll need to make.

Another question for those in Quadrant D is whether and how they'd like to grow. Are you ready to take on new employees? Would it make sense to broaden your services or the areas of expertise you bring to your clients? Growth doesn't always need to show up in the bottom line. Always put your passion and happiness first.

The upper right quadrant may be an ideal location from the standpoint of most 2x2 matrix models, but that doesn't mean you won't have constant work, decisions to make, and new knowledge or skills to acquire.

"On Your Own" Doesn't Mean "Alone"

By Rich Douglas, Rich Douglas Consulting

Many consultants start their own practices because they want to work alone. No more staff meetings, performance reviews, or any other burden that comes with being in an organization or business. It's just them, their clients, and the work.

But being on your own doesn't mean you're all by yourself. You'll need to wear many different hats as a consultant, and you might want help with some of them! Some of the different roles a consultant must play include subject matter expert, analyst, designer or developer, implementer, evaluator, administrator, accountant, advertiser, project manager, web designer or IT support, and investor.

That's a lot of hats! But you don't have to wear them all yourself. You can partner with businesses and individuals who specialize in any of these areas to get everything done. And there are some things you should not do unless you have this expertise (so you'll need to work with an accountant and attorney). You can work with:

- Other practitioners who have expertise you don't
- Course and product designers to shape your ideas into something deliverable to clients
- Administrative assistants (virtual and otherwise) to maintain your schedule, answer the mail, pay the bills, and cash the checks
- An accountant to do your taxes and set up your legal structure as an LLC or corporation
- An attorney to act as a legal representative and handle things like a trust
- An advertiser to promote your practice or products
- A web designer to set up your website, maintain it, post content, and improve its search engine optimization (SEO)
- A cash flow source to set up and sustain your business, like a lending institution
- Other consultants and consulting companies

These are just some of the roles you need to perform and the kinds of people and organizations you can work with to do them. The message here isn't the specific list, however. It's that no matter what challenges you face as a consultant, when you're on your own, you don't have to go it alone!

Your Position Isn't Static

Keep in mind that the quadrant you find yourself in on the Entrepreneur Readiness Matrix is simply where you stand today. If you were to do this exercise again after some research and experience, you'd likely move to a different spot on this matrix.

It's also important to remember that this is not an exhaustive list of everything you'll ever need to make your consultancy or business venture successful. Entrepreneurship is a journey with twists and turns, and even experienced businesspeople need to continue to stay on top of industry trends and develop new business skills.

Moving From Left to Right: Growing Subject Matter Expertise

Because you're reading a chapter about the consultant as an entrepreneur, odds are good that you are passionate about your work, and you believe you could be really good at it. Perhaps you're self-taught or recently came across a specific aspect of your expertise that you've seen others use to start their own business. Becoming an expert (which is represented by moving from left to right on the quadrant) takes time, drive, focus, and experience.

Moving From Bottom to Top: Growing Business Acumen

If I haven't made the point clear by now, I'll say it one last time: Just because you are really good at your area of expertise, you're not automatically going to begin a profitable venture by sharing it with the rest of the world. Knowing stuff and creating a business around that stuff represents two very different competencies. Running a successful, profitable, sustainable business will not be a journey along a straight line; you will face twists, turns, dips, and hills. You'll need to embrace the fact that running a business requires resilience and perseverance.

Summary

One thing you should always remember as a business owner and entrepreneur is that you should never be standing still—and that includes your position on the matrix. There is always something new to learn about running a business or a way to advance in your area of expertise. So, even if you are satisfied with your position on the matrix, think about how you can continue learning. You may need to learn new things just to maintain the place on the matrix that you deem critical to your success.

No matter where you are on the matrix, quadrant mobility is critical. Think about the actions you should take now to fill in your gaps.

Actions You Can Take Now

- **Find a mentor in the field.** You don't need a formal mentor–mentee relationship, but finding someone who has been in the industry long enough to have seen fads come and go, new trends emerge, and turned concepts into concrete practice will be an invaluable resource. Invite the individual to coffee and start a conversation.
- **Do your homework.** Whether that means listening to a variety of podcasts on the topic, reading a book, taking a class or workshop or certificate program, or seeking out and talking to others in your field, you'll need to increase your knowledge foundation. This can also help you determine whether you could be passionate about the area you've chosen for the long term.
- **Determine where you fall on the Entrepreneur Readiness Matrix.** Use the short questionnaire posted online at td.org/handbook-for-consultants to help assess your business acumen and subject matter expertise and plot where you fall on the matrix.
- **Align with the important people in your life.** Running a business can be an intense experience, not just for you but also for those closest to you. Talk with your spouse, partner, children, or others with whom you're close, and make sure you're aligned on how much you'll be working (especially if working evenings or weekends is not currently part of your routine), whether you'll have to travel, and how you'll address financial considerations that may arise.
- **Build your network.** Where will that first client engagement come from? It's easier to land gigs through referrals and people you know, but your connections need to be authentic. No one will want to hear your sales pitch out of the blue, no matter how well you knew them prior to your entrepreneurial journey. Begin having authentic conversations about what your plans are and why you're passionate about this topic area, and don't forget to ask your connections if there's anyone else you should be connecting with.

About the Author

Brian Washburn is the co-founder and CEO of Endurance Learning. This small-but-mighty instructional design firm serves as an extra set of hands for organizations large and small, helping them design and develop learning experiences that are engaging and lead to change. He got his start in both entrepreneurship and instructional design as a Peace Corps volunteer in Paraguay, training farmers on small business skills to improve their local agricultural co-ops while increasing their family's incomes. If you'd like to talk about training or entrepreneurship, Brian is always happy to grab a virtual coffee. Drop him a line at brian@endurancelearning.com.

SECTION III

Delivering Results
The Work of a Consultant

What does a consultant do? They exist in every industry, for every position, to support every task, and to solve every problem. You've probably heard of management consulting, IT consulting, marketing consulting, human resource consulting, talent development consulting, image consulting, tax consulting, cybersecurity consulting, nutrition consulting, financial services consulting, retirement consulting—you get the idea! Your area of expertise forms the basis that defines your consulting practice. Depending on what your client needs, you will play many roles, from identifying the problem to implementing the solution and anything between. You can read more about this in chapter 15.

Our luminary consulting author, Marshall Goldsmith, has been ranked the world's number 1 executive coach and a top 10 business thinker for eight years. He is one of a select few executive coaches to have worked with more than 200 major CEOs and their management teams. Marshall's consulting firm focuses on coaching, but that's really an understatement of the work he does and the impact he's had on so many businesses.

In this section, we explore more about what a consultant does. For example, Tonya Wilson shares what you can expect as an OD consultant and Dolores Kuchina-Musina discusses what you need to know if you want to consult with the US federal government. Lei Comerford explores how to use instruments with your clients, and Diana Howles provides six keys to help you build a successful consulting career. Greg Owen-Boger and Dale Ludwig wrap up the section with a reminder that you need to work both *in* and *on* your consulting business.

4 Mistakes to Avoid as a Consultant

You're a successful employee and you're tired of watching training consultants sashay in, conduct training, and waltz out with a big check. You've always wanted to be a consultant. You know you can do the same—but better. Today's gig economy excites you and you want to be a part of it. Is it time to finally start thinking about striking out on your own to do what you love?

Maybe! But you need more than an exciting idea and a passion for what you do to create a sustainable business. You need to avoid the four mistakes that many new consultants make. Review these typical blunders and determine how you can prevent them.

1. Overlooking the Planning Process

Yes, planning can be boring and it takes time. However, starting your consulting business without a solid plan is like driving in a foreign country when you can't speak the language, don't know which side of the road to be on, and forgot your map and GPS! To get started, you'll need at least three things: a business plan, a marketing plan, and a financial plan.

Of course, these won't need to be as detailed as those required by a large corporation, but you will need them to have enough details to serve as a road map. You need a plan that keeps you focused and heading in the right direction. You don't have time or money to waste on dead ends, wrong turns, or detours. Planning helps you answer questions such as:

- What kind of consulting will you do?
- What services will you offer?
- Who is your ideal client?
- How will you locate clients?
- What tools will you use for marketing?
- How much startup cash do you need?
- How much should you charge?

Don't skip the planning process. If you do, it may be the costliest mistake you make.

2. Relying on Your Area of Expertise to Be a Successful Consultant

Whether you are an expert in communication, leadership, cybersecurity, or artificial intelligence, you likely know your industry intimately; most consultants do. But your expertise alone will not lead to success—most consultants underestimate what it takes to run a business.

You are no longer a trainer; you are a business owner. If you want to be in business a year from now, you will need to gain all the skills required of a successful entrepreneur:

- How do you market your services?
- What do you say on a sales call?
- How do you manage cash flow?
- What taxes do you pay?
- How will you know when to hire someone to help you?

Don't think your expertise will automatically skyrocket your business to success. You can't just print your business cards and wait for the phone to ring. It won't.

3. Setting Your Fees Too Low

First-time consultants rarely set their fees high enough. If I asked five new consultants to put a price on their heads, there is a 90 percent chance that I'd recommend they double it. What?! How can that be?

There are a lot of factors to consider when determining your fee. You no longer have the protection of a company to pick up your insurance premiums, fund your retirement plan, pay for your days off, pay for conference fees, and provide office supplies. You'll have to pay for your own taxes, office rent, copying costs, utilities, accounting and legal fees, equipment purchases, and myriad other things. Go ahead. Add up the expenses necessary to run your business. . . . Surprising, isn't it?

It's easier to establish an appropriate salary when you first get started than it is to increase your fees later. Besides, from your client's perspective, a higher fee is often an indication that you will add value and you are confident in your ability to produce quality results.

4. Discounting the Value of Making Personal Connections With Clients

Staying top of mind with your clients is one of the best ways to keep these relationships vibrant and healthy. This is true for current, past, and potential clients. Building a personal connection with my clients is important to me; here are three ways I do it:

- **Physically be in their presence.** When working on-site with a client organization, I like to pop in to visit the CEO, president, HR director, or whoever hired me (with their favorite coffee order in hand), even if we were not scheduled to meet. Some consultants are sure to shudder at my lack of formality, but it represents who I am. Those who hire me know that I make these visits out of a desire to achieve excellent results for the organization. Granted—not everyone may appreciate this approach. You may need to schedule meetings in advance. The key is to make time for maintaining your relationships and getting to know your clients well enough to remember their favorite brew.

- **Share permanent, practical annual gifts.** I always look for something unique and special to send my clients on a regular cadence. Some consultants do this at year's end, others as a New Year's gift, and others at Thanksgiving. My company has gained a reputation for creative, practical gifts—one year we sent miniature mugs filled with gold paper clips. They were high quality, useful, and kept our company logo on our clients' desks every day.

- **Stay on their radar.** Keep yourself in front of your clients by periodically sending useful information or notes. For example, I send clients articles, notes of interest, books, announcements, cards, seasonal greetings, and even cartoons! Whether it's a new hire for your company, a new baby for your client, an award for the organization, or a promotion for someone you work with in your client's company—always look for opportunities to connect with your clients and contacts. Don't miss it.

The ideal situation for any consultant is for your clients to speak highly of you and recommend you to other clients. Nothing—absolutely *nothing*—is more valuable to you than a client's recommendation. You earn that by exceeding their expectations, adding value at every point, producing the highest quality results, building trusting relationships, and modeling the highest ethics. In other words, you earn it by doing a good job. Do good consulting!

The ebb associates' vision statement says, "Our clients are so satisfied that they market for us." Although it took time to achieve that vision, we have. In fact, we can trace more than 80 percent of our business back to three of our original clients!

Staying in business as a consultant depends on your ability to maintain a steady flow of business while projecting a positive image and an ethical reputation. Provide each client more value than they paid for, and you will have repeat and referral business. It's a guarantee that you will stay in business for life.

Your job as a consultant is to deliver results via a successful consulting business. To accomplish that, you need to create a plan, manage your business like an entrepreneur, compensate yourself adequately, and nurture every client relationship.

Coaching
Try Feedforward
Instead of Feedback

MARSHALL GOLDSMITH, *LUMINARY CONSULTING AUTHOR*

As an executive coach for more than 40 years, I've worked with leaders around the world who understand the critical importance of providing their employees with opportunities for improvement. Excellent leaders have a significant impact on the success and growth of their organizations, and providing feedback has long been considered an essential skill for leaders. As employees strive to achieve the organization's goals, they need to know how they are doing. They need to know if their performance is in line with what their leaders expect, and they need to learn what they have done well and what they need to change.

Traditionally, this information has been communicated in the form of downward feedback from leaders to employees. But these conversations are awkward to approach and difficult to have if leaders are pointing out the mistakes and flaws of the past. And, leaders just don't want to have them! Having consistent conversations about an employee's performance is critical, but leaders often drag their feet when tasked with providing feedback.

So, let's change the game. I'd like to share an idea called "feedforward."

What Is Feedforward?

Beyond a leader's reluctance, there is a fundamental problem with feedback: It focuses on the past, on what has already occurred—not on the infinite variety of opportunities that can happen in the future. As such, feedback can be limited and static, as opposed to expansive and dynamic. As a coach or a consultant, you are probably always searching for new methods and different ways to support the people you train or coach. In this chapter, I'll share a suggestion for reframing performance conversations.

When clients receive feedback, they get information about how they are currently performing. Feedforward is the reverse—it replaces positive or negative feedback with future-oriented actions. This means focusing on the future instead of the past. Feedforward can provide ideas for individuals to learn how to avoid repeating mistakes. It helps them learn different, more effective ways to solve problems. People typically leave a feedforward discussion feeling motivated and supported.

However, I want to be clear: My intent here is not to imply that consultants and coaches (or leaders within organizations) should never give feedback or that you should abandon performance appraisals. I simply want to show how feedforward can be preferable to feedback in day-to-day interactions. But first, let's look at an example of a feedforward session.

A Feedforward Activity

Over the past several years, I have observed more than 30,000 leaders as they participated in a fascinating experiential feedforward exercise in which they are asked to play two roles. In one role, they are asked to provide feedforward—that is, to give someone else suggestions for the future and help as much as they can. In the second role, they are asked to accept feedforward—that is, to listen to the suggestions for the future and learn as much as they can.

The exercise is part of a group event and typically lasts for 10 to 15 minutes. Each participant has six to seven dialogue sessions and are asked to follow these instructions:

1. Participants define a behavior they would like to change—one that would make a significant, positive difference in their life. They should then formulate a one-sentence statement such as, "I want to be a better listener."
2. Participants pair up and describe this behavior to their partners in one-on-one dialogues.
3. After stating what they want to improve, each participant should then ask for feedforward (in the form of two suggestions for the future that might help them achieve a positive change). If teams have worked together in the past, they are not allowed to reference that or give any feedback about the past. They are only allowed to give ideas for the future.

4. The individual who asked for feedforward should listen attentively to the suggestions and take notes. They are not allowed to comment or critique the suggestions in any way—not even to make positive judgmental statements, such as, "That's a good idea."

5. The individual thanks the other person for the suggestions.

6. The pairs then reverse roles so the other individual can state what they would like to change.

7. Now it's their partner's turn to provide feedforward in the form of two suggestions.

8. Teammates should thank each other for the suggestions, replying with a simple, "You're welcome." The entire process of giving and receiving feedforward usually takes two to three minutes.

9. Participants find another person and repeat the process until the facilitator ends the exercise.

I like to ask participants to share one word that best describes the experience, once we're finished, by completing the sentence, "This exercise was . . ." The words provided are almost always extremely positive, such as "great," "energizing," "useful," or "helpful." One of the most mentioned (and least expected) words is "fun!"

Consulting Tip

Use the feedforward exercise during your next leadership development event. It also works well as a meeting warm up activity.

Yes, the activity is fun, but as a coach you should focus on all the other reasons for perfecting the feedforward skill. When you know the difference between feedforward and feedback, the benefits are easy to see. It will make you a better coach and your clients will benefit greatly. Always remember, the past is unchangeable; the future is ripe for change.

10 Reasons Coaches Should Try Feedforward

Coaches play a unique role in developing others. They don't give information; they ask questions and tap into their clients' experiences and thought processes. They typically don't give recommendations, but they do empower clients to make their own decisions.

ATD's *TDBoK Guide* (Talent Development Body of Knowledge) defines coaching as "partnering with clients in a thought-provoking and creative process that inspires them to maximize their personal and professional potential." The *TDBoK Guide* also describes coaching as "an essential capability for any TD professional that has the power to catalyze breakthroughs to enhance individual, team, and organizational performance." Coaching is an interactive process that helps individuals explore possible future scenarios or develop more rapidly toward a preferred future state, produce results, set goals, take action, make better decisions, and capitalize on their natural strengths. It requires using active listening, asking powerful questions, evoking awareness, and creating action plans. Coaching sounds almost magical, doesn't it?

The leading credentialing authority in the coaching profession, the International Coaching Federation (ICF), has set standards for training in the core competencies and ethics of coaching. ICF defines coaching as, "partnering with clients in a thought-provoking and creative process that inspires them to maximize their personal and professional potential."

While feedback can be used to help your clients see what happened in the past and why, feedforward is a better way to help your clients plan for their future. Afterall, coaches are at their best when they help their clients tap into what they already know and enable them to make their own decisions.

Feedforward may be a new idea you hadn't thought of before. Let's review some of the reasons I believe consultants and coaches should use feedforward.

1. We can change the future. We can't change the past.

Feedforward helps people envision and focus on a positive future, not a failed past. Athletes are often trained using feedforward and positive visualization techniques to complement their reviews of past performance recordings. For example, racecar drivers are taught to look at the road ahead, not at the wall. Basketball players are taught to envision the ball going in the hoop and to imagine the perfect shot. By giving people ideas about how they can be even more successful (as opposed to visualizing a failed past), you can increase their chances of achieving this success in the future.

2. It can be more productive to help people learn to be right, than prove they were wrong.

Negative feedback often becomes an exercise about proving someone was wrong or did something poorly. This tends to produce defensiveness on the part of the receiver and discomfort on the part of the sender. Even constructively delivered feedback is often seen as negative because it necessarily involves a discussion of mistakes, shortfalls, and problems. Feedforward, on the other hand, is almost always seen as positive because it focuses on solutions—not problems.

3. Feedforward primes successful people to become even more successful.

Successful people like to focus on ideas that will help them achieve their goals. We accept feedback that is consistent with the way we see ourselves, so many successful people will push back against hearing about their past shortcomings. Successful people often have a very positive self-image. I have observed many successful executives respond to (and even enjoy) feedforward. I am not sure that these same people would have had such a positive reaction to feedback.

4. Feedforward can come from anyone who knows about the task.

It does not require personal experience with the individual. You would be amazed by how much you can learn from people you don't know! For example, if you want to be a better listener, almost any successful person can share ideas on how to improve. They don't have to know you. Feedback requires knowing about the person. Feedforward just requires having good ideas for how to achieve the task. Thus, as a consultant or coach working with an employee or group of employees, you don't necessarily have to know their entire performance history before using the feedforward approach.

Consulting Tip

Try feedforward for yourself. Find another consultant who knows what you do. Walk through the feedforward process and make sure you both get to be on the receiving end. After your feedforward session, get back in your roles as consultants and process the activity. Ask: What did you learn? How did the process feel? How might you each use it in your consulting practice?

5. People don't take feedforward as personally as feedback.

In theory, constructive feedback is supposed to focus on the performance, not the person. In practice, almost all feedback is taken personally (no matter how it's delivered). Successful people's sense of identity is highly connected with their work. The more successful they are, the more this is true. Thus, it is hard to give dedicated, professional feedback that is not taken personally. Feedforward cannot involve a personal critique because it is discussing something that has not happened yet! Positive suggestions are seen as objective advice, whereas critiques are often viewed as personal attacks.

6. Feedback can reinforce negative self-fulfilling prophecies.

Feedforward can reinforce the possibility of change. Feedback can reinforce the feeling of failure. How many of us have been helped by a significant other, parent, or friend, who seems to have a near-photographic memory of our previous shortcomings, which they choose to share with us to point out the history of our flaws? Negative feedback can reinforce the message that this is just the way you are. Feedforward assumes that the receiver of suggestions can make positive changes in the future.

7. Most people hate getting and giving negative feedback.

I have reviewed summary 360-degree feedback reports for more than 50 companies. The items, "provides developmental feedback in a timely manner" and "encourages and accepts constructive criticism" both always score near the bottom on co-worker satisfaction with leaders. Traditional training does not make a great deal of difference. However, if leaders got better at providing feedback every time the performance appraisal forms were improved, most should be perfect by now! Leaders are not very good at giving or receiving negative feedback. It is unlikely that this will change soon.

8. Feedforward can cover almost all the same content as feedback.

Imagine that you just gave a terrible presentation in front of the executive committee. Your manager is in the room. Rather than make you relive this humiliating experience, your manager might help you prepare for future presentations by giving you suggestions, which can be very specific and still be delivered in a positive way. In doing so, your manager can cover the same points without feeling embarrassed and without making you feel even more humiliated.

9. Feedforward is faster and more efficient than feedback.

An excellent technique for giving ideas to successful people is to say, "Here are four ideas for the future. Please accept these in the positive spirit that they are given. If you can only use two of the ideas, you are still two ahead. Just ignore what doesn't make sense for you." With this approach, almost no time gets wasted on judging the quality of the ideas or proving that the ideas are wrong. By eliminating judgment, the process becomes much more positive for both the sender and the receiver. Successful people often have a high need for self-determination and will accept ideas that they buy while rejecting ideas that feel forced upon them.

10. Feedforward can be used with just about anyone.

Use feedforward with your coaching clients, whether they're managers, peers, or team members. As a coach, this is a great way to open your clients up to thinking about their future and empowering them to consider new solutions. Rightly or wrongly, feedback is associated with judgment. This can lead to negative—even career-limiting—unintended consequences when applied to managers or peers. Feedforward does not imply superiority of judgment (which you should never do as a coach). Instead, it is focused on being a helpful fellow traveler rather than an expert. Therefore, it can be easier to hear from you as a coach because you're not in a position of power or authority. Feedforward is also an excellent team building exercise—pair up team members and have them ask, "How can I better help our team in the future?" Once they listen to feedforward from their partner, they can reverse roles.

My experience has been that people listen more attentively to feedforward than feedback. One person who experienced feedforward told me, "I think that I listened more effectively than I ever do at work!" When asked why, he responded, "Normally, when another person is speaking, I am so busy composing a reply that sounds smart that I am not fully listening to what they are saying. In feedforward, the only reply that I am allowed to give is 'thank you.' Because I don't have to worry about composing a clever reply, I can focus all my energy on listening!"

Practical Advice for Your Coaching Practice

Pamela J. Schmidt, courageUP

For many years, I wondered if I had what it took to fly solo as a leadership and transition coach. I had spent 40 years collaborating in the trenches to make things happen for others. How valuable was my experience? Was I ready to build a coaching and consulting practice? It was time to own my decision. After much sage advice, I realized it was my choice and my chance to do what I loved doing—helping individuals, teams, and organizations realize their full potential! I finally understood that I did not have to take a full leap into the next chapter of my life. I could walk gracefully forward and experiment with my definition of the work and my niche.

My niche focuses on people who are eager to make big shifts and changes at work or at home; my job is to help them find alternative options that might be outside their experience and comfort zone. I believe that ideas, possibilities, and answers are already present if we have the courage to experiment. And that inspired the name of my company: courageUP.

I provide professional services to help bright and passionate people find their courage to own their goals, whether they are business or personal goals or both. This ownership leads them to take the first necessary steps to achieve those goals. But I also had to coach myself to find the courage to create the lifestyle I wanted for my new direction.

I believe these practices make me a better coach and can help you too:

- Pace yourself.
- Realistic optimism is crucial; look for the silver lining in all circumstances.
- Growth takes time and patience. Dark and quiet places help ideas germinate. It is easy to think going dark means something is buried, but in fact, it's actually been planted for growth.
- Benchmarking is a helpful tool until you compare yourself out of your definition of success. Use it wisely.
- Get an accountability coach. It's easy to change plans, but it is harder to hold tight and be patient. Check your thinking with someone you trust before making big changes.
- Clarity is a gift, so remain clear on your definition of growth.
- Enjoy the work. If you aren't, you are not doing something right.
- Be like an owl! They have exceptional hearing and amazing long-range sight. Listen intentionally and keep your eye on your horizon.

I encourage you to make your own list of practices to consider how to become a better coach.

Summary

Quality communication between and among people at all levels and in every department and division is the glue that holds an organization together. By using feedforward—and encouraging others to do the same—you can dramatically improve the quality of communication in the organizations where you work as a consultant and coach. Feedforward ensures that the right message is conveyed and that those who receive it are receptive to its content. The result is a much more dynamic, open organization—one whose employees focus on the promise of the future rather than dwelling on the mistakes of the past.

Actions You Can Take Now

- **Practice feedforward.** Identify a friend with whom you could practice feedforward. Follow the instructions in this chapter. Be sure to do two rounds—one for each of you.
- **What's holding you back?** Are you thinking about being a consultant who coaches others? What's holding you back? Make a list of all the skills you have that make you a good coach. Share this list with someone and ask for some feedforward to move you to the next step.

About the Author

Marshall Goldsmith is the Thinkers50 number 1 Executive Coach and *New York Times* bestselling author of *The Earned Life, Triggers,* and *What Got You Here Won't Get You There.* His books have sold more than 3 million copies and have been translated into 32 languages. He was ranked the world's number 1 executive coach and top 10 business thinker for eight years and is one of a select few executive coaches who has worked with more than 200 major CEOs and their management teams. Marshall served on the advisory board of the Peter Drucker Foundation for 10 years. He has been a volunteer teacher for US Army Generals, Navy Admirals, Girl Scout executives, and leaders of the International and American Red Cross (which also named him National Volunteer of the Year). Among his numerous awards and acknowledgments, Marshall was chosen as the inaugural winner of the

Lifetime Award for Leadership by the Harvard Institute of Coaching. Marshall's mission in life is to share all he knows with as many people as possible. With that in mind and working with Fractal Analytics, he is developing his own AI computer bot, MarshallBOT. It will share all he knows for free in multiple languages. You can find hundreds of free articles, interviews, columns, and videos at MarshallGoldsmith.com, and you can reach him at Marshall@MarshallGoldsmith.com.

CHAPTER 15

The Client Interface
Your Role in the Consulting Process

ELAINE BIECH

When I first started as a consultant, I was woefully ill-prepared. I had applied for my boss's job and when I didn't get it, I decided to become a consultant instead. I guess that reason was as good as any other! (There's more to that story, but for another time.) However, I quickly realized that I had no idea what I was getting myself into. I didn't know how to find clients, how to open or close a sale, how to schedule a client call, how to market, what role I would play, how to gather data, how to identify or solve problems, how to determine my legal responsibilities, how to build a client relationship, how to run a business—you get the picture.

Perhaps you are in a similar situation. You may even have a first client in mind or lined up. Now comes the hard part. What does it mean to be a consultant? How do you get started with your client? What is the work you do? Many of the questions I had when I started out are answered in other chapters in this book. But when working with your clients, you need to be clear about two things: the role that the client expects you to play and the process you'll use to complete the task. In this chapter, I'll help you gain clarity on these two things.

Your Role as a Consultant

You'll play numerous roles as a consultant because you typically enter a project whenever a client needs your help, rather than always starting at the beginning. To understand how to best help your client, you need to be clear about the role your client expects. Let's consider five common roles based on the type of work you may have to perform:

1. **Identify the problem.** You may enter a project when a client knows something is wrong, but cannot identify what that is—morale is down, communication is poor,

turnover is high, or profits are declining. In this case, you may be asked to identify the problem. To do so, you'll probably gather data, interview people, study the big picture, recognize interfaces, and benchmark other organizations. The roles you will play include interviewer, analyzer, synthesizer, categorizer, and researcher.

2. **Identify the cause.** You may enter after the client has defined their problem—sales are down, time from concept to market is too long, or defects are high. The client knows the problem but not the cause. In this case, you may be asked to identify the root cause of the problem. To do so, you'll need to understand the basics of problem solving, how to uncover the root cause, how to communicate with process owners, and how to challenge the status quo. You may also need expertise in the industry. The roles you will play include expert resource, auditor, devil's advocate, mediator, and problem solver.

3. **Identify the solution.** You may enter when a client knows there is a problem and has identified the cause—sales are down because the competition has introduced a new product, time from concept to market is too long because the staff doesn't work well together, or defects are high because the supplier is unreliable. In this case, you may be asked to identify a solution or solutions. You will probably need to research outside initiatives in the same or related industries. You may need to locate other resources or facilitate open discussion. You will also need to help others identify potential ideas. The roles you will play include processor, idea generator, facilitator, and adaptor.

4. **Implement the solution.** You may enter when a client knows there is a problem, has identified the root cause, and has determined the solution—they need to attract a new customer base, they need to work better as a team, or they need to improve supplier communication. In this case, you may be asked to create and implement the solution or change. You will be expected to make things happen. If you must install the new, you may also be required to dismantle the old. To do so, you'll need to deliver information and assist others to communicate effectively. You may need to supervise installations and reconfigure the workforce. The roles you will play include catalyst, implementer, change agent, mentor, communicator, and coordinator.

5. **Assist with a specific project.** When support is needed or an organization senses that it doesn't have the expertise to complete a particular job or project, it might bring in a consultant—the company may hire a consultant to bolster the marketing department during a seasonal campaign or to design a succession planning process. Your objective analysis is valued by the hiring organization. In addition to consultants, the people taking on these projects might be called gig workers, contractors, or part-time employees.

Your Consulting Process

No matter what your role is or where you enter your client's situation, you need to be ready to go when a client calls. Every consulting project—no matter what you're asked to do, how long it lasts, or what the price tag is—will go through a series of phases. I learned that the hard way, but you don't need to if you use a consulting process that works for you. Using a specific process has several benefits:

- It will keep you focused so you don't jump ahead or forget a step.
- It will keep your clients focused on the phase you are in and what needs to be completed.
- It builds your credibility with your clients.

Numerous models exist to conduct the consulting process, and all follow a similar process. Let's review ATD's 5D model (Figure 15-1), which I designed for ATD's Consulting Skills Certificate course. It is based on the ebb associates' consulting model. We'll discuss the five phases here, but ATD's Consulting Skills Certificate course goes into much more detail.

Figure 15-1. ATD's 5D Model and Phases

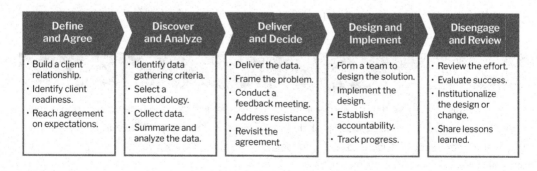

Define and Agree	Discover and Analyze	Deliver and Decide	Design and Implement	Disengage and Review
• Build a client relationship. • Identify client readiness. • Reach agreement on expectations.	• Identify data gathering criteria. • Select a methodology. • Collect data. • Summarize and analyze the data.	• Deliver the data. • Frame the problem. • Conduct a feedback meeting. • Address resistance. • Revisit the agreement.	• Form a team to design the solution. • Implement the design. • Establish accountability. • Track progress.	• Review the effort. • Evaluate success. • Institutionalize the design or change. • Share lessons learned.

Phase 1: Define and Agree

The define and agree phase provides a starting point to prepare you for learning more about the project. Peter Block calls this phase "entry and contracting." Whether it's because of a decision from the C-suite, the result of another project you led, or simply a serendipitous meeting while networking, this should be treated as the first step in the consulting process.

You'll want to plan ahead for your initial exploratory meeting with any potential client. I like to research the client for background and then use that information to establish a set of questions before the meeting. This accomplishes two things. First, it provides a foundation for building our relationship. Second, it ensures I obtain the information I need to either proceed with the project or determine that it isn't for me.

The most important advice I give new consultants is to begin building a relationship with your client at your first meeting. And the best way to do that is to spend time learning about each potential client prior to your first meeting.

The exploratory meeting is an opportunity for you to learn more about the project and present yourself as a credible consultant. As an external consultant, you bring knowledge and ideas from other companies and a clean slate unfettered by any internal baggage. All this builds credibility. But you'll also want to do more learning than selling in this meeting. Plan to accomplish several things:

- Establish a positive relationship with the client.
- Understand the scope of the project.
- Identify what the client expects of you.
- Identify the resources required.
- Discuss the processes you will use.
- Reach agreement on next steps.

Consulting Tip

Let me say this again: Your first meeting will be more successful if you take time to learn about your client and plan what you need to accomplish during the meeting. You can find a meeting planner worksheet and a contract checklist at td.org/handbook-for-consultants to help you prepare for your next meeting and evaluate yourself afterward.

The Value of Client Research

It was in 1985 and I had a contract with NASA's Langley Research Center to deliver an online webinar, "Leading Effective Meetings," to NASA's 10 field centers. Everyone at Langley was on edge because this was the first time they'd ever tried to do anything like this. Failure was not an option. I got wrapped up in their nervousness. The HR director, Bill, and his colleague, Pat, wanted me to invest every second into preparation to ensure success. Remember, NASA doesn't like failure! They loved to say they were going to "beam me up" across the nation.

Perhaps to ensure my commitment, they promised to introduce me to executives at Newport News Shipbuilding (NNS) after the webinar. I was from Wisconsin and had never heard of NNS—the shipbuilders in my state built boats out of their garages. However, Bill and Pat kept me too busy to research this shipbuilding company.

Well, I was "beamed up" with much success and celebration. Following the session, Bill and Pat drove me to the shipyard. On our way, I asked where this shipyard was located. Bill replied, "We've been going past it for the last mile." Oh, oh! As I looked out the window and saw US Navy carriers and huge cranes, I realized my lack of preparation was a mistake. The second clue that I'd made an error by not doing my research came as we pulled into the parking lot and I saw the sign saying, "Newport News Shipbuilding, a Tenneco Company." Now, Tenneco was a company I'd heard of and I knew it was large. My third clue came as we entered the boardroom and I saw 10 men dressed in suits sitting around the largest round oak table I'd ever seen. Introductions were made and I suddenly realized that the suits expected me to say something. So, I asked my first question: "How many people are employed here?" The response of 32,000 employees was almost five times the size of the small Wisconsin town I lived near!

Fortunately, my impromptu questions led to an excellent discussion and I was hired to design the NNS's first process improvement program. That was followed by several other training programs, and ultimately, I did consulting work for the company for 10 years. I built a strong relationship with NNS and hundreds of its employees.

But make no mistake—that first conversation could have gone in the opposite direction because I didn't do any potential client research. Don't risk a lucrative and gratifying client relationship! Always prepare for your first meeting.

Agree on What?

Reaching an agreement is a communication process, which is why asking questions is a critical part of phase 1. You should gather the following information about the project:

- Logistics, such as administrative and support steps (including who will be responsible for making copies, taking notes, developing agendas, compiling questionnaires, scheduling meeting rooms, and serving as a contact)

- Expected outcomes and agreement on the scope
- A timeline that includes actions prior to beginning the project, target dates, progress report dates, and other due dates
- Resources provided by both the client and the consultant
- Confidentiality agreements regarding data and other pertinent issues
- Commitment and support expected, including agreement on time availability
- Communication desires for the client, consultant, and other stakeholders
- Processes that will be used, including data gathering
- Your role in the process and the one specific person who is your client

These decisions may be made in one meeting, or they may require several. They may be either verbal or formally documented in an acceptance agreement, which can be as detailed as you wish. However, the need for an acceptance document is entirely up to each organization and your preferences. You may also be expected to write a proposal. (The decide and agree phase should lead to decisions that provide enough information for you to write a proposal, which is discussed in more detail in chapter 25.)

Consulting Tip

Don't write a proposal or sign an acceptance agreement unless you are certain you have a clear understanding of the project and its deliverables.

Phase 2: Discover and Analyze

Once you have defined the problem; initiated a working relationship; signed a contract, agreement, or proposal; and agreed on the next steps with your client, it's time to gather data. Your primary role in this phase is to identify the cause and prepare to share it with your client.

Data gathering will help you decide what kind of problem you are addressing. Is it a problem that can be solved by training? Or is there another root cause? You may be asked to develop training because of an incident; for example, because the cafeteria is getting an unusually high number of customer complaints, the company wants you to develop a customer service skills program. Although it may be tempting to quickly put together a customer service training program, it would be much wiser to first determine whether there is really a need for it. A needs assessment can help you do that.

The goal of gathering data is to determine the current state and the desired state. Then you'll be able to see what must change by looking at the difference, or the gap between the two. If it is a training problem, this gap is translated into the learning that must occur and it becomes the basis for a good training design.

Be prepared for unanticipated consequences and issues that may be uncovered during this phase. A consultant must objectively review the data and present it candidly and honestly. What you learn may take you back to the beginning to revisit the timeline, resources, and perhaps even your agreement with the client.

There are a dozen or more techniques for collecting data, so it's up to you to decide which ones work best for you. Be careful that you do not get stuck continuing to obtain data in the same way. Or even worse, decide that because you have worked with the organization before and know them, you do not need to gather data.

Interviews, focus groups, questionnaires, observations, and performance data are popular data collection tools. You can learn more about them online at td.org/handbook-for-consultants. Each tool has its own advantages and disadvantages. And you may have to use multiple tools in concert to gather all the data you need.

When selecting a tool, the criteria you need to consider include:

- **Time.** What is your turnaround time?
- **Cost.** How much money is available for the assessment?
- **Comfort level and trust.** What is the climate within the organization? Which assessment tool will ensure candor and accuracy?
- **Size of the population to be surveyed.** How many people need to be involved in the assessment?
- **Confidentiality.** Is confidentiality an issue for individuals in the department or organization?
- **Reliability and validity.** To what extent is this critical? How will the assessment methodology affect its reliability and validity?
- **Organizational culture.** What have employees used in the past, and how might different methods be perceived?
- **Location of those to be surveyed.** Are many people located remotely?

Analyze the Data

Next, you'll need to examine the data you've gathered. When faced with the stack of notes from your data collection efforts, begin by entering everything into your computer. Look for relationships and connections between the data points. Once you have input all the data, you will generally have the beginning of several themes. If you started with a model in mind, begin with that model and plug the information into it.

Once you can see the themes, read through the document one more time to see if any additional themes pop out and determine if an overview comes to mind. Then go through the document again to extract phrases and quotes that demonstrate the theme. Finally, if it is your responsibility, identify recommendations. In some cases, you may organize the data and provide examples so that a feedback meeting team can identify their own themes and recommendations.

Phase 3: Deliver and Decide

The previous phase flows directly into this one. In phase 2, you identified the cause of the problem. In phase 3, you begin to identify the solution. Deliver and decide refers to delivering your findings, which you gathered and analyzed during the last phase, and deciding what will happen next.

Both deliver and decide may occur within the same hour-long meeting or they may occur over several meetings. However, the preparation up to that time may be lengthy. The key to this phase is being organized so that the data sells itself. The ultimate goal of this phase is ensuring you have a well-organized meeting where you can deliver your assumptions about the data you gathered.

Frame the Issue

You will identify themes using the data you analyzed in phase 2. Depending on your client and the problem, this step may be completed before, during, or after a meeting with your client.

Identifying themes is also called framing the issue. If you are working with an internal team, they may help you establish themes, patterns, or relationships that frame the issue for easy understanding. Models can also help you frame the data and present it in a cohesive, logical way.

A model for training might be a sequential design, levels of expertise (beginner and advanced), or relational (leading yourself, leading your team, or leading your organization). You might also use organizational design models such as:

- Weisbord's Six Box Model (purpose, rewards, relationships, leadership, structure, and helpful mechanisms)
- Appreciative Inquiry
- McKinsey's 7-S Model (skills, strategy, structure, systems, style, staff, and shared values)
- Matrix Grid Reports
- SWOT analysis (strengths, weaknesses, opportunities, and threats)
- Value Chain Analysis (nine primary and support activities)
- PIPE (procedures, information, people, and equipment)

If you have a lot of numbers and statistics, visualizing data in a bar chart, graph, or another graphic design can make it easier for everyone to comprehend. You may also wish to separate the data into chunks. One method that works well is to divide the information into the following categories:

- **Findings.** Verifiable information, statistics, and evidence in the form of both quantitative and qualitative data creates a rationale and can be presented in a bulleted list.
- **Options and opportunities.** The conclusions drawn from the findings can be presented as options and alternatives, pros and cons, or another simple grouping.
- **Recommendations.** These are the results of data gathering and analysis and can be presented in incremental levels of acceptance, by department, or in any other logical grouping.

You use the data that you've collected, framed, and displayed during the feedback meeting. You may also be expected to provide a report summarizing the data. Depending on your agreement with the client, this report may be completed before the feedback meeting or after (as a summary of what occurred in the meeting).

Prepare for Resistance

The feedback meeting—where you share the data and what you uncovered—can create positive energy in an organization and a path toward change. However, it may also raise other issues including resistance. Because you and your client work as partners, you should meet with them to share the information before you release it to the rest of the organization. This allows your client time to prepare how they will react to and address the data in the feedback meeting. This is one of the reasons I recommend using a specific design.

If working with an internal team, you may want to meet with your client separately before sharing the feedback with the entire team. This is especially important if you've learned sensitive information. On the other hand, resistance can occur at any time, so beware of a client who:

- Seems to have a hidden agenda
- Has unrealistic expectations
- Withdraws commitment from parts of the project
- Fails to provide data and information as promised
- Is slow to approve work
- Shifts gears in the middle of the project
- Ignores your recommendations
- Requests that you change or omit information from a report
- Brags about controlling or taking advantage of others

When resistance to what you present in the feedback meeting occurs, try taking a rational approach first—state your observations and do not back down from touchy issues. And make sure to practice good listening skills. Remember, resistance is not something to overcome; it's something to be understood and expressed.

Consulting Tip

Peter Block says that resistance means you are "dealing with something that is important to the client." So, learn why the resistance occurred. What important aspect did you uncover?

Ensure Alignment

For good measure, schedule a meeting with your client as soon as possible after the feedback meeting. During this follow-up meeting, you should:

- Revisit the data and decisions to ensure that you are aligned on the project's goals.
- Reach agreement on the process that will be used to move forward.
- Decide how you will measure success.

- Determine immediate next steps.
- Begin thinking about how to evaluate the change that will be implemented.

During phase 3, your role is to help your client decide *what* to do. In the next phase, you will help your client design *how* to do it.

Phase 4: Design and Implement

Designing and implementing your recommendations is the culmination of a successful consulting project. Depending on the project, your job might actually end at this point if you initially decided to turn the implementation over to the client. For example, they may have brought you in to identify the root cause of a problem and recommend a solution, such as the need for a training program, but they will design and deliver the training program. However, I find that this is becoming less common as companies more frequently keep consultants on contract to design the solution and facilitate the implementation.

Designing the plans for change is an exciting step. If this is a small project, you may own most of the responsibility for the design. If it is a larger project, you would be wise to gather a team of internal employees to help establish the design. Tap your project management skills to get started.

Consulting Tip

One way to help employees accept the change is to make them a part of it. This is one reason why I recommend using a team to design and implement the next steps.

Manage the Change

In phase 4, you move into a change manager role. Because the projects on which you consult will almost always involve a change, understanding the ins and outs of change management is critical. You'll design the change based on the data you discovered and analyzed in phase 2 and the recommendations from phase 3. Your team will assist with a good portion of the thinking and some of the legwork while you coordinate. And, you will all establish targets or goals for what success looks like. These targets are the reason you are involved.

Consulting Tip

Read a book or two about change management—John Kotter's *Leading Change* is a good place to start. Or, check out ATD's Facilitating Organizational Change Certificate program, which will not only help you with this aspect of consulting but also help you prepare for CPTD certification.

This part of the project will require you to tap into a variety of skills and roles, and you may be involved in many different actions, such as:

- Ensuring that milestones are met
- Negotiating between different departments
- Fostering collaboration among employees and between diverse groups
- Tracking timelines and tasks to ensure timely delivery
- Managing organizational politics
- Facilitating meetings
- Motivating employees, managers, and leaders
- Encouraging involvement
- Updating management
- Creating effective transition strategies
- Engaging stakeholders

Decide on the Change Target

Data gathering and the feedback meeting are critical because they lay the foundation for the effort's target. In some organizations, the target may also be called the strategic imperative, the sense of urgency, or the compelling reason. Whatever it is called, the change target provides the direction and goal for phase 4.

For example, if the organization is concerned about its talent management efforts, it might focus on improving succession planning and recruitment. This would be the change target. The specific goals that demonstrate whether the organization has achieved its target might include statements such as:

- By May 2028, there will be a minimum of one ready candidate for every key position.

- By July 2028, we will have identified the best universities for recruiting entry-level scientists.

It is up to the consultant to create (with the client partner) an environment conducive to making the change happen. But know that change may take longer than you anticipate and it may not go the way you've planned. Change initiatives require strong leadership, and there is no one right way to do them, so you must be prepared for anything. As a consultant, you are in a precarious place—you are responsible for success but are seldom managing the resources required for implementation. You have the opportunity to influence but are not a decision maker. This means it is imperative that you work through your client partner and other leaders in the organization.

Implementation is the exciting step in the process in which the client and the consultant begin to execute the changes to reach the preferred future. The strategies may include things you've conducted in the past or something that is totally new to you. It may affect a few people, a work team, a department, or the entire organization. Implementation may take a very short time for small projects or multiple years for large organization-wide projects.

Some strategies and tools consultants use include:
- Human performance improvement (HPI)
- Change management
- Work redesign
- Team building
- Process improvement
- Coaching
- Survey feedback
- Impact studies
- Talent management planning
- Reorganization and restructuring
- Career development
- Process reengineering
- Compensation planning
- Developing and clarifying values
- Feasibility studies
- Succession planning
- Establishing a vision

- Strategic planning
- Risk assessment
- Communication process redesign
- Creating value propositions
- Designing training
- Leadership development
- Conflict resolution
- Customer service planning
- Leadership development
- Large group interventions
- Hybrid workforce planning

Tracking your progress will be immediately helpful to ensure the actions are completed on time. And assigning accountability makes it more likely that employees will complete their tasks. More importantly, though, tracking and completing steps on time will help build your credibility. An accountability tracking chart can be helpful at this stage. You can find an example on the handbook website, td.org/handbook-for-consultants.

Ensure Implementation

Even if you aren't involved in the implementation phase, you can still help your client ensure that the initiative becomes part of the organization's future. Share some of these ideas with your client:

- Keep everyone involved in the process.
- Continue to discuss the effort.
- Report on successes—large and small—and share them broadly.
- Remove old ways so employees have no choice but to use the new methods.
- Establish red flags for regressive behavior.
- Articulate the connections between new behaviors and organizational success.
- Ask people for ideas about new initiatives or refining what has been done.
- Use the credibility and success of this effort to address other processes, procedures, and roles, as well as other parts of the organization that do not align with the vision.
- Adjust all procedures, pay and benefit systems, and other recognition efforts to support the new design.

- Implement a monitoring plan and assign someone to report on it regularly.
- Establish a follow-up plan that focuses on key transition areas.

Phase 5: Disengage and Review

This last phase examines the project's accomplishments. Don't take this phase lightly. It provides several ways to look at evaluation—reflecting on what you learned, celebrating your successes, bringing closure to the process, and reminding your clients of what they have gained. These actions ensure that you and your client continue to get better and better at what you do.

Evaluate the Results

Whenever you end a project, you should evaluate what occurred based on the meaningful metrics, linked directly to the project goals, that you agreed to with the client. An evaluation can identify areas that still need to be addressed or that were uncovered during the implementation phase. It can also build your client's confidence in the process, which can then increase executive support.

As a consultant, you can benefit from an evaluation beyond the project's outcomes. Evaluations can foster improvement in future consulting projects and provide credibility for marketing your consulting services.

When developing an evaluation plan, consider:

- What behavior or result is the metric intended to reinforce?
- What is important to the client?
- How will the information be used? For what purpose? Who will receive it, in what format, and how often?
- How will evaluation data be collected, validated, and analyzed?

Consulting Tip

Start setting up the measurement process and systems early—during the second or third phase of the consulting process—so it's easier to track your progress.

If you come from a training perspective, you might be familiar with Kirkpatrick's Four Levels of Evaluation. Be sure that you strongly consider their idea of return on expectations, the degree to which what you delivered met what the client expected. Determine your consulting success by contemplating the following questions:

- **Did you do what you said you were going to do?** Did you meet the target you and the client set at the beginning of the project and then refined during the feedback meeting?
- **Did the change create an impact?** At the end of the deliver and decide phase, you and the client determined what to measure. Those items often focus on impact and will include both qualitative and quantitative data, such as lower costs, faster turnaround, reduced rework, higher profit margins, increased sales, or reduced overtime.
- **Would you do it again?** How satisfied is your client? How satisfied are the employees? How's company morale? Would you use the same process again? Would you accept a project like this again?
- **What did you learn that you can use in the future?** Gather both written and verbal feedback to ensure that you and the team you worked with experience personal growth.

Continue Learning

In addition to a formal evaluation plan and methodology, it's also a good idea to invest time in a discussion about the project once it's complete. This provides feedback but is also a good way to gain closure on the project. My military clients call these meetings after-action reviews (AARs) and use these questions to facilitate the discussion:

- What went well that we would do again?
- What problems did we encounter that we could have prevented? How can we prevent them in the future?
- What would we do differently?
- What insights did we gain about how we work together?
- Were the right people involved?
- How did we keep interruptions for customers and employees to a minimum?

- Did employees receive training, development, and coaching as needed?
- What did we do well that we can use in the future?
- What personal issues prevented a smooth effort?
- How did we link the results to organizational strategy?

Have a process in place to store and retrieve your lessons learned. Then, refer to them every year and ask yourself, "Did we really learn those lessons from last year? How did we implement them?" Here are some other thoughts related to lessons learned:

- Foster your client's independence and ensure their self-sufficiency.
- Develop a system of continued communication.
- Develop ways to promote continuous learning.
- Establish communities of practice or learning.
- Create opportunities for dialogue.
- Promote systems thinking.
- Apply continuous improvement processes.
- Use feedback for the next initiative.
- Celebrate success.

Consulting Tip

Determine how to review, organize, and use your lessons learned from each consulting project for continual improvement of your consulting company, its employees, and yourself.

Summary

To be successful in your consulting practice, your clients need to be confident in your abilities at the beginning and satisfied with the results at the end. Every consulting project requires you to know your role and understand the process, like ATD's 5D model, to ensure your clients get what they expect. When your role is clear and your process is in place, both you and your client will have a shared sense of what you need to concentrate on. Focus on the process and it will create a path to your success.

Actions You Can Take Now

- **Evaluate yourself.** Complete the Consultant Contracting Checklist at td.org /handbook-for-consultants. Look at those you marked as "no" to determine why you did not do them and what you can do differently next time.
- **Declare your role.** Review the five roles consultants play. Which roles do organizations hire you most often for? Do they match your strengths? Are there other roles you'd like to play more often? Identify five things you could do proactively to be hired for those roles.
- **Take a course.** Consider registering for the ATD's Consulting Skills Certificate course to gain more in-depth knowledge of the ATD 5D model.

About the Author

Elaine Biech, CPTD Fellow, is a consultant, facilitator, and principal author of the *TDBoK Guide.* She also authored the *Washington Post* number 1 bestseller *The Art and Science of Training* and 88 other books with 14 publishers. ATD calls her "a titan of the training industry." Elaine is the recipient of numerous awards from many organizations including four national ATD awards: 2020 Distinguished Contributor, Bliss, Torch, and Staff Partnership Awards. A sample of her ATD volunteer experiences includes being a member of the national ATD board of directors and the executive board, a member of NAC, ATD 2000 International Conference & EXPO design chair, and president of the SW Wisconsin Chapter. Elaine has presented at ATD's International Conference & EXPO for 38 consecutive years; she also initiated and chaired the conference's consultant's day for seven years. She serves on CCL's board of governors and is ATD's first CPTD Fellow Honoree. Elaine was honored with the Wisconsin Women Mentor Award and received ISA's 2022 Thought Leader Award. She is a dedicated lifelong learner who believes that excellence isn't optional. A consummate TD professional, Elaine has been instrumental in guiding the talent development profession throughout her career.

CHAPTER 16

6 Keys to Consulting Success

DIANA L. HOWLES

The big day had finally arrived for the video shoot. A large financial organization had contracted our company to consult on an educational offering for its large sales department. Initially, the client had a few ideas, but they weren't sure how to move forward. After our initial discussions, we explored more of their needs and worked to uncover any assumptions they didn't even realize they had. In the end, a custom sales video emerged as the best solution. My business partner and I were asked to oversee the scripting, so we asked for input from several other sales staff and project team members. We also provided input on the shoot location, approved the on-camera talent, and were on set the entire day to oversee the video's production. Along the way, we strategically fostered a fun, professional consulting relationship with this client, which made the video shoot day fun for everyone. But it was even more rewarding to be able to help our client be successful by providing a targeted solution that was just right for them.

We all have our own consulting process. We tap into our experience and expertise to deliver what our clients need. However, in my career, I've found that there are a few key principles for unlocking greater consulting success. You've probably heard of them, although some aren't commonly practiced:

1. Prioritize people.
2. Take a solution-agnostic approach.
3. Uncover your client's vision and assumptions.
4. Gather feedforward and then feedback.
5. Collect multiple perspectives.
6. Adopt a continuous evaluative mindset.

These six keys are related and align to a people-centered, collaborative, and results-focused consulting approach. They will help you improve your consulting relationships, grow your business, and build a successful consulting career. In this chapter, we'll explore the six keys to better understand what they mean and why they're important so you can apply them to your own consulting practice.

Key 1. Prioritize People

When you practice a people-first policy, you can build positive and healthy relationships, which makes your consulting work more enjoyable, efficient, and effective. I recommend leveraging your personal power with likability. The law of liking says that if a person perceives that you like them, they tend to like you in return. Other people skills to hone include caring, practicing authenticity, asking good questions, showing genuine interest, observing, being patience, actively listening, and finding a shared commonality.

Get to know your clients as people before asking about their business titles—learn their names quickly and use them right away. Find out what's important to them. What excites and interests them? If you see them as humans first, rather than sales prospects, you're much more likely to build genuine, rewarding relationships. It also helps put clients at ease, which means they'll be more likely to share their thoughts, ideas, and concerns.

You also want to cultivate psychological safety with those on your project teams. This safe environment allows your clients to feel more comfortable taking risks, expressing doubts, sharing new ideas, asking hard questions, and, if needed, respectfully disagreeing.

When dealing with difficult clients, try building a rapport and establishing a common communication style. Notice how they interact with others, and then tailor your approach to match theirs. For example, I was struggling to establish a rapport with one of my clients, who also happened to be a very fast talker and moved at a rapid pace. Because people often have natural affinity with those like them, I adapted my style to match her faster pace. As a result, we successfully discussed her vision, explored her concerns, and, ultimately, built a positive relationship that continues today.

Good consultants also have high emotional intelligence. When relationships get emotionally heated, it may be necessary to take a break and reconvene on a different day. Once all parties have calmed down, you can have the difficult conversation. Empathy is also a part of emotional intelligence and an essential people skill. When we practice empathy, we try to adapt to the other person's perspective in terms of how they think, feel, and respond. This builds trust. By approaching challenging conversations with empathy, you are better positioned to resolve conflicts and maintain positive relationships with your clients.

As a learning consultant on a project, I once worked with a client (let's call him John), who unknowingly frustrated many of his internal colleagues with unclear and long-winded communications, undecided tendencies, and seemingly scattered ideas. This lack of clear communication and resulting rework caused many to avoid working with him as much as possible. Even though I saw and experienced those same issues while working on projects with John, I also appreciated how much he taught me about his area of expertise. One day, I called him to ask a few questions; once we were finished, I genuinely thanked him for the impact he'd had and everything he'd taught me during the project. Then, something remarkable happened. John began to open up and talk honestly about his experiences at the organization, some of the challenging obstacles he had encountered, how he viewed the importance of his work, and his passion and commitment to the role. Thankfully, I was able to listen more than talk and empathize with his perspective.

When we ended the call, I knew our relationship had changed forever. The openness, raw honesty, and support we shared had blossomed to a higher relationship of trust and mutual respect. From that day forward, we became close confidants. In little ways, I noticed differences too. For example, John began responding to my emails more promptly and positively, our meetings were more productive, and he became easier to work with overall. Real connection changed everything!

Ultimately, prioritizing people and elevating interpersonal skills are necessary to build effective relationships using personal power, psychological safety, rapport, emotional intelligence, and empathy. This will become the foundation on which you build your consulting business, and it will help you deliver rewarding and successful projects to your clients.

Key 2. Take a Solution-Agnostic Approach

Do you consider yourself a skilled problem solver? If so, it may feel natural to offer solutions as soon as problems are presented to you. For example, when a client explains a challenge, you might immediately think of a solution. In the same way, your clients and prospects may be quick to present their preferred solutions—a common example is when clients say, "We really need a training class."

Before recommending a solution, you need to fully understand the problem. Unfortunately, in the L&D space, a training program is often the hammer that sees nails all over the place. But what if training really isn't the best solution for the situation? And what if the client's challenge isn't actually the core problem? In these cases, moving forward with a training solution would likely result in little or no impact on workplace performance.

For example, if a client says they need a virtual training course on customer service, you may be tempted to offer a customer service class as an off-the-shelf product. However, if you pause and dig deeper, you may discover that all but one or two call center staff members are currently receiving good customer service ratings. So, in this case, wholesale training isn't appropriate—instead performance management, mentoring, or coaching with these low-performing individuals will address the core problem, as well as save time and resources.

Another reason to avoid rushing to a solution is the temptation to run with the first good-sounding solution offered. I'll bet that some of your initial instincts when presented with a problem are to quickly propose solutions. Having an answer makes us feel smart and competent. However, research shows that these early decisions are often not the best ones. In his book, *Thinking, Fast and Slow*, Daniel Kahneman explains that people often make decisions quickly using intuition and heuristics based on incomplete information. They also tend to be overly confident about their prescribed solutions.

As a consultant, when presented with a client problem, it's important to take a solution-agnostic approach *initially*. Resist the temptation to run with a solution. Instead, slow the process down. Ask questions, probe, and talk with other people. In design thinking, this is the exploratory phase of problem solving. Your task is to uncover, define, and fully understand the root cause of the problem through exploratory and front-end analysis interviews. Only then, once the problem is clearly defined, can you begin to explore and ideate solutions.

Key 3. Uncover Your Client's Vision and Assumptions

Remaining solution-agnostic until you've discovered and defined the problem's root cause is not your only task. As you move forward with clients, it behooves you to unveil some other informational nuggets too.

Everyone has assumptions, and too often they need to be challenged. Be careful not to assume you know what your clients need. In your initial conversations, make sure the client is doing most of the talking. While clients typically have ideas about what a solution should look like, these assumptions and their vision often remain hidden. You might be thinking, "Well, can I just ask them?" Unfortunately, it's not that easy. Many clients will tell you they are open to anything, and they'll believe that too. Your job is to lift the veil and reveal their vision for them. You want to fully understand this vision and, if needed, calibrate or help them re-envision it another way.

One of the most effective strategies for uncovering assumptions is to ask open-ended questions. Ask questions that begin with *how, describe, tell me about, what if, what,* and *why.* Then, use their answers to generate more questions. This way, you (and they) discover what they really want, uncover any underlying biases, and identify any blind spots that might warrant further exploration. For example, encourage a client by asking, "What does success look like for your employees once this project is done?" or "Can you describe what you want staff to do that they're not doing now?"

Another strategy for uncovering assumptions is to actively listen and closely observe body language and nonverbal cues. If you are meeting virtually, ask that everyone uses their camera so you can leverage both the visual and verbal modalities. Pay attention to not only what your client says, but their paralanguage or how they say it. For example, if a client seems hesitant when exploring an aspect of the project, it may indicate an underlying concern that should be discussed. With close observation, you'll gain valuable insights to help you better understand your client's expectations for a project.

Consulting Tip

Get comfortable with silence. If you are doing more than half the talking, you've probably already lost whatever the discussion is about.

By leveraging strategies like asking open-ended questions, active listening, closely observing nonverbal cues, and collective ideation sessions, you can unpack your client's assumptions and ensure the project meets their vision for success.

Key 4. Gather Feedforward and Then Feedback

As I mention in my book, *Next Level Virtual Training: Advance Your Facilitation,* feedback often comes too late in our fast-paced work environments. Because proposed solutions and plans typically go into development quickly, by the time you ask senior leadership or customers for feedback, it's difficult to return to the drawing board to rethink assumptions.

This can create issues because your team is already invested in the solution they're working on. If you wait until the solution is nearly complete to request feedback, you'll find that customers are reticent to offer improvement ideas to something that already looks polished. And even if they do want to see changes, the project team won't want to make them due to the added work they'd require. This late in solution development, new ideas are usually shelved, due to the added time required to implement them, even if they would improve the quality of the solution.

Getting feedforward is quite different because it occurs in the solution formulation phase after you've defined the problem and all relevant situational factors. As a consultant, you will need to embrace uncertainty. Ask for input and reactions from target end users—such as members, customers, or internal clients—while your potential solutions are still in their rough form. Feedforward is an iterative, collaborative process in which you share tentative ideas to see how they resonate or could be improved. Lead with the prompt, "What if we could . . . ?"

The idea is to gather comments, insights, and ideas before you've finalized your prototypes and design. At this stage, people are not attached to the solution and they know that it can still be changed easily, which means they're less reticent to withhold comments. Feedforward in these earlier stages saves exponential amounts of rework because you can fail early and fast, with minimal time and resources invested.

I frequently apply the feedforward strategy in my work. For example, when a client contracted me to consult on a learning solution for new hires, I collaborated with them and we sketched out ideas together. Once we landed on a potential vision, I ran a paper and pencil sketch of this same vision by a few new hires who had just started a week or two prior. They reviewed the sketch and asked questions based on their experience as a new hire. Later, we ended up using those questions for the main menu of the learning solution. Ultimately, new hires chose the questions that most resonated with them to learn the answers. The final result benefited from early input.

As you begin constructing the solution or product, your vision becomes more tangible and can be expressed through rapid prototypes or specification documents. At this point, you shift into feedback mode. Now that your solution is grounded and solid, it's time to use feedback to calibrate and tweak the prototypes. Sketch ideas, run them by stakeholders, iterate, ask for more input, modify, and iterate again. In short, you'll use feedforward conversations first to determine your solution; then, once you build the solution, you can refine it with feedback.

This is a principle of design thinking—you go slower initially to go faster, smarter, and more confidently later. As consultants, we need to let go of our egos early when developing solutions. It's OK to have an uncertain start. While that initial period might appear to be a struggle, it will yield better results in the end.

Key 5. Collect Multiple Perspectives

When my company was approached by a large financial services organization to design and create a physical escape room learning experience, it seemed like a daunting task. The client wanted its sales staff to start thinking in more agile and innovative ways to help them maintain their market share in a fast-growing competitive environment. They wanted the learning experience to reflect this while also being engaging and participatory.

The result was successful and all 300 sales staff were able to complete the escape room in small teams. Many variables contributed to this project's success, but the participant debrief at the end was probably the most meaningful. Led by a skilled facilitator, participants were asked to deeply reflect on what they'd learned and how it applied to their sales market situation.

In addition to the debrief, I credit the program's success to the design process, which incorporated collecting multiple perspectives from the outset and user testing. Gathering multiple perspectives enabled us to better acquire a people-centered and relatable understanding of the problem. In the case of the escape room, we began by having conversations with key sales leaders from the field to discuss how sales staff were used to thinking in old, routine ways. We wanted to challenge them to become more agile and innovative in their sales approaches.

In addition, we invited members of the sales staff into these initial meetings to ensure we were hearing from a diverse set of voices. They were willing to help us brainstorm and eventually vote on the overall theme, as well as help us build and test the skill practices. It's well established that better solutions to complex problems come from groups rather than one or two individuals. The key is involving the right people in the collaborative process.

Once we started to design the physical escape room, I insisted we test it multiple times. I knew the value of running small groups of people through an activity during this initial development phase. It's important to bring the people on the receiving end of a product or service into the design process. Sure enough, our test users found the first clue too quickly, so we were able to adapt the level of difficulty as well as a few other tweaks inspired by these tests.

Finally, gathering multiple perspectives also helps build ownership. The escape room was well received and embraced by all involved, and many became champions for marketing it. This cultivated a shared sense of accountability for the project's success. We noted that many of the sales staff who offered different perspectives early on became test users later.

Gathering multiple perspectives is part of what is referred to as participatory design. Adopting this approach creates an engaging, memorable, and vibrant design process and learning experience.

Key 6. Adopt a Continuous Evaluative Mindset

A consultant should keep an evaluative mindset throughout the life cycle of a project to help make data-driven decisions. Author Michael Quinn Patton (2010) calls this "developmental evaluation." Examine what's working and what's not working in situations with greater complexity.

Once I was contracted on a project as the lead learning design consultant. It was post-pandemic and hybrid training approaches were growing in popularity. Although some employees were beginning to return to the workplace, those who had transitioned to working remotely no longer had a designated office space. My charge was to create an online scheduling system to manage daily desk space rentals for the hundreds of employees who may occasionally come into the office. My company was also tasked with training staff on how to use it.

In the initial exploration process, we found that different groups—especially the IT staff—were advocating for several conflicting solution approaches. Some even insisted theirs was the right solution. We needed more evaluative data. So, I created a quick reference guide for the new system and asked potential users to use the guide when reserving their desks within the system. More than 75 percent of those test users experienced crashes that disabled their system. I brought this data to the team and used it to explain why we needed to shift solutions. The team leader was convinced to change the procedure and adopt a different system for reserving workspaces. For the next six months, there were zero calls about this new reservation system to the help desk. The new solution was a huge success and employees no longer experienced system crashes. Instead, it saved time, money, and frustration.

Remember, evaluation doesn't just come at the end, especially for complex projects with uncertainties. Evaluation is basically determining the worth of something through objective measures. This can be done by a skilled consultant who serves as an evaluator at critical decision points during project development. As you can see, this final key builds on many of the prior consulting keys, such as having a solution-agnostic approach and gathering input into solutions before your client rolls them out.

Consulting Tip

You should regularly and formally ask the client if you are meeting or exceeding their expectations. How often do you take the time to do that? Check in with your client today to evaluate their satisfaction.

Finally, a continuous evaluative mindset helps establish credibility. By demonstrating a commitment to ongoing improvement, consultants can position themselves as respected partners. Therefore, adopting an evaluative mindset is essential to achieving success.

Summary

Overall, you have learned many strategies to help sharpen your consulting skills. These six keys are tightly interwoven and use a people-centered, collaborative, and results-focused consulting approach. Be sure to leverage these insights to help take your consulting career to new heights.

Actions You Can Take Now

- **Get feedforward.** Are you starting a project? Proactively seek feedforward on your ideas and designs in the very early stages while they're still a work in progress. This way you'll ensure that your ultimate solution benefits from early iterative work.
- **Add diversity.** Actively bring in multiple perspectives to your current project. This variety of voices will offer fresh perspectives you may have missed.
- **Evaluate, evaluate, evaluate.** As a consultant, wear the evaluator hat throughout and apply developmental evaluation. Today—not tomorrow—ask evaluative questions about the project you are conducting.

About the Author

Diana L. Howles is an award-winning speaker, Amazon bestselling author, and global virtual and hybrid training expert who has more than 20 years of experience in the learning industry. As a world-class facilitator, she has led virtual programs in more than a dozen countries. She is the author of the award-winning *Next Level Virtual Training: Advance Your Facilitation* (2022), and is a contributing author to the number 1 international bestseller *Resilient Women in Life and Business* (2023). As CEO of Howles Associates, Diana is a sought-after and popular speaker at international conferences and events. Contact her at howlesassociates.com.

CHAPTER 17

The Many Roles of an OD Consultant

Engaging for Organizational Health

TONYA WILSON

One of the greatest joys an organization development consultant can experience is to see positive transformation with real outcomes that influence organizations and individuals for good! I had this experience with my client Carl, an IT executive for a technology services company with about 30,000 employees. As Carl and I presented at an IT symposium on the power of mastering transformative communication to drive data team effectiveness, it was clear that integrative OD made a difference in his team's performance.

His was a story of challenges with team communication and some dysfunction that was influencing performance, psychological safety, and stakeholder management. After learning more about his team's challenges, we used a communications intelligence tool to create a new language and common understanding about each team member. Then, we followed with a team and leader integration process that clarified the team's roles, expectations, and outcomes. Finally, a refresher change management workout training helped create more effective stakeholder mapping and engagement. In addition to increasing his great place to work scores, Carl also saw improvements in these areas:

- Employee resource optimization
- Employee to leadership relationships
- Employee to employee relationships
- Employee and organization to customer relationships
- Improved collaboration and continuous improvement
- Greater organizational agility and resiliency

This transformation enhanced interpersonal relationships and team cohesion. In addition, it influenced overall organizational health, which was important because the company was moving quickly toward an important cloud strategy.

The health of any living organism is essential to its performance and desired outcomes. And while organizations are not living organisms, it is a useful metaphor for describing the role of OD consultants and practitioners and the influence they can have on organizational performance and outcomes. Similar to medical practitioners, who attend to the human mind and body, OD consultants attend to the organizational body, looking at its various functions and interdependencies. Applying a functional and integrative medicine approach to organization development involves adopting a holistic perspective that emphasizes the organization's overall health, balance, and optimal functioning. Just as the human system has a mind–body connection, a mind–body connection plays a significant role in an organization. This connection recognizes that the physical and mental well-being of individuals in an organization are intertwined and mutually influential.

Consultants use tools to examine functions and systems for intake and release to ensure that each part of the organization is healthy and operates interdependently to optimize performance. Just as physicians use traditional methods and nontraditional integrated approaches with their patients, OD consultants use traditional and nontraditional approaches, combined with assessments, data collection, and collaborative conversations.

In this chapter, we'll look at the work OD consultants do through the lens of a popular framework for organization design and the questions you should be thinking about and asking your clients. Then, we'll tackle a few specific OD topic areas.

Examining the Health of an Organization

An organization's mission, vision, and values are the foundation of its strategy. The consultant's role includes supporting the organization as it moves toward its aspirational goals, which are often called strategic plans. Executing on strategy requires significant work, and the outcome is capacity building and the creation of competitive strength. OD consultants base their work on data and perform an analysis of qualitative and quantitative inputs to gain insight into organizational health implications.

In their book, *Organization Development and Change*, Thomas Cummings and Chris Worley (2015) define *organization development* as "a system-wide application and transfer of behavioral science knowledge to the planned development, improvement, and reinforcement of the strategies, structures, and processes that lead to organization effectiveness." This definition provides a consistent view of the diagnostic approach to organization development.

However, organization development is also beginning to be considered more dialogic. Coined by Bob Marshek and Gervase Bush, the term *dialogic organizational development* takes into consideration the changing needs of the individual, team, and organization. It brings focus to the benefit of integrating stories, narratives, and an understanding of dynamic, real-time views of organizational life. This approach addresses the complexities associated with ever-changing organizational structures and demands and is the one I use most often.

Successful consulting includes an integrated view of organizational life. OD consultants use employee engagement surveys, exit interviews, diversity climate surveys, leader multi-rater assessments, and compensation assessments to measure the organization's health. Much like a healthcare professional, OD consultants have to examine every aspect of the organization:

- Assessments of knowledge management, knowledge transfer, and learning are aligned with the function of the organization's brain. It also helps the strategist understand the networks and pathways required to achieve the organization's goals.
- Listening to the organization's heart tells the OD consultant what that company is focused on, how it invests, how it provides resources to its teams, and how it ensures its people have what they need to be effective.
- By examining the organization's lungs, the OD consultant can understand how it gets fresh ideas and makes space for creativity and innovation, how it adapts to culture and leadership changes, and what efforts are necessary to ensure that there are systems to support the airflow for ongoing growth and development.
- The organization's digestive system helps the OD consultant determine how the company nourishes itself by developing staff to increase capacity, capability, and greater levels of engagement or dealing with cancerous relational growth.

The tools an OD consultant uses are designed to assess alignment between values and strategy, soundness of structure, efficiency in processes, care for people, and signs of dysfunction. Consultants must be aware of the organization's collective wellness as well as the health of individual employees. The integration of strategies to manage stress—including mindfulness, breathing techniques, and self-care—is essential to fostering greater levels of performance when stress and anxiety are high.

This integrated OD evaluative process can be intimate and uncomfortable at times—much like a visit to the doctor—and establishing a sustainable relationship requires trust. Authenticity, excellent communication, credibility, and confidentiality are critical.

Your clients may believe they have a solution based on their own diagnosis of the problem—much like patients who self-diagnose and then suggest possible treatments and remedies. For example, if the organization has a retention issue, your client may think that training is the best and only solution. Unfortunately, if training only treats the symptoms, it won't heal the cause. OD consultants use surveys and assessments, interviews and conversations, workshops, data gathering and analysis, focus groups, observations, or benchmarking and insights from professional associations to validate the real problem and prescribe an effective solution.

The Star Model

Organizational theorist and consultant Jay Galbraith developed the Star Model to provide a lens to organizational health and life (Figure 17-1). The Star Model examines five essential organizational components: strategy, structure, processes, rewards, and people.

Figure 17-1. Galbraith's Star Model

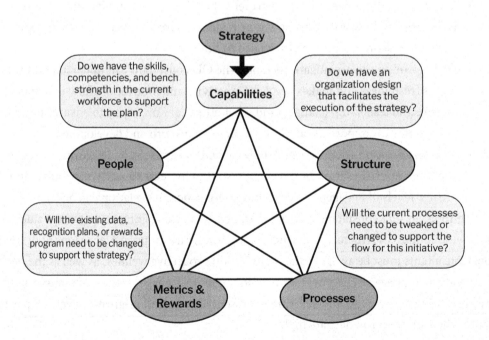

Using the Star Model is like using a stethoscope on the organization—it provides a gauge for understanding more about its vital functions and needs. While this model is typically used to align organizational change and design, you can also use it to formulate questions for your clients. Asking the right questions is essential for connecting with client needs and gathering meaningful data in the journey toward a healthy organization. Let's review the Star Model components in more detail.

Strategy

It begins with strategy—the work that must be done and its direction and objectives. As a consultant, it is essential to understand the work and its purpose. Posing questions about the strategy for the team and the organization provides insight. As a consultant, it's also important to link the organization's strategy to the task you've been asked to address. Surprisingly, while clients may understand that an activity needs to happen, they may not know how to connect those activities to the organization's strategy.

Questions to ask include:

- How do you describe your organization's strategy?
- What are three to five major goals your business needs to achieve in the next 12 to 18 months?
- Do people at all levels of your organization have a common understanding of the strategy?
- How would you describe the organization's strengths, weaknesses, and gaps?
- What are your desires for the organization?
- What work output and related capabilities are necessary to ensure the strategy's success?

Structure

Examining the organization's structure as it relates to its ability to support and execute the strategy is important for learning about the client. The fundamental question here is whether the structure (that is, the organization's positions, departments, and decision points) supports its strategy. For example, unproductive silos may indicate structural issues. If you don't resolve these structural issues, it will impede the organization's ability to meet its objectives.

Questions to ask include:

- Does the organization have the right structure to support your customers and drive your strategy? Why or why not?
- What do you wish you could accomplish through your structure that you are not accomplishing now?
- What changes in the structure have you thought about, if any, that might improve the organization's effectiveness?
- What capabilities could you develop through partners?
- Is your organization aligned with centralized or decentralized structures?
- Do you have people in the right geography from a talent and cost perspective?
- Does a remote work structure align with internal and external needs?

Processes

The third component of the Star Model relates to processes, which work better when aligned with structure. OD consultants can use process reviews to gather information about how budgets and resource allocations are made. This is an opportunity to examine efficiency and effectiveness.

When changes are made in the organization's direction or structure, processes must also be reassessed to ensure the information flow and communication are consistent with decision points. In addition, a breakdown of the communication process can create a significant point of failure, so using communications assessments or flow diagrams to outline the process can help ensure cross-functional support. OD consultants can use data from the customer, customer satisfaction surveys, and supplier satisfaction feedback to gain further insight into the effectiveness of process flow.

Questions to ask include:

- How are decisions made about the organization's budget and resource allocation?
- How do you typically receive communication about the organization, priorities, and the future?
- What top three actions can be taken to improve communication in the organization?

Metrics and Rewards

Looking at metrics and rewards helps you determine how success is measured and behavior is incentivized. The measure of success should be linked to the strategic direction and goals of the organization. Motivations and rewards influence levels of effective commitment, which is why many organizations establish key performance indicators (KPIs) or objectives and key results (OKRs), or management by objectives that point to what is important in the organization. As the old adage says, "What gets measured gets done." Therefore, it is essential for decision makers to consider whether what they are measuring aligns with the strategy to provide a clear line of sight for employees. In addition, rewards can influence retention and performance. While clients may question why reviewing metrics and rewards is essential, OD consultants understand that they may be sending unintentional messages about the value and priority of the work or their people.

Questions to ask include:
- What metrics should go on the business dashboard?
- What incentives will drive the right behavior?
- How can you use data from employee engagement surveys or exit interviews to determine employee perceptions around metrics or rewards?
- Have you benchmarked rewards against comparable competitive markets?

People

The people component is absolutely critical to the organization's health, so you may be wondering why people is the last component of the model. After all, many organizations encourage a people-first value set.

People are listed last in the model so that you can be intentional about aligning the people component with the organization's purpose, mission, vision, and values, which are part of its strategy. One way to do this is to use the talent wheel to understand how effectively people strategies are supporting the organization (Figure 17-2). OD consultants should be using the Star Model to ask questions about every element of the talent wheel to better understand the needs and the health of the people component.

Questions to ask include:
- What talent is needed to support the strategy? (This is especially critical with the rise of digitization and AI.)

- What HR or talent practices and routines are critical to your capabilities?
- Do you have a people plan or a people strategy? What updates are needed?
- What gaps are you seeing in talent today? What concerns you about the future?

Figure 17-2. The Talent Wheel

The Star Model, like the stethoscope, helps OD consultants examine basic and critical areas of the organization's health. But you can also use other tools in combination to assess the performance of the organization's systems. For example, you might find yourself using system thinking tools such as SWOT, Appreciative Inquiry, PEST, Lean, or Six Sigma.

Gathering information during the intake process or even the initial interview process allows you to meet the client in spaces that they may not have considered, which facilitates meaningful dialogue around strategic and operational concerns. Once you have collected the data, you can begin to look for themes and patterns to determine which areas are functioning optimally and which are not. You can download a guide for using the Star Model at td.org/handbook-for-consultants.

> **Consulting Tip**
>
> It's important to remain objective. Don't buy into your first impressions—think about cause and effect between data points. Themes such as poor goal clarity, poorly defined roles, or poor communication might be starting points for deeper inspection, but don't make any assumptions about their cause.

The Many Hats and Multiple Specialties of the OD Consultant

OD consultants have to wear many hats to support their clients. While consultation may be the primary reason for engagement, you'll often need to serve as a coach, facilitator, subject matter expert, and, on occasion, an organizational therapist. Of course, one essential responsibility is understanding your role and the client's expectations concerning deliverables. Defining your scope lays the foundation for a successful engagement.

Managing the scope of the work is essential to ensure appropriate prioritization and to meet the client's agreed-upon deliverables. Because OD consultants look holistically at the organization, you may see multiple areas that must be addressed to support the client. Engaging in collaborative consulting with the client (and their HR partners) creates a space for conversation and validation of priorities. It also allows you to have authentic conversations about new areas the client didn't realize were causing performance challenges. This new awareness can result in scope creep.

After completing the diagnostics, you'll provide a treatment plan. While it may seem prescriptive, this plan is typically developed collaboratively with a lens of practicality, human behavior, and science. Consulting in OD often requires shifting mindsets for optimal performance through change, which is integrated into the plan to create more effective outcomes and impacts. The OD consultant's approach typically includes systems thinking and appreciative inquiry, as well as data collection. Data is necessary for understanding organizational needs and to assess the value and outcomes of your work.

The field of OD is vast, spanning many topics that influence organizational life. Let's examine seven common areas of consulting within the OD field.

> **Consulting Tip**
>
> Integrate themes with examples (remembering to protect anonymity) in your reports, insights, and conversations with your clients. You'll be more successful when your action plans and solutions result from highly collaborative engagement.

Change Management

Joanna is a senior leader with a large healthcare organization that has recently gone through a significant merger and acquisition. As the organization was implementing a strategic human resources capability, Joanna was tasked with leading the new employee relations department supporting 20,000 employees. She reached out to me for help with change management very early in the design phase, and we chose to pilot the new system with one division before rolling it out to the whole company. As a consultant, I walked through each element of the change plan to ensure I had a clear view of each step necessary to implement the system. Joanna used her coaching skills and a new change management toolkit to develop a comprehensive charter for this project and secure buy-in from senior leaders. Once the scope and impact of change was clearly defined, a readiness assessment and user acceptance test soon followed. The extensive plan and change network engagement played a significant role in this change initiative's success.

Change management is always at the core of organizational effectiveness and development consulting. Consider the impact of the change on people, whether it is small or enterprise wide. To help the client, a consultant must be aware of what changes are needed, what changes have already been made, what changes are desired, and what's been unsuccessful in the past.

Understanding the client's desired outcome in moving from a current state to a future state is important as the vision becomes clearer. An impact assessment will allow you to assess the current state and the potential impact of the desired future state by providing additional insight into how the change will affect the people, processes, tools, systems, and environment. This all becomes part of the diagnostic process and helps develop influence strategies.

Change is constant; however, people often behave like it is a one-time event. Although change is typically complex and not linear, it's often treated in a very compartmentalized project-focused way. And while some significant programs and projects require a high level of investment in support of the change, most organizations are making multiple changes simultaneously, which leads to change fatigue. Thus, consultants must work with organizations to maintain a pulse on engagement and mitigate any potential burnout associated with change. If you're not careful, the ongoing waves of change may even influence the organization's overall wellness in the form of a lack of productivity, unwanted attrition, erosion of trust, and failed implementations. These consequences always lead to costs.

OD consultants can use stakeholder mapping and assessments, with client input, to plan the full spectrum of the change's impact and determine levels of readiness. It's helpful to get your client thinking about how the change will affect key stakeholders. One way to create strategies to deal with resistance to the change is to have the client list every stakeholder who will be affected by the impending change, and then ask those stakeholders to answer the following questions:

- What is a win?
- What is a loss?
- What is the concern?

Consulting in change requires you to share strategies for greater adaptability and agility. Encourage your clients to shift their mindset so each change supports the next one, rather than being a completely separate event. All leaders must see change management as a required core competency. Additionally, they should design processes and assessments to ensure organizational infrastructure is adjusted accordingly.

Consulting Tip

Change is always accompanied by some level of transition. *Change* is the event moving from the current state to the future state; however, *transition* is the emotional side that helps those affected by the change move from the ending of one thing (such as a process, project, or organization structure) to the beginning of a new thing. Managing the transition is just as important as managing the change. William Bridges's research has been a huge help in marrying strategies for change and transition.

Diversity, Equity, and Inclusion Consulting

Diversity, equity, and inclusion (DEI) consulting requires the consultant to be aware of the client's aspirations compared with their level of commitment to change. While the client may look to training as a solution, it typically won't take them beyond unconscious bias training and awareness.

While unconscious bias training and awareness are vital, they do not facilitate the change necessary to support greater equity in organizational processes. It's critical to integrate change principles and create psychologically safe spaces through interviews, focus groups, and questionnaires with senior leaders, organizational influencers, groups of diverse workers or volunteers, and potential customers. Reviewing data, values, charters, strategies, and business cases associated with DEI efforts is also vital to the process. The assessment process will include reviewing qualitative and quantitative data and the diversity climate assessment. Although there are many great models and frameworks, the Global Diversity Equity and Inclusion Benchmark (GDEIB) developed by the Centre for Global Inclusion is a comprehensive evaluation you can use.

Recommendations for a DEI outcome-based strategy will include external opportunities—such as supplier partnerships, organizational alliances, and community collaboration—to connect with the DEI ecosystem. And the DEI ecosystem must be part of an iterative process: OD consultants should continually evaluate quantitative metrics, visualize the impact of these strategies, and iterate the changes to the model based on the assessments. Building awareness, implementing the strategy, assessing the outcomes, and revising the model, if required, are critical to shifting mindsets, overcoming biases, and driving behavior change across the organization.

Consulting Tip

Whether or not you plan to do DEI consulting, the Centre for Global Inclusion is an excellent resource. You can register for their mailing list at centreforglobalinclusion.org.

Some clients are more inclined to develop an activity-based strategy than an outcome-based one. Note that activity-based strategies may have more short-term impact implications and yield a different ROI than an outcome-based strategy.

Team Performance and Effectiveness

Team performance depends greatly on competent leadership, clear direction, established operating rhythms, defined roles, trust, and excellent communication. When tasked with assessing and diagnosing declining team performance and effectiveness, OD consultants can look to those areas to help teams establish fundamental operating principles. The Tuckman Model of team development continues to be a useful model of performance as teams form, storm, norm, perform, and adjourn.

Leader and team integration activities—such as new leader assimilation, team integrations (for new products, projects, or programs), and HR assimilation (for remediation)—are still particularly effective in enhancing team performance when done thoughtfully and collaboratively. If these activities are used in an organization, you may want to understand whether they are simply checking the box or if leader and team action plans are followed through in a post-activity environment.

Cross-functional or matrixed relationships may also influence team performance. OD consultants can help the team gain greater clarity around their goals, roles, processes, and interpersonal engagement (GRPI). Richard Burkhardt developed GRPI to help teams become more effective and productive in their engagement. Figure 17-3 is my adaptation of Burkhardt's GRPI model.

Figure 17-3. The GRPI Model

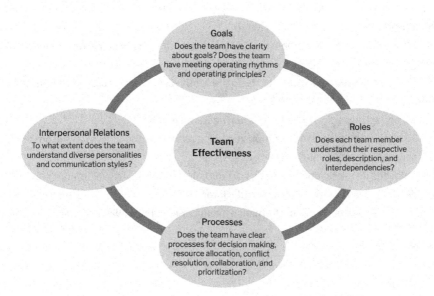

223

Leadership Development

Organizational performance will be significantly influenced by its leaders' capability, competence, confidence, commitment, and character. Helping organizations develop and align their leadership values and competencies is essential work for you as an OD consultant. Leaders who model healthy behaviors bring significant benefits to their teams and the organization as a whole.

Any leadership development effort should begin with a fundamental review of the organization's culture and its mission, vision, and values. That information and the amount of available resources will help inform the program's design and the organization's expectations.

OD consultants can use leadership frameworks or programs to improve leadership performance. Multirater instruments, sometimes called 360-degree assessments, help align organizational values and required leadership competencies.

Guidelines for Using 360-Degree Assessments

- Select a 360 assessment with reliable and valid research that provides data on the results over a period.
- Consider what is being measured to ensure it aligns with your client's leadership competencies.
- Talk with the client about anonymity; it is critical for candid and accurate feedback.
- Be clear about the size of feedback groups; generally, you need a minimum of three people to protect anonymity.
- Remove any specific jargon in open-ended statements that would point to the identity of the respondent.
- Do not provide the feedback report to the leader of the assessed employee without their consent.
- Provide feedback in person or virtually when necessary.
- Provide a copy of the report to the employee being assessed one or two days in advance.
- Share insights with the employee being assessed.
- Help employees develop action plans as part of their professional development plan.
- Schedule a follow-up review 12 to 18 months later.
- Don't use 360 assessments for performance management or disciplinary actions.

As an OD consultant, your leadership development work may lead to leadership or executive coaching work. It is essential for you to be clear about your scope and communicate expectations to your client.

Consulting Tip

Don't forget to meet people at their point of need. Operate with humility, communicate with empathy, exhibit courage and accountability, embrace adaptability, build trust, and extend grace. These qualities, when paired with leadership skills, are essential for sustainable success.

People Strategy

An organization's people strategy captures how its talent-related capabilities aligns with immediate and long-term business needs. OD consultants often collaborate with HR business partners, HR leaders, and business leaders to understand more about the organization's people strategy and formulate strategic initiatives to execute it. The people strategy generally includes business priorities, workforce implications, skills gaps, resources or rewards, demographics, the hiring plan, succession plans, risk of attrition, and other elements.

As a starting point, ask your client whether the organization has the right people, in the right places, at the right times, with the right skills, doing the right things for short- and long-term needs. If there's a technology road map, you'll want to partner with the technology leader to address any resource gaps. However, those questions can only be answered once you've completed a clear and thorough assessment using a sound methodology. This process evaluates risks and costs related to talent, which are aligned with the organization's priorities for customer, operational, and workforce success. It's also recommended that you collaborate with leadership outside the HR function. The people strategy provides a playbook for people alignment and is a remarkable tool for onboarding new leaders and managers. It is also helpful for finance or during a merger or acquisition.

When integrated into the business strategy, the people strategy aligns the external business view with an internal view for successful planning and execution. The right questions provide insight into the goals. If there are specific position considerations, it's also important to ask internal and external questions.

Example internal goal questions include:

1. What is the level of risk to the company if the position is left vacant for an extended period?
2. To what extent does the position:
   - Drive revenue and influence bottom-line financial results?
   - Involve developing strategy, designing new products, or creating growth opportunities for the organization?
   - Require broad decision-making authority?
   - Involve relationships with external customers and key stakeholders?
   - Influence the performance of or manage other critical positions?

Example external goal questions are:

1. What is the current market value of the position? How has the value changed over time?
2. How is the position valued by other companies?
3. What is the degree of competition for qualified candidates for this position in the marketplace?
4. To what extent does the position:
   - Require the use of rare or unique capabilities and skill sets?
   - Need data derived from the people strategy?
   - Inform leaders of critical risks and opportunities that may shift technology or operational road maps?

Process Redesign

When conducting assessments, OD consultants may find process breakdowns or inefficiencies, especially if the organization is restructuring or introducing new technology. The continuous barrage of change creates a need to assess whether the processes are still relevant in the changing environments. Lean, Six Sigma, and TQM (Total Quality Management) make it easier to redesign processes, which may involve streamlining, centralizing, decentralizing, and even balancing. When done well, a process redesign can lead to a competitive advantage for the organization. You may need to facilitate or coach your client on process design. It's also imperative that you collaborate with the finance team and any team members responsible for process improvement because this type of work can result in quantifiable savings.

Process redesign considers the flow of information and its impact on decision making. It begins with understanding the inputs and how they are transformed for the necessary outputs. Critical questions in process design are:

- What is the desired future outcome of the process?
- Who are the customers and suppliers of the process?
- Where does the process start and end?

The use of process mapping is essential for clarifying each step within the process. You'll begin with a specific line of activities that are closely associated with outputs and behaviors, and then consider who is responsible for each. One method of end-to-end process design includes swim lanes, which identify the critical functions engaged in the process at each activity and crucial decision points within the process. You'll also be able to identify interdependencies, redundancies, and potential inefficiencies. A great benefit to this process redesign is understanding responsibilities, accountabilities, and more effective communication. Redesigned processes can result in transformational change.

Organization Design

Organization design or redesign can feel like a very daunting engagement, yet organizations are constantly changing and restructuring their teams. Helping the client perform a job analysis to better understand the organization's needs will lead to a more thoughtful design that brings tremendous value.

I recall the significant distress and weightiness of my client Jason's task to restructure his medical imaging business unit. Jason was senior vice president of the imaging business unit, which was very successful with its innovative offerings to customers in the healthcare industry. However, they were struggling to align to the corporation's new vision and direction. Jason needed to create a new, decentralized structure that could operate with greater levels of autonomy. This was a significant departure from the existing structure and created complexity and changes for thousands of employees. I was engaged to work with the business unit leadership team on a redesign that might even eliminate some of their roles. We were able to use the Star Model to highlight the many needs of Jason's team.

After spending months refining design criteria, hosting comprehensive interviews and focus groups, reviewing job and role descriptions, carefully considering interdependencies and decision-making authority, completing extensive impact assessments, redefining processes, and realigning infrastructure, a new organizational design finally took shape. Jason, filled with delight, commended his team for their exceptional work. Unbeknownst to them, the redesign not only exceeded expectations but also fulfilled an undisclosed objective: preparing the business unit for sale. The successful outcome ultimately resulted in a beneficial transaction for all parties involved.

As consultants, we may not always be privy to every objective or motive behind a project, but we should always leverage our skills, knowledge, tools, and techniques to deliver the utmost value and meet the diverse needs of our clients.

Chris Worley, a recognized global leader in the field of organization development, agility, and organization design, does a phenomenal job clarifying the need for agility in the organization design process when he reminds us that we are building organizations for change. This mindset shift requires us to be fluid in this ever-changing landscape that is demanding more and more transformation. The use of Galbraith's Star Model is also helpful in this work.

It is essential to ensure clarity around the design criteria and decision rights before beginning the design. Two key questions often overlooked in the organization structure's design are "What will be needed to integrate the new structure across the core business and functional units?" and "What will be required to integrate with suppliers and partners?" Understanding interdependencies in this process will support effective design. Organization design is not a quick process; it requires considerable cross-functional engagement.

Summary

Although we looked at several organizational effectiveness and development consulting areas, OD consulting is not always compartmentalized. Think of the organization as a living system—similar to how healthcare professionals view the human body—with the diagnostic and dialogic lens to assess how it can function more effectively. While this adds complexity to the work, it also sets the client up for greater success. Ensuring your clients have healthy organizations where people can experience success is a key objective for OD consultants.

Action You Can Take Now

- **Be a star.** Select one of the seven areas where an OD consultant works with clients. If you are still an internal employee, use the Star Model to determine how to approach an assignment with your company. If you have a consulting practice, choose one of your clients and do the same. Imagine that you have a contract with them. What data do you need? What questions would you ask?

- **Examine yourself.** Use assessment tools (such as your communications or personality assessment) to learn more about yourself in preparation for client engagements. Bill O'Brien says that "the success of an intervention is often dependent upon the interior condition of the intervener" (Scharmer 2016). The more we know about ourselves, our strengths, our triggers, the things that bring us joy, and the things that frustrate us, the better prepared we are to help others navigate new pathways.

- **Offer help, not work.** In the consulting world, we can show up as an expert, a collaborator, or a pair of hands (Block 2022). Clients who are experiencing pain or those who are just trying to navigate the barrage of change or challenge of inefficiency simply want help. When we show up as partners to help, rather than bringing a ton of overwhelming theories or models, client receptivity increases exponentially. The best results happen when we integrate these theories, models, and frameworks in practical and efficient ways as we partner with and help our clients.

About the Author

Tonya J. Wilson, MAIOP, CPM, is president and founder of AFC Consulting Group. A consultant, coach, organizational psychologist, speaker, and author, she has expertise in organizational effectiveness and development, change management, and DEI. Tonya has worked in manufacturing, aerospace, telecom, government markets, and healthcare, and has held leadership positions at McKesson, Change Healthcare, Meggitt, and AT&T. She is a DEI subject matter expert, consultant, OD advisory committee member, and facilitator for ATD. Her mission statement is "setting you up to win." Tonya works with leaders to drive alignment between business and people strategies specializing in DEI strategy, change management, communications, team integration, organizational health, and design. You can learn more at afcconsultinggroup.com or connect with her at linkedin.com /in/tonya-j-wilson-maiop-cpm-b4663898.

Using Instruments and Tools for Your Clients' Success

LEI COMERFORD

There are thousands of tools and instruments for consultants to use within their practice. And if I asked you how many you actively use today, the list may include a select few or it may be expansive. While this chapter does not provide an exhaustive list of every tool and instrument, I hope it provides a good starting point for you to consider trying something new. We will explore how using tools and instruments can support your client's success and discuss a few areas to be aware of as you build or expand your consultancy.

As a coach, I use assessments on a regular basis to open the door to new insights for my clients. Through these assessments, my clients gain greater self-awareness, build confidence in their strengths, and identify development areas that are critical to their leadership success.

As we move forward in this chapter, I challenge you to think about the tools you are using and identify any gaps. We will:

- Explore different types of instruments and tools to support client success.
- Discuss how to select the support tools that work best for your business.
- Understand the importance of collaboration with other consultants.

Types of Instruments and Tools

Let's begin by examining four types of instruments and tools, including those that can be used with your clients, specific HR tools, training instruments, and coaching tools.

Client Instruments and Tools

These tools are used to stay connected to and inform or educate your client base. Depending on the size of your business, you may have already implemented a few of them. If not, no worries; each element will become important as the pain point exceeds your current situation. In other words, as your business grows, efficiency will become more important to your success, scalability, and work-life harmony. That's when you know that a tool might be the best way to become more efficient.

Management Systems

Do you need a CRM, CMS, PMS, or LMS? I know, so many acronyms, and there are even more. These systems offer specific benefits for managing your business, which I've summarized in Table 18-1 for easy reference. You may find them overwhelming, and based on my own experience, I recommend that you go at your own pace and do what feels right for you. Just remember that stretching your comfort zone can be a good thing.

Table 18-1. Management Systems Summary

Client Tool	Acronym	Purpose, Use, and Definition
Client relationship management	CRM	A technology system for managing your company's relationships and interactions with current and potential customers
Contact or client management system	CMS	Offers a business the ability to manage and track client contact details and interactions
Practice management system	PMS	Allows a business to organize and automate its backend system, including contact management, online billing, website, and marketing
Learning management system	LMS	Software designed to manage all aspects of a company's training efforts to create, share, and track status and completions for specific learning assignments
Calendar and scheduling systems		Systems designed to manage your calendar and schedule appointments
Billing systems		Systems designed to track billing, create and send invoices, and collect client payments
Email marketing systems	EMS	Software designed to manage all aspects of your email marketing, including designing, sending, and tracking email communications

If you are just starting your consulting business or are in the first year or two of business, managing these efforts manually is quite doable! It's remarkable how efficient an excel spreadsheet can be if it's well organized. On the other hand, even if you don't need these tools, make sure you're familiar with them because your clients likely are.

Calendar, Scheduling, and Billing Systems

A consultant can quickly become overwhelmed by the available options for calendar management. The best recommendation I can offer is to connect with other consultants that are doing similar work to your own and ask what they are using, why they like it, and what they don't like.

Another helpful question to ask another consultant is, "What do you wish you had implemented but didn't?" Billing systems and software functionalities may be stand-alone products, or they may reside in a suite-like offering that combines backend solutions in an all-in-one system. Personally, I've found that maintaining QuickBooks is effective for billing certain types of clients if the customization is not available in my all-in-one system.

Consulting Tip

Looking for ways to gather testimonials from your clients? Boast is a tool that collects video testimonials. The best part is it's easy to use.

Communication Systems

There are so many options for communicating with current and prospective clients, including the email marketing system. Researching and asking other consultants what they use is my first recommendation to land on your solution. Some of the most popular options include MailChimp, Constant Contact, and HubSpot, and the list is growing daily. There are free and paid subscription options. You can also check to see if your CMS includes this functionality. For example, I use Coaches Console, which offers the ability to send email communications. Understanding the size of your client and prospect base, as well as how frequently you plan to send communications, will help determine which solution is best for you.

Other forms of communication to support your clients outside email might include newsletters, blogs, podcasts, videos, social media posts, and mobile applications. Technology provides ways to implement almost any option in your consultancy. I like to occasionally experiment (although I would not claim to be a risk taker) and am currently using a few options for video including Zoom, Loom, BombBomb, and my iPhone. Zoom and Loom offer free and paid subscriptions; however, BombBomb requires a paid subscription following a free trial.

I use different solutions depending on what I'm trying to accomplish. For example, if I want to send a "Hey, I was thinking of you" video, I'll use BombBomb because I can send it directly from the program and embed the video in an email. If I'm sharing a how-to or instructional video, Loom is a great option because I can share my computer screen to explain a process. If I'm recording a short video for social media or to post on my website, I'll use Zoom or my iPhone.

Mobile applications also provide quick solutions for communicating with clients. Two apps I use are WhatsApp and Voxer. WhatsApp is a free service that allows you to communicate with text and phone; Voxer, which has a free and paid subscription model, works like a walkie-talkie (sending your verbal communication while you're speaking) and also has the ability to text.

Human Resources Instruments and Tools

HR tools measure employee performance, potential, and engagement and are used widely by consultants who focus on traditional HR components. These tools may be part of your primary consulting toolkit, or they could be models you designed and use as your unique go-to-market solution. Or maybe your client requests that you use a specific instrument to collect, interpret, analyze, and present a proposal to solve a challenge they are experiencing.

This section presents high-level explanations for a few common HR tools, but if you want a more in-depth description, review the Instrument and Tools Reference Guide at td.org /handbook-for-consultants. Of course, you can also do a quick internet search for more information about any of these tools.

9-Box

First created by McKinsey in 1970, the 9-Box model is used to measure employee performance and to identify employees with leadership potential. There are several different versions of this model and they use a variety of category names; however, the overall outcome is the same. The higher an individual falls on the boxes, the more potential they show for growth; the farther right they fall, the better their performance reviews. On the other hand, those who fall on the low side of the grid show less potential; and the farther left they fall, the worse their performance reviews. To summarize, employees who fall in the lower left are the lowest-rated performers and those in the upper right are the highest-rated performers.

There are pros and cons to using the 9-Box model. When done accurately, this model highlights high-potential employees for succession planning and provides organizations with a view into existing and future development needs. However, it relies on human perspective. The results may be subjective and include bias and discrimination that leads to limiting an employee's future opportunities. You will find an example in Figure 18-1.

Figure 18-1. The 9-Box Grid

Develop	Develop or stretch	Stretch
Low performer High potential	Moderate performer High potential	High performer High potential
Observe	Develop	Stretch or develop
Low performer Moderate potential	Moderate performer Moderate potential	Higher performer Moderate potential
Observe or terminate	Observe	Develop
Low performer Low potential	Moderate performer Low potential	High performer Low potential

Potential ↑

Performance →

Adapted from Gupta (2022).

Competency Models

A *competency* is a required ability that is specific to an assigned role. Competencies identify specific behaviors that define proficiency within an organization, position, or in a professional's career and are usually specific, observable, and measurable knowledge, skills, or abilities. Organizations use competency models for recruiting, career development, culture development, and learning to recognize success measures. Effective competency models include clear descriptions and examples of relevant activities and behaviors associated with each element to support the understanding of expectations. Ensuring that you are continuously adding value to your clients should be of the utmost concern. Becoming an expert in and applying competency models could be a valuable service to offer organizations of any size.

Engagement and Exit Surveys

Engagement and exit surveys are used to collect periodic feedback from employees regarding what's working and what isn't, as well as challenges employees are experiencing and organizational blind spots related to employee engagement. In 2021, Gallup, the leader in the engagement survey arena, reported that the US had experienced a decline in employee engagement (meaning that more employees were actively disengaged in the workplace) for the first time in more than a decade (Harter 2022). This statistic is important because companies that are experiencing declining employee engagement will likely be looking for a consultant to help determine what happened and what they can do about it. Another popular survey is *Great Place to Work*, which is done in partnership with *Fortune* magazine on an annual basis.

Over the past 10 years, an influx of organizations focusing on employee engagement efforts, and with the declining engagement levels in the US workforce, these organizations will continue to be critical to your clients' success. Activities to engage employees include fitness programs, recognition programs, workplace parties, team building events, off-site events, special training offerings, and extra days off, just to name a few. By understanding your client's current employee engagement scores, their survey results, and their appetite for change, you will be better equipped to propose activities and initiatives to increase engagement within the organization.

Training Instruments and Tools

Training tools are used to educate and engage employees during live, hybrid, or virtual learning events. They can also be used outside training programs for interactive purposes between team members. There are many options on the market, and having a general understanding of them will be helpful as you support clients who have their own preferences.

Presentation Formats

PowerPoint was the training industry presentation standard for many years, but Google Slides has become more common. (Personally, I still prefer PowerPoint for my presentations.) Formats like Prezi, Canva, or Visme provide more creativity and freedom when creating presentation materials. Each option offers unique functionalities and challenges. The benefit of understanding how to competently use one or several of these tools will come into play when you are asked to create a proposal presentation, training deck, key performance indicator (KPI) update, closing presentation, or some other presentation. You'll find more information in the Instrument and Tools Links reference guide at td.org /handbook-for-consultants.

Consulting Tip

Always practice using any new presentation software to fully understand how it works prior to going live in front of an audience.

Collaborations Spaces

Miro, Mural, Google Jamboard, and ClickUp bring visual collaboration to life and offer teams the ability to share thoughts, images, documents, and real-time collaboration without the constraints of geography or time zones. ClickUp goes beyond the other examples I've listed; it focuses not only on visual collaboration but also on productivity by including project management tools, real-time reporting, and time tracking.

While working with a national pharmacy benefit management organization, I selected Google Jamboard to allow space for ideation within a newly formed team to set expectations, identify desired outcomes for a large project, and gain consensus on how they would hold themselves and each other accountable. When you shift the client's mind by opening the door to collaboration, anything is possible.

Remember to consider mobile application options for collaboration if voice messages or texts are the best solution for connection and collaboration. A few tools that support audio messages one-on-one or in groups are WhatsApp, Signal, and Voxer. Your clients will all require different levels of interaction, and any of these options may be your best solution to meet or exceed their expectations!

External App Engagement

These tools are meant to engage your audience, test their knowledge level, and confirm through quizzes that they are absorbing the content and messages you are sharing. I've experienced a few as a participant in training events and I've also used some as a facilitator. What I like most about some of these tools is their competitive aspects, which naturally increases interest and engagement. If you're a consultant who does most of your work delivering live or virtual training, you might consider playing with these tools.

Slido, Kahoot, Quizizz, and Poll Everywhere are just some examples of these external application tools. Understand why you want to use these tools and practice using them once you select the best solution. Getting comfortable with facilitation application tools can make the difference between a successful workshop that everyone is raving about or one that never hits the mark.

Consulting Tip

Although these apps are fun and obtain lots of participant engagement, they can also lead to an increased volume of the room. Watch out for this if you're in close proximity to other more quiet environments, like a hotel meeting room or client office meeting space.

Virtual Meeting Platforms

Choosing a virtual meeting platform can be tricky. As a consultant you may have a preferred virtual platform; however, the clients you work with will have their own preference, and they may require you to use that platform instead. For example, Zoom is a popular, easy-to-use virtual platform, but there are other companies with a stronghold on the market, including Cisco WebEx, Google Meet, Microsoft Teams, BlueJeans, and Adobe Connect. And others continue to enter the market all the time.

I recommend asking your clients what platforms they prefer and then doing your homework to show up confident and competent when leading virtual meetings. Yes, this means getting to know other platforms and testing out the features on a regular basis to ensure you're using them effectively. It also means understanding which features are available on the most popular platforms so you can recommend solutions to your clients that best meet their needs.

Luckily, there are many articles and YouTube videos to help you get up to speed on these platforms and they are only an internet search away.

Feedback and Survey Tools

Feedback and surveys offer real-time positive and constructive information that will help you determine if you are delivering on the client's expectations and where you might flex moving forward. A few best practices that I implement when creating surveys include:

- Understand what your goal is for asking each question and how you will use the feedback.
- Ensure rating scales are simple and consistent. A five-point scale allows for more specific feedback than a 10-point scale.
- When incorporating positive and negative rating scales, start with positive first— strongly agree, agree, neutral, disagree, strongly disagree. Raters who quickly skim the survey will likely assume that you're starting with a positive, so if you start with the negative, your data may get skewed.
- Keep the survey short and provide an estimation of how long it will take to complete.
- Ask only a few open-ended questions that require a text-based response.

When I keep these best practices top of mind in my survey design, I find that the completion rate is much higher.

Evaluation

Basic to all consulting work is the ability to evaluate what happened. Kirkpatrick's Four Levels of Evaluation is one standard for leveraging and validating talent investments (Table 18-2). This model has evolved over six decades and applies to evaluating onboarding, product and program launches, leadership development, safety, security, succession planning, and DEI.

Whether you use the Kirkpatrick Model or another one, the next question you need to ask is how to collect feedback from your clients and participants. There are many options to choose from, including SurveySparrow, Typeform, HubSpot, SurveyMonkey, Qualtrics, and Google Forms. You'll find more information at td.org/handbook-for-consultants. It boils down to doing your research to understand which solution is best for you based on your unique criteria.

Table 18-2. The Kirkpatrick Model

Level 1: Reaction	The degree to which participants find the training favorable, engaging, and relevant to their jobs
Level 2: Learning	The degree to which participants acquire the intended knowledge, skills, attitudes, confidence, and commitment based on their participation in the training
Level 3: Behavior	The degree to which participants apply what they learned during training when they are back on the job
Level 4: Results	The degree to which targeted outcomes occur as a result of the training and the support and accountability package

Source: *Kirkpatrick and Kirkpatrick (2016).*

One additional element to keep in mind is security and the Global Data Protection Regulation (GDPR), especially if you are working with clients outside the United States. In fact, many US organizations have also adopted GDPR policies. A best practice is to discuss this topic with your client and include any necessary details in your contract. A few questions to keep in mind are:

- Will you own the survey process, or will the organization manage it and share the feedback with you?
- Are there survey solutions your client organization prefers to use?
- In what format does the client want to receive the findings if you are responsible for administering the survey?

Coaching Instruments and Tools

Coaching tools are used to evoke awareness and, in many cases, improve a client's skill set. This section is near and dear to my heart and business. As an executive and leadership coach, I'm certified in a variety of assessment tools and use these activities and exercises with my clients on a regular basis. One piece of advice I offer is to be intentional when suggesting the use of any of these tools. You want to be able to articulate your reason for using them. I believe assessments and exercises can open the door to amazing new perspectives and awareness, but if your clients have already completed similar tools, you should review those results before moving onto new assessments. You may find that your client won't benefit from or doesn't want to complete yet another assessment.

Assessment Tools

Table 18-3 highlights some of the most common assessment tools in the industry; yes, I'm partial to a few because I'm certified in them. However, I've also included others to demonstrate the variety that exists—there are more assessments than you could possibly imagine.

Table 18-3. Common Talent Development Assessment Tools

Assessment	Type	How to Access	Purpose and Common Uses
Herrmann Brain Dominance Instrument (HBDI)	Thinking style	Through a certified practitioner only	This four-quadrant model is focused on natural thinking preferences, not competency or skill. It allows for improved communication, better relationships, and increased influence and buy-in. People are whole-brained and therefore have the capacity through thinking agility to stretch and show up in lesser preferred quadrants when the situation requires it. The 116-question assessment leads to understanding your normal and under-pressure profile. It can be used with individuals, pairs, teams, and organizations.
Myers-Briggs Type Indicator (MBTI)	Personality, psychological type	Online and requires certification to debrief	The MBTI assessment helps you understand your communication preferences and how you interact with others through the identification of four dimensions of type. The 93-question self-assessment results in the identification of extraversion versus introversion, sensing versus intuition, thinking versus feeling, and judging versus perceiving.
DiSC	Behavioral	Through a certified practitioner only	This four-quadrant model helps you understand management style strengths and weaknesses to improve leadership capacity. The results explain the percentage of each style you are and how you handle challenges, interact with others, and approach life, as well as how others perceive you. It can be used with individuals and teams. Note: There are different versions of the DiSC assessment on the market.
Positive Intelligence (PQ)	Mental fitness	Through a CPQC-certified PQ coach and online	This tool measures the strength of your positive mental muscles (sage) versus negative mental muscles (saboteur), which leads to the ability to unlock your natural potential by increasing your mental fitness. By answering 54 questions, you receive a unique profile report indicating the strength level of nine saboteurs.

Table 18-3. (cont.)

Assessment	Type	How to Access	Purpose and Common Uses
True Tilt, Tilt365	Personality	Through a certified practitioner or online	This model helps you discover your natural personality and how to balance character strengths through validated science that is playfully deployed. Four lizard characters portray each of the four quadrants of the Tilt Model: connection, impact, structure, and clarity. It can be used with individuals and teams.
Lumina Spark	Personality	Through a certified practitioner only	This 144-question personality self-assessment reveals your whole personality. Use it to increase self-awareness, reveal hidden potential, and cope better under pressure. Improve communication, teamwork, and leadership. The profile measures 24 qualities and three personas.
Clifton Strengths	Strengths	Online	This survey uses 177 paired statements to identify your talents and natural patterns of thinking, feeling, and behaving. You can elect to receive your top 5 or the full 34 strengths in a report.

One additional type of assessment that is beneficial to many coaching engagements is the multirater instrument. Offering positive and constructive feedback through a series of open-ended questions and standard questions, the multirater instrument (commonly called a 360-degree assessment), was originally created by the Center for Creative Leadership (CCL). It obtains anonymous feedback from the individual's manager, colleagues or peers, direct reports, and other groups. The client rates themselves and then compares this self-assessment to others' assessments, which helps identify strengths and gap areas for future development. Many versions are available online and it can also be performed individually through interviews with a coach. You should choose an instrument that is validated and reliable when you measure something as important as an individual's strengths and weaknesses.

Before you rush to become certified in one assessment or another, start by understanding your business and the consulting challenges you solve for your clients. I suggest assessing your current clients (or conducting market research if you're just starting out) to determine which assessment tools they will benefit most from. This is also a good time to reach out to other consultants and coaches to ask how they are using assessment tools within their businesses. It's amazing how supportive other consultants are when you request a short meeting to learn from them. I've built lifelong relationships by taking the time to reach out, network, learn from others, and, when possible, give back!

Instruments and Exercises

Within the coaching industry, there are also many instruments and exercises designed to increase learning and awareness. I've found that the ones I use most often were first introduced to me during my coach training programs. They are simple to explain and offer deep insight for everyone who completes them.

Although there are many available on the market, here are three that I find helpful:

- The Wheel of Life exercise helps clients quickly understand how balanced or fulfilled their life is in up to 10 categories; the results can then lead to development plan actions.
- Values exercises help clients identify their core values and what's most important to them to ensure alignment in their life and career. You could also consider doing a values card sort.
- Mission and vision statements align teams and organizations. Do you have your own personal or consulting mission and vision statement? Your clients and the teams you work with should create these statements to better guarantee alignment with the tasks and activities you and your client teams address.

Tool Selection Process and General Understanding

With thousands of tools and instruments available, how do you decide which ones you need and which are the best? It starts with truly understanding your clients' needs. Check the cost and what you are getting. You should also know whether certification is required.

Understand Your Clients' Needs

Assess your clients to fully understand what they need to achieve, their objectives, and what they want to be different. I've worked with many leaders who came to me saying they wanted one thing and by the time we completed our discussion realized they had a very different need. You may conduct a needs assessment to determine any gaps between current and desired outcomes, which provides valuable insight into your client's processes and highlights areas for improvement. Many data collection methods exist, including quantitative techniques (surveys) and qualitative techniques (focus groups).

When conducting a needs assessment, Sardek Love (2016) notes that "asking the right questions helps you deliver maximum value to your consulting projects." Use these seven highly effective questions to start on the path to a positive, bottom-line impact that your clients will love:

- **The diagnostic question**—What is the problem?
- **The metric that matters question**—Which metrics are you trying to positively affect?
- **The performance gap question**—What are employees doing that they shouldn't be doing?
- **The timing question**—When did it first begin? When does it occur?
- **The location question**—Where does the problem occur?
- **The scoping question**—How big is the problem in measurable terms?
- **The powerful closing question**—What questions should I have asked but haven't?

After completing the needs assessment, you will have the critical details to determine the best solution or tool to use moving forward. In most cases, you will look to your own internal toolkit, which includes instruments, tools, models, and assessments that you use regularly. However, in some cases, you might determine that you need to adopt a new solution to best support your client. In this case, you may need to refer them to another consultant with the required expertise, or you may simply need some additional education, research, or training to remain the best resource for your client.

Vetting Tool and Instrument Organizations

Every consultant gets overwhelmed by the options and tools available to support their clients. How do you select the best? A few best practices that I implement include doing my own research, reviewing the tool or instrument's website, reading reviews, reading user testimonials, and taking advantage of free trials to better understand the tool and the benefits it might offer my clients. You will find many of these websites offer chat functionality to answer questions or provide a phone number to connect with a team member for a demo or to dive deeper into your questions.

Ask yourself, "Is there an industry standard that I need to ensure I implement or offer to my clients based on my consulting type?" Would you benefit from implementing assessments that are already widely used by other consultants? Or would you benefit from adopting a newer, fully vetted, lesser-known tool or instrument for differentiation in the market?

Business Investment and What Does It Cost?

This is when the rubber meets the road. What is your out-of-pocket cost to use or share these tools and instruments with your clients? For your internal systems, these expenses fall into the cost of doing business that you will justify over time. For assessments and other direct client tools, the cost will differ and could require formal certification, which varies from minimal investments up to thousands of dollars. In these cases, a decision to pass on the expenses to your client is a common one. You should think about any markup or true pass-through that makes the most business sense. These are all elements to consider upfront and require making an intentional decision about how you want to move forward.

Certification Requirements

A training certification is required to use many assessment tools or debrief the results. These investments vary by tool and organization and may require an annual contract commitment based on usage (such as the number of seat licenses you are committing to purchase). This is when knowing what your clients require and truly understanding how you want to use the tool to address their needs is critical to ensure you are incorporating the best solutions with the best return on investment for you and your consultancy.

Collaborate With Other Consultants

Consultants are fabulous collaborators. We all want to grow and develop our practices, and I have found that we grow by sharing and helping other consultants. I've been attending Consultant Networking calls for several years—calls happen weekly, but even attending a few times a year is valuable. We all want to share our experiences, knowledge, and expertise with one another. We are all fully living in the mindset of abundance, and by contributing to others, you are contributing to yourself.

> ### Consulting Tip
>
> Join a consultant community such as the Consultant Connection Coffee Chat Community (C5). The group provides consultants with peer support, mentorship, ongoing learning, and networking opportunities. Register with no cost or obligation at c5consultantconnection.com.

Having your own consulting business can feel like you are on an island by yourself, with a fantastic team of one. If you take the time to attend and participate in regular networking opportunities and connect with like-minded consultants, you will find that your motivation, inspiration, drive, and success all benefit exponentially. You don't have time to test, try out, and demo every tool on the market, but you can ask your consulting colleagues for advice. Leverage your connections and you'll find that many become trusted confidants. It's the best way that I've found to identify instruments and tools for my clients' success as well as discover new opportunities I can provide as a consultant.

Summary

The thousands of tools and instruments on the market can be overwhelming to wade through. As a consultant, you'll first want to know what kind of tools you are looking for. How will you use them? Which clients will you use them with? What do they need? How will these tools benefit your consulting business? The tools and instruments you use will support your client's success and can help you build or expand your consulting practice. Whether you are exploring a specific tool your client wants you to use or experimenting with tools that help your business grow, tap your consulting colleagues for advice. You may be surprised to learn how many have experience and expertise with tools that are exactly what you need.

Actions You Can Take Now

- **Be a friendly researcher.** Reach out to three to five consultants you admire or want to get to know better and ask them questions. Then compile a list of their answers and share with everyone. It's a path to an instant network. Here are some suggestions to get you started:
  - ° What backend systems have you implemented to support your business?
  - ° What tools and instruments do you use regularly? What do your clients say about the value they bring?
  - ° What's one thing you know now but wish you had known or had in place when starting or expanding your consultancy?
  - ° What networking communities are you currently a member of?
- **Grow your community!** Find out which consultant networking groups are in your local area. What about ones that meet virtually? Join some groups so you can learn from others and contribute.

About the Author

Lei Comeford is a highly effective ICF executive coach, master facilitator, and learning and development consultant with experience in helping organizations improve productivity, effectiveness, and engagement. With more than 20 years of strategic and operational experience in healthcare as well as more than five years in hospitality, Lei partners with individuals, teams, and organizations to amplify and elevate their communication skills, strategic relationships, and leadership effectiveness. She is known for being a thought partner and has a passion for helping leaders reach beyond their goals through increased self-awareness with an objective to empower effectiveness and engagement with each client. You can reach out to Lei at Lei@Leicomerford.com.

Consulting for the US Federal Government

DOLORES KUCHINA-MUSINA

In today's complex and rapidly changing world, the US government faces a variety of challenges that require specialized knowledge and expertise. As a result, many government agencies and departments rely on the services of consultants to navigate these challenges. Being a government consultant can be a rewarding and challenging career that requires a unique set of skills and abilities. To start providing services, it is essential to research the field, obtain required skills training, develop a network, craft a business plan, and market your services. You could also join the ranks as an employee of a top-tier firm that provides consulting to government agencies such as McKinsey & Company, Accenture, Bain & Company, Deloitte, KPMG, and EY.

As a consultant performing work as a government contractor, you will fit into one of two broad categories: prime contractors and subcontractors. Prime contractors bid on and win contracts directly from government agencies, while subcontractors join prime contractor teams, usually to provide a specific capability or product. For your small business to serve as a prime contractor or subcontractor, you'll need to legally qualify as a small business and register as a government contractor. After you establish and register your company with your state, you'll also have to register it to do business with the federal government.

This chapter discusses steps you can take to set yourself and your company up to succeed as a consultant for government clients.

Registering Your Business With SAM

The government requires businesses to be registered within the System for Award Management (SAM), which verifies that they have the necessary eligibility and credentials to compete for and win federal contracts. Once registered, companies receive a unique entity identity (UEI) number and a commercial and government entity (CAGE) code; these two numbers are critical for your organization to be recognized as a business that can support federal government contracts.

In addition to identification numbers, SAM registration includes core information about your company such as an address, point of contacts, bank information, acceptable forms of payment, and, most importantly, your ability to comply with specific requirements unique to the federal government. These requirements are captured in the representations and certifications (which are compilations of statutes) and federal acquisition regulations (FAR) and defense federal acquisition regulations supplements (DFARS; which indicate to the government the level of compliance of the federal contractor). Lastly, SAM captures your company's self-election of applicable North American Industry Classification System (NAICS) code and product service code (PSC) that apply to their products and services, which makes it easier for the government to find based on required needs. NAICS codes are used by federal agencies to classify businesses when collecting, analyzing, and publishing statistical data about the US economy; PSCs are four-digit codes that describe a product, service, or research and development activity purchased by the federal government. The PSC Manual lists all existing product and service codes and is maintained by the General Services Administration (GSA). Just think of these codes as keywords and categories the government can use to find your organization when they are searching for specific goods and services.

If you are already feeling overwhelmed, it is understandable. I have supported dozens of SAM registrations, and even with all my experience, it still takes me two hours to complete one. Then, it can take more than a month to receive final approval from SAM, with minimal communications along the way. If this complex process is making you reconsider your desire to work with the government, remember that the time spent creating this will be worth it. After all, you won't be paid for your work if you are not registered. If that is not motivation enough, imagine getting the news that your $50-million contract could not be awarded because you were not in SAM! (Based on several true stories.)

Consulting Tip

If you want to work with the federal government, start your SAM registration as soon as you can. It's required to compete for government contracts, and while there's no cost, it's a lengthy process. Visit sam.gov to get started.

Abiding by FAR Guidelines and Its Supplements

Working with the federal government can be extremely complicated—mostly due to extensive and unusual jargon. (No chapter on anything government related would be complete without an alphabet soup of acronyms!) You also need to learn the rules . . . and the rules about the rules. These rules ensure that anyone doing business with the government is treated fairly and equally.

You need to understand the jargon to understand the rules; if you don't follow the rules, you will be immediately disqualified at that specific point in the process. I believe that the best way to learn the jargon and the rules is to read the FAR.

FAR is the principal set of rules regarding government procurement in the US and is codified in chapter 1 of title 48 of the Code of Federal Regulations (CFR); you can access them at acquisition.gov. FAR covers many of the contracts issued by the Department of Defense (DoD; such as the US Navy and Army) and civilian federal agencies (including the Department of Health and Human Services). The largest single part of FAR is part 52, which contains standard solicitation provisions and contract clauses. A *solicitation*—which can be a request for information (RFI), request for quote (RFQ), or request for proposal (RFP)—is how the government requests solution proposals from consultants. Solicitation provisions are certification requirements, notices, and instructions directed at firms that might be interested in competing for a specific contract.

The clauses contained in the solicitation control everything—including the scope of work, the length of the contract (also known as the period of performance), milestones, required deliverables, acceptance criteria, and other contractual clauses. Their purpose is to provide a set of consistent policy procedures within the federal acquisition process to keep the government contracting ecosystem flowing smoothly. Government acquisition professionals must follow the FAR, internal policies, and their agency supplements, such as DFARS, the general services acquisition regulation supplement (GSARS), and the National Aeronautics Space

Administration FAR supplement (NASFARS). It is also important to note that these clauses and the requirements may change based on the type of company the government wants to engage. For example, relevant parts for small businesses include part 19, small business programs. The regulations dealing with government contracting programs for small businesses are outlined in title 13, part 125, of the CFR.

Now that we've covered registration and government regulations, let's jump into how you capture, bid on, and win these opportunities. As you have already learned from the rest of this book, it is important to understand your offerings and potential clients. Some of the approaches of B2B interactions have crossover to winning government contracts, but there are important nuances that you need to know.

Acquiring Federal Business

For all consultants, it's critical to properly position your organization and its services to your customers. It is up to you to gather as much information as possible to implement your probability-to-win strategy and bid or no-bid strategy. This means that you have done enough research to fully understand where you can position yourself in the market to determine if an opportunity is a good fit and you can perform the work. You should know if there are potential incumbents, if this is recompete work, if it is a new capability, whether you have the skills for the project, and whether you will need other consultants or employees for support. Marketing to government agencies, much like marketing in the commercial sector, is about building relationships. And just like in the commercial sector, at the end of the day, government buyers buy from people and companies they know and trust. However, unlike private industry, the government is required to select the lowest bidder unless a clear rationale is provided.

Building a reputation as an expert in your industry, fostering relationships with potential customers and partners, and getting face time either at industry events or meetings are all just as vital in government business as they are in private sector sales. However, it's essential to recognize some of the rules and limitations specified by the acquisition regulations. For example, once an RFP is released, government communications and interactions with industry contractors are very restricted. It's generally impossible to have one-on-one discussions with the government post-RFP, so it is critical to establish relationships and build trust long before a solicitation is released. If contracting officers had more flexibility to speak with the industry,

Five Steps to Start Doing Business With the Federal Government

Steve Maier, Management Concepts

While selling to government agencies and organizations requires significant effort, there are rewards if you are diligent and have the patience to attract the attention of government buyers. In my experience, these are the steps that businesses need to take to effectively sell to the federal government:

1. Start by performing some market research, especially if your business has already had inquiries from the government. Investigate what the government is buying, which agencies are buying it, and the contract vehicles they're using. Your research should also identify key competitors and help you understand what prices the government is paying for similar services.

2. Register your established business into SAM, the official US government database. The system will assign you a unique ID, like your DUNS number.

3. If you're a woman, veteran, disabled veteran, or a minority business owner, you should also apply for disadvantaged business status with the Small Business Administration.

4. Establish a schedule contract with the GSA. These schedule contracts streamline the government sales process because they have pre-established pricing, terms, and conditions that government buyers can use to purchase from a company. They even provide schedule templates, such as the professional services schedule (PSS) and the human capital and training services (HCaTS) schedule, which are both designed for the training industry.

5. Complexity defines this step because you are essentially responding to an RFP from the GSA, so you'll need to provide a business description, technical documentation demonstrating that you're an established business with systems and internal controls in place, the prices you are offering, and documentation showing that you have already sold your services commercially. You must also adhere to the most favored nation clause in your contract—which essentially guarantees that no commercial customer will receive a larger discount off your prices than the one you provide to the government. Not managing your private sector discounting practices can create liabilities if you're audited in the future.

6. Learn about requirements for the Cybersecurity Maturity Model Certification (CMMC) 2.0 program, which will require a cybersecurity certification of any internal systems that store information deemed sensitive by the US Department of Defense and that you meet the internal control requirements specified in the certification.

It's a robust process that yields robust rewards to businesses that perform all the steps with discipline and diligence. Good luck!

they would. Unfortunately, however, many contracting officers (COs) have to "go dark" on contractors during the solicitation stage to ensure fair competition. Don't take it personally; it's not you . . . it's the FAR (or the supplement).

What to Do Once the Solicitation Has Been Published

Now that you are armed with information and know a government contract would be a good fit for you, you also need to know that just because something is published and you can submit a bid does not mean you have to. This is when contractors fall into a dump and chase mentality, which occurs for many reasons, including wanting to cast a bigger net and capturing large amounts of funds. This is not the optimal method to win work because writing proposals is a tedious and time-consuming process. A compliant, well-written, targeted proposal is much more likely to win than a half-effort one. Therefore, having a solid strategy and proper decision-making process is essential if you want to do business with the government.

The next step is actually reading a solicitation. A typical solicitation includes the performance work statement (PWS; section C), the response requirements (section L), and the evaluation criteria (section M). The government will use the solicitation as the contract upon award. Three sections (K, L, and M) will not be included.

Reading a solicitation can be intimidating. When I read my first solicitation, I started on page one and read through the remaining 249 pages (cover to cover). It was exhausting, mind-numbing, and required a lot of internet searching to understand the terms and type of work. My manager was impressed I made it through the whole document and then showed me a trick, which I will share with you. When you are reviewing a solicitation, first check the response requirements (section L) and the evaluation criteria (section M). These might be separate attachments if they are not the standard form, so keep that in mind. These two sections help you determine quickly if you are eligible to bid. They also tell you key dates (such as the timeframe to pose questions to the government and submission dates) and how to outline your proposal. You'll use these sections to create an annotated proposal outline. And once you have that, you can start going through the statement of work (SOW) or PWS to fill in the outline with additional ideas and content. If you are working alone, this process helps keep you organized as you work through your proposal. If you are working with a team, it will help guide your subject matter experts on the performance expectations they need to describe.

Consulting Tip

When responding to a solicitation, read it for content, but also for the nuances in the words that are used. Government agencies use different words than the private sector. Always use the common words found in the solicitation when responding to an RFP, RFI, or RFQ.

The government typically allows 15 to 60 days for responses, depending on the size of the request. The number of days it can take to make the award can also vary—some agencies have made awards in as little as five business days, while others can take up to 700 calendar days. This timeframe can be prolonged if someone challenges the award, which is called a *protest*. Until the protest is resolved, the work on the contract cannot begin and everyone who bids on the effort has to wait for the final determination for the next steps.

What the Contract Award Process Entails

At this stage, let's assume the best-case scenario—you've won the contract! Now what?

Generally, once you win a contract, the government will send you the contract document and a timeline for the next steps. Your first task is to read the contract! I cannot stress this enough: Do not sign the contract without reading it.

Do your due diligence to review your contract and compare it against your proposal. If there are any discrepancies between your submission and the solicitation in the award, contact the CO or contracting officer representative (COR) and outline your concerns in a clear and concise manner. This is why having an experienced contract manager in your company is key. This initial review is critical to ensure you understand the terms, conditions, deliverable expectations, acceptance criteria, and how you will be paid. Keep in mind, work should never begin without a signed contract or written authorization provided by the government to proceed. If you are unsure if work has been authorized, contact your contracts manager or legal support to review.

After your base award is signed, the next steps are to perform the work, keep documentation pertinent to the effort, manage any contract modifications, and make sure to do timely contract close out at the end of the period of performance. If you have a good relationship with the client, I recommend starting your next solicitation prior to this contract ending, so you can try to continue the relationship.

The How and What of Government Contracts

The government writes many types of contracts, and each one has advantages and disadvantages for both the contractor and the government customer. The type of contract depends on the cost type—is it a firm fixed price or cost reimbursable—and is defined by the expectations, obligations, incentives, and rewards for both the government and the contractor during an acquisition.

The contract type also determines:
- The degree and timing of the responsibility assumed by the contractor for the costs of performance
- The amount and nature of the profit incentive offered to the contractor for achieving or exceeding specified standards or goals

Fixed-price contracts provide a firm price for the work completed or items supplied. However, an adjustable price level is sometimes used for a ceiling price, a target price (including the target cost), or both. The government may also choose a variable fee structure (profit) for this type of contract to be fixed, upon award, or incentive depending on the effort being performed.

Cost-reimbursement, or *cost-plus*, is a type of contract in which a contractor is paid for all its allowed expenses up to a certain amount. In addition to cost, there is also a fee structure so the company can make a profit. Cost-reimbursement contracts carry additional obligations for the contractor in how they account for the costs they are seeking for reimbursement, so make sure you understand what you're getting into. This type of contract has additional compliance obligations, such as cost accounting standards (CAS), that many small businesses find costly and strenuous.

Compliance and Ethics

Public sector contracting is governed by an important set of rules. Both the government and its contractors must follow numerous rules and regulations, including FAR, the Procurement Integrity Act, and Defense Contract Audit Agency (DCAA) CAS. Additionally, contractors (both prime and sub) must avoid conflicts of interest, improper influencing of contract awards or federal employees, and a variety of other improper appearances, omissions, and actions. General government ethics guidelines have historically called for a high degree of public trust, a high standard of conduct, avoiding conflicts of interest or any appearances of conflicts of interest, complete impartiality, and lack of preferential treatment.

Registering on SAM and abiding by FAR and any of its supplements is a great start, but it does not reach the extent of your compliance. Across your organization, your internal programs and personnel must be compliant with the agencies you do business with; otherwise, you could face some of the ramifications listed in this chapter. The DCAA and the Defense Contract Management Agency (DCMA) were both established to ensure that businesses were compliant with FAR policies. The DCAA performs contract audits for the DoD and other agencies, while the DCMA provides contract administration functions, product acceptance and inspection, and cost or price negotiation support.

If contractors ever find themselves in a noncompliant situation, the results could be extremely costly. Ramifications of noncompliance include civil or criminal penalties, voided or terminated contracts, and debarment (never being able to win a government contract again).

Every contractor is responsible for maintaining compliance with any government rules and regulations that apply. If contractors aren't compliant, they run the risk of paying the government the full extent of any damage incurred, plus costly penalties. Compliance and keeping up to date on federal government contracting policies are essential if you want to be a successful federal contractor.

Your duty to ensure compliance and the highest ethical standards is critical because the money spent on government contracts is taxpayer money, which means it's your money. You have a responsibility to the United States populace to ensure you are providing a fair and reasonable price and performing work of the highest quality. I have worked on small contracts with a value of $5,000 and large contracts worth more than $6 billion; each one required oversight for compliance and understanding of proper ethical behavior. If someone is not performing, organizations and people can report them for unethical behavior, which can cause companies to lose their ability to do business with the government. As you can imagine, a negative reputation follows you much more closely than a good reputation. So, be mindful of your business practices and perform work as if it is your money because, chances are, your taxes contributed to your ability to get that contract.

Summary

Working for an agency in the US federal government can be satisfying and rewarding. Although it may seem complicated at first, it can also be fun once you learn what's expected. You will almost always need to write a proposal, so polish your proposal writing skills. A benefit of working with the government is that everyone, no matter who you are, is treated fairly. Winning a contract is not about who you know, but what you know. So, if you are the best at what you do, you may win over other contractors who have more experience. One way to get started is to act as a sub to another contractor.

Actions You Can Take Now

- **Read about procurement.** Government contracting can be confusing. If you need more information about the process, read Jack Pitzer's *Introduction to Public Procurement.*
- **Ask yourself if government contracting is right for you.** Review the self-assessment questions associated with this chapter online at td.org/handbook-for-consultants. The process will give you an idea of whether government consulting is right for you.

About the Author

Dolores Kuchina-Musina, PhD, MBA, PPCM, CFCM, NCMA Fellow, is the chief disruptor at REXOTA Solutions, a company in the Washington, DC, metropolitan area focused on strategy, planning, pursuit, capture, management, and administration of federal contract and agreement awards. Dolores has more than 10 years of experience in federal, state, and international public procurement, specifically directing and managing strategic pursuits in collaboration with business development, proposal development, and change management initiatives for federal procurement acquisitions. She's also served as a strategic partner in providing risk management support for federal compliance contracts. Dolores has been published in several academic journals and is the author of *Public Procurement for Innovation: Research and Development at the US Federal Level.* If you have any questions, please reach out to info@rexota.com or visit rexota.com.

CHAPTER 20

Planning Priorities

The Challenge of Working
in and *on* Your Business

GREG OWEN-BOGER AND DALE LUDWIG

Are you a sole practitioner working in an independent consultancy, or are you part of a small partnership? Are you just starting out, or have you been in business for a while? Are you wondering how you can accomplish all the tasks on your action item list? Are you looking for a way to make sense of it all? This chapter will help put everything in perspective no matter what kind of consultancy you have or stage you are in. For example:

- You may be just getting started and wondering about the challenges ahead.
- Your consulting business may be growing and experiencing the challenges of scaling up.
- Your consulting practice might be experiencing stagnation, and you know that something needs to change so you can move forward successfully.

Since Dale founded Turpin Communication in 1992, and Greg came on board in 1995, we've worn many hats. We have been in, moved through, and fallen back into all of these phases during our more than 30 years in business. If we've learned anything, it's that change is a constant, workload and priorities shift regularly, and being overwhelmed is sometimes a way of life.

When we're on-site with a client, it's important to us that the client believes they are our top priority. The challenge for Greg is that he's also the primary salesperson. Not too long ago, we were leading a three-day communication training program for one of our favorite clients. As it happened, there were also a few deals in the pipeline, and one of them was urgent, sizeable, complex, and needed his immediate attention. His only option was to work on the proposal, which involved other Turpin team members, before breakfast or after dinner. Making matters worse, our team members, one in finance and another an account manager, were spread across multiple time zones. By finding time when he could, and having a dedicated team willing to work with his schedule, Greg was able to get the proposal out the door.

This is a common challenge among consultants because we wear so many hats throughout the day. Turpin is at the point in our company's evolution where we are able to hire employees to ease the burden on the two of us, but it wasn't always that way. So the question is this: With all the responsibilities you have as a business owner, how do you balance the client-facing work that you're being paid to do with the demands of running your business?

We have learned to place our work into two categories. Sometimes we work *in* the business. Other times we work *on* the business. Throughout this chapter we will attempt to make sense of this and provide examples from our own business-owning journey along the way.

Working in Versus on Your Business

First, some level setting. Working *in* your business involves using your expertise to deliver successful training or consulting to your clients. It focuses on helping clients achieve their goals, and it's how you make your money. Working in your business is what most consultants assume will be their primary focus. And, during busy stretches when a lot of work is coming in, it is. Working *on* the business involves all your additional operational responsibilities. It requires thinking like a business owner, not a consultant. Unlike working in the business, working on it may not come naturally and often requires spending money, not making it. Table 20-1 outlines the activities that fall into these two categories.

Table 20-1. Business Activities for Turpin Communication

Working *in* the Business	Working *on* the Business
Client-facing activities: • Consulting • Instructional design • Delivering training • Executive coaching • Sales* • Client and account management • Writing blogs and books for the benefit of clients	Operational responsibilities that support the business: • Strategy and project management • Marketing and social media • Website design and maintenance • Contracting • Finance • Writing as part of marketing, including blogging • Onboarding new employees

*For some companies, sales might be part of the operational side, but for us, it's client facing because of our consultative sales approach. This means that everything we do is tailored to the client, and in our case, tailoring starts during the sales process.

Balancing and Prioritizing the Workload

If you've chosen to be an independent consulting practitioner, most of the work will fall to you at the start. You may outsource some of the legal and accounting work, but chances are good that you'll do the rest. As your consultancy matures (and ideally grows), you should be able to outsource more and more of the nonconsulting work to others. The people you choose may be contractors or vendors. Others may become employees. Regardless, you'll need to answer these questions:

- What should be outsourced?
- When is the right time to hire some help?

To help answer the first question, do what we did (and continue to do from time to time): Make a list of the work that you do, including all tasks and responsibilities. Next, create a matrix—the horizontal line represents who could do the work, while the vertical line separates the work you like to do from the work you dislike. (See Figure 20-1 for an example.) Place your tasks on the matrix, and label each one as either "on" or "in." This will give you a snapshot of where your business is today.

Figure 20-1. Example Matrix of Prioritizing Your Workload

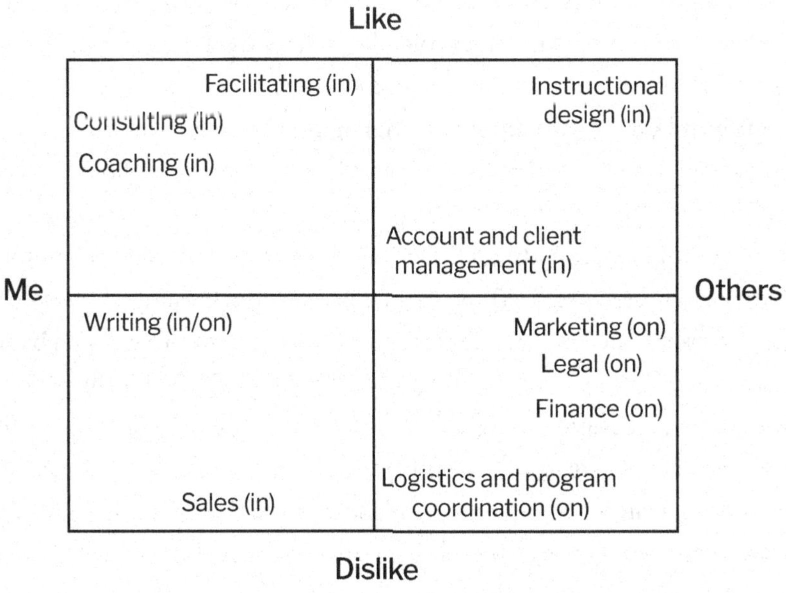

In this example, everything on the left-hand side—consulting, coaching, facilitating, writing, and sales—should remain with the business owner because they are instrumental in supporting the quality of the work. These tasks are all examples of working *in* the business, so it's logical that they are left to the consultant. If and when these tasks become too overwhelming, you'll know it's time to find a partner to share the workload.

The tasks that fall on the right-hand side are all good candidates for outsourcing because they can be done by someone else. In this example, logistics and program coordination, legal, and finance are easy choices for outsourcing because the consultant doesn't enjoy doing them. These tasks are all examples of work that is done *on* the business to keep it running smoothly.

Let's take a closer look at four of the tasks in this example:

- **Writing.** Depending on what you're writing, it could be considered something you do either *in* or *on* the business. Writing marketing copy and blog articles designed to boost website traffic is an example of working on the business. Writing a book, on the other hand, is an example of working both in and on the business. Ideally the book will make money (in), but it's also a great marketing tool (on). In either case, because this consultant enjoys writing (mostly), it is not something to outsource at this time.

- **Sales.** Because closing deals requires a business mindset, it is an important part of the business. Thus, sales falls into the *in* bucket for a consultancy. While the consultant doesn't enjoy the sales role, they currently don't have an alternative option. This may change as the business evolves.

- **Account and client management.** Managing clients and their accounts may not fall into their sweet spot, but in the example, our consultant should continue doing it. At least for now.

- **Instructional design.** Sitting all the way up in the upper right quadrant, instructional design is something this consultant really enjoys; however, it could be done by someone else. While it may seem counterintuitive, it can be necessary to prioritize what's best for the company over your likes and dislikes. So, finding an instructional designer to lighten the load may be in our consultant's future.

The question about when to find help comes down to finances. Do you have money in the bank, and is cashflow good enough to allocate some of it to these responsibilities? If the money is there, the decision is easy. If the money isn't there, you'll need to plan for improving profitability.

When our consultancy started growing, our first employee took over logistics and workshop coordination. Later, we added a bookkeeper, operations manager, marketing manager, and someone to manage sales. Then, as our earlier story illustrated, Greg took back the sales role, and our workshop coordinator moved into an account management position to help balance Greg's workload. Now that we have other people on the team, Dale remains steadfast in his role as founder and lead trainer and consultant. He also writes every day and works on the business by participating in staff meetings and strategy discussions.

You will find a matrix like this one at td.org/handbook-for-consultants. Download it and use it to determine what you need to do yourself and what you could outsource. We recommend revisiting this exercise from time to time. As your business grows and changes, you'll want to re-evaluate what work needs to be done and by whom.

Mission-Critical Responsibilities and Collaboration Opportunities

There are a few business-owner responsibilities that fall into the working *on* bucket that are so important you should stay involved even if you outsource them. This work, which is about how you present yourself in the marketplace and differentiate yourself from the competition, includes:

- Establishing yourself as the expert
- Defining your brand
- Managing sales and marketing
- Building your thought leadership

Let's look at these responsibilities in more detail. It may seem daunting for one person to manage, but you can look for opportunities to collaborate with people in your network or other creative ways to outsource.

Establishing Yourself as the Expert

Keep the focus of your business narrow. The temptation to be everything to everyone is strong, especially in the beginning. However, it's better to stick to what you do best and be recognized for that, rather than go outside your comfort zone just to make more sales.

There are two reasons for this. First, the quality of your work will likely suffer if you stray too far. It's hard enough to get things right when you're doing what you know best. Branching out into areas you aren't as comfortable with runs a real risk. Second, a narrow focus gives you the opportunity to finetune your methodology, develop depth of experience, and clearly explain your points of differentiation to clients.

For us, establishing and maintaining our expertise involved two steps:

- **Developing an approach to our work that was unique in the marketplace.** Turpin was founded on the notion that the presentation skills training available for businesspeople was broken and fundamentally missing the mark. By "fundamentally," we mean that our competitors were delivering training on the wrong process—teaching people to deliver speeches when they really needed to learn how to manage a conversation. We call them Orderly Conversations. The ramifications of this distinction are broad and deep, and every advancement we've made in our methodology has grown from this idea. Our work is about correcting misguided assumptions, unlearning techniques that don't work, and replacing them with simple, practical recommendations.

- **Consistently communicating that approach to our learners, clients, and potential clients.** We write a lot. One of our first big writing projects was a whitepaper laying out our guiding principles. And writing our first book, *The Orderly Conversation*, helped clarify our thinking while setting the stage to establish our thought leadership. Since then, we have written books, book chapters, blog articles, and several magazine articles. We've also spoken at many industry conferences and webinars. In each situation, we work to communicate a consistent, thought-provoking message that helps people not only do things differently but think about things differently as well.

Sometimes it's difficult to truly understand your expertise and what makes it unique. Fish don't see the water in which they swim, as they say. We have the benefit of being able to bounce ideas off one another. If you don't have a partner to talk to, try talking with people who are familiar with your work. Their insights on your business may help you narrow in on your niche.

Defining Your Brand

Defining your brand begins by determining how you want to be perceived by your clients. What values do you want your work to embody? What is the mission that only you can achieve? What is your vision for the future? How do you want clients to feel when they work with you?

Thinking at this level may feel unnecessary when you're starting out, but the work you do to define your brand will have long-term benefits. You'll establish guiding principles for your work, lay a solid foundation for your marketing, and be better positioned to judge whether a project is appropriate for you.

We engaged a marketing company when we rebranded in 2009. Through collaboration with them, we hung our new brand on the image of single malt Scotch, which led us to use descriptors such as "sophisticated," "wise," "nuanced," "understated," 'best-in-class," and so on. This exercise informed our color palette, tone, and even our decision to remove exclamation points from our writing. After all, a single malt Scotch never yells. Instead, it gets your attention by being the best of its kind. Our brand has essentially stayed the same ever since. It influences what we do and how we show up in every situation.

Keep in mind, defining your brand doesn't have to be a laborious process. It simply requires you to take a step back to identify what you want to accomplish and how you want your business to show up in the marketplace. It defines your why.

Consulting Tip

It may be helpful to read *Start With Why* by Simon Sinek when going through this process. He encourages readers to consider their motives and purposes to determine their "why."

You should honor and protect your consultancy's brand throughout the life of your business. If something is off, people will know, so it's important to make sure that every member of your team understands the brand and their responsibility for supporting it.

At some point as the business grows and matures, you may find it beneficial to do a brand refresh. We refreshed ours in 2018. We wrote new and more compelling positioning statements and developed a more sophisticated website. We were delightfully surprised to find that this led to larger and more sophisticated clients engaging with us.

You should also do a SWOT analysis from time to time to identify your company's strengths, weaknesses, opportunities, and threats. The business world, economy, and even the TD industry shift, and your business is no exception. By conducting a SWOT analysis, you're more likely to stay in front of these shifts rather than playing catch up.

Managing Sales and Marketing

It's easy to assume when starting a new business that once you've completed a few engagements, your quality will be recognized by everyone and the work will pour in. You may also think that your professional network is broad enough to keep you busy. While some new business may come to you in these ways, relying on it without additional marketing is risky.

Your marketing materials are an extension of your brand. Once you've established your brand, start developing marketing messages. To attract the right clients, answer these questions before you start marketing your services:

- **What business problems are you solving?** What are you able to do for your clients? How do you make their lives better? The types of business problems we solve have evolved over the years. In the beginning, we marketed ourselves as a presentation skills training company. Now, our focus is both broader and more focused. It is broader in the sense that we market ourselves as business communication consultants and trainers. It is more focused in that we emphasize the benefits of our work, which include career development for individuals and filling leadership pipelines for our clients.

- **Who are your target client companies?** Do you want to focus your work on a particular industry? Or can you be successful in a variety of business verticals? As much as it frustrates our marketing company, we focus on a variety of industries because the skills we develop are applicable in all situations. If you take a similar approach, be ready for the question, "Do you work with financial institutions (or healthcare, or engineers)?" Some buyers assume that expertise in their field is required. This is, of course, not the case for us. Having industry expertise may benefit some consultancies.

- **Who is your ideal buyer?** For example, do you find the most success with people in an HR role or people working in separate business units? Buyers in different roles make decisions in different ways and at different speeds. Understanding this will help you determine how to react to each of them. We have two types of ideal buyers. The first type are leaders within L&D who make buying decisions across the entire organization. These engagements are often sizeable, and we enjoy repeat business year after year. Our second type of ideal buyer is managers looking for training for their teams. They have urgency, budget, and specific needs. In some situations, the initial work with one manager leads to deeper penetration within the organization.

Once your brand, messaging, and ideal clients are identified, you'll be able to create supporting materials such as business cards and brochures, your social media profile, and a website.

In the beginning, most of your leads will come to you either through your network or your website. When these inquiries come in, it's time to close the deal. The sales process you follow will be unique to your consultancy. Your price point and the number of decision makers involved will also play a role. Regardless, it's important that your sales message is an extension of your marketing message. Establishing trust is key—if the buyer doesn't trust you, you won't close the deal.

Another thing to consider is whether or not the prospect is a good one. A potential client who is clearly buying on price, for example, may not be the best fit. We've learned not to waste time on low-quality leads. Your time is precious, so spend it where it's likely to benefit you and the business.

Here are some things to do:

- **Develop a clear, easy-to-use website.** For many people, your website is your introduction and will be the first indicator of what it will be like to work with you. A good website encourages potential clients to reach out to you. A poor one does the opposite. Focus on making your website easy to navigate and easy to understand. Make sure that it supports your brand.

- **Describe what you do in terms of how it benefits prospects.** You want your message to be something like, "I can make your meetings more collaborative, efficient, and successful," rather than, "I have expertise in meeting management."

- **Create brand distinction.** Keep track of your competitors, not to imitate them but to be able to differentiate yourself. How do they distinguish themselves? What are their values?

- **Stick to your values and your brand.** Don't cheapen your business by taking on work that doesn't align just to make money. In the beginning, we supplemented our income by subcontracting for other consultants or organizations, which gave us a financial cushion so we could turn down work that wasn't right for us.

Building Your Thought Leadership

As your expertise grows, it's important to communicate it outside your circle of clients. Here are a few ways to build your thought leadership:

- **Publish a blog on your website.** It's a great way for potential buyers to understand your thinking and approach. Blog topics may include case studies, new ways for buyers to think about the problems they face, and solutions for common business problems.
- **Speak at conferences.** This is a great way to build your credibility with a broader audience.
- **Write for industry publications.** This will help you reach a broader audience than you already have.
- **Publish whitepapers on your website.** Whitepapers establish your expertise in an objective way that's free from an overt sales message. *Writing White Papers* by Michael A. Stelzner is a great place to start. Interestingly, our first whitepaper helped us close a deal in 2011. We continue to work with that client today, and they have become the most profitable client in our history.
- **Use social media.** Make sure you've got a credible social media presence that reinforces your brand.

Establishing your thought leadership may not lead to more sales immediately, but the reach of these activities is long. We have had potential buyers contact us and say, "I remember hearing you speak at a conference five years ago, and now I have a need for your services."

Consulting Tip

Tap into your network of professional friends to help with the work described in this chapter. Bouncing ideas off people you trust, asking them to facilitate a conversation about your brand, having them lead a SWOT analysis, and providing help with mission and vision statements can bring a useful and objective perspective to the work that needs to be done.

Publish or Self-Publish?

By Rich Douglas, Rich Douglas Consulting

Publishing a book is a great way to establish your position as a thought leader. If you're convinced that writing a book will help your practice, a big decision will be whether to find a publisher for your book or to publish it yourself. There are advantages and disadvantages to each option.

Working with a publisher means that there's a larger presence behind your book. They'll take care of editing, getting it printed, having it distributed, promoting it, and so on. Then, there's the prestige of having a book selected for publication. But publishers typically put out just a few hundred titles per year and reject thousands more. Your fantastic book might not make the cut. Also, you may lose some control over content and how it's presented—and if you want to update the material, the publisher might not support a new edition. In return for the publisher managing the book's production, you may also give up a considerable portion of the sales—in most cases, you're paid in royalties, which are derived from a percentage of revenue.

Self-publishing changes that dynamic. You have greater control over the content, style, and everything else that goes into the finished product. Plus, you keep a greater portion of the money it generates. However, with that control comes the responsibility of being writer, editor, publisher, promoter, and anything else to make the book a success. And, typically, sales of self-published books are far lower.

The Risks of Only Working *in* the Business

The work you do *on* the business ultimately helps the work you do *in* it. You can clarify your focus, define your ideal clients, know how to answer the big questions about your work and values, and gain comfort in your industry.

However, there is a common trap: Spending too much time *in* the business can lead to unintended consequences *for* the business. Examples include:

- A large client takes most of your time (and produces most of your income). If this goes on for too long, you are essentially in a contractor role and at the mercy of that client.
- Your first big project (the one that led you to become independent) dominates your energy and thoughts, which limits your growth potential.
- You avoid sales and marketing because you're busy with other responsibilities, and besides, you don't feel comfortable with them anyway.

The consequence of focusing too much of your work *in* the business is that you lose sight of operational tasks and responsibilities, which are necessary for consultancies to thrive. We know this firsthand. During the Great Recession of 2008, our business was booming. We were in the middle of our largest contract to date and enjoying the benefits of nonstop work. Toward the end of 2009, that contract was finished. After taking a few weeks for some much-needed rest and relaxation, we realized our sales pipeline was empty. There wasn't a single prospect on the horizon, and our website was in dire need of updating. Thankfully, we had cash reserves to tide us over, but it took years to fully recover from that oversight. In hindsight, however, we're glad that happened because we were better positioned than most when the COVID-19 pandemic hit in 2020.

As scary as it may seem, always assume that things like recessions, setbacks, and even pandemics are on the horizon. This will remind you to carve out time in your schedule to work on your business and be ready for what may come.

Summary

No L&D consultant starts a business with the burning desire to learn accounting software, market themselves, design a website, or prepare tax forms. That's not where your sense of professional fulfillment comes from, and it's certainly not where your expertise lies. So, the work you do on the business, as important as it is, will not be the most satisfying work you do. But if you think of it as the price of your independence, as the work you do to make it possible to do the work you love, you will face the challenge, learn new things, and know when to take on new responsibilities and when to give up others. Consider it a lifelong stretch assignment.

Actions You Can Take Now

- **Collaborate early.** Ask a friend you trust to role play a sales meeting with you. Have your friend ask the questions that you expect to get (and even some you don't expect). This will build your confidence with the conversation and help you be more focused, concise, and benefit oriented.
- **Consider outsourcing.** Review all that you need to do and determine what you could outsource. For example, the amount of help you need with sales and

marketing depends on your experience and expertise. How could you use an outside perspective to guide you? Could you outsource writing projects? Everyone needs a proofreader. Everyone. No matter how good your writing is, always have someone look at important documents to ensure clarity, correct grammar, word choice, and punctuation.

About the Authors

Dale Ludwig is the founder and president of Turpin Communication, a presentation and facilitation training company based in Chicago, Illinois. Since 1992, he and his team have developed methodologies that challenge much of the conventional wisdom in the field. Dale has a PhD in communication from the University of Illinois at Urbana-Champaign. He is a co-author of *The Orderly Conversation: Business Presentations Redefined*, *The Virtual Orderly Conversation*, and *Effective SMEs: A Trainer's Guide for Helping Subject Matter Experts Facilitate Learning*. This is his third contribution to an ATD handbook.

Greg Owen-Boger is executive vice president and co-owner of Turpin Communication, joining the organization in 1995. He leads sales, marketing, and operations at Turpin, as well as working as a trainer and coach. Above everything else, Greg is dedicated to the idea that effective, efficient workday communication is possible for everyone. He was the president of the ATD Chicagoland Chapter in 2015. Greg is a co-author of *The Orderly Conversation: Business Presentations Redefined*, *The Virtual Orderly Conversation*, and *Effective SMEs: A Trainer's Guide for Helping Subject Matter Experts Facilitate Learning*. This is his third contribution to an ATD handbook. Learn more about Turpin Communication at turpincommunication.com.

SECTION IV

Developing
Business
Finding and Keeping Clients

Starting your consulting business is the first critical decision, but creating a continuous flow of clients will be the defining challenge that determines whether you stay in business. Finding and keeping clients is always the top priority. But it is not just about selling—developing business is also about pricing, marketing, networking, and producing results.

Our luminary consulting author, Michael Zipursky, is an expert at staying in business—so much so that he's helped almost 900 consultants throughout the world earn six- and seven-figure incomes. Michael introduces possible pricing models and then discusses why you should consider the powerful value-pricing method and how it works. He is an expert in this area, and I am delighted that he agreed to author this chapter.

Selecting how to price is critical and tied to many other related topics. Fortunately, we have you covered! Wondering about the importance of a niche? Wendy Gates Corbett is the expert here. How about marketing and selling? Halelly Azulay and Joe Trueblood provide answers to all your questions. Holly Burkett shares her secrets for writing a winning business proposal, and Michael Ferraro and Kimberli Jeter will chime in on the value of volunteering and networking. Finally, Rich Douglas helps you create a path to passive income.

7 Super Sales Secrets to Developing Business

To stay in business, you must sell. Unfortunately, this makes many consultants uncomfortable, and they would prefer to avoid anything that appears to be a sales call. Why? Because our minds are racing with these concerns:

- How can I stand out? I'm only a solopreneur!
- What do I do to prove myself?
- What should I ask?
- How should I handle objections?
- What if they say no?

I've got seven secrets to help you overcome these internal objections and nail your next sale. Let's get started.

1. Listen, Listen, Listen

Probably the most important secret is to listen during your sales call. Don't talk. Don't force your sales pitch on your prospect. Listen. If you are doing more than 50 percent of the talking, you've probably already lost the sale. The prospect is just waiting for you to stop talking so the meeting can end. Are you listening—truly listening—to your potential clients?

2. Raise Your Price

Most people assume that a lower price will help make a sale, but that's wrong. Buyers often assume that a lower price equates to lower quality. I experienced this firsthand during my early years as a consultant. I was overwhelmed with work and decided to raise my rate to reduce the number of projects. It's a simple supply and demand problem—right? Wrong! The increased fee suggested that I was more valuable, and I was quickly overwhelmed by even more work. What does your pricing say about you?

3. Be a Partner, Not a Vendor

This tip comes from Bill Treasurer, an expert consultant and author of chapter 5, who says that a vendor does the minimum amount of work for the maximum amount of money. When you are a vendor, your clients try to control you with vendor management. Don't bring a you-need-to-do-this attitude. It's better to be a humble partner and co-create with your clients right from the start. Your client's ownership will be higher, and it will build your relationships. You will find that relationships matter a great deal in consulting. Do such a great job that they are excited to bring you in for future projects! (See also Mike Kent's advice in chapter 34.)

4. State the Cost of Not Buying

Research shows that humans are more interested in avoiding pain than acquiring pleasure. When applied to selling, you could interpret this to mean that sharing the negative reasons to buy creates a more compelling argument than sharing the positive reasons. For example, "If you don't accept this offer, turnover will double this year," is more compelling than "You'll reduce turnover by 50 percent if you move forward on this work."

5. Hearing No Can Be Good

Wait, what? Remember all the times that you followed up and followed up and followed up again with a client who kept stringing you along? That was a waste of your time. If you accept a wishy-washy uncertain noncommitment, you'll need to chase the client. It's better to just be candid and say, "It doesn't seem like this is a fit for you. Is that right?" This gives the prospect an out and gives you a final answer so you can move on to another potential client.

6. Communicate Two Things

Of course, you want to share all the features and benefits you're offering, your past experience, and the expertise you bring, but all your prospects need to know is this:

- What problem you will solve for me?
- What do I need to do next?

Make sure they know what problem they have that you will solve. Sometimes when clients state a problem, it isn't accurate. In that case, you may need to help them clarify what the problem is. You also need to make sure that they know what they need to do next to engage your services, so tell them how to set up your next meeting, sign a contract, read your proposal, or whatever steps are necessary to take their yes to the next level.

7. Confirm Next Steps and Follow Up

Before you leave the sales call, make sure to solidify what happens next. A great way to do that is to ask prospects, "What date works best on your calendar for our next meeting?" Without a next step, you haven't closed the sale. Your own next step is a given: Sending a thank-you note is a requirement. Follow up is critical.

That's it! Seven super sales secrets that will help you keep your consulting pipeline filled and business booming. After your first sale, you should immediately focus on the second one. That means you should do such a fabulous job for the client that they ask you back for their next project and sing your praises to other potential clients. Which of these seven secrets will you focus on first?

Increase Consulting Fees Exponentially With Value Pricing

MICHAEL ZIPURSKY, *LUMINARY CONSULTING AUTHOR*

Consultants leave hundreds of thousands of dollars on the table every day, but it's not because they haven't mastered LinkedIn, have the wrong outreach strategy, or don't have the fanciest website. It's not that those things aren't important; however, they aren't the biggest needle movers if you want to earn more.

If you want to double your firm's revenue this year—and you could only focus on one thing in your business—what would that be? Most consultants might respond with one of these ideas:

- "I'd work on my lead generation."
- "I'd hire a salesperson."
- "I'd become a master at writing proposals."

These aren't bad answers, but they're usually not the best place to start.

The single biggest opportunity for consultants to earn more is by raising their fees. I know it almost seems too simple. Is it really that easy? Sure, just double the price in your consulting proposals. But the thing most consultants struggle with is the justification for the fee increase.

What should you charge your clients? Determining your fee may be the most difficult decision a first-time consultant makes. However, it is a decision that you must make before you can start soliciting business. Your client will likely want to know what a project will cost them before they'll agree to work with you. And even after you've determined a pricing strategy, you'll continue to deal with the question of what to charge or how to charge.

I'm a big proponent of increasing your fees. It's a high-leverage move that enables you to earn significantly more without having to work more hours or take on more projects. In this chapter, I'll share a strategy for raising your consulting fees exponentially. We'll examine:

- Different pricing models for consultants
- Understanding value pricing
- How to conduct the value conversation
- How to put it into practice, including the specific steps you'll take to implement value pricing in your business

Available Pricing Models for Consultants

Before you implement a better pricing strategy, it's useful to understand the most common pricing methods for consulting work: an hourly or daily method, a fixed-rate or project method, and the value pricing method.

There are other pricing methods, such as retainers or performance-based pricing, but this chapter focuses specifically on value pricing because it provides one of the greatest opportunities for consultants. To illustrate the different methods, let's look at Acme International Tax Consultants, a company that provides tax consulting to small businesses.

Hourly Method

The *hourly method* means that you charge by the hour for your consulting services. You set an hourly rate, track your hours, and then bill your client for your time. It's a very common method for new and inexperienced consultants. A *daily rate*, often used by training consultants, is a variation of the hourly method that is usually dependent on an hourly rate and how you define "daily."

Acme began offering their consulting services for $250 per hour. In the early days, this worked well. It seemed like a premium rate. However, Acme noticed that using hourly fees incentivized them to take longer to complete a project, even if the client wanted the project done faster. Their incentives and their client's incentives weren't aligned.

Acme also spent a lot of time and energy tracking their hours—time they could be spending creating more value for their clients or developing their intellectual property and content. Finally, many clients balked at their hourly rate. As an hourly rate, $250 seemed like a lot. And the price alone didn't convey the value Acme offered.

So, Acme decided to switch from an hourly rate to a fixed rate.

Fixed-Rate Method

The *fixed-rate* (or *project-based*) *method* means that you charge by the project using a predetermined rate.

Acme switched from charging an hourly rate of $250 per hour to charging $5,000 per project. Their clients loved the switch. With the hourly method, clients had no idea how much they'd end up paying. With the new fixed rate, they knew exactly what they would be getting and how much they would be investing.

However, Acme's consultants had some issues with this pricing method. Because of each project's unique nature, it was hard to estimate how long each one would take, and they always took longer than expected. While their fixed fee was based on an estimated 20 hours total for a project (which works out to $250 per hour), in reality, it usually took about 35 hours to complete a project (which brings the hourly rate down to $143). They also had difficulty handling scope creep. They wanted to create the best result for their client, but they had to ensure each project was profitable, and that meant saying no to some client requests.

Acme also noticed they were still spending a lot of time on administration. Despite charging a fixed price, they were still conscious of how many hours they were spending on each project. Ultimately, the fixed-rate method wasn't much different than the hourly method, and they were leaving money on the table.

Was there a pricing strategy that aligned their incentives with their client's? That's when Acme decided to try a new pricing strategy: the value pricing method.

Value Pricing Method

The value pricing method removes the focus from time and deliverables and instead bases payment on results and outcomes you create for your client. In most cases, this is the best way for consultants to maximize their fees. So, how does it work?

With value pricing, you start with the client's needs. Once you discover the value you can create for your client, you can price your consulting services based on that value. With hourly or project-based pricing, you start with the service and price it based on how much it costs to deliver. Hourly and project-based pricing are not nearly as flexible because your service's price is based on how much it costs to deliver (and not the value it creates). This means that you also have to convince buyers that it's worth the price. Value pricing allows you to price each project independently, based on the value it creates for each client, which is a much easier sell.

So, instead of simply charging $250 per hour or $5,000 per project, Acme sought to understand how much money they would save their clients before thinking about how much they would charge. Then, they'd use that information during their sales conversations. For example, rather than saying, "Our fee is $250 per hour," the Acme consultants began saying, "We have a specific program for taking you through the process. It will save you $500,000 each year in taxes, and the fee is $50,000." There was no mention of hours. One of their clients said, "I don't care whether it takes one day or a few weeks. As long as I'm saving that kind of money, let's do this."

By using value pricing, Acme could spend fewer hours, earn more for their services, and still have happy clients. And their clients saw both the tangible value (money saved) and the intangible value (not having to stress over taxes). Despite the higher investment, it created a significant return on investment (ROI) for clients. That's one of the most rewarding outcomes of value pricing.

Creating a Value Pricing Mindset

But why does value pricing work? Let's start by thinking about why clients are paying you—it's not for your time, deliverables, or even your expertise. They are paying you for the results and outcomes you create.

Acme's clients weren't paying them to spend 20 hours completing paperwork or having conversations about international taxes. Their clients were paying them to save money, be more profitable, and create greater wealth. The number of hours or deliverables it took to create that outcome was irrelevant. In fact, the quicker Acme created that result, the happier the client was.

Think about going to the dentist. A dentist might charge $500 for a tricky, possibly painful 20-minute procedure. That may seem like a high price for a short amount of time, but would you rather the procedure take longer? No! You want to have it done as quickly as possible and to ensure the problem doesn't resurface. You're paying for the result, not the time. And the quicker you get the result, the better.

This is a key mindset when using value pricing: understanding that you are paid based on the value, results, and outcomes you create. Until you understand this principle, you can't effectively put it into practice.

The power of the value pricing approach is *leverage*. If you can deliver a million dollars' worth of value, you'll find many opportunities to earn $75,000, $100,000, and $200,000 for those projects, even if they only take you a few weeks to deliver. Earning that same level of compensation as a consultant using hourly fees is difficult.

Unfortunately, many consultants who get to the proposal stage don't know how to use value pricing. This happens because they haven't gone deep enough into the value conversation before designing the proposal, which means they also don't fully understand the value they'll create for the client. You need to learn how to have a value conversation with your client so you can agree on what value means to them.

The Value Conversation

To use ROI and value-based fees, you must conduct meaningful conversations with your clients. In these conversations you will do two things: Agree on what value means for the client and demonstrate the potential ROI to them. Show them the value and outcome they will receive from moving forward with the engagement you propose.

Acme consultants told their clients that they would save money on their taxes, but that was just the start of the conversation. In a value conversation, consultants must determine several other elements. For example, it was important for Acme to find out the following information:

- How much money the client was currently paying in taxes each year
- How much time they were spending each year dealing with their taxes
- The stress, unease, and concerns the client experienced throughout the year related to their taxes and finances
- What they were and weren't doing regarding their taxes and how they could legally save a considerable amount each year with a proper tax strategy
- What they planned to do with the money they saved each year once the new tax strategy was in place (such as invest in growth, hire a new team member, or go on a holiday with their family)

You should identify similar elements for each of your clients. The best way to discover this value is by asking your prospective clients deep, penetrating questions. The object of a value conversation is to peel back the layers to find the value they're after. How you conduct this conversation depends on your industry, your offer, and your relationship with the prospective client.

We provide consultants with a value conversation script they can use in different types of situations. This general framework of questions helps identify the value the buyer cares about. Let's look at some examples of these questions along with explanations of why they work:

- **"Imagine we're talking 12 months from today—you've achieved your goals and are thrilled with your progress. What does your team, life, or business look like?"** This question helps frame the conversation about value by asking the client to reveal their desired future state. It works great for prompting them to tell you the primary value they seek. Use it early in your conversations to reveal what the client wants; then, use that information to dig deeper, ask more questions, and get more specific about the value they seek.

- **"What is your number 1 priority for this business during the upcoming fiscal year?"** By asking them specifically for their top priority, you can help clarify whether that should be their number 1 priority. Then, you can look at how to help them achieve it. This also gives you the opportunity to document their priorities to refer back to if your client ever gets off track or unfocused.

- **"What options have you looked at to achieve this?"** There is no need to reinvent the wheel. Understanding what your client has done so far, or what they are thinking about doing, can help you uncover things you may not have thought of yourself that are worth trying. Or, you may be able to make recommendations for how they can try again but in a different way that you know will produce a better result.

- **"What is the main value you are looking for by doing X?"** Will this help the company make an extra $5 million? Will they save tens of thousands of dollars each month? Will they get a promotion? Will their top team members stay longer at the company? Will this reduce their stress level? You should adjust how you frame this question based on your area of expertise and the type of work you're doing. When you and the buyer understand what's at stake and the value that you're creating, you can position your offering and structure your proposal so that it aligns with the value you are delivering. While you should always identify the financial upside of a project, it's also important to ask what a successful project would mean to them as an individual. Sure, it might make the company an extra $5 million, but if it's also going to make the decision maker's life easier by dramatically reducing their workload and stress level, you want to make it known that you understand, so communicate that the project will accomplish both of these goals. There are several questions you can ask that lead to this type of discussion.

- **"Is there anything that you or your employees are doing that may be getting in the way of achieving this result?"** It's not uncommon to find that clients are unintentionally taking actions that are harmful to their business or getting in the way of the progress they want to make. By getting the client to speak openly about this, you can figure out how to help them deal with the issue, remove the roadblock, and overcome the challenge.

- **"If you don't fix it, how long can you manage to stay with things the way they currently are?"** Get your client to picture how things will look if nothing changes. This can create a strong sense of urgency and positions you as the one who can fix it and help your client avoid dealing with the problem longer than necessary.

- **"Is there any reason you wouldn't want to move forward with implementing X?"** It's better to find out now what might prevent the prospective client from moving forward with the project than to wait until you get to the proposal stage. This is the perfect opportunity to answer objections on the phone or in person rather than through a string of emails.

When you're asking these questions, don't be too shy to challenge the prospective client on their responses. The more you dig, the easier it will be to find the core issue. This means that you will be able to help them discover and enjoy an even greater value.

Consulting Tip

Meet with another consultant. Explain value pricing and practice asking questions. Both of you could brainstorm a list of meaningful questions that lead to the results you desire.

When Acme asked these value questions, they gained a much better understanding of why the client wanted to get help with their taxes now, how much money they could save each year, and the amount of time and energy they were currently wasting on their taxes. Combined, these answers gave Acme a very good understanding of the value for the client and allowed them to position their services and offer to deliver great value for the client and an outstanding ROI while earning substantial compensation for their expertise.

Remember: The value conversation takes practice.

Asking these questions may feel uncomfortable at first. However, it not only helps you and the client identify the value they care about, it also ensures you're both aligned on what success looks like. The conversation itself is also a valuable eye opener for the prospective client. By asking thoughtful questions, you will almost always get your clients to think about things they haven't thought of before, as well as see opportunities or dangers they hadn't considered. Therefore, this becomes a valuable conversation for both you and the client.

Putting Value Pricing Into Practice

How can you put a value pricing approach into practice? The art of conducting a value conversation with a buyer hinges greatly on the groundwork you've laid before the interaction takes place. It begins with your proactive efforts to showcase your consulting expertise and demonstrate value even before being introduced to the buyer. Perhaps they had the privilege of witnessing your captivating speaking engagement at a conference, and your insights and knowledge left a lasting impression.

Alternatively, the buyer might have stumbled upon an enlightening article you wrote in a renowned industry publication and instantly recognized your depth of understanding and thought leadership. In another scenario, you could have initiated contact through an online platform, like LinkedIn, going the extra mile to offer a valuable resource tailored to the buyer's needs and interests.

These pre-engagement interactions serve as crucial building blocks that establish a foundation of credibility and trust for a meaningful value conversation between the consultant and the buyer.

Here are some value pricing approaches you can put into practice for your consulting company:

- **Practice the ROI mindset.** When you're hyperfocused on creating value for your clients, it will be reflected in your pricing. Start by highlighting the value your work creates. Consider how you can use your expertise to help your clients:
  - Make money.
  - Achieve better results in less time.
  - Save money or time.
  - Boost emotional well-being or status.
  - Remove stress and problems.
- **Learn to ask meaningful questions.** You can't set a price based on value without having a value conversation built around deep, meaningful questions that uncover the value your client cares about.
- **Present strategic offers.** With value pricing, you don't need to present a single offer. Instead, you should provide multiple options. Clients appreciate choices. Present three options that, respectively, deliver greater value and an increase in price.
- **Practice makes perfect.** Like anything else, value pricing takes practice. You may not get it right on your first try, but don't stop—you will get it to work, and when you do, you'll find that you're able to earn significantly more, often working fewer hours.

Summary

Although there are many ways to grow or improve your consulting business, value pricing is one of the best ways to both raise your fees and provide greater results and value for your clients.

Actions You Can Take Now

- **Understand how you help.** List all the ways that you help your clients save time or money. Identify exploratory questions you could use to start a conversation around these savings.
- **Work it out.** Use the Value Pricing worksheet at td.org/handbook-for -consultants, and begin to think through a plan for how to use this technique.

- **Find one.** Identify one client with whom you could initiate a value-based pricing discussion. Conduct the discussion and evaluate the results. What did you do well? What could you still improve?

About the Author

Michael Zipursky is the co-founder and CEO of Consulting Success, an organization that specializes in helping entrepreneurial consultants grow profitable, scalable, and strategic consulting businesses. He has advised organizations like *Financial Times*, Dow Jones, and RBC, and helped Panasonic launch new products into global markets. Additionally, he's helped more than 850 consultants from around the world in more than 75 industries add six and seven figures to their annual revenues. More than 48,000 consultants read his weekly consulting newsletter. Michael is the author of the Amazon bestsellers *ACT NOW: How Successful Consultants Thrive During Chaos and Uncertainty*, *The Elite Consulting Mind*, and *Consulting Success*. You can learn more about his work and download a consulting blueprint by visiting consultingsuccess.com.

CHAPTER 22

Finding Your Niche

WENDY GATES CORBETT

Before you can find your niche, you have to know what you're looking for. So, what is a niche? There are two parts: what you do and for whom. The *what* is the product or service you offer that solves a problem for your target audience (the *who*). You can also think of it as your special sauce—the unique, amazing solution you provide your clients. The *for whom* is the target market that your product or service is best suited for. This is usually an organization, a group of people, or an individual.

Here are a few examples of niches:

- Connection Catalyst, founded by Chris Coladonato, provides nature-based wellness coaching to individuals who want to reconnect with themselves and others through nature.
- Lighthouse Learning Solutions, owned by Brian Lanza, provides small companies with instructional design and e-learning development for people skills training.
- Signature Presentations, my company, provides employees with simple, actionable ideas to foster a sense of belonging in their workplace communities.

In this chapter, we'll explore the reasons for defining your niche and some ways you can start homing in on the niche you want your business to reside in.

My Niche

I left a long career in technology training to start my first business, Refresher Training, in 2013. My niche was providing slide design services and training for TD professionals. The idea for the business came during a workshop I took with a prominent, seasoned professional. His content was fabulous, but his slides were so carelessly designed—they looked like he'd thrown them together that morning. I was so disappointed by the mediocre quality of his slides, which was such a far cry from the stellar quality of his content, delivery, and reputation. It still upsets me that the poor quality of his slides was the most memorable part of my experience. It stayed with me long after the workshop (Can you tell?), and I realized there was a market for helping trainers make their presentation slides more visually engaging. I could create a company that refreshed training materials (the what) for training professionals (the who) and provided slide design training programs.

After a few years, my niche expanded to include professional speakers, many of whom are also trainers. I loved helping them make their inspiring, motivating messages more meaningful. It was at this point that I rebranded my company as Signature Presentations. As I continued developing relationships with my speaker clients, they began to ask for guidance on crafting their message and on polishing their delivery. Now my what was expanding beyond polishing slides to improving all facets of a speaker's presentation, including messaging, delivery, slides, and handouts.

Then, as I sought to understand the process my speaker clients were going through to prepare a new presentation, I discovered that I was also interested in being a professional keynote speaker. So, I added keynote speaking about belonging and professional presence to my what.

In recent years, I have expanded my niche yet again to include organizational culture and belonging work, which combines keynote speaking, consulting, and training with employees at all levels of an organization. All my niches benefited from a definition process.

Why You Should Define Your Niche

Defining your niche is helpful for both you and your target audience. It provides you with a way to clearly communicate how awesome you are at providing your product or service. Describing what you do and for whom lays the foundation for your website copy, marketing campaigns, social media posts, how you introduce yourself, and all of the ways you tell the world what you do. This, in turn, allows your potential clients to self-identify as your target audience. The more clearly you demonstrate that you understand your audience, the more you will stand out from the competition. By communicating with your target audience using their language, you're telling them, "I know you, I understand your problem, and I have the perfect solution for you." For example, let's say you write a LinkedIn post about your recent project revamping a new-hire orientation program to reflect your client's new hybrid work environment. Someone reading your post may be revamping their own new-hire program and decide to contact you for help.

Time is your most valuable asset, and it is finite. Investing hours in a potential client only to discover that they're not a good fit is frustrating. A clearly defined niche will save you time and effort because you can use it to answer these two questions:

- This is the problem I can solve. Do they have this problem?
- This is my target audience. Are they a member of this audience?

By focusing on a unique product or service that addresses a specific need your targeted audience has, you can become known as an expert in that area. As your knowledge and expertise expands, you establish your credibility as a thought leader in your space. And being recognized as a thought leader will lead to a faster sales cycle—prospective clients will more quickly decide to work with you because they feel like they already know you. This benefits everyone!

Imagine Joe and Maria are friends who work for different companies. Over coffee, they discuss their struggles revamping their new-hire programs. Joe asks Maria, "Do you know anyone who can help us revamp our program?" If you are a generalist without a declared niche, you have a much lower chance of being on her radar.

Misconceptions About Declaring Your Niche

For me, it initially seemed counterintuitive to declare a niche. My first business provided presentation design consulting and training. This meant my initial target market was everyone because everyone needed better, more effective presentation slides. The problem with trying to target everyone, however, is that it's impossible to market to everyone and it's very costly to try.

There are many common misconceptions about choosing a niche. Let's examine three.

1. Declaring My Niche Limits or Restricts My Potential Client Base

Many consultants want to cast a wide net and appeal to a broad audience so they can attract a lot of clients. Unfortunately, trying to reach a broad audience actually does the opposite. Clearly communicating your specific product or service will attract the right audience for your business. And don't forget that your niche is simply your *primary* target audience; it is not your *only* target audience.

When I declared my niche—helping professional speakers make their presentations more memorable—I generated more business, not only with professional speakers, but also other audiences! Much of my new business came from conversations with people who asked, "Do you conduct slide design training for salespeople (or executives or *<fill in the blank with other audiences>*)?"

2. Defining My Niche Will Limit the Kind of Projects I Do

Many consultants like doing a variety of projects. For example, you might enjoy working on instructional design and training delivery. Or maybe you like delivering leadership development and customer service training. A common concern is that by defining your niche, you will only attract opportunities directly related to that area. The truth is, as you become known for what you do, and as you develop relationships with your clients, they will turn to you for additional opportunities, regardless of your niche.

For example, in my belonging consultancy practice, employees are my target audience. My clients, however, have also invited me to consult with their senior leaders, speak at their conferences, and provide training to their employee resource groups. As a result, I get to experience a lot of variety in my projects.

3. Once I Define My Niche, I Will Be Stuck With It Forever

Choosing a niche is a commitment. You are declaring to the world, "This is what I do and for whom I do it." However, it does not mean that you can never choose another one. The talent development field is broad and filled with opportunities.

Think of it this way: Some TD professionals start their career as instructional designers but adjust their path after discovering the joy of training delivery. The same can be true for you as a consultant: Your career path is subject to change—we're all constantly evolving!

Consulting Tip

Ask three consultants you know to define their niches. If they have a niche, can you clearly define what they do? If they don't have a niche, did they use any of these misconceptions as an excuse?

Ways to Define Your Niche

There are countless ways to specialize what you do and for whom. Refer to the examples in Table 22-1 to spark your thinking. For instance, your niche might be providing a blended approach to leadership training and consulting for new frontline managers in the United States.

Table 22-1. Ways to Define Your Niche

Topics or skill sets	Leadership, inclusion, virtual delivery, change management
Demographic	Early career, customer service managers, new managers, senior leaders, students, higher education administrators
Industry	Healthcare, financial services, biotech, government agencies (federal, state, or local)
Development tools	Articulate, Captivate, PowerPoint, Camtasia, Adobe
Delivery modality	In-person instructor-led training (ILT), virtual ILT, e-learning, blended, mentoring, consulting
Content developed	E-learning, ILT materials, facilitator guides, microlearning, videos, job aids
Geographic location	United States, Asia Pacific, Latin America

So, how do you actually determine your niche? Let's review a few approaches for identifying your niche. Some of these involve going outside yourself by talking with others or searching the internet; other approaches involve going within to look for answers.

Identify What You Enjoy

Identify the skills, passions, expertise, and interests you thoroughly enjoy. Think about your favorite aspects of your current job, as well as your previous positions. This exploration can help you identify some natural areas and audiences to serve as your niche.

Ask yourself these questions:

- What do I most enjoy doing in those roles?
- What tasks or projects do I dread?
- Who do I enjoy working with?
- Who do I work well with?

For example, when Chris Coladonato started Connection Catalyst, she initially planned to do what she had done in a prior corporate role: Help leaders cultivate productive, supportive virtual and hybrid teams. She was great at it! It seemed like a no-brainer decision. In fact, it was a no-brainer decision. But, even though Chris was an expert in hybrid teams, the idea of spending more time helping organizations tackle their hybrid and remote team challenges drained her. Maybe it wasn't a no-brainer after all?

So she asked herself where she found the most joy in her day. The answer was in nature. When Chris really thought about it, she realized how much happier, healthier, and clearer she felt when she took time to reconnect with herself in natural settings. As a result of time spent outdoors, she had more clarity and focus, and she was more productive. This revelation led her to refocus her business from helping hybrid teams to helping others reconnect with themselves in nature for self-restoration and renewal.

It's not enough to identify what you like to do or what you're good at. Your niche needs to include a solution to a problem your target audience has. Take your exploration a step further to make sure what you like to do actually solves a problem or addresses a need. Ask yourself:

- What types of challenges am I the go-to person for?
- What advice do people come to me for?
- What problems or challenges do I like tackling?
- What problems am I most successful at solving?

Research Your Market

It doesn't matter how great you are at solving a problem that no one has. Part of finding your niche is identifying any unmet needs that you can address, which will help you determine the demand for your solution. To find out what kinds of problems your target audience is experiencing, you'll need to do some market research.

Let's look at five ways to do market research:

- **Have conversations with trusted colleagues, friends, and advisors in your network.** Ask for their perspective on how prevalent the market is for your niche.
- **Do an internet search using keywords related to your niche.**
  - The volume of search results is an indicator of its popularity. For example, as an organization consultant focused on belonging, I did keyword searches on "organization culture," "disengagement at work," and "psychological safety at work." There were millions of matching results—including

companies, blog articles, videos, podcasts, and news articles—which confirmed a significant audience was also searching for those topics.

- ○ You'll find the names of companies and individuals who are associated with your niche. This gives you an idea of your competition, potential collaborators or partners, and how you can differentiate yourself.

- **Explore your competition.** Who is already doing what you want to do? Review their websites, read their blogs, follow their social media posts, and check out articles published on LinkedIn. Examining what others are doing in your space can help you generate ideas for differentiating your solution so it stands out.

- **Read industry reports and data from established, trusted professional organizations for insights into current and future trends.** For example, ATD's *State of the Industry* report reviews annual trends in talent development, such as spending and priorities. This data offers insights into where your potential clients are spending their budgets and what their priorities are.

- **Review conference agendas for session topics and presenters.** Conference selection committees choose sessions based on their promise to offer effective solutions to today's challenges. Look closely at each session's description and learning objectives to see how they relate to your niche. You may uncover solutions that are already out there, which will give you more details for how to differentiate yourself and your solution.

Ask the Right Questions

Defining your niche often involves asking and answering thought- and insight-provoking questions of yourself and others, including trusted colleagues and potential clients. Your trusted colleagues will have insights about your skills, talents, and superpowers that you don't see.

Ask yourself and them:

- What do I love doing?
- What could I do all day long, even if I wasn't getting paid?
- What problems or challenges do I get excited about solving?
- What unique talents do I enjoy putting to use?
- What problems or challenges have I solved using my expertise that I would love to help others solve?

Next, speak with people in your network—especially members of the target audience you are considering. Have conversations with them, or use surveys or polls to get more information about your potential path.

Ask them one or more of the following questions:

- What work challenges are keeping you up at night?
- What is the biggest problem you're facing right now that, if resolved, would bring you the greatest relief?
- Is [*the problem you want to solve*] a problem you're facing right now?
  - If they say, "No, I've resolved the problem," follow up by asking, "How did you solve it?" Find out if the problem was sufficiently resolved or if other issues have surfaced.
  - If they say, "Yes, this is still a problem," follow up by asking, "Where does this challenge fall on your list of priorities?"
- Are there other challenges related to [*the problem you want to solve*] that you're currently facing?
- What related challenges do you see arising in the next 12 to 18 months?

Because I frequently speak at conferences, I was concerned how conference organizers and meeting planners would interpret my decision to transition from presentation design to belonging consulting. Would they assume I was simply trying to capitalize on the trendy diversity, equity, inclusion, and belonging (DEIB) topic? I needed some advice and reassurance, so I reached out to my friend Bridget, a conference planner I've known for years. I shared my concerns and asked for her candid perspective. In addition to cheering me on for following my soul's calling, Bridget saw my transition as an evolution and reassured me that others would likely see it that way too. She reminded me that as TD professionals, we are all about developing people, including ourselves! Her perspective, as someone in the industry, was incredibly helpful.

Summary

This chapter provides you with ways to define your niche. This may be one of the most important things you can do to guarantee your consulting practice is a success. If you identify a niche that truly represents you and what you enjoy, it will show up in your business results—your clients' success and yours. Remember to get others involved as you address this important aspect of starting your business.

Actions You Can Take Now

- **Take a first shot.** Brainstorm two or three ways you could fill in these blanks to start defining your niche: I do [*this—the solution*] for [*whom—your target audience*].
- **Use the power of questions.** Identify two or three people to ask the questions in the 10 Questions to Find Your Niche worksheet at td.org/handbook-for -consultants. Reach out to trusted colleagues, potential clients, and professionals in the space you want to enter.
- **Go to a conference.** Find a conference related to your niche. Review the keynote and breakout session descriptions. Look at who is speaking, what their topics are, and how the topics differ from your niche.

About the Author

Wendy Gates Corbett, CPTD, is an organization consultant, international keynote speaker, and belonging researcher. She works with employees at all levels to foster belonging in their own workplace communities with simple research-based practices. As president of Signature Presentations, she is a recognized talent development leader and a past member of the international board of directors for the Association of Talent Development. Wendy holds a BS in psychology and an MS in industrial and organizational psychology. In addition to speaking, training, and executive consulting, she serves as an adjunct professor of management and leadership at Duke University. You can learn more by visiting her websites, wendygatescorbett.com and signature-presentations.com.

It's All About Marketing

HALELLY AZULAY

Many consultants never think about marketing until something goes wrong. The company that was your bread and butter has just been bought out by its competitor. The person who hired you to conduct an organizational assessment was offered a better job and the new guy wants to bring in his own consultant. The market has taken a downward turn and your regular clients aren't calling you. . . . Guess it's time to think about marketing.

Instead of thinking of it as a "break in case of emergency" to-do item, you should always be thinking about marketing. And not just marketing your business—marketing yourself. Defining your expertise and establishing your credibility are important business activities that bring you a steady flow of prospects. Being visible via your inbound marketing activities helps your ideal clients discover you, fall in love with you, and decide to spend their money on your services. Your online presence (website and social media assets), your in-person presence (networking and speaking efforts), and your inbox presence (regular, proactive email interactions) are all a critical part of your future success. Ignore them and you'll be forgotten at best, ignored or rejected at worst. Nurture and develop them and you'll reap the rewards in greater client exposure and conversion.

In this chapter, you'll see how marketing is tied to your image, why you must be deliberate about your image, and how to build your brand success. Your branding needs to be intentional. This chapter shares several effective strategies you can use develop your brand.

Branding and Thought Leadership: Expert Credibility and Visibility

Many professionals make the mistake of believing that their work will speak for itself. They keep their heads down, produce quality results, and hope that the word will get out and new opportunities will appear.

But that's not how the world works. Rather than word spreading about their work, they remain a best-kept secret and miss out on some amazing opportunities. If you think branding and thought leadership are contrived, insincere, or unappealing, you may need to work on changing your mindset before you can become a truly successful consultant.

Word-of-mouth marketing and referrals are a great source for finding new clients, but you can't count on only that—especially if you want to grow your consulting business. You must actively engage in marketing all the time, especially when you're busy with work; otherwise, your client spigot will run dry, and you won't have primed the pump with any new connections or leads. Plus, you'll miss opportunities if you don't share your brilliance with the world in a proactive way. The people who need your help will either not know about you or forget you exist when the time comes. This means you must take the initiative to stay visible. You need to proactively pursue branding and thought leadership as the long game.

Before moving on, let's define *brand* and *thought leadership*. Here's what a few experts say about the concept of a brand:

- "A brand is a name, term, design, symbol, or any other feature that identifies one seller's good or service as distinct from those of other sellers." —American Marketing Association
- "Your brand is a perception or emotion, maintained by somebody other than you, that describes the total experience of having a relationship with you." —David McNally and Karl D. Speak, *Be Your Own Brand*
- "[Your brand is] how people see you, feel you, understand you, and make assumptions about you when you are not in the room." —Marc Ecko, *Unlabel*

What about thought leadership? *Thought leadership* is a way to add value by sharing more of your expertise with more people using a variety of channels and media. It's what takes you from just being an expert to being someone who people think of when a topic is mentioned because they believe that you possess a clear and dominant point of view.

Very few ideas are truly original. However, thought leaders use language and style to articulate their perspectives in a new way. They harness multiple platforms to reach a broad audience. Thought leadership is a combination of expertise, voice, visibility, and reach for brand recognition.

Creating Your Brand

The good news is that your brand is constantly being made and remade. The bad news is that you're adding to or subtracting from your brand all the time with everything you do, say, write, project, or express.

You already have a brand. The question is, are you aware of it and do you own it? What are you doing that helps your brand? And what consistent and clear message are you transmitting about yourself by how you dress? Treat others? Ask (or don't ask) questions? Carry yourself? Perform your work? Sign your email? Respond to inquiries or requests?

Your Current Brand Assets

Implicitly or explicitly, you are constantly conveying information to the world about who you are and what you have to offer. Are you quantifying your many assets, growing them, and being intentional about communicating them to your potential and current clients?

Brand assets include your knowledge and information, strengths, skills, values, experiences, mindset and approach to learning and change, qualifications, social networks and relationships, credibility, mentors, good habits, and what you share online. Spend some time increasing your own awareness of your brand assets and how you might grow and express them more proactively. You will find downloadable worksheets at td.org/handbook-for-consultants to reference as you work to improve your branding techniques.

Also, remember that your clients and prospects are a part of your brand story—either as brand ambassadors or brand destroyers.

Brand Levers

How do you communicate your brand? While brand assets are the content of your brand, *brand levers* are the mechanisms you use to share your brand with those who could benefit from your services and become your ideal clients. They include your social media posts, your blog posts, and even your introduction when meeting someone new. What levers can you pull to get your message out there? How can you change or grow what you're doing now? Begin by creating taglines and crafting your elevator speech:

- **Taglines.** Develop a short tagline that describes what your business does in terms of the benefits, the value you create, and the results you produce. Look at taglines for your favorite brands to find inspiration and ideas. For example, the tagline for my company, TalentGrow, is "developing leaders that people want to follow." Taglines can be used in many places including your website, your media profile, and after your email signature.

- **Elevator speech.** Also known as an *elevator pitch*, the *elevator speech* is a short memorable introduction. It's called an elevator speech because it should last no longer than an elevator ride from one floor to the next. It readily answers the question, "What do you do?" or "What is your company all about?" in a meaningful way so the listener can formulate a follow up question. The elevator speech should also be compelling enough to keep them asking questions to learn more about you and your business. You could use something similar to your tagline, but add a little more detail and make it a complete sentence or two. Your elevator speech should be short and sweet, informative, and interesting, and infused with your personality to make it more compelling.

Your Biggest Brand Barrier

One of the biggest brand barriers I've seen is your own mindset. Many new consultants fail to toot their own horn or hustle in their off hours to create content or amplify their ideas and thoughts. (Or perhaps they don't know this is something they need to do?) Brand development and amplification take effort and confidence. Some people believe or hope that it's not necessary, whether because they don't want to do the work or because they're shy or feel like an impostor.

The latter feelings bring thoughts like "Who am I? What do I have to add? Why should I speak out about this? There's probably lots of people who know so much more about this than I do." Unfortunately, this kind of thinking gets in your way. Bestselling author Brené Brown has written and spoken about this kind of fear and playing small or being plagued by impostor syndrome. She suggests that rather than asking, "Who am I to think that I can do *X, Y,* and *Z?*" the real question you should ask is, "Who am I *not* to think that I have gifts to be able to share with the world?" If you've been working in an organization for a long time, it may have been a while since you heard anyone say how fantastic you are because you've been too busy just working.

There are other barriers to developing your brand too. Take a minute to identify any barriers that are getting in your way of building a personal brand and establishing your thought leadership. Then, brainstorm ways to overcome them.

Brand Development

Brand development requires intention and focus. Take some time to reflect on what you know and who needs to hear it. Begin to identify your target audience. Then, look for anyone who is connected to that audience because you'll want to build a community of people who can cheer you on and champion you as you build and amplify your thought leadership. You don't need to do it alone.

Make sure you're intentionally conveying the right brand to your ideal clients. Leverage the tools and techniques we've discussed here. Which levers have you tried? Which ones will you try in the future?

Sharing Your Brand

Once you've established what your brand is, your next task is to share it with the world. You can do this through many marketing strategies, including networking, content marketing, search engine optimization (SEO), your website, and social media.

Networking

Many people think networking is a waste of time. It's collecting business cards you'll never use. It's schmoozing and brownnosing, and no one likes a fake who does that. However, you've got the wrong mindset if you think networking lacks purpose, and you're probably missing out on some incredible opportunities.

I define *networking* as building and maintaining long-term, mutually beneficial relationships. While I would not consider a superficial, one-off transactional interaction or a one-sided conversation to be networking, you also never know when these experiences can transcend into long-term relationships. So it's always good to put in the effort.

Networking can bring enormous value to your success and that of your clients and colleagues. It builds your relationships and opens new channels for information, resources, ideas, and business possibilities. Plus, it connects you with potential clients and reconnects you with existing ones.

Networking allows you to add value beyond what you can do alone, thus growing your influence and the impact of your work. It's one of the most useful ways for both new and experienced business owners to survive and thrive in the marketplace and in client organizations that are inherently political and socially interconnected. One of the keys to more fulfilling and effective networking is having the right mindset.

Here are a few more things to enhance your networking strategy:

- **Adopt an abundance mentality instead of a scarcity mindset.** Networking is full of possibilities rather than a zero-sum game of winners and losers. Share your knowledge, ideas, and time with others generously, and in return, you will generate more knowledge, ideas, and opportunities in direct and indirect ways.

- **Use the trader principle.** By adopting a trader principle approach—seeking to create an equitable (win-win) value exchange over time—the value you offer in any relationship will always be equal or greater in exchange for the value you receive. The value of what each person offers to trade is measured from the receiver's perspective, and it can include many things, such as time, input, gratitude, recognition, feedback, appreciation, introductions, and opportunities.

- **Give first and give often.** Noted organizational psychologist Adam Grant suggests that those who give without the direct expectation of any reciprocation are often found at the top of the success ladder. Conversely, those who take more than they give don't experience lasting success. Be a giver.

- **Small habits make a big difference over time.** Networking, in this context, can be a collection of small actions that you can habituate in ways that don't require a big investment of time or energy. It does not have to be a huge gesture. It can be as small as making an introduction, sending a thank-you note, or reaching out to see how someone is doing today.

Consulting Tip

All consultants understand the idea of asking current clients for referrals, but few follow through. Ask early—you don't need to wait until the end of a project. As long as you are not planning to work with their strongest competitor, clients are usually happy to provide a referral.

Networking has helped me in undeniable ways, and it can help you too if you consciously engage with the right mindset using practical strategies. Mutual benefit must exist, so consider what you can offer others. Your value proposition could be your skills, connections, ideas, energy and enthusiasm, or many other things. The clearer you are about these factors, the better your chances of successfully networking. Just make sure to think strategically. You're always going to leave an impression—like it or not. It's up to you whether the impression or brand you create is intentional (by design) or unintentional (by default).

Inbound Marketing

Seth Godin created the term *inbound marketing* in 1999. It is a strategy to manage marketing by bringing customers to you rather than seeking them out using traditional marketing techniques like advertising, cold calling, and direct mail. With inbound marketing, you instead attract customers using content marketing, SEO, and branding.

The are many benefits of inbound marketing, including:

- Building trust and credibility
- Enhancing your professional brand
- Generating social proof
- Increasing your visibility, reach, and exposure
- Demonstrating generosity and triggering the reciprocity effect
- Showcasing your expertise
- Building a group of raving fans and champions

For now, we'll focus on *content marketing*, which is creating, publishing, and disseminating helpful content online (such as articles, blog posts, videos, or podcasts) to a targeted audience to create brand awareness, attract potential clients, and convert leads into clients. Bestselling author and social media expert Gary Vaynerchuk (2013) suggests using content marketing to "jab, jab, jab, right hook." In other words, give away free, useful, generous content several times before ever trying to ask for anything in return and always giving much more than you ask.

The possibilities are plentiful and growing all the time. Here are just a few of the content marketing and thought leadership channels that are available to you:

- Writing blog posts, newsletters, articles for social media such as LinkedIn or Medium, articles in industry magazines, or books
- Speaking in a conference breakout session, at a chapter meeting for a professional association, in a TEDx or TED-style talk, or in a webinar
- Audio such as podcasts, radio shows, or an audiobook
- Video such as a video post or live broadcast you host on YouTube, Facebook, Instagram, or other social media sites

- Media use including TV interviews, podcasts, radio show interviews, or being mentioned in a media article (try HARO)
- Hosting a peer-led mastermind group, a mastermind dinner or CEO roundtable, a Facebook group, and networking groups, events, and meetups
- Interviewing others for articles in publications (such as ATD Links) or on social media sites
- Sharing others' content directly (via email or word of mouth) in your social media channels, liking and commenting on others' content, or answering questions and commenting in online discussion forums found on LinkedIn, Facebook groups, and Quora.

Email Is King

With changes in algorithms and entire platforms disappearing, social media should not be the main focus for your client communication or marketing. The most important tool, the one that converts better than all the others, is email. That's why every entrepreneur must make it a priority to collect email addresses for all current and potential clients. Then, you should keep in touch with these people through consistent, relevant email communication.

For example, recent changes to the Facebook algorithm caused posts from Facebook business pages (which you should have) to only reach 2 percent of their followers—and even that number has been steadily declining for years (Wagner 2021). You need to spend money on ads (whose costs are increasing) to actually get your content seen by anyone who has opted in to view your content on Facebook. But emails are delivered to your contact list reliably, and if you create compelling messages and subject lines, you'll get much better open rates.

In short, don't invest all your time and money building an audience on someone else's platform—it's like building houses on someone else's land. You own your email list and will forever. LinkedIn owns its platform and could change its rules or shut its doors tomorrow—if that happened, your followers and connections would go away too.

Consulting Tip

Create an email address that points to your dedicated domain name (like halelly@talentgrow.com) instead of using something generic, like gmail.com or outlook.com. This instantly creates a more professional image.

I suggest collecting email addresses as soon as possible—even before you launch your business. Nurture that list by sending consistent, targeted updates and useful information to keep them opening your emails. It's easier to build trust and credibility over time. Then, when you have an offer to make, you're more likely to reach them and find them interested and open to working with you.

> **Consulting Tip**
>
> Spacing your emails at consistent time intervals is important. However, know your audience and the purpose of your email campaign. Emails that lack a purpose and occur too frequently can be a turnoff to your audience.

Your Web Presence Is Queen

If email is king, your website is queen of your online presence and your access to your current and potential client base. This is your first impression for current and would-be clients, members of the media, and anyone else searching for your kind of services or your subject matter expertise. A website is essentially a virtual brochure sharing information about your company, who you are, and what you offer. It's a place to house any free content, such as your blog, podcast, or other content marketing assets. You want to make a good impression to get them interested, and then keep them on your site by providing compelling content and a positive experience.

According to online marketing experts, your website's number 1 job is to capture the email addresses of your potential customers using a lead magnet offering; that is, giving away something your ideal clients would find of great value in exchange for sharing their names and email addresses. Also called "opt-ins," lead magnets can be an e-book, a PDF download, a video tutorial, a mini e-course, checklists, templates, and more. Use your imagination—but even better, observe and ask your ideal clients what problems you can help them solve immediately, and then offer something for free that does that. They'll be glad to give you their email addresses and once they do, you can continue nurturing the connection and converting them to paying clients.

Remember, most people who are seeking the type of solution you provide won't be ready to make a purchase decision the first time they land on your site. So, while your website can convert leads into sales, your focus should be on building trust and credibility, educating visitors about what you can do, and then nurturing that connection and building that trust. This is what will eventually convert them into clients.

Your site should convey an image of your brand that is consistent and designed to appeal to your ideal clients. It should look professional and clean, but it doesn't have to be expensive—especially not when you're just starting out. And it must be mobile-optimized. Many, if not most, web searches are now conducted on mobile devices, and Google actually *punishes* sites that are not mobile-optimized by demoting them in the search results algorithm (if not completely removing them from the results list).

But don't worry! There are lots of website building platforms that allow you to create a beautiful and functional website for very little money and with little to no web design skills. Just don't compromise so much that your website looks amateurish because it will inhibit your potential buyers. That amateur image will be projected onto you and your services as well.

Consulting Tip

Choose a dedicated domain URL as soon as possible. Today is not too early to begin looking.

As your business and revenue grow, you can invest in a more elaborate website with more bells and whistles. However, you always want to make sure your website is logical, simple, and user friendly, with a consistent layout throughout. On the current version of my website, I minimized the number of pages to make it easy for visitors to find content. It's also important that you maintain control of your website so you can easily make changes and updates yourself; otherwise, make sure your web designer is able to make changes quickly and inexpensively.

SEO

What do you do when you have a problem? Most likely, you go to the internet to search for the right information or solution provider. Your potential clients do this too. The goal is to have your website or social media accounts rank as highly as possible on the search results. How does this happen?

Most search engines have an algorithm that determines what websites they offer as a match for each search query. Then, they'll offer about 10 sites on each page of results. The narrower your niche, the fewer competitors you likely have, and therefore you'll probably rank higher on the results. The more common your service, however, the more likely you'll get buried in a sea of comparable providers.

Optimizing your website and other content marketing for your keywords is one way to increase your chances of being featured on the right search results and gaining prominence. Figure out which main keywords your potential clients are using when searching the type of services you offer. Once you've pinned those keywords down, use them in the body, titles, and even meta tags of all your website pages and published content. Search engine crawlers will find those keywords on your website, and their algorithms will see you as an expert or a good fit for any searches with keywords that match yours.

Consulting Tip

You can learn more about SEO optimization from free online courses at HubSpot Academy or by downloading Google's SEO Starter Guide. Other websites such as Moz and Backlinko also offer information about SEO.

Marketing in the Era of Social Media

Social media is a general name for a variety of digital content sharing and networking platforms. Specific platforms come and go, but the biggest platforms for most business-to-business service providers (including TD consulting businesses like yours) are LinkedIn, X (formerly Twitter), and Facebook. You should also consider creating accounts on YouTube for sharing video content, Instagram for sharing quick video stories and graphics-based content, and Pinterest for sharing graphic-based content such as quotes.

To fully leverage these platforms, offer helpful content that is not just your own, generate engagement with your content, and engage with others' content by liking, commenting, and sharing. You can join or host groups on LinkedIn and Facebook that provide a space for interacting with others around a shared interest. Such groups offer the opportunity to build community, provide support to others, and showcase your expertise in a way that is generous and not salesy or pushy. Many groups even have community rules around not sharing sales pitches or being self-promotional, so be sure to read and honor any ground rules.

Leverage a social media management tool such as Hootsuite or Buffer to make sharing content less taxing. But remember, social networking requires actual engagement and interaction, not just pushing out content in a one-sided transaction. Sometimes it's better to just choose one or two platforms where your potential clients hang out and focus your energy on interacting there, rather than trying to have a presence on all of them.

> **Consulting Tip**
>
> As you consider which social media platforms you'll leverage, remember to maintain the benefits and minimize the drawbacks.

Build a social media habit with boundaries by budgeting a portion of each day—perhaps 15 minutes in the morning and 15 minutes in the afternoon—to monitoring your platforms. This will ensure that you don't get sucked into a social media rabbit hole and find yourself wasting precious time with no ROI to show for it.

Stay on the Cutting Edge

Tech tools, software, apps, media platforms, and gadgets continue to morph. It seems like new ones come on the market daily if not hourly. It can be daunting to keep up. Find a curation source you can turn to regularly for trustworthy updates on the latest and greatest tools and technology. Some read *Wired* magazine; others turn to websites like Mashable or listen to podcasts focused on such topics. While you shouldn't obsess about it, you also don't want to get left in the dark and miss out on opportunities to innovate and stay ahead of the curve. For example, how are you using ChatGPT?

In addition to tech tools, make sure to stay current on new research and changes in your field of expertise—as well as other related fields that share trends and opportunities—so you can prepare yourself and your clients for them. Subscribe to blogs, podcasts, and YouTube channels, and follow great curators on social media to see what they're reading and sharing, what they recommend, and what they're buzzing about.

Inbound Marketing Tools and Resources

Email and Client Contact Management Tools

Email services—like MailChimp, MailerLite, Constant Contact, HubSpot, and ConvertKit—are either free or cost a nominal monthly fee and provide analytics, ways to segment and tag your email list, and tools for creating a variety of email campaigns (including regular weekly or monthly newsletters, nurture campaigns, and one-off special offer messages).

Website Building Tools

Two of the most popular tools for building websites are WordPress (which offers predesigned themes) and Squarespace (which offers predesigned templates). Make sure to set up your website to have a dedicated domain URL, rather than one that shows the hosting platform name in the domain (which often happens when people opt for cheaper options like Wix). The latter looks amateurish.

SEO and Keyword Research Tools

Check out LongTailPro, Ahrefs, or Semrush for ideas about long-tail search terms that you might be able to leverage.

Social Media Graphics Creation Tools

Canva and Pablo are two programs for easily creating shareable graphic memes or cards.

Social Media Management Tools

Buffer, Hootsuite, MeetEdgar, Zoho, and ContentStudio are just a few of the tools available to help you share the same content to multiple social media channels simultaneously. (In other words, you publish once and the tools push the content out at the ideal times and frequency native to each platform—it doesn't have to be synchronous.) This can save you a lot of time and allows you to be present on multiple social media channels, which increases your reach and exposure.

Summary

Internet marketing has its place—as long as you remember that it is good for marketing but not for selling. You can have a blog, 10,000 followers on LinkedIn, and a regular presence on Facebook, but you still need to find a way to take the last step—you need to close the sale. And that rarely happens online.

Try these closing thoughts to most effectively market your consulting business and get yourself in front of the decision makers:

- Maintain a presence on both Facebook and LinkedIn, where four of five users drive decision making.
- Turn likes into leads by determining where your audience hangs out—explore Instagram, X, and other social media sites.
- Follow at least a dozen thought leaders in consulting or your area of expertise.
- Listen to your audience's issues and concerns and provide value.
- Experiment with premium content that solves your potential clients' problems.
- To be successful, blogging is a weekly commitment. The payoff is that it positions you as the expert, builds a following, and helps to raise your profile. Consistency is key.
- Provide a way to drive traffic from your social media platform to your website. For example, if you advertise on Facebook, focus on getting people to visit your website to download a free whitepaper.

Actions You Can Take Now

- **Write your elevator speech.** This short memorable introduction to your consulting company says what you do, for whom, and why in two or three sentences. It should evoke questions from your listeners and encourage them to continue the conversation.
- **Build your brand.** Think of three to five of your brand role models. Why do you hold each as a role model? Now think of company brands that you admire and why you admire them. What important branding insights can you bring to your brand building efforts? What is your desired brand as a consultant? Who is the most important audience that your brand needs to compel?

About the Author

Halelly Azulay is a leadership development strategist at TalentGrow, a consulting company she founded in 2006 to develop leaders who people want to follow. She has published two books, *Employee Development on a Shoestring* and *Strength to Strength*, and is a contributing author to numerous books about talent development, including *ATD's Handbook for Training and Talent Development* and *The Art and Science of Training*. Halelly offers actionable leadership insights on her blog and podcast, the *TalentGrow Show*, where she has interviewed such legends as Daniel Pink, Beverly Kaye, and Elliott Masie. She published the popular LinkedIn Learning courses "Leveraging Your Strengths" and "10 Mistakes Leaders Should Avoid." In 2019, she partnered with Elaine Biech to create the online course "Building Your Successful Consulting Business" for new and aspiring consultants. Halelly and Elaine Biech also started the Consultant Connection to provide consultants with peer support and networking opportunities at the start of the pandemic. Learn more about Halelly's work at talentgrow.com.

Consummate Consultative Selling

JOE TRUEBLOOD

A true consummate sales professional helps others achieve their desired outcomes. It is never about selling someone something they do not need or want. Instead, consummate sales professionals enable client organizations to make informed decisions relative to what they buy and with whom they work to successfully address their business needs. In this way, the role of the consummate sales professional and that of a consultant are quite similar. Consultants also offer advice and expertise to client organizations to help them improve their business performance, and this often occurs through sales conversations between the consultant and client.

I have had the good fortune to lead many high-performing sales teams and led the Americas in a multibillion-dollar global sales performance improvement company. In this capacity, I've been able to access several research studies that were conducted on the top performing sales organizations worldwide displaying what works when selling. In 2006, I founded my company to assist clients in growing their businesses through selling. In this chapter, I'll share what I've learned about selling and what will work for you.

Before You Can Sell, Do Your Homework

Successfully selling your products and services—your expertise—first requires you to complete a market analysis. A detailed assessment of the organizations that are best suited to derive value from your services, your market analysis should be both qualitative and quantitative. The quantitative piece estimates your number of prospective clients, which helps determine the size of the business opportunity; for example, the number of businesses within a defined geography and vertical market. The qualitative piece is used to evaluate which prospective clients would be more conducive to the value proposition. You might ask, "Does the value proposition have a higher rate of success in certain industries?" Manufacturing, finance, retail, or pharmaceuticals are a few examples. From this list of target clients, you will create a primary, secondary, and tertiary grouping so you can limit your focus while also maintaining the knowledge of your full market potential. You should identify and focus on only the industries and types of organizations that are best suited to receive value from your offerings.

Next, evaluate the competitive landscape to identify your direct and indirect competitors. This will help you determine your competitive differentiator, your value proposition, and your distinct point of view. In other words, why would a client choose you versus one of your competitors? Differentiation is always challenging, so knowing you can't be all things to all people is key. Asking clients why they chose to work with you may prove invaluable in refining your message to the marketplace and acquiring new clients.

Once you've decided which organizations to focus on and how to differentiate yourself, you'll need to consider all the potential business issues your services will address. Think of a *business issue* as any work-related problem, opportunity, trend, goal, strategy, mandate, change, or state of affairs that people in an organization want to address, need to address, or should be addressing.

Most business issues fall into one of three categories:

- **External**—events outside organizational boundaries over which the organization has little to no control. A few examples are inflation, interest rates, employment level, federal or state laws, increased competition, consumer demand, and the overall state of the economy.
- **Organizational**—internal events affecting the organization as a whole. These issues have implications or consequences in various organizational functions. A few examples include reorganization, mergers, profitability, productivity, market share, new objectives, goals, and targets.
- **Functional**—issues that must be addressed by people at a functional level; for example:
  ° Manufacturing could involve improving quality control, reducing unit costs, increasing productivity, or controlling expenses.

- ◦ Sales could involve increasing sales volume, client satisfaction, or account penetration or onboarding.
- ◦ Marketing could involve developing new products, differentiating products, advertising, or social media.

Be sure to align your website, social media, marketing, and sales collateral to create a consistent message around your value proposition and the business issues your organization can successfully address to support your business development efforts. This alignment will help set your business up for success when you begin engaging with clients and selling your products and services.

Client Relationship Process

Consultative selling is based on creating and using an overarching client relationship process that enables you to consistently interact with your clients. You'll need to make this detailed process second nature—from how you initially earn the right to do business with a client to how you nurture and maintain a mutually beneficial long-term relationship. And each phase must be defined, including client expectations and key activities (what, why, and how).

Consulting Tip

Do not mistake technology for the client relationship process itself—your approach for working with clients to establish a mutually beneficial relationship will always produce a consistently superior experience. It's more than a sales process. It is an organization-wide approach to meeting and exceeding client expectations from initial contact to closing a sale to successful implementation and follow-on work.

I've shared the client or customer relationship process I devised for my business in Figure 24-1. (A quick internet search will result in other examples.) Let's look closer at each phase in my process. As we review each one, I'll share the phase goals, as well as client expectations and key activities. I've also included a fictionalized example from my work with XYZ Company to further your understanding.

Figure 24-1. Amplify Growth's Customer Relationship Process

Phase 1. Earn the Right and Build Trust

In phase 1, you want to learn about the client's most critical business needs, establish a mutual purpose for continuing, and agree on next action steps. Communicate your results-oriented approach in a manner that piques the client's interest, meets them where they are, inspires confidence, and creates a positive impression.

- Goal: Client agrees to move forward and allow a deeper exploration of their needs.
- Client expectations:
  ○ Did you demonstrate your knowledge of the client's business, industry, outlook, and trends, as well as their culture and political and social environment?

- ° Did you provide an agenda, ask for input, and seek permission to continue the conversation?
- ° Did you build trust and confidence and create credibility?
- Key activities:
  - ° Before meeting with the prospect, research the client organization, industry, and current trends.
  - ° Define meeting objectives.
  - ° Create an agenda and map out the dialogue and questions you will use to uncover the client's business issues, the circumstances involved, and potential next steps.

For example, my initial research following these steps indicated that XYZ Company, a multinational retail organization, needed interviewing and selection assistance.

Phase 2. Analyze and Gain Agreement on Business Issues

Next, exchange information to develop a clear, complete, and mutual understanding of the client's needs and requirements for an effective solution. Agree on the gaps between what is and what could be, and then further qualify the viability of the opportunity.

- Goal: Reach agreement on needs, decision-making criteria, and next action steps.
- Client expectations:
  - ° Did you demonstrate insight through analysis?
  - ° Did you consider all existing information and develop a complete picture of the situation and challenges?
  - ° Did you exhibit behavior that helped build trust, confidence, and credibility?
  - ° Did you recap the discussion to ensure mutual agreement on needs, circumstances, prioritization, and appropriate next steps?
  - ° Did you establish the next meeting date and time?
- Key activities:
  - ° Interview the prospect to determine their vision, objectives, and requirements.
  - ° Gather information on the prospect's structure, decision-making process, capabilities, budget, and other important factors.

° Analyze, interpret, and synthesize information to determine the gap between the current and desired state.

° Determine the scope and type of initiative to successfully address the gap.

° Ensure mutual understanding.

It may take more than one business meeting to move from phase 2 to phase 3. For example, upon further analysis of XYZ Company, I found that the extremely high employee turnover rate was due to a leadership issue that went from the top of the organization all the way down to the store manager level. Always ensure that you have determined the specific needs of the organization in phase 2 before moving on. The prospective client may try to move you to phase 3 before you are ready—do not fall into this trap.

Phase 3. Develop and Agree on Solutions

Once you've progressed from phase 2, you'll collaborate with the prospective client to develop a mutually agreed-on solution. This might mean creating an implementation process to plan for and address the client's business needs and desired levels of improvement.

- Goal: Client accepts your recommendation and agrees to work with you.
- Client expectations:
  ° Did you design solutions that clearly link to the mutually agreed-on business needs?
  ° Did you present credible, practical solutions in an easy-to-understand format?
  ° Did you provide a proposed work plan including process steps and key milestones?
  ° Did you gain commitment from key stakeholders?
- Key activities:
  ° Plan your recommendation to ensure you have identified all stakeholders and the business and personal needs of each one.
  ° Prepare your presentation with each stakeholder in mind and share a draft proposal outline with the key stakeholder to ensure you are on the right track.
  ° Present your recommendation to the stakeholders and gain agreement to work together.

XYZ Company and I followed these steps and mutually agreed that the solution was to address interpersonal communication skills and behavior modification training. We also agreed that coaching was required.

Phase 4. Communicate and Implement

Phase 4 is when you'll communicate, execute, and support the implementation plan to ensure the client's ownership and the agreed-on solution are fulfilled in such a way that they achieve the results the client values. This phase isn't over until both you and the client fulfill your respective commitments.

- Goal: Client says, "Delivered as agreed."
- Client expectations:
  - Did you communicate the implementation plan to all client stakeholders in all locations?
  - Did you execute an implementation plan that includes performance standards?
  - Did you support the client with any logistics and reinforcement issues that may have developed?
  - Did you provide consistent messaging and assist in marketing the implementation internally?
  - Were you flexible and prepared to respond to the unexpected?
- Key activities:
  - Plan the implementation rollout, including the vision, messaging, scheduling and required resources, and logistics.
  - Establish a process for monitoring progress.
  - Gain final clarification about invoicing, travel, and business expenses.

XYZ Company and I agreed on an implementation plan in which we started by training and coaching the executive team and then worked down to the store manager level.

Phase 5. Demonstrate Success

In phase 5, collaborate with the client to analyze agreed-on outcomes and milestones, and, if necessary, adjust the plan to ensure you deliver the desired results.

- Goal: Client says, "We can clearly see the results, and we value this relationship."

- Client expectations:
  - Did you assist the client in analyzing and interpreting the results of the agreed-on milestones?
  - Did you help measure the success of the implementation?
  - Did you assist with any benchmarking?
  - If needed, did you develop action plans for adjusting the process?
- Key activity:
  - Collect and analyze data.

Take appropriate action to communicate success with all involved and adjust as needed. To implement phase 5, XYZ Company and I agreed to communicate success via the company newsletter and key regional meetings. Following the program, turnover was no longer an issue, employees and customers were happier, and the company saw increased profitability.

Phase 6. Grow the Relationship

With this last phase, mutually sustain the initiative and stay informed about the client's business so you can anticipate their ongoing business challenges and assist them with any other business issues. Continue to nurture your overall relationship, both personally and professionally.

- Goal: Continue the relationship.
- Client expectations:
  - Did you keep the client abreast of developments that are relevant to their business?
  - Did you offer innovative ideas?
  - Did you create networking opportunities with other clients who have similar business issues?
  - Did you anticipate the client's needs to help them avoid pitfalls?
- Key activity:
  - Nurture and optimize the relationship.

Yes, I was able to continue and grow the relationship with XYZ Company. This huge success enabled me to be part of their strategic planning team for their "store of the future."

Initiating New Business Relationships

A necessary and challenging aspect of business development is securing appointments with potential clients. While all aspects of professional selling have their challenges, the prospecting phase is one of the most difficult. Be prepared to experience a lot of rejection.

Most prospecting efforts fail due to one of these reasons:

- You haven't conducted research or market analysis in advance.
- Your initial communication asks the prospect for an appointment before adding any value.
- You assume the prospect has a specific need based on stories or your intuition, which gives you an unsubstantiated sense of security without any confirmation.

On the other hand, most successful prospecting efforts follow these examples:

- Involve research on the prospective client organization and the key contact with whom you want to have a conversation.
- Provide value in advance of making an ask, such as articles of potential interest or an invitation to an event.
- Involve a well-thought-out email campaign with the understanding it usually takes up to seven touches before obtaining a response.
- Ask friends, associates, or other clients to provide a referral—or better yet, an introduction.
- Offer to provide a virtual cup of coffee or tea.
- Ask for an appointment for a minimal amount of time—say 15 minutes versus 30 minutes or an hour. When your 15 minutes has nearly ended, acknowledge it and request a date and time to have a follow-up appointment. The prospect may say, "I have a few more minutes now, so let's continue our discussion."

The Art and Science of the Client Conversation Process

First and foremost, one of the key differentiators in the success or failure of a client relationship is the person conducting the conversation. Good salespeople are worth their weight in gold, but anyone can become better at selling if they prepare and rehearse in advance. Whether the conversation is virtual or in-person, the process remains the same.

Once you have earned the right to have a conversation, you have four key objectives:

- Build a relationship (with all things being equal, people conduct business with people they like being around, they trust, and have confidence in).
- Uncover business issues and the circumstances involved.
- Identify the business issues your services will be able to successfully address or resolve.
- Earn the right to continue to the next appointment and key action steps.

Let's look closer at how to accomplish these objectives.

Pre-Call Planning

As with all things in life, solid preparation can give you a leg up on the competition. Rather than treating initial client interactions with the same standard spiel, always tailor them to each prospective client.

Start by identifying whom you will meet with. What are their roles and responsibilities? What is your plan for conducting the conversation? What are your primary and secondary call objectives? (While your goal is to achieve your primary call objective, ensure you can also achieve your secondary one.) What information and insight did your research provide—both about the prospective company and the individuals you will meet with?

Agreeing on the Call's Purpose

Just as you would with any successful meeting, once it is time for the small talk to come to an end, put the client at ease by opening with a proposed goal for the conversation. Obtain mutual agreement about what you plan to cover or accomplish. You can propose an agenda, state the value to the client, and check for acceptance. Based on their feedback, make adjustments as needed.

Interviewing

Begin the interview process using the questions you prepared in advance, but remember that you don't have to ask all of them—it's typical to have more questions than required. Also, make sure the process is conversational versus only questioning. The most successful sales calls usually involve the salesperson talking much less than the prospective client.

Successful salespeople do these six things:

- Ask exceptionally good questions that require the client to think and provide an appropriate level of explanation.
- Show some form of acknowledgment that they heard the client; for example, nodding their head or giving a verbal comment.
- Ask good follow-up questions to ensure a mutual understanding of the business issues and the circumstances influencing them.
- Create a mutual understanding of the current situation and the desired future state.
- Potentially expand the client's vision of what the future state may be.
- Always ask for a referral, whether internal or external to the client's organization. Simply ask, "Is there anyone else I should meet?"

Some examples of good interviewing questions to ask include:

- What is the current situation?
- What has brought about the current situation?
- What are you looking to accomplish?
- What have you tried or thought of trying to address the current situation?
- What is your desired outcome? Tell me more.
- Why is that important?
- What do you mean by . . . ?
- How do you feel about . . . ?

Consulting Tip

If you find yourself talking more than 50 percent of the time, you have likely already lost the sale. Let the client do most of the talking.

Preparing for Follow-Up

Successful salespeople know it usually takes more than one sales call to:

- Gain a complete, mutual understanding.
- Uncover additional business issues or think through the most appropriate way to assist the client.

- Gain access to and have conversations with other key stakeholders.
- Understand the client's decision-making process.
- Determine the client's budget.
- Take the necessary time to develop trust and confidence.

Turn to the Business Issues Worksheet at td.org/handbook-for-consultants to help track the business issues, business needs, desired state, and what you've mutually agreed on with the client. This must occur before you can provide your solution.

> **Consulting Tip**
>
> Clients may ask about your skills, but they're actually evaluating how you communicate and whether they can trust you. Your personality, not your expertise, will land most sales.

At the end of each conversation, it is important to mutually agree on the next appropriate action step. In sales terms, this is referred to as "closing." Inexperienced salespeople usually find this to be the most difficult step, while successful salespeople realize it is a natural step in the process. Like any successful business meeting, recapping the meeting's agreements—especially what will be done, by whom, and when—is critical for continued success.

Closing, by its very definition, means something must first be opened. Thus, the art and science of the conversation is all about opening. Gaining mutual agreement on the business issues to be addressed, developing trust and confidence, and assisting the client to create their desired future state are all essential to this process.

Of course, the ultimate close is when the client agrees to conduct business with you. This takes time and hard work. The average sales cycle for business services that require a consultative sales approach usually takes longer than others—anywhere from three to 18 months. On the positive side, the average investment price of the deliverable is usually higher.

Summary

It doesn't matter how good you are—you can't be a consultant if potential clients are not aware of you or if you are unable to persuade them of your value. Sales are critical to your very existence. The simple six-phase model presented here starts before the actual sales meeting with preplanning. Don't underestimate the value of being prepared. Every consummate salesperson enters a sales meeting with the right frame of mind—positive, helpful, and ready to build a trusting relationship.

Actions You Can Take Now

- **Answer four key questions.** Take time to answer these questions to get your sales process started:
  - What is your primary targeted market?
  - What business issues does your value proposition successfully address?
  - What is your business development process?
  - Why should clients choose to work with you?
- **Obtain feedback.** If possible, ask clients what went well and what you could have done better. Use this input to improve your customer relationship process.
- **Learn more.** Participate in a sales training workshop to obtain specific feedback about your behaviors and what you can do better.

About the Author

Joe Trueblood, CEO of Amplify Growth, is an authentic, strategic leader with a proven ability to develop and implement changes in processes, structures, individuals, and team development to increase profits for organizations around the world. He quickly sizes up situations, understands what needs to be done, and makes it happen. No unnecessary fanfare or long-winded dissertations—just results. Joe has been leading positive change that delivers business growth for more than three decades. He has a track record of bringing order out of chaos, successfully restructuring, revamping, and realigning resources for optimum efficiency and effectiveness. From growing a Fortune 500 company to leading the Americas for the world's largest sales performance improvement company, Joe transforms underperforming sales organizations, turns around troubled companies, and fuels business growth by executing winning strategies that increase internal and external satisfaction. A coach at heart, he gains commitment, not just compliance, with an enthusiastic leadership style that brings people on board and into the process. Learn more at amplifygrowth.com or reach Joe at jtrueblood@amplifygrowth.com.

6 Keys to Writing a Winning Business Proposal

HOLLY BURKETT

You've just finished an invigorating call with a prospective client. You're clear about their challenges and how you can help. The fit, timing, and opportunity all seem ideal. Now you just need to follow up with a winning business proposal to cinch the deal and ensure they are as motivated as you to move forward together. Are you sure of what needs to be included to win business based on a proposal? Do you know what the client will expect to read? Are you even sure why you need a proposal?

In this chapter, we'll explore what a business proposal is, why you need it, and how to craft one that's sure to win the business you're seeking.

The What and Why of a Business Proposal

A *business proposal* is a document designed to persuade an organization to buy your service or products. When you're anxious to get on with the real work of consulting, writing a business proposal can often seem like busy work or a waste of time. Some consultants don't even go through the effort—but that's a mistake.

Keep in mind, however, that a business proposal is an essential document for any consultant wishing to establish a new business opportunity or expand an existing one. For starters, the process of writing a proposal forces you to think strategically about your potential client and how you can best meet their needs. It helps you to outline the project's goals and objectives and present a plan of action to achieve them. A proposal also compels you to communicate your unique value to the client as a potential business partner, advisor, and solution provider.

For your clients, a business proposal helps inform decision making about how and when to allocate money and resources to the project.

In short, no matter what type of consulting practice you manage, a well-written business proposal is critical to your very livelihood because it helps you do the following (Stenger 2016):

- Make realistic plans.
- Secure funding.
- Determine direction and structure.
- Clarify your strengths.
- Put everyone on the same page.

Types of Business Proposals

Let's look at several different types of business proposals.

Informal Proposals

Informal proposals are generally short, straightforward documents. They describe a project and its estimated costs and are typically used to propose a specific solution to a problem or a request for products or services.

Formal Proposals

Formal proposals are more involved and often require extensive research and planning. These are typically used to secure contracts or large grants.

Solicited Proposals

With a *solicited proposal*, an organization is either actively seeking proposals that meet a specific need or reacting to an offer to consider a proposal. Types of solicited proposals generally include:

- **Request for information (RFI).** This is a screening tool designed to help the buyer understand which vendors are in the best position to provide what's needed. It often precedes the proposal solicitation process.
- **Request for proposal (RFP).** These are used by organizations to solicit proposals from potential vendors. They contain specific information regarding the project, the requirements, and the evaluation criteria for selecting the successful proposal.

In addition to outlining what the client needs and wants, an RFP also details how the proposal information should be organized and presented.

- **Request for quote (RFQ).** These are used when price is a primary factor in the purchasing decision, but not the only one. The buyer might also need information about product availability, delivery times, and other specifics. Proposals responding to RFQs are often shorter than those for RFPs.
- **Invitation for bid (IFB).** These are used to solicit services based primarily on price. Put simply, they're a request for a response to the question, "What would you charge to do this?"

Consultants responding to any solicited proposal should follow the buyer's preferred, stated format. Because proposals can be as short or as long as necessary to communicate the required information, they typically range in length from one to 50 pages. Longer proposals are typical when responding to a solicited RFP.

Unsolicited Proposals

An *unsolicited proposal* might result from a lunch conversation at a conference. A consultant might tell a prospect they have a solution to their problem and ask, "Would you like me to submit a proposal for that?"

Common Elements of a Business Proposal

The format of your proposal will largely depend upon the project and the client. However, a standard business proposal is generally structured to include the following elements:

- Cover letter
- Title page
- Purpose statement
- Presenting situation
- Project objectives
- Approach
- Timelines
- Responsibilities
- Qualifications
- Deliverables

- Critical success factors (optional)
- Your investment
- Terms of agreement
- Signature field
- Appendix (optional)

Cover Letter

Most proposals have at least two distinct pieces: a cover letter and the proposal document itself. These two pieces are combined into a single submission that's usually between six and eight pages in length.

Many consultants use their cover letter to highlight the essence of the proposal in an abbreviated fashion, to emphasize their qualifications as a bidder, and to formally request the project. Your cover letter is one of the first impressions a potential client will have of you, so it's important to appeal to them quickly and succinctly.

A cover letter is outlined as follows:

- **Header.** Include date and contact information.
- **Salutation or greeting.** Use the name of the person reviewing the proposal. Address your letter to this person with a common business greeting, such as "Dear [*first and last name*]" or "Dear [*position title*]." Avoid using "To whom it may concern."
- **Opening paragraph.** Explain your interest in the project and the organization. Show you've done your research.
- **Middle paragraph.** Give a brief overview of your background as it relates to the project. Include key achievements, skills, and specialties that make you particularly well suited as a consultant. Focus on one or two and provide specific details about recent successes, including measurable impacts you made. Use keywords from the RFP or pulled from your conversations with the client.
- **Closing paragraph.** End with a short paragraph summarizing why you are submitting your proposal and why you would be a great fit.

The closing paragraph often includes a *call to action* (*CTA*), which is a common marketing and sales tool for ensuring customers enter the next step in the purchasing life cycle. In a proposal or cover letter, the CTA is typically a brief statement asking the reader to take a specific action, such as visiting your website, viewing your testimonials, or reading related blogs or articles. For example, your letter might include the following:

- **Click here to learn more.** This can be used to take readers to specific pages of your website, like the company profile page or a client list.
- **Learn why our service is right for you.** Use this to direct readers to links with video clips of you in action or testimonials from clients in like industries or with similar challenges.
- **Sign up for our newsletter.** Use this to enable readers to enter their email address and sign up for your newsletter or other publications.
- **Follow us on social media.** This statement is typically accompanied by links to your company's social media accounts. Providing a place where users can view all your links at once and asking them to follow the accounts directly can make doing so more convenient.

When using CTA requests in a cover letter, I recommend you limit yourself to only one to two statements. Generally, the best advice for writing a winning cover letter is to keep it short and to the point!

Title Page

The *title page* will include the name of the proposal—such as, "A Proposal Prepared for *<Company Name and sometimes the person requesting the proposal>*"—the date, your company name, company logo, and contact information.

Purpose Statement

The *purpose statement* is a high-level summary of the presenting issue and your reason for submitting a proposal.

Presenting Situation

The *presenting situation* summarizes your understanding of the client's pain point and the business issue they are trying to solve. This section may be a few sentences or it may require a couple paragraphs. The goal is to show that you fully understand the client's unique challenges and opportunities. Here's an example you can tailor to your needs:

In response to *<concerns, questions, complaints, or constraints>*, the *<company, department, or group>* initiated a series of *<history of previous solutions, if applicable>* in *<year or month>* to enable *<strategic goal>*. With assistance from *<HR, OD, L&D, or other consultants>*, each *<department, team, or region>* within the *<company>* completed the *<previous solution or implementation plan>* with *<sessions, meetings, or plans>* spanning a period of *<timeline>*. Recent conversations with *<name or title>* suggest that much of the preliminary work from *<previous solution>* has not been sustained due to *<issue, constraint, or challenge>*. Given *<current situation and driving force>*, there is renewed interest and urgency in developing a *<solution>* that will achieve *<strategic goal or future vision>*.

Project Objectives

The *project objectives* describe the consulting engagement's high-level objectives and confirm assumptions about the stated business needs. Your objectives should all be action oriented. Here are some examples of primary objectives from a project with the talent development team:

- Analyze key factors driving employee turnover.
- Design a customized climate survey to collect immediate feedback.
- Evaluate survey results among select participants.
- Provide recommendations for a comprehensive engagement strategy.
- Collaborate with stakeholders to develop tools, systems, and processes for tracking and improving engagement and retention.

Approach

The *approach* section summarizes what you plan to do to address the client's pain points, meet their critical business needs, and achieve their desired objectives. Use this section to describe how your skills, perspective, and approach will add strategic value as a solution. You should also briefly state the general philosophy, principles, and best practices that guide your approach; for example, the ADDIE (analyze, develop, design, implement, and evaluate) model, the HPT (human performance technology) model, return on investment (ROI), or CliftonStrengths.

Include high-level details about how the proposed approach will be carried out, along with the estimated schedule, scope, and resource requirements needed to complete key tasks. Your level of detail should be sufficient enough to convey what will happen without becoming entangled in minutiae. Improve the clarity of this section by breaking it up into subsections that describe the specific phases of your methodology or service; for example, using headers like data gathering, design, implementation, and evaluation.

Finally, aim to ground your proposed approach in a framework that the client will understand and trust (that is, limit your use of jargon).

Consulting Tip

Use simple visuals like infographics, icons, or graphic images to illustrate your approach and help your proposal stand out.

Timelines

Timelines can be stated in many ways. Some consultants describe timelines in association with specific phases (Table 25-1). However, it's not always possible to define specific dates, especially with long-term engagements, so it's best to state timelines as estimates or targets, rather than absolutes.

Table 25-1. Estimating Timelines With Phases

Estimated Timeline	
January 3–January 30	**Data Gathering:** Conduct interviews and focus groups.
February 2–March 15	**Design:** Design and develop pilot, and vet design with stakeholders.
March 20–30	**Implementation:** Launch pilot program.
April 1–May 25	**Evaluation:** Collect, analyze, and report post-program data.
June 1–25	**Follow-Up:** Determine next steps with pilot group.

It's also important to remember that your project approach and timelines are based on preliminary assumptions, and these circumstances can be easily disrupted. For example:

- Sponsors might leave.
- Project members might be reassigned.
- Budgets might be cut.

- You may unexpectedly have to learn new subject matter, software, or technical skills.

These changing business demands will influence your project's success or failure.

> **Consulting Tip**
>
> As a written safeguard, end the timeline section with a statement like, "Any change to this proposal's scope and resource requirements may affect target timelines and completion dates."

Responsibilities

The *responsibilities* section provides a high-level description of the sponsor, stakeholder, project team, and consultant responsibilities during the implementation of the proposed approach. It's important to use this section to emphasize the role of shared ownership and joint accountabilities to achieve the desired results.

Qualifications

The *qualifications* section is typically a brief paragraph highlighting your relevant skills and experience, with an emphasis on communicating the key benefits of working with you. It also provides a place for you to highlight your unique value proposition.

In lieu of including this section in the proposal, many consultants opt to attach a one-page "About the Consultant" profile to the appendix. Wherever you choose to cite your qualifications, be sure to stress *why* a client should do business with you versus your competitors.

Deliverables

The *deliverables* section describes the specific outputs of your overall approach or of its distinct phases. Sample outputs may include assessment tools, training curricula, job aids, evaluation plans, competency frameworks, e-learning modules, culture audits, reports, or survey templates.

Critical Success Factors

The *critical success factors* section is optional, and is often used to underscore success factors, such as engaged sponsors, access to subject matter experts, or transparent communication practices. It typically ranges from one to three sentences.

Your Investment

Your *investment* section can include the cost of the entire project from beginning to end, or it may divide costs into fees for each phase of service delivery. In *The New Consultant's Quick Start Guide*, Elaine Biech (2019) recommends using the word "investment" rather than "cost" so clients can focus on the benefits of working with you.

Terms and Conditions

The *terms and conditions* section specifies an effective date for your proposal's terms. Including your terms and conditions is important because the client's business conditions, as well as your fees, approaches, or availability, may change over time. It also minimizes the chance that a client will keep you dangling (Biech 2019).

Consulting Tip

Cite a timeline for your proposal's acceptance. Tell the client that fees and terms will be honored for 30 (or 60) days, and after that time, a new proposal may be required. Manage your time and compel the client to make a decision within a reasonable period to protect their investment.

Signature Line

The *signature line* should show the printed names and titles of the decision makers who are authorized to approve the proposal, along with the dates of approval.

Appendix

An optional section, the *appendix* may include one or more parts with charts, graphs, figures, or any other supplemental material including:

- Relevant work samples
- A biographical profile describing your qualifications

- Contact information for references
- A partial client list
- Select testimonials from previous clients

You can find a job aid with a sample consulting proposal that includes many of these items at td.org/handbook-for-consultants.

6 Keys to a Winning Proposal

For every RFP you respond to and every proposal you generate, your competitors are working just as hard to win the business too. So, what does it take to stand out from the crowd? Follow the six keys in Figure 25-1 to stay on target and surpass the competition.

Figure 25-1. Six Keys to Writing a Winning Business Proposal

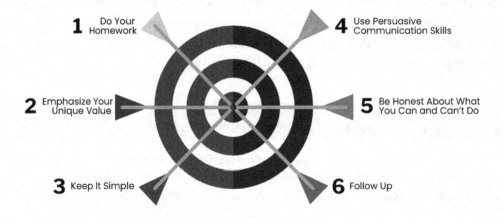

1. Do Your Homework

From a client's perspective, a winning proposal is one that's responsive. The client wants to see that you have done your homework to truly understand what they need and want and have carefully responded to all aspects of the consulting request or RFP. All things being equal, responsiveness is ultimately much more of a differentiator than a proposal's visual appeal or even the fluidity of its writing.

To show you understand the business issues from the client's point of view, collect as much preliminary information as you can and tailor your proposal to the specific situation. The more information you have about the client and the problem they want to solve, the better. In *The New Business of Consulting*, Elaine Biech (2019) says, "You will write your best proposal if you listen to what your client says and take good notes."

Questions you should address when doing your due diligence include:

- What does the company value most?
- What is the company's vision and mission?
- How does the company's leadership function?
- How does the company describe its strengths?
- How does the company describe its immediate and future challenges?
- What barriers interfere with meeting these challenges?
- How does the company measure success?

If you need more information, schedule a brief follow-up interview with the potential client before you submit your proposal. If you're responding to a solicited proposal, use the client's RFP as a guide.

Consulting Tip

A high level of personalization will put you at an advantage over your competitors and help add value early. It shows that you were listening to your buyer's needs and understand key challenges from their perspective.

2. Emphasize Your Unique Value

Your client will hire you (or your firm) because of your promise to add value and solve their problems. Be clear about *why* a client should choose *your* services instead of someone else offering the same or similar services. Emphasize any strengths, experiences, products, or processes you offer that your competition does not. Then, instead of listing the number of services you provide, highlight their benefits.

Here is an example of how you might craft your value statement in a business proposal.

Qualifications

As experienced business partners, we are uniquely qualified to implement this approach. Here are some key reasons why Company X will benefit from working with us:

- **Expertise.** We have a track record of helping healthcare organizations like yours successfully improve employee engagement and retention through integrated talent development solutions. We also have specialized expertise in designing and analyzing climate surveys to inform engagement and retention strategies.
- **National presence.** We are a national service provider with highly qualified associates from coast to coast. We can provide flexible, customized, and agile staffing for this project no matter the timeline or specific challenges.
- **Shared values.** We believe that an organization is only as strong as its employees and leaders can't achieve their mission and vision without commitment from an engaged, talented, and thriving workforce. Advancing the health and well-being of the organizations, teams, and individuals we serve are the values that shape how we work as strategic partners.

3. Keep It Simple

Don't go overboard with complex language, trendy jargon, or niche expressions. Instead, be as clear and concise as possible. While it can be tempting to pump your proposal full of helpful information and all the reasons your client should choose you, the longer it is, the less likely they are to read it all.

Erica Holthausen of Catchline Communications cautions consultants to "be aware of the curse of knowledge." She says, "As experts, we have a very hard time imagining what it's like for someone else not to know something we know. We are so steeped in the logic, methodology, or approach we developed or were trained in that we forget to spell it out or supply the necessary details for our clients. The greater our expertise in a certain area, the more likely we are to forget what it is like to be stuck in the muck."

As you write your proposal, make sure you're creating a document that is easy to read and concisely brings forth your key points. Use plain language and incorporate headings, callouts, graphics, and a clean format to make it more compelling and engaging.

4. Use Persuasive Communication Skills

Winning proposal writers use persuasive written communication skills to convey their value. If you can't effectively show your insights or expertise in writing, it won't matter how innovative your ideas are or how qualified you are as a consultant. A client won't know what you can do unless you tell them in words, images, and terms they understand. When writing a proposal, always have the client in mind: Use language that mirrors what they have used in conversations or reports.

Persuasive communication also involves the ability to organize writing topics in easily digestible chunks that stick to any stated guidelines. Following the guidelines includes everything from submitting by the deadline to making sure you've not written past the page limit.

Before submitting your work, proofread your proposal! Grammatical errors and spelling mistakes communicate sloppiness and a lack of attention to detail. You might also ask someone who doesn't know your company to proofread your proposal and provide feedback. Check that you've covered communication basics and addressed these key questions:

- Is this proposal well written, professional, and clear?
- Is this proposal aesthetically pleasing? (The look of your proposal matters more than you may realize.)
- Can this proposal be easily read on a mobile device? (Proposal software can make it easy to create mobile-friendly documents.)
- Have I supplied the required and relevant information?
- Does this proposal incorporate key themes around the client's pain points and strengths?
- Does this proposal have a unique voice that's specific to me and my company?
- Does this proposal anticipate questions about the approach, resource requirements, and costs?

Consulting Tip

Create a proposal checklist to review before submitting any proposal.

Some consultants use proposal software or proposal writing services to develop their writing skills, create actual proposals, or review unsuccessful past proposals to see how they could be improved in the future. The Association of Proposal Management Professionals (APMP) suggests using certified proposal writers with experience submitting at least 50 proposals (ideally 100).

Proposal software resources include Loopio, PandaDoc, and Twenty5, among many others. For example, Qwilr helps users embed and play videos within a proposal to bring personal messages to life (see pages.qwilr.com/Proposal-Look-Book-2022-Edition-tu3B0CzOSly3). ChatGPT is another resource that you can use to outline a proposal. Keep in mind, however, that ChatGPT may be able to describe how a requirement *ought* to be addressed, but it will not describe how *you (or your team)* would address it in the real world using your knowledge about your client's needs and the skills you possess.

5. Be Honest About What You Can and Can't Do

You must be ready and willing to avoid submitting for projects that are beyond your skills and expertise. For instance, if you don't have significant experience leading efforts in the areas identified in a client request—such as designing a climate survey or creating a competency framework—then it's best to defer or refer that request to someone else. A bid-on-everything approach wastes resources that you could be investing in other more appropriate or winnable opportunities.

That's not to say that you shouldn't pursue stretch projects. In those situations, however, it might be helpful to partner with a more experienced colleague and craft a proposal that combines both of your skill sets. Here, your partnership role should be one that adds value to the client, not just your own professional development. Generally, if you have something to learn, you should learn on your own time.

Saying no may also involve turning down requests that you consider to be inappropriate or too labor intensive once your proposal has been accepted and you've started putting your approach into practice. For example, you could be asked to omit feedback from one key segment of an employee population when gathering data in a discovery phase, or you could be asked to use unfamiliar technology that requires a steep learning curve. Anticipating possible changes to project scope, approach, or resource requirements will help you frame the critical success factors statement in your proposal.

6. Follow Up

Writing a follow-up email after sending a proposal to a potential client is important because it can help remind them of your proposal and potentially restart your communication. You can also use follow-up emails (or calls) to confirm your interest in the project, clarify something about your proposal, ask for a status update, or gain additional client information.

Guidelines for follow-up communication include:

- **Keep a schedule.** Follow-up emails are often most effective when sent three to five days after submitting your proposal. Use a client contact log to track potential and actual proposals, along with your scheduled follow-up dates (Table 25-2).
- **Keep it brief.** Short, direct messages allow your client to quickly and clearly understand your purpose. The average follow-up email is only a few paragraphs long.
- **Personalize it.** Show the potential client that you paid attention and understand their unique needs. Emphasize information about why your proposal is well suited for their current or future challenges.

Table 25-2. Sample Client Contact Log

Organization Name	Contact Person	Date of Proposal or Contact	First Follow-Up Date	Second Follow-Up Date	Third Follow-Up Date	Comments

Adapted from Biech (2003).

Consulting Tip

Put your potential client first. Start all of your follow-up emails with "you," not "I."

What Is a Good Win Rate?

Win rates vary for each consultant and highly depend on factors like areas of expertise, your tenure and brand identity as a consultant, your size and scope of operations, targeted industries, personal preferences, and geographical location, among others. Given the many factors involved, "There is no such thing as an average proposal win rate" that is universally applicable (Siebert 2023).

To decide what rate is ideal for you, consider the following example: If you're submitting a large number of proposals, a low win rate may actually be proportional to the volume you've submitted. If you have a win rate of 80 percent or higher, you may want to ask yourself if you're taking enough chances on opportunities to grow your business and take you out of your comfort zone. You should also consider how much time you spend writing proposals. What is the cost of the investment?

Keep the following guidelines in mind when looking to assess and improve your proposal win rates (Siebert 2023):

- Build relationships with buyers before an RFP comes out. Relationships build trust and help clients know who you are and what you have to offer.
- Take care of your existing clients. It's much easier to keep an existing client than it is to find a new one.
- Avoid writing proposals for projects you have no realistic chance of winning.
- Be proactive and future focused. Instead of saying, "How can I win this opportunity right now?" say, "How can I win this contract (or one like it) when it goes out for bid in two years?"
- Don't compare yourself to some external, subjective standard. Look internally and reflect on things you can do to improve.

Summary

A well-crafted proposal is essential to growing your business and communicating your value as a service provider. A winning proposal will help you stand out from the competition and go from being one of many fish in the sea to being the fish that everyone wants! Use this chapter as your road map to greater success.

Actions You Can Take Now

- **Create or refresh your proposal template.** Pay special attention to how you communicate your unique value and define the benefits of choosing you as a consultant. Focus on why you stand out from the competition.
- **Critique your most recent proposals.** Identify the winning aspects of proposals that were accepted and make a note of improvement opportunities for ones

that were rejected. Set a realistic goal for increasing your win rate by a specific percentage and date.

- **Plan ahead.** Identify business development opportunities or clients whom you'd like to work with in the next two years. Connect with colleagues in your network who may be doing business with them or working on projects that appeal to you. Ask for informational interviews to explore tactics for increasing your access to those clients or special projects.

About the Author

Holly Burkett, PhD, SPHR, is an accomplished talent builder, change leader, and workplace learning professional with more than 20 years of consulting experience. She is passionate about developing resilient leadership capabilities that enable high engagement and performance. Her clients include Apple, SEVA, and Premera Blue Cross. A certified change practitioner, associate of the ROI Institute, certified Stakeholder Centered Coach, and member of Forbes Coaches Council, Holly is a sought-after coach, speaker, and facilitator with a doctorate in human capital development. The award-winning author of *Learning for the Long Run*, she regularly contributes to industry resources, including the *TDBoK Guide, ATD's Handbook for Training and Talent Development,* and *ATD's Organization Development Handbook.* You can reach Holly via email at holly@hollyburkett.com.

Volunteering
A Path to Clients

C. MICHAEL FERRARO

During my career, I've served in a volunteer capacity for many organizations—from business and industry groups to professional associations to not-for-profit organizations and even educational institutions. I've also volunteered for a couple of government associated organizations and groups. And while I had a strategy and a plan for many of them, I also joined some of these organizations just for fun.

It takes a lot of time to volunteer, so you have to decide what works best for you and how much time you can spend on each opportunity. I also try, whenever possible, to learn a new skill or concept as part of my volunteer work to enhance my personal and professional development.

This chapter is organized around the different volunteer opportunities available to TD professionals. I've also peppered in my experiences and lessons learned to help you develop a strategy for using volunteering to build your consulting business.

Volunteer With Local Training, Development, and HR Associations

The first group I volunteered with was the ATD Metro DC Chapter—my local chapter for the Association for Talent Development. I joined the events committee, which was responsible for planning our monthly meetings and the annual local chapter conference, booking speakers, and welcoming those attending our events. I also ran for, and was elected to, the ATD Metro DC Chapter Board.

This experience allowed me to learn about industry trends from other local internal training directors and facilitators. I also met my first consulting client at a monthly chapter meeting. She initiated the conversation, which led to a cup of coffee at her office and chatting with some of her managers about what I could offer.

Consulting Tip

Don't just join a community organization—show up, join a committee, and volunteer.

I also joined the local chapter of the Society for Human Resource Management (SHRM), which led to joining the HR Virginia Annual Conference committee. In that capacity, I worked with volunteers for a large three-day statewide event attended by more than 500 HR professionals, which enabled me to have many meetings and discussions about my business with volunteers and attendees.

When you put in the time to build relationships, you also build trust, which leads to conversations and often new clients. I have found over the years that as many professional colleagues move from company to company, they may not need my services today, but I can help them at their new company in the future by building these local relationships now.

Join Your Local Chamber of Commerce

Joining local business and industry groups will expand your network with other business executives and help you grow your business locally. By engaging with your local economy and industries, you can learn about your community's workforce development needs. You will also meet executives who are passionate about this topic and eager to talk about their challenges to professionals in the training community.

I joined the Northern Virginia Chamber of Commerce because I wanted to expand my network to other business groups in the area. In the first month after I started my business, I received an invitation to attend a prospective member event at the Fairfax County Chamber of Commerce. This event had more than 100 people in attendance, and the speakers promoted the importance of membership and getting involved. While networking before and after the event, I could see how different it was than the networking at ATD or SHRM meetings. Chamber members were encouraged to do business with other members, and we all exchanged business cards and scheduled meetings. I joined on-site that day.

I joined three different committees—membership, education and workforce, and partnering—that then set the stage for more community engagement, which also led to new clients:

- The membership committee called on potential local businesses to pitch them on a chamber membership. I reached out to some large corporations, met with many, and was able to convince them on membership. During each conversation, I would also share information about my firm and, in many cases, was able to connect with the person in charge of training. The chamber's motto was "help yourself as you help the chamber." I would never have been able to make that connection if I wasn't there on behalf of the chamber.

- The education and workforce committee worked on partnering the business community workforce needs with the education system to prepare future employees. My engagement there led to connections with many HR professionals. This committee also hosted events and symposiums on connecting with HR and business leaders, which led to many great conversations and opportunities with businesses that were concerned about their future workforce. I also served as the chamber's representative on the Counties School and Business Advisory Board, which opened more opportunities to engage with business leaders concerned about the workforce pipeline.

- The partnering committee was responsible for connecting larger member companies with smaller businesses within the chamber. Once a year, we held a partnering event in which purchasers from large businesses set up displays and had speakers on panels. I was invited to be the keynote speaker at this conference several times, and my presentation on selling skills led to many opportunities for new business.

Consulting Tip

Joining a chamber of commerce can jump-start your business. Also, consider offering to be a speaker at a business organization for free.

Ultimately, these volunteer efforts paid off early in my firm's development. After winning several volunteer service awards at the chamber's annual chairman's luncheon, I was asked to serve on the Fairfax County Chamber of Commerce Board of Directors. That board had more than 100 community leaders at the time and was a fantastic opportunity for making more connections. For example, during a board of directors lunch meeting, I met an executive at a large consulting firm that had just been awarded a training project with a government agency, and he wanted to know if I was interested in contracting for him. I agreed to meet with his team, and they hired me to spend several months on this contact training project for their managers across the country. Thanks to this project, I was able to secure enough funds to build my company's first website and keep business positive for the first year.

Shortly after joining the Fairfax County Chamber of Commerce, I joined the local Greater Reston Chamber of Commerce. The chairperson at the time asked me to join her board of directors and help with membership recruiting, which was something I had successfully done at the Fairfax County Chamber of Commerce. Eventually, I became chair of the board—a huge responsibility that took up a great amount of time (sometimes daily work). Between all the board meetings, committee meetings, ribbon cuttings, networking events, meeting with elected officials, and more, I had less time to work on my business. However, part of my job as chair was to meet with businesses that were either current members or prospective members of the chamber. To my surprise, many of the potential members were very interested in introducing me to their HR and training departments, which led to many new clients.

The Greater Reston Chamber of Commerce was also responsible for hosting several festivals in the local community that raised a great deal of money for the chamber. During these festivals and events, I was responsible for meeting with all the sponsors and vendors.

Join Other Local Business Groups

I also wanted to learn more about the predominant businesses in my local community, which in Northern Virginia is the technology industry. Therefore, I joined the Northern Virginia Technology Council (NVTC) and used a similar playbook to guide my involvement as I did with the local chambers of commerce.

I started by volunteering on the membership and workforce committees. At the time, workforce and workforce development were huge topics of concern to Northern Virginia business leaders. The workforce committee was tasked with connecting the people who hired and trained employees in organizations with those who prepared students for the workforce.

As a volunteer on the workforce committee, I helped make connections with member businesses and attended many meetings and conferences. This committee also facilitated panels of HR leaders and their counterparts in the education community who were trying to figure out how to connect the workforce pipeline to help businesses with their workforce needs. I eventually co-chaired the workforce committee and was asked to serve on the NVTC Board of Directors. Through these volunteering efforts, I was able to develop more clients over the years.

Consulting Tip

Join a workforce committee with an industry-based organization to reach different industries.

My time as a member and volunteer with local chambers of commerce and business groups opened up countless invaluable doors for me that led to consulting work. If you are trying to build your business locally, you must engage in the local economy.

Engage in the Public Workforce System

In 1998, the US federal government passed the Workforce Investment Act, which required state and local governments to create workforce investment boards to allocate millions of dollars to help improve the community's workforce development skills gaps. These boards were typically populated with local business leaders, members of the local government, educators, and other training service providers.

The presidents of the Chamber and NVTC both nominated me to serve on the new local workforce investment board for our region, and I joined as vice chairman of the board for a four-year term. This led to the opportunity to serve on the Virginia State Workforce Board during Governor Mark Warner's administration. This experience added a new highlight to my professional resume and showed potential clients in Northern Virginia that I was very involved in serving the state.

Serving on the state board also led to a very interesting opportunity with ATD. My work with local and state boards piqued my interest in the ATD policy council and its agenda regarding working with the public workforce system. Although the members of this volunteer public policy council were mainly from larger member companies, I was asked to serve as the lone consultant company member (under the condition I would not try to sell to members of the committee, which I agreed to).

As a member of the public policy council, I was able to speak at many ATD conferences, including the annual International Conference & Exposition and the Annual Chapter Leaders' conference, to discuss the public workforce system. Over the years, I was also able to take groups of ATD members and chapter leaders up to Capitol Hill to meet with their state congressional representatives and staff to discuss workforce development issues. In the eight years that I spent speaking at conferences and with chapter leaders, I built many relationships that led to new clients.

Consulting Tip

Volunteering with ATD and speaking at its conferences can immensely expand your network.

Engage in Community-Based Leadership Programs

As a member of the chambers' boards and the NVTC board, I was encouraged to apply to the Leadership Fairfax Institute (LFI) program. This is a well-respected community leadership program, similar to others throughout the country, that brings local business, education, government, and nonprofit communities together to learn about and engage in the community. I highly recommend looking for a program like this in your local area. After graduating from the LFI class in 1998, I was asked to serve on the volunteer LFI board of directors, which gave me an opportunity to expand my own personal skills. I decided to join (and eventually became co-chair of) the organization's development (fundraising) committee because I wanted to learn more about fundraising. Because the organization regularly reached out to large firms in the community for donations and sponsorships, I saw it as another opportunity to network with new firms—I was once again able to help myself, when appropriate, while helping the organization.

I was also asked to co-facilitate the opening retreat for LFI's incoming class. After a few years, I was asked to conduct a half-day DiSC training session for each new class every September. Through my work volunteering for LFI, I get to share my professional work with a new group of community leaders and share what I can do for their teams and organizations. I frequently run into LFI alumni at community events in the Washington, DC, metropolitan area, especially here in Northern Virginia, who approach me and ask, "Aren't you the DiSC instructor?" or "Can you do that for my team?"

Consulting Tip

Volunteering your time to facilitate or run an off-site event for a community group can lead to new client opportunities.

Engage With the Education Community

Through my volunteer work, I developed a nice working relationship with Sister Gallagher, the president of Marymount University in Arlington, Virginia. She once invited me to her office for lunch and to chat about workforce development and the public workforce system. When she asked for feedback about what our community was missing around workforce and human resources, I told her that I thought organizational HR functions weren't recognized in our community as much as they should be—and perhaps we could develop a recognition program to rectify that. Sister Gallagher thought this was a great idea and said that her school would take the lead. Then, in a follow up conversation, she "voluntold" me to lead the development of an awards program! I couldn't turn her down, although I didn't really know what I was getting myself into. She also asked if I would volunteer on the School of Business Advisory Board.

The first event for the Human Resources Leadership Awards of Greater Washington was held 18 months later. I spent the next four years as co-chair and was subsequently introduced at later annual awards dinners by the current co-chairs as a founding co-chair. Over the 15 years of the program, I was able to connect with and be recognized for this volunteer work by many HR professionals. Even today, people in the HR space remember my work with the program and thank me for it. Starting something new in my community and establishing myself as a community trustee in my profession created a bit of a legacy for me here in the Washington, DC, area.

Volunteering for Fun and Making New Contacts

While professional and business volunteering opportunities abound, and I always had fun while volunteering, it's important to volunteer just for fun too. You'll be able to meet new people, expand your network of contacts, and gain new clients too. Here are some examples of fun volunteering experiences I've had.

I am a member of the Tower Club in Northern Virginia, which is a business club that's part of the national Club Corporations properties across the country. After being accepted, I volunteered and joined the club's membership committee, helping invite and sell membership on the club's behalf. I was able to expand my network while helping the committee organize prospective member events. I eventually served on the Club's board of governors for six years. But much of my time with the club (whether on or off the board) was focused on just having a fun place that I could enjoy with my family. For example, we attended events such as the Santa Brunch and other holiday brunches for Easter and Thanksgiving.

Another fun activity was serving on the Celebrate Fairfax Board of Directors, the community-based program that used to put on the annual Celebrate Fairfax! Festival and still hosts other events to celebrate the county and community. During my two terms, I attended the festivals and worked many hours while wearing my large board of directors' badge and polo shirt. As I walked around the festival grounds helping individuals, staff, vendors, and volunteers with whatever they needed, I had a lot of fun and gained a sense of satisfaction with my ability to help out in my community. The new contacts with sponsors and vendors was just an added bonus.

Finally, serving on the Goodwill Board of Greater Washington gave me the opportunity to develop my knowledge of finances in nonprofit organizations. I was recruited for that board in part for my retail skills—I spent 25 years in retail prior to starting my business—and as you may know, Goodwill runs many retail stores. However, Goodwill is also a workforce development business that trains their clients to be self-sufficient, in addition to giving them job opportunities in Goodwill retail stores and through grant programs. I spent six years on the finance committee and learned a great deal about cash flow in a nonprofit, as well as how to diversify and manage income and investments. While I did develop some new contacts and connections, this was not a business development opportunity. Rather, it was something I was enthusiastic about that I could do to learn new and important skills.

Summary

As you can tell, I began actively volunteering in my community soon after starting my business. I intentionally joined groups to help expand my network and knowledge about the workforce development and training issues facing the organizations in my community. I also focused on learning how to grow my business in my county and state. Along the way, I was also able to enhance my skills and continue growing my knowledge in those areas where I needed to learn more. There were days early in my new business life that I would go from board meeting to committee meeting to another event and then another meeting all in the same day. It took a lot of energy and time, but I had a strategy, and I worked hard to build my network of contacts. However, and more importantly, I was (and still am) a community trustee—I'm concerned about keeping my community a great place to live, work, and raise a family.

I also found many executives and HR professionals who felt the same way, and although they could work with consultants anywhere in the country, they wanted to work with someone local. They wanted to help a small business in their community. This is something to think about as you volunteer and grow your network.

Use the job aid on the website, td.org/handbook-for-consultants, as you start your volunteer efforts. It will help you secure more client relationships that will lead to new business for you, as it did for me.

I am less active today with my community volunteering efforts, but I am still involved in some organizations. My business is at a satisfactory place with many wonderful clients, so I've focused my volunteer efforts on my family foundation. In 2010, I helped my daughter form the Bite Me Cancer Foundation five months after she was diagnosed with cancer at 17 years old. While she was growing up, she watched her family be involved in so many community volunteer activities that it just seemed normal for her start her own foundation! I am now able to use the skills I learned through 27 years of volunteering and apply them to our foundation, which helps teenagers with all cancers while also directly funding thyroid cancer research grants.

Actions You Can Take Now

- **Join today.** Join the local chapter of ATD, SHRM, and other professional associations to start building your professional network.
- **See who needs help.** Next time you're in a local coffee shop or grocery store, take a minute and examine the bulletin board. Who is looking for volunteers? What opportunities are out there?

About the Author

C. Michael Ferraro founded TRAINING SOLUTIONS (TSI) in 1995. TSI offers a variety of programs and products, along with Michael's more than 40 years of experience, to help improve employees' skills and develop more positive and productive workplaces. Michael has facilitated many people skills training programs throughout the country for a variety of clients from large corporations to small and mid-size companies to nonprofits and universities. He also offers a skills-based executive coaching program that includes 360-degree feedback. Michael is an active volunteer in the Washington, DC, metropolitan area, with a focus on building relationships to help create new clients for his company and positively contribute to his community. He is currently chairman of the Bite Me Cancer Foundation, which was started by his daughter Nikki in 2010 to support teenagers fighting cancer and to fund thyroid cancer research. Reach out to Michael at ferraro@trainingsolutions.com.

CHAPTER 27

Networking Is Necessary for Consultants

KIMBERLI JETER

Why is networking necessary for consultants? Because you have big dreams and amazing gifts. You are only limited by your imagination and the depth and diversity of your network. Networks are the key to helping individuals, teams, organizations, and communities thrive.

I am sure impostor syndrome is real for some people, but I have been the biggest impostor of all—I've designed and sold products and services with zero experience. When I was 23 years old, I designed a five-day training program for women entrepreneurs in Russia, which turned out to be a great success and was used to train more than 10,000 entrepreneurs around the globe. The key to this success was a network of trainers who made the content come to life. I then went on to design programs for corporations to build sustainable communities in the highlands of Guatemala and supply chains for oil and gas companies in Africa. When I started this work, I didn't have any experience in these areas, but I knew people who did. Thanks to my networks, I've helped my organizations and our clients successfully launch big, bold internal and external initiatives throughout my career.

According to the Bureau of Labor Statistics Business Employment Dynamics statistics, the failure rate for startups and private sector businesses in their first year is nearly 20 percent, and it's higher for consulting businesses.

To help you avoid becoming part of that 20 percent, and to navigate the uncertain and sometimes overwhelming journey of being a consultant and business owner, you can leverage your network for support. Networks will help you find the clients you need, but did you know they'll also help manage operational risks? You can tap your network for information about software and tools to run your business, manage your pipeline, and learn about cashflow.

Ask them when to hire employees, outsource, or partner. Networks also help you pivot and survive economic downturns. If you fill your network with the right people, they will work overtime to support your success.

You can find networks to promote your consulting business almost anywhere. Consider some of these likely places:

- Consultant communities, online groups, and small business development centers to find partners and share pricing strategies, tools, best practices, business tips, and camaraderie
- Professional associations, chambers of commerce, and local business groups to identify experts, learn trends, elevate your brand, and generate referrals
- Accountability partners who you select to help you achieve your goals by being someone to talk to and cheer you on
- Trusted experts, advisors, coaches, and mentors who engage professionals and entrepreneurs to offer sage advice and recommend financial advisors, bankers, insurance agents, attorneys, graphic designers, marketing professionals, IT experts, and any other expertise you may need
- Friends, family, neighbors, college acquaintances, and colleagues who offer moral support, fresh perspectives, and client referrals
- Serendipity also creates luck—tell your story to everyone, and one day, out of the blue, you might get a call with a great opportunity

Serendipity? Yes. When you connect with someone and discuss new opportunities, you generate energy in your network, which creates a pull that brings more people to you. One example of serendipity happened to me at a conference while walking the expo floor. I stopped at a booth and talked to an amazing woman. We shared community impact stories. I told her about some of the challenges my colleague in Africa and I were working on. It was exciting and led to a conversation between my colleague and the company. My colleague ended up with an opportunity to attend a training course for free. Now all three of us are connected, inspired, and energized when we think about how our relationships started and have evolved. One random conversation led to an introduction and another conversation, which created an opportunity.

Networking occurs anywhere there are people who want to share ideas with each other. For example, Neal Bloom, entrepreneur, investor, and community builder in the United States leads monthly hikes for founders. Hikers meet entrepreneurs from diverse industries, build connections, enjoy nature, and support one another.

Ready to network, but not sure where to start? For more than 25 years, my network has powered my success across countries, cultures, and industries. We've helped thousands of entrepreneurs and small business owners succeed locally, regionally, and in global supply chains. To help those businesses succeed, we connected and strengthened networks of local consultants to help businesses tackle any situation. So, when I was approached to write this chapter, I connected with my network and they answered the call. Here you'll find networking tips from consultants representing six continents—we've got you covered.

The What, Who, and How of Networking

We toss the word *networking* around and talk about it freely, even though no two people may define it the same way. Many of us see networking as both a positive and a negative—a social activity to meet others in our profession or people who share a common interest. However, at its core, networking is the exchange of ideas and information between individuals. As Shakti Saran of India says, networks are "the essence of existence and life."

What Is Networking?

You may think of networking as identifying professional contacts, but at its heart, networking is relationship building that often goes beyond those professional connections. Your network also includes the relationships you build throughout your life.

However, despite understanding the importance of networking, a lot of people struggle with it. To understand why, I launched a global survey. You could say I was networking about networking.

Ivett Casanova Perozo, of Being You Consulting, helped me deploy a two-question poll with the Consultant Connection Coffee Chat Community (C5). We found that when people think of networking as stressful, uncomfortable, or smarmy, they were typically focusing on "the ask" at large, in-person events. However, when those same people described someone in their network, they used words like joyful, creative, kind, nurturing, thoughtful, inspiring, helpful, and supportive. The key to successful networking is a growth mindset. You will be more successful when you approach networking as an exciting learning opportunity that introduces you to people who are helpful, supportive, and energizing. When you find the right people, you will solve problems faster, add more value to your clients, build innovative partnerships, and bring big ideas to life.

As you network, tell your story to everyone—why you created your business, what problems you solve, and why you're excited. Share it energetically and enthusiastically. Your network will quickly become your brand ambassadors and champions bringing you to the attention of potential clients and partners.

Who Is in Your Network?

Even though we haven't talked in 30 years, Flavia Perez, my friend from the Uruguayan American School, responded when I asked for ideas about networking. She said, "Your network is your whole life." Yes, it's everyone you've known throughout your life: family, friends, teammates, colleagues, clients, and others. Flavia is a successful consultant who believes her success is due to her relationships. For example, she has two partners who met each other while taking a course on coaching.

Flavia said the first clients she and her partners had were the result of telling everyone they knew about their plans. Their network of friends wanted to support them in their first entrepreneurial venture, and some identified clients and invited them to consult for their companies. Flavia says that networking was critical in starting their business, and although the people in their network liked them, it went beyond that. Their network believed in them, knew they were capable, and trusted them to do good things. She believes that their network was key to ensuring their consulting partnership is successful today.

So, the people in your network are determined by everything you've ever done. Like I did with Flavia, don't hesitate to contact someone you knew in school 20 years ago if they make you smile and do work you find interesting. Call to reconnect and be open to serendipity. You may be surprised by the conversation. For example, when Flavia found out I was doing research on social impact partnerships, she immediately shared several organizations in Brazil that would add unique perspectives to my project!

How Do You Network?

You can meet people online, at in-person events, through colleagues or friends, and through everyday activities. For example, I asked a parent at a sports event what he thought about networking—the resulting 10-minute conversation with a stranger led to useful insights. Quick interactions can be considered networking, but it's the relationships and trust you build over time that drive success. To be effective, networks need to be developed, maintained, and leveraged. Most importantly, networking requires an attitude of generosity—giving and helping first.

Because sincere networking is mutually beneficial, be sure to examine the benefits you can give as well as those you get. No one expects networkers to be altruistic, but helping others can be rewarding in multiple ways. For example, the benefits that you can give might include helping others with their careers, developing new friendships, or becoming a mentor to someone.

The best way to learn how to network is to try it. Look up a local professional association such as your local ATD chapter or the chamber of commerce. Sign up and attend an event. Set a goal to talk to two people. Then, try these tips from Australia's Renée Hasseldine, CEO and founder of ThinkRAPT:

- **Seek quality over quantity.** Don't race around the room trying to meet everyone. Focus on building quality relationships.
- **Give first.** Don't focus on what you can get or making a sale. Focus on giving something that the other person wants or needs.
- **Be strategic.** Don't lose sight of the bigger picture. Focus on events that have the right people in the room.
- **Practice self-compassion.** Don't burn yourself out by doing too much. Focus on the events that feel good and fill your tank.

Mastering several skills will help you be successful at networking—especially during planned networking events. Consider these additional tactics for being the best networker you can be:

- **Listen skillfully.** Because networking is a way to build and maintain mutually beneficial relationships, it is more important to listen than to talk. Build trust by listening.
- **Demonstrate a positive attitude.** This should come through in your words, tone, body language, and outlook on life. Always consider what impression you are leaving.
- **Plan strategically.** Just as a business makes investments to gain a return, investing in networking should deliver the return you desire.
- **Practice authenticity.** Don't pretend to be someone you aren't. If you are only in it to take, you will be discovered.

- **Remember names.** Networking is about building relationships for the future. Remembering names isn't easy, but there are tricks you can use to improve name recall.
- **Ask interesting questions.** Networking is about getting the other person to talk. Ask questions that find the passion in others: What excites them, what's the best thing that's happened, what are they looking forward to, and what's important to them?
- **Get out of your comfort zone.** Tell yourself that you are at an event for a reason. Sometimes you have to just go for it and introduce yourself to the biggest name at the event. Don't be afraid to take a risk.
- **Model your values.** Project the right tone when you meet someone. Be aware of the energy you bring to the conversation.
- **Follow up.** The best networking occurs after the networking event is over. Make the follow-up immediate and personal.

Consulting Tip

Use a journal or online tool to track your conversations, make notes about each person, plan follow-up actions, and document ideas generated. Check out the sample networking journal at td.org /handbook-for-consultants.

Conversation Openers and Builders

Breathe, smile, and find someone to engage with. I usually start with the host (who will typically introduce you to someone else), someone in line waiting for a beverage or to register, or someone who sparks an idea. (The last is my favorite.) Start a conversation—be curious, funny, wry, and just be yourself. Some of the conversation openers I use include:

- How do you feel about networking?
- What lights you up, gets you excited, or inspired you to come?
- I am new to this group. Do you have any recommendations for what I should do or who to meet?
- I'm curious about . . .
- Love your shoes; I love this song.

Once you've started the conversation, good networkers will continue to build it. Your new contacts will notice if you get them to tell you about themselves first. One way to do this is by not answering the "What do you do or what are you working on?" questions first. I learned this the hard way. For example, I lost a potential opportunity to do more work with a favorite client because I excitedly shared a different project I was working on. The client gave me great feedback on that project, but we ran out of time just as they were sharing what they were working on. It was an amazing project. I would have loved to work on it, but I blew the opportunity!

Clay Ostrom, owner and lead brand strategist of Map and Fire, saved me from future mistakes by sharing this hot tip: When someone asks what you're doing, respond with, "Oh, I can tell you more about me later. I'd really love to hear about you instead."

Make a list of questions or phrases you can use to engage with curiosity, generosity, and gratitude. Here are a few conversation builders that I use:

- What challenge are you going to tackle this year?
- What are you learning or reading?
- That sounds interesting, where can I learn more about it?
- Who do you recommend I follow if I want to learn more about . . . ?
- What recommendations do you have for . . . ?
- What metrics are important for your business? (This is my favorite to ask people in different roles and industries.)
- Thank you for sharing.

Always end with a thank-you. If you like the person, ask to connect on LinkedIn. Your follow-up connection note should include the event name and reflections from your conversation. The goal is to trigger memories of you, not just the event. Is there too much to remember? Check out the networking wheel tool at td.org/handbook-for-consultants.

Consulting Tip

Practice gratitude by recognizing cleaning crews, volunteers, security teams, and other people who are not in the spotlight. Use their names, smile, and recognize the value they add to the event. If you struggle with meeting people at events, start by thanking the people who work at them. This short effort makes it easier to approach someone new for a longer conversation.

Develop a Networking Strategy

I've encouraged you to attend a networking event and provided some guidelines about how to be successful. Once you're ready to take the next step, you can develop a network strategy that supports your growth.

4C Networking Framework

Use the 4C Networking Framework to strategically invest your time and energy to build a network that supports your life goals as an individual, a business owner, a service provider, and a community leader (Figure 27-1). Hassan Dassat, a consultant and trainer from Mozambique, works with multibillion-dollar corporations and local and global partners to develop local businesses and improve the lives of Mozambicans. He suggests "aligning networking strategies with your professional and personal goals." What great advice—and you can use this framework to do just that.

Figure 27-1. The 4C Networking Framework

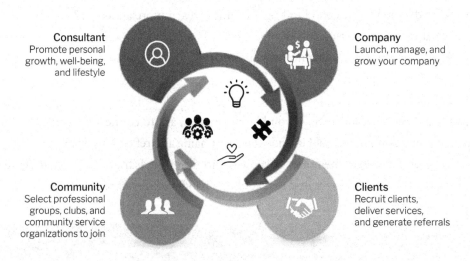

As you develop your strategy, ask yourself questions in each of the four areas—consultant, company, clients, and community. Let's start by looking at some of the questions I ask myself, as well as some insights for how I would answer them.

Consultant

Questions to ask:

- Why do you want to be a consultant?
- What will this career transition do for you personally? For your family?
- What will you do to maintain your overall well-being?
- Are you an athlete, artist, activist, a parent, or a caretaker? Consulting can be a demanding career, so find ways to build networking activities into your lifestyle.

I became a consultant to help clients design social impact programs and partnerships that drive change at scale, and I wanted to be able to work at a pace that fit my life. When I started consulting in 2020, my father lived in Florida and had terminal cancer, my family had moved from Colorado to California, and my kids needed support to manage the transitions and loss. Because I needed to be available for family, my networking strategy was focused on discovery and low-touch activities like training, webinars, virtual conferences, and occasional one-on-one meetings. As my family demands decreased, I was able to shift to more high-touch community-building activities to build trust-based relationships and my brand. By working at the pace of my life, I was able to balance my professional and personal demands while building a global network of trusted advisors to support my company, add value to my clients, and engage community stakeholders.

Company

Questions to ask:

- Will you be a solopreneur or an agency owner?
- How can you find others whom you'd like to work with?
- What skills and knowledge should you look for in an accountant, lawyer, and banker?
- How can you learn the skills required to run the business side of your consulting practice?

You are creating a company, so your answer to this question will determine your networking strategy. If you're a solopreneur, you may look for potential partners, subcontractor roles, or long-term contracts. As an agency owner, you may be scouting potential employees, identifying HR firms to manage employment issues, or finding legal and banking support to navigate international contracting and banking laws. The decisions you make may also influence where you invest your time. If you are a solopreneur, your local ATD chapter is a great place to network. If you are building an agency, you may want to join the board of an organization that attracts a diverse group of community leaders (the Red Cross is a great example). You may also want to attend more events with your local chamber of commerce.

While I'm currently a solopreneur, I'm also building an agency. Before I hired consultants from Africa, I leveraged my network to ask for advice. I was given sample contracts, banking recommendations, and advice on how to navigate key regulations. My network also recommended a lawyer who could help me adapt my contract to the relevant country context. As River Wolf Group grows, we will continue to hire employees and seek B Corps certification. Through my startup and impact investor networks, I've already identified two founders willing to coach me through the hiring and certification processes.

Clients

Questions to ask:

- Who is your ideal client? Are you targeting individuals, companies, government agencies, or nonprofits?
- What products or services will you deliver?
- What problems will you solve for your clients?
- What do you need to learn about your clients' industries, competition, challenges, and performance drivers?
- How will you measure success for your business?
- Will you have a few clients or hundreds?
- What revenue and customer satisfaction targets are important?

Your answers to these questions will influence where you should invest your networking time. For individuals, you might work on promoting your online presence. If you are focused on companies, invest time developing a network in specific industries. If you're an executive coach, prioritize events and activities that help you build connections with CEOs and other members of the C-suite.

River Wolf Group clients include companies, foundations, and associations investing in long-term initiatives (more than five years). We are engaged to support vision and strategy and startup, pilot, pivot, or scale-up activities. Our key metrics include relationship length, referrals, and repeat business.

Whether we focus on client recruitment or retention, we use the same networking strategies. We invest in long-term relationships by engaging several times a year to share a resource, express gratitude, send a care package, or celebrate a milestone. We have fun building these relationships and our clients appreciate the effort we make. They know we are committed to their success, whether we are paid or not. The approach often results in new contracts or referrals.

To reach prospects, I attend foundation events in my community; provide free training; engage in corporate social responsibility (CSR) and environment, social, and governance (ESG) groups on LinkedIn; and attend in-person and virtual conferences that have sessions on corporate-nonprofit partnerships.

Community

Questions to ask:

- Do you currently volunteer with or donate to community organizations?
- What award ceremonies could you attend?
- Do you engage with professional organizations or business communities?
- How might engaging in the community elevate your brand?

Volunteer service, giving, and engagement activities are great ways to tap into your purpose while building your network. However, make sure you provide services to your community because you want to and because it's a part of your consulting practice's purpose. People will know if you aren't doing it for the right reasons.

To build connections and add value to my network, I need to stay on top of key trends influencing businesses and understand problems from a wide range of perspectives. The quickest way to do this is by networking in the community and showing up in unexpected places. Whether I am attending a board meeting, a startup event, an ATD chapter meeting, or a community conversation, I always look for new people who spark aha moments and share new insights. The connections I make and the resources they share can be directly applied to my business, shared with my network, or filed away for future opportunities to add value to my network.

Create Your Networking Strategy

Set aside a half-day to create your networking strategy. Focus on your goals, milestones, and timelines. Begin by answering the questions under each of the 4Cs.

Then, check in with yourself. How are you feeling about your answers? Are you excited? Nervous? Overwhelmed? These feelings will help you set your networking goals. For example, if you are nervous or overwhelmed, what do you need to do or learn to mitigate that?

Finally, set your networking goals. Remember, you are not alone on this journey—your network will help you. So, let's ask the who, why, what, where, and when questions to develop your short- and long-term goals.

Who and Why

Who do you need to find and why do you need to find them? Prioritize the contacts you want to make. For example, I want to meet CEOs because they are my target client and a key source of referrals. I also need to meet their assistants, who can help me gain access to my target client. I also want to find conflict resolution, change management, and communication experts to partner with on large corporate turnaround projects. And I want to find a writer to coach me to become a faster and more succinct writer.

What

What problems came up during the 4Cs exercise? What problems do you need to solve to run your business? Who will help you solve them? What is your business model?

Where

Where will you find the people you need? Do they need to be local or can you find them online? Refer to the 4C Networking Framework to help identify the best places for meeting the people you need. Co-working spaces are a good resource for learning about what is going on around town. You can also use keyword searches to find events, meetups, and associations on the internet. Check out the Sample Networking Planner online at td.org/handbook-for-consultants.

Ladan Manteghi, president of Manteghi Global and Georgetown University's Business for Impact senior advisor, suggests showing up to network where you are not expected. For example, go to places where what you have to say, sell, or advocate for is new but relevant. Show up where the decision makers and those who control the money are. If you can offer new research, data, products, or insights that have value to this audience, you will be seen, heard, and invited back.

When

Finally, draft a yearly networking plan with a focus on the next 90 days. Use the information you've worked through, and include key timelines and targets for any high-priority activities. Don't procrastinate. Hold yourself accountable by sending a personal e-mail or handwritten note to four people now. Share a possible connection, forward a resource, and express your gratitude for them.

Consulting Tip

Hold yourself accountable for your networking plan by doing two things. First, block time to review your strategy and timelines monthly. Update your strategy based on what is working and what has changed in your business or your life. As you grow your business, you may find your priorities changing in response to new opportunities; therefore, adjust your network goals and strategy accordingly. Second, share your networking plan with an accountability partner to maintain your focus.

Summary

As you've read in this chapter, there are many ways to network. To be the most efficient, keep a networking journal to track who you meet, when, how, and what made each person unique. List any ideas that were sparked through networking. Did you identify a new idea for a product or service? Did you learn about a new tool to use in your business? Keep notes and thank people by telling them how they helped you. You may also want to track when you'd like to follow up. Perhaps, it was a good conversation but wasn't relevant for your business (yet). In that case, thank them and make a note to follow up in a year. You should also note how you could help them.

The benefits of networking are many and varied. The beauty of it is that networking can be anything you want it to be. When you're aligned with your networking purpose, you benefit personally and professionally. You should also make sure that you make time for the activities that move you toward achieving your networking goals. You will never simply find time because it's already there. As with any other goal worth pursuing, you must make time for working on networking.

Finally, always feel free to contact me. I can help you build a network that is as rich and rewarding as mine.

Actions to Take Now

- **Network now.** Consider who is in your network and who you want to add. How could you meet them? Who do you know that could connect you?
- **Join a group today.** Find an association, mastermind group, ATD chapter, wellness group, or other community to join. Check the resources at the end of this book. The Consultant Connection Coffee Chat Community is one of my favorite groups for networking with other consultants.
- **It's in your hands.** (Use this book!) Dive into building your network by connecting with other authors in this book.
- **Reconnect.** Identify five acquaintances you haven't connected with in at least a year. Purchase a nice card or write a note on your consulting company's stationary recalling a memory, their impact on you, or something else to connect. Tell them you want to follow up and learn what's new with them in a week. Then do so.

About the Author

Kimberli Jeter founded River Wolf Group, a social impact consulting firm, to enable individuals and their businesses to do good through social impact strategies that generate sustainable value for their people, brand, communities, and the planet. For more than 30 years, she has held a wide range of local and global positions focused on activating purpose, building partnerships, and creating impact ecosystems that help individuals and communities thrive. Kimberli builds and nurtures her global network of partners through her kids' activities, the Consultant Connection Coffee Chat Community, ATD, and social impact and CSR communities. Connect and network with Kimberli on LinkedIn at linkedin.com/in/kimberlijeter and on her company's website, riverwolfgroup.com.

Passive Income

Make Your Consulting Products and Services Work for You

RICH DOUGLAS

Remember the story about the shoemaker and the elves? The shoemaker and his wife were exhausted and at the end of their rope. They had materials to make one more pair of shoes—and then they didn't know what would happen to them. They went to sleep, and in the morning, miraculously, there was a brand-new pair of shoes! The shoes were so beautiful, they sold immediately . . . and for a very good sum. This allowed the shoemaker to purchase enough materials to make dozens more shoes. Once again, he and his wife went to sleep and the next morning their shop was filled with shoes! Their business was revitalized, and they were set for the future. Amazing!

But how? What was happening while they slept? It turned out a few industrious elves appeared each night and made the shoes; once the shoemaker and his wife were set, the elves moved on.

Wouldn't it be great to have that kind of help? And to have your business working (and earning) while you sleep? Well, sorry. We're fresh out of elves! But there are ways for your business to work without you working for it. Some people call this *passive income*.

In this chapter, we'll review the difference between creating custom solutions for your clients and having products—different sources of passive income—the reason for creating these products, the roles you play, and why you might want to consider putting passive income to work for you.

What Is Consulting?

There are as many definitions of consulting as there are, well, chapters in this book. That's an indication of its complexity, not its vagueness. However, whether you're an external consultant or an internal consultant working within the confines of an organization, you partner with your clients to help them meet their business or organizational objectives. Consultants provide value because they are experts or have resources that help clients reach their goals.

Edgar Schein, in his wonderful book *Humble Consulting*, describes two levels of consulting. The first level is transactional—you find a need and meet it. But the second level—where the relationship between the consultant and the client comes first—is where trust lives. That trust has your clients turning to you not with a request or an order, but with their challenges and goals. In many cases, the consultant finds these things out along with the client!

Whether you work at the transactional or relationship level, consulting is typically a very hands-on, labor-intensive process. In short, it requires a lot of *you*. But operating a successful consulting business—one that brings in recurring revenue—doesn't always have to mean that 100 percent of your revenue comes from actively engaging with clients. That's where passive income can help you.

Creating Passive Income Streams

It's possible to turn your expertise and experience into passive income—an income stream that (largely) doesn't involve you in the process. The idea is that your practice earns revenue without requiring you to be present during the engagement between the customer and your product or service.

As you'll see, this isn't usually the case, especially starting out. But you can think of it like a machine: Once it's up and running, it can crank out sales and profits all on its own.

Throughout this chapter, you'll learn about the real-life origin story of Next Element, a global consulting firm co-founded by Nate Reiger. We'll use their example to examine some potential passive income streams and how Nate and his partners made those streams work in their business.

Before we dive in, let's meet Nate and Next Element:

Nate Regier, PhD, spent 11 years as a clinical psychologist before becoming an entrepreneur. He was managing a multistate employee assistance program (EAP) and noticed a prevalence of mental health problems in the workplace. More importantly, he recognized that most of the problems were either caused by miscommunication or drama and could be solved by improving the relationships between leaders and employees. He believed he could make a bigger difference by coaching, consulting with, and training leaders in companies rather than waiting for the fallout to show up in his therapy office.

So, in 2008, Nate left his job and joined three other consultants with a similar passion to form Next Element. Their mission from day one was to bring more compassion to every workplace. Next Element focused on interpersonal communication skills and negotiating healthy conflict because they seemed to be at the root of most problems. When they started, they had no tools of their own, but Nate and his partners were all certified trainers in the Process Communication Model (PCM), a terrific behavioral model of communication that teaches specific behavioral strategies for connecting, motivating, and resolving miscommunication with different personalities.

Assessments

Have you ever taken the Myers-Briggs Type Indicator (MBTI) assessment, a leadership assessment, or gone through a 360-degree evaluation? Well, someone designed those products and sold them, and now they're generating plenty of passive income while users, coaches, and trainers put their assessments to work.

Creating an assessment comes with a couple benefits. First, there's selling the instrument. If your clients value what the instrument can tell them, they will purchase and use it. You can design it so that the administrative work of reporting and explaining the results is completely automated online. So, all you need to do is create the next StrengthsFinder and sell a couple million copies, right? Well, maybe (or maybe not). But creating this type of tool can generate passive income while also leading to other sources of active income, like training programs delivered by you. It may seem like a lot of work, but once established, it's possible for an assessment to run on autopilot.

As certified trainers, licensed to teach PCM to others, Nate's team started by purchasing assessments and training materials from their distributor, Kahler Communications Inc. (KCI). As Next Element grew, they started spending more and more on materials. This ignited a dream to create their own model, certify others to teach it, and then sell materials to others around the world as a form of passive income. To accomplish this goal, the partners focused on four ways to increase their passive income: becoming a distributor for PCM, earning a reputation as thought leaders through publishing, delivering outcome research, and creating their own model for better margins.

Courses and Licensing

So much of what consultants do involves developing others. Whether it's through training, coaching, facilitating, or mentoring, we help organizations perform better by developing their talent. We also help individuals in their careers in the same way: We prepare them for greater challenges. Training courses are a direct way of doing this. We determine what participants need to know, be able to do, and value. Then, we can offer learning experiences that meet those needs.

Training can be split into two categories: synchronous and asynchronous. *Synchronous training*—whether online or in the classroom—happens with everyone participating at the same time. So, if you're the instructor, you must be there and actively teach your clients the course content. *Asynchronous training*, on the other hand, can be designed with you as an active (but not real-time) facilitator, managing discussions, delivering instruction, and answering questions. Or—and this is the good part—you can create training that is hosted on a website and delivered to your clients on demand. Creating and delivering online asynchronous training is a great way to reach a worldwide audience that learns on their time.

Another way to make your content and intellectual property work for you is to license it to others for their use. In doing so, you document what you do (including the content, methods, and tools) so someone else can replicate the process and deliver the program. And they'll pay for the right to use your content. Say, for example, you've developed an innovative way to design and deliver sales training. You could license your method to other consultants who then use it with their clients—or you could license it out directly to a company to use to train their own salespeople.

By 2015, Next Element had established itself as a global leader in PCM and was invited to become a US distributor of the program. This allowed them to train others to teach PCM and resell training materials to their network of certified trainers. This became their first source of passive income. Next Element currently supports a US network of 50 PCM-certified trainers, who purchase digital training materials from them via an online assessment portal.

Nate also wrote the book, *Seeing People Through*, which is a leader's guide to applying PCM in an organization. This book added credibility and reach to their work with PCM; when people discover it, it opens doors for more consulting. In addition, the book led to an invitation from KCI to develop leadership-specific PCM training materials for use around the world. Next Element receives royalties on the sales of these materials, which added another source of passive revenue.

Consulting Tip

Make a list of all the content you have designed and delivered. How many of those programs could be packaged and sold to others?

By 2016, Next Element Consulting had developed its own model for healthy conflict called Leading Out of Drama (LOD). As CEO, Nate supported the model by writing and publishing another book, *Conflict Without Casualties*.

The company also created a suite of online assessments and digital training courses along with a very thorough and replicable train-the-trainer certification process. Their global network of more than 100 trainers, coaches, and consultants could purchase assessments, get individualized digital participant training materials, and track program outcomes, all within the MyNE online portal.

By charging an annual network membership fee, Next Element was able to provide generous and comprehensive support to their trainers. LOD became a third source of passive income for the company, which had grown consistently over the past eight years.

One thing that's important to note when developing materials for licensing and distribution to a larger audience is IP protection. Nate is very adamant about this, noting that "you must protect your IP if you are going to license it and put it in other people's hands. It's necessary for your own credibility but also for those who are working with your tools."

> After using the term *compassionate accountability* for about five years, Next Element decided to trademark it. Recently, they started seeing it show up in similar applications as theirs, and now they encounter someone potentially violating their trademark about once a month.
>
> "It's not fun to address these infringements," explains Nate, "but to us, this is a sign that we created something 'sticky' whose time has come. One of the reviewers of my book told me, 'You have given a name to something we've all been talking about forever, but never quite could identify.'"

Videos

Videos can generate revenue for your practice directly or indirectly. They can be embedded within other training materials or designed to stand alone. Can you think of ways to use stand-alone videos to generate passive income for your consulting practice?

Creating and selling videos is easier today than ever before. No longer do you need a recording studio with expensive equipment, nor a publisher to manufacture, advertise, and sell your videos. You can create professional-looking videos on your own. You just need a computer, software, a good camera (or smartphone), a nice background, and your own good looks and charm. Later, you might get more sophisticated by adding graphics, sound, and even animation, but those aren't necessary to project a professional image and deliver value to clients. Your customers will typically find your videos online through YouTube. But remember, they might not be searching for you—unless you're already famous—but for content on subjects like the ones you excel in. So make sure they're able to locate and view your content because you've uploaded it where they can find it.

How does this create passive income? Videos posted to YouTube are often accompanied by advertising. If you generate enough *hits* (views of your content), you can earn money from the ads on your videos. Some content creators even have sponsors that pay them to advertise their products and services within the video. Either way, the more your video is viewed, the more you get paid.

Beyond being a source of passive income, videos can provide support and credibility to your practice. Viewers may watch your content and decide they want to work with you. Or someone considering working with you might look for your content online. Making this available to potential clients is a great way for them to see you in action.

> Next Element has its own YouTube channel and has curated a variety of playlists. During the COVID-19 pandemic, they developed a free, biweekly webinar series to provide customer support and generate interest in their solutions. Next Element even submitted a video to a LinkedIn competition and received recognition as a finalist.
>
> The handout for this chapter, which can be found online at td.org/handbook -for-consultants, has links to several of their YouTube videos, including:
>
> - The playlist for *Compassionate Accountability* includes the book trailer and a variety of shorts. While these videos don't produce any revenue, they help generate interest in the company and the book.
> - The playlist for their flagship enterprise-level product—The Compassion Mindset—has several promotional videos designed just for marketing, including Next Element's official two-minute promo video.

Books

Writing a book can enhance your business either directly or indirectly. Catch lightning in a bottle—write the next bestseller—and you'll sell thousands of books! Unfortunately, the vast majority of books sell far fewer copies. So, why do it? A book can bring indirect benefits to your practice. You can use it as a prestige piece to give to potential clients. Or, you might have a great idea you want to document and present. Perhaps you'd like to include the book on your website to add legitimacy to your message. Whatever the reason, publishing and selling your book can directly generate revenue while also adding some oomph to your professional practice.

> Nate's book *Compassionate Accountability* supports Next Element's Compassionate Mindset framework and enhances the company's credibility to provide consulting and assessment services for larger clients.

But what about all the free content you're giving away? While most people won't do business with you just because they read your complimentary book or viewed your video, a few people will! And don't worry about giving away content for free. You certainly can deliver a lot more value to your clients than what you put into a free sample. (And if you can't, you may need to rethink your business.)

Stay Informed

Just because your passive income plan is producing revenue, that doesn't mean you should ignore it. Stay aware of what's happening in your industry and whether you need to change or remove any income streams as a result.

> Since the COVID-19 pandemic, Next Element's mission has become more focused on finding ways to expand the reach and impact of compassion in every workplace. They elevated *Compassionate Accountability* to become their unifying framework—the company's umbrella brand.
>
> To meet the growing demand for compassion and accountability in leadership and organizations, and increase their passive revenue potential, Next Element developed an enterprise-level program called The Compassion Mindset. This program is built to scale within organizations by certifying in-house L&D teams to use their materials, which means that Next Element isn't responsible for leading the training programs. Their train-the-trainer certification process is relatively short (eight to 12 hours), and the curriculum is accessible and easy to apply right away. Certified trainers are quickly able to help their leaders deal with difficult situations more effectively and improve their interpersonal leadership skills.

Getting Started

So, all you need to do is throw a program together, stick it on your website, and watch the cash roll in, right? Well, not exactly. There are many different roles involved in this process. As we review each one, think about who in your company can bring their experience to the role. And for you solopreneurs out there, realize that, while these roles must be performed, you don't have to do them all yourself—so think about what you bring to the table and where you will need help.

Project Manager

Someone has to coordinate the work. And that someone is likely you. Whether you do all the work yourself or partner with others, you'll need to ensure it gets done correctly. Planning, designing, delivering, and evaluating the results are all necessary to hit the three key marks: a product that's high quality, on time, and within budget. You can get help with these things, but if it's your practice (or you lead a department for internal consultants), it's on you.

Subject Matter Expert

Your subject matter expertise forms the basis for any passive income sources. You should build products and services designed for passive income around the same subjects you focus on in your consulting work.

Designer

Depending on your skills, you might be able to design the products and services you hope to sell as passive income sources. However, most consultants are not also book designers or video producers or assessment validators, so you might need to partner with a designer to shape what you know and can do into a product or service. You'll need to determine what degree of quality you want to put forward and how much that might cost you in upfront expenses.

Host or Administrator

After creating the products you're going to sell to produce passive income, you have to put them somewhere. Your products must be located where customers can find them, buy them, and use them. You could host them on your company's website, as Nate did, or you could partner with a company that specializes in doing this.

Marketer

You will need to get the word out so your customers can find you and your content. If you host the product on your website, you will need to learn more about search engine optimization to ensure it's visible. You should also link your content (wherever it's hosted) to other places people find you, like Nate did with YouTube and other social media platforms. And you should probably offer a lead generator to offer value first. Some of these may generate revenue, but they should also generate leads for your more complex consulting offers.

> Next Element created a free 18-lesson e-course to use as a lead generator. It's delivered through email and helps people experience their compassionate conflict methodology.

Evaluator

Even with passive income sources, consultants should consider how to evaluate whether their products are delivering the intended outcomes for their clients. Whether it is learning about their experiences through a poll, measuring what they learned, or even seeing whether they used the content, it is vital for consultants to know if they're achieving what their clients seek. Otherwise, your book might go unread, your videos unwatched, your assessments untaken, and your licensed products unused. So, whether you evaluate your own products or get help, do it! You should also evaluate whether any passive income streams are still serving their intended purpose.

> Use evaluation to help make business decisions. For example, in 2022, Next Element looked at the webinars they'd delivered in 2020 and 2021 and unlisted the best ones from YouTube. Now they offer these recordings as paid webinars or license them to clients who are looking for short training content. While this isn't a major source of revenue, it's a nice option for clients who aren't ready to hire the company in person.

All these roles need to be completed, but you don't have to do it alone. Reach out through your network or ask fellow consultants for leads on other experts who might be able to help. Be sure to check out the Are You Ready to Launch a Product? self-assessment online at td.org/handbook-for-consultants.

> Next Element now has several tested and proven sets of behavioral technologies to bring more compassion to every workplace. They have plans to scale and increase passive revenue by licensing their IP to organizations that might want to share it with their customers or integrate it into their offerings. Through it all, the company's mission remains the same: Bring more compassion to every workplace while making a living doing it. (You can learn more about Next Element on their website, Next -Element.com, or by contacting Nate directly at nate@next-element.com.)

Why Consider Passive Income?

Going from working for your consulting practice to having it work for you—or, more likely, doing both—sounds like hard work. And it is. But as Next Element's example shows, it can be done incrementally, and you don't have to treat it as an all-or-nothing prospect. Many of these ideas can be tested on a trial basis.

In return, there are real benefits to taking this approach, including:

- The most important reason is an increase in revenue. Passive income is the solution to making money without counting the hours. Or, as many say, "Making money while you sleep."
- When you create products and services to generate passive income, they are generally sold as off-the-shelf products—what you see is what you get. However, they can sometimes be modified to meet specific clients' needs, which is referred to as "customized off the shelf." Whether you customize your products is largely driven by the customer's needs and the scale of the work. In most passive income situations, you'll stop at an off-the-shelf product. But for big clients, you might decide to customize your offer to fit their needs—you won't have to build from scratch; instead, you'll modify it for their needs.
- By making your offer less about you, it will be more flexible in the long run because you'll be able to add licensing, sell it, or leave it to others. Having passive

income streams makes your business more valuable. It also creates a company that is bigger than you, which means it doesn't have to go away when you do!

- Creating passive income streams doesn't have to affect your more client-centric, active consulting practice. You can have the best of both worlds. You can continue consulting and make money while you sleep. The existence of these additional income streams gives your practice more gravitas.

Summary

In this chapter, we explored the concepts of generating passive income by creating stand-alone products and services that don't need your active participation. Books, courses, videos, and many more products can do this for you. We also examined the roles that need to be performed and who can do them. Finally, we looked at some of the reasons why a consultant might want to create paths for passive income.

As consultants, we're accustomed to being hired for our experience, expertise, and insights, but there are other ways to enhance your businesses that don't require constant attention and involvement. It doesn't have to take a huge effort or risk to try one of these ideas to see some results. So, go out there and put passive income to work for you!

Actions You Can Take Now

- **Pick one.** Review the different ways to create passive income and decide which interest you the most. Select one item, create an action plan, set a deadline, and share your plan with an accountability partner.
- **Take a consultant to coffee.** Identify a consultant who produces the kind of passive income you would like to produce. Take them out to coffee or lunch, and ask them all the questions swirling around in your head.

About the Author

Rich Douglas is a performance consultant and principal of Rich Douglas Consulting. He has extensive experience in training, leadership, and delivering solutions for AT&T, the CIA, NASA, the Department of Homeland Security, and others. A retired US Air Force officer, Rich has also been a faculty member for several universities. He holds a PhD in higher education from Union Institute and University and a DSocSci in human resource development from the University of Leicester. He is certified in human resources (SPHR) and talent development (CPTD). He is also a Professional Certified Coach (PCC). You can contact Rich at rich@richdouglasconsulting.com or view his website at richdouglas consulting.com.

Focusing on Your Future

Define Success Your Way

During his 67-year career, Ed Schein authored dozens of books, including *Humble Consulting*, on career dynamics, organizational culture, group dynamics, and interpersonal interactions. His model of organizational culture and writings on relationships and trust are still used by managers today. Ed was perceptive, insightful, intelligent, and able to see what others could not.

Although his book *Career Anchors* may have brought the most recognition, Ed's eyes always lit up when he was talking about organizational culture. And that's why I invited Ed to write one of our luminary chapters. He and I were working together (with the help of Berrett-Koehler) to clarify exactly what would be in his chapter; one evening, he reached out to let me know that the fifth edition of *Career Anchors* would be coming out at the end of March. He was so excited about it. And then the next morning, I learned that he'd passed away. That so epitomizes Ed—contributing to the profession until his last breath. He was 94 when he died.

We are honored that his son, Peter, agreed to step in to write the luminary chapter for this section. As a co-founder of the Organizational Culture and Leadership Institute, Peter has dedicated his work to advancing organization development. If you are an experienced consultant, I encourage you to read Peter's chapter, which focuses on four sticky notes he found in his father's office after he died. To consider yourself a consummate consultant, consider how your profession must align with your life.

The last section of this handbook is all about defining your own personal success. One of the reasons you likely became a consultant was to do what you love and to add value. I believe that no one should get up and go to work every day. Instead, you should all love what you do so much that it feels like play. Use this section to pause and think about whether you're still excited about the direction you are going. Do you still feel like you are playing every day?

In her chapter, Christie Ward reminds you of this very thing, as well as the importance of doing consulting your way. Then, Steve Cohen cautions you to avoid common mistakes that consultants make, while Kevin Marshall and Rusty Shields encourage you to look back, reflect, and determine whether you need to refocus your strategy. Mike Kent discusses how consulting is a relationship business. The final chapter by Beverly Crowell, who currently works with Peter Block at Designed Learning, provides the perfect bookend to this handbook. She offers best practices and poignant lessons for building trusting relationships with clients that start with the contracting meeting.

5 Surefire Ways to Build Trusting Relationships With Clients

Why do consultants need to build trusting relationships? Consultants solve problems, typically without tangible products, which means that the service they're selling is invisible. And when consultants do their job well, their clients usually get the credit for what they do. But that's a good thing! Your clients are paying you for your expertise and should at least be rewarded for finding you to solve their problems. But what does this have to do with building relationships?

Because it's rare for consultants to receive organization-wide acclaim or recognition for their work, you'll need to build relationships based on a foundation of trust. These trusting relationships will lead to additional assignments, referrals to new clients, and repeat business. Clients are more likely to trust you with their problems if they trust you as a person.

Let's look at a few different ways you can build trust with your clients.

1. Keep Your Word

This is a logical place to start—do what you say you're going to do, follow through with action, and keep your promises. A no-brainer, right? Well not necessarily if you are building a relationship with a client. Consultants want to be helpful, but there may be times when you just can't do what you thought you could. It happens to all of us. If (when) this happens to you, don't put off delivering the bad news; do it as soon as possible.

One suggestion is to combine the bad news with information about what you've done already and your plan to alleviate the situation. For example, imagine you learned about a regulation that was part of the solution, which was going to cause you to miss the deadline. You could tell your client that although you're going to miss the deadline, you've already started to fulfill the requirement and are adjusting the schedule by doing a couple tasks in parallel. Of course, you want to always keep your word, if possible, but things happen. Do what's right.

2. Make Trust Your Signature
Consider how you can build trust everywhere—it should be a daily occurrence. Don't expect immediate results, but don't do it as a gimmick either. Build trust because it's the right thing to do. It fosters collaboration and inclusiveness. What do you do every day to demonstrate honesty, reliability, consistency, integrity, and discretion? You can make trust your signature in all that you do and build a reputation of trust.

3. Show That You Appreciate Your Clients
A critical part of building a trusting relationship is to show appreciation for your current clients, past clients, and potential clients. Yes, it takes effort to maintain a relationship with everyone, but there is a huge payoff. Stay in touch with past clients by sending a note to ask how they are doing. Stay in touch with current clients by checking in with them during your project. How about potential clients? Consultants who are just out to make money probably won't take the effort to maintain relationships with clients who don't purchase their services. But that's a mistake. Don't be the consultant who disappears after hearing a couple nos. If you think that you can help a potential client, stick to it and remember that the best salespeople only spend a small percentage of their time selling. Instead, they invest in learning about the client's challenges, discovering what problems need solving, and building the relationship.

4. Go the Extra mile
No, I'm not saying that you should allow scope creep to slip in—instead recognize that everyone needs help now and again. This also does not mean taking responsibility for other's problems because that means you are taking control and preventing your clients from

learning and developing themselves. Instead, build trust by helping them learn to trust and improve themselves without building dependency. This means being kind, providing a listening ear, or pointing them in the right direction. Others will notice if you offer help when it provides no direct benefit to you.

5. Admit Your Mistakes

It's hard to admit your mistakes, but it is crucial for building a trusting relationship. Don't hide them. Don't make excuses. Don't blame others. When you accept and acknowledge mistakes, you'll provide another opportunity to build trust. By demonstrating your vulnerability, admitting your mistakes, and sharing what you learn from them, you demonstrate that you are human too. It's impossible to build trust if others see inconsistencies between what you do and say.

Building trust isn't easy and it takes a long time. And the sad thing about trust is that it can be wiped out with one careless action—a white lie, an upcharge for travel expenses, or an exaggerated fact. Don't do it. Building a trusting relationship with your clients is part of your brand. It is your reputation. What do you do best and how can you make it a part of your brand?

CHAPTER 29

Big Ideas on Little Notes

Central Themes in the Work of Edgar H. Schein (Author of *Humble Consulting*)

PETER A. SCHEIN, *LUMINARY CONSULTING AUTHOR*

When Ed moved his office to California in 2011, he filled it with mementos, images, ideas, and inspirations, creating a fertile environment for him to write, consult, and create. One of the walls in that office was covered with nearly 50 colorful sticky notes—visible reflections of what was important to him. These notes captured many vital themes of Ed's work, including thinking, analyzing, sorting out, and fretting about people in groups and organizations. What follows are my reflections on time I spent with Ed, along with some of his big ideas captured on four of those little squares.

Embrace the Personization Journey

About 70 years of Ed's scholarship are captured in this first note. Let's start with what looks like a typo—the word is *personization*, not *personalization*. We introduced this word in *Humble Leadership* (2018) because the interpersonal process is very different from the more mechanistic idea of personalization or customization. Certainly, it is possible to create a bespoke future where everything we consume is tailored to our individual

> *Personization. . . . The manager's journey to the human side of enterprise!*

needs, but a manager who wants to become a leader must do more than tailor directions to teams to get their attention and get results. *Personization* means forging a whole-person-to-whole-person relationship—not just between peers, but most importantly in reporting relationships up and down an organizational hierarchy. The manager who wants to become a leader needs to motivate and inspire to catalyze forward progress and achieve desired results, and they recognize that a critical part of that is having a personal connection, empathy, and insight into the tailwinds and headwinds each individual is facing at work and at home.

While this leadership mindset may sound very 21st-century, it can be traced back directly to thought leadership from the mid-20th century and post-Taylor industrial optimization and efficient organizational portfolio thinking. "The human side of enterprise" was how Douglas McGregor described what more broadly might be called *humanism* in organizations today. He was the one who recruited Ed to MIT in the 1960s, and he clearly had a foundational impact on Ed's thinking. McGregor's Theory X and Theory Y were never far from Ed's mind in any intervention with an organization grappling with people problems. Does the organization think of its employees as resources, nodes, or cogs in a machine, who are motivated by direct incentives, coin-operated, or otherwise not inclined to productivity unless the implicit contract offers a fair day's work for a fair day's pay? Or, does it think of its employees as motivated, purposeful, and responsible adults sharing a common vision for a successful future? Although Theory X or Theory Y, varies by industry, geography, history, and maturity of the organization, Ed found that he could get a good sense of which theory held sway not too long into his initial encounter with a leader.

"Journey" may be the most important word in this note. It is unusual for the forces propelling Theory X and Theory Y to remain constant or static in an organization because its cultures are continually evolving based on the changes in and within those in charge. Generally, the rate of these kinds of changes has only increased. Any manager hoping to become a leader today must embrace the journey, the troubled waters and shifting sands, knowing that it's only possible to come out better off in the end if they are taking stock of the turmoil and figuring out how to get through it with the help of those around them. The benefit of personization is what they're able to learn along the way. A manager and a group build openness and trust in the process of personization, and through that collective journey, they learn how to better anticipate, elevate, or correct for the contributions of one another so that next time the sand shifts, they already know how to better face the challenge together.

It's important to recognize that Ed did not say personization would get you to the human side of enterprise. He said it was a journey because the human side is not a place, it is way of thinking when confronting the next set of challenges. Great leaders who started as managers are great learners—they've been able to learn from both their own journey and the journeys of others alongside them.

Consulting Tip

To become truly successful, you must seek to develop whole-person relationships with your clients. Only through the kind of openness and trust that emerges through personization can you deliver not just the results your clients want, but the ones they need.

Build a Culture of Asking, Not Telling

Aren't great leaders supposed to inspire and direct by telling their followers everything they know? Knowledge from experience is power, and experience needs to be taught to others. This is fundamental to the modern leadership mindset, particularly in technology-centric industries in which deep content knowledge can be pivotal to leadership decision making. Ed referred to this mindset as the "culture of tell"—leaders believe they know a lot, and the obligation of leading is telling others what they know will help make the firm successful (Schein 2013).

Telling me turns me cold. Asking me warms me up.

The reality, however, is that others in the room may know more than the nominal leader. Ed's sticky note reminds us that, at the group level, telling creates a disparity or asymmetry—a situation when those who know are advantaged and those who don't are disadvantaged (or left feeling cold). When people feel like they're being "told to," especially when it's something they already know, Ed's notion of turning cold also means turning inward and, most perilously for the group, not sharing what they know. Too much telling leads to very little sharing. By talking at the group for the sake of coming across as the most informed and authoritative, the leader or the consultant may end up leaving the group cold toward one another rather than warmed up to tackle a challenge collectively.

At the individual and consultant level, telling before asking only widens the distance between people rather than drawing them together. Think about it. When you are told something you already know or feel like you are being lectured to, you probably start wondering why that person is acting that way toward you, rather than thinking, "This person seems interested in me. How can I help them?" Again, Ed's notion of cold can be interpreted as distant, while warm suggests growing closer together.

In the second edition of *Humble Inquiry* (2021), we referred to "drawing someone out" not in a manipulative sense but in a collaborative sense. It's important to remember that we can draw someone out through skilled inquiry and warm them up to work with us rather than alongside or against us. Ed spent a lot of time teaching how humble inquiry does not mean asking questions—it means strengthening openness and trust, or warmth, with each other. The simplest example is asking a yes or no question—what you're actually doing is telling the other person that you know so much you can narrow the answer down to two options, yes or no. Because you usually don't know that much, a yes or no question (or response) can feel just as cold as if you were told something. Why? Sharing begets warmth. We need to realize that sharing does not start with telling—it starts with inquiring.

As a professor, Ed spent a great deal of time in his last couple decades thinking about the complex dynamic of telling and inquiring. His own struggles (isn't it the professor's role to tell people stuff) no doubt contributed to his belief that we must be mindful of when we are truly inquiring versus telling, even in the form of a question. If there is one underlying theme in our Humble Leadership book series, it is the call to all of us (as managers, leaders, and even spouses and partners) to be conscious of the US culture's inclination to tell. Authentically developing what we call "level 2" relationships of openness and trust requires learning humble inquiry skills. The simplest test we can apply in any situation is simply asking ourselves, "Am I asking a question that I truly do not know the answer to?" This draws the inquirer and the other person closer together because implicit in such a question is the acknowledgment of mutual interdependence, or as Ed said, warmth.

Consulting Tip

Plan to ask more than you tell, especially when you start working with a new client. Always bring a list of thoughtful questions to your first meeting to ensure you're helping them solve the right problem.

Remember Humanity's Innate Social Talents

This note was on Ed's wall many years before we knew that generative AI in forms such as ChatGPT would be better at being a human than a human could ever be at being a machine. I will never bet against a machine's ability to assimilate vast amounts of information and assemble a rational argument more efficiently than a human. However, while it is not in this note per se, efficiency is the operative word here, which Ed and I talked about all the time. The concern that people would become more machine than human was centered on Ed's concern that we would soon focus more on efficiency than effectiveness.

The danger is not that machines will become human, but that humans will become machines.

Imagine a two-by-two matrix with "known" and "unknown" down the vertical and across the horizontal axes. In the upper left-hand corner are the known knowns. Here the question is how well we can process and decide based on known parameters and known values. It is hard to argue that humans are better at this set of calculations. For example, think of the efficiencies we have gained in the last half century by letting computers handle these bounded tasks, like spreadsheets and databases in accounting and finance.

In the upper right-hand corner, our challenge is the known unknowns. Here again computers are far more efficient at crunching through all the permutations. We know the variables, but don't know the values; computers can cast the possibilities at lightspeed and perhaps even determine their probabilities with rapid clarity. Think of how scenario planning has been aided by this gained efficiency.

It gets a bit trickier, however, in the lower left-hand corner (the unknown knowns). This is where ChatGPT could come into play—constructing a position, an argument, or a stance by generatively assembling clauses and phrases that lead to a known acceptable conclusion. The efficiency of AI's ability to creatively assemble those subarguments so well that we don't realize a computer was doing it has awed and perhaps terrified us all. The idea that ChatGPT can write a college-level English paper or that generative AI can pass the LSAT is disconcerting. But, can we feel a little better knowing that we are still dealing with newly found assimilation efficiencies in supercomputing over lightspeed networks and massive storage arrays. Isn't it still in the realm of content assimilation, rather than perception or interpretation?

It is in the lower right-hand cell, the unknown unknowns, where the human ability to process context alongside content must be revered and protected. Ultimately, this is the crux of Ed's note: Humans lose if we spend too much of our waking and working hours chasing efficiency because it's a race we will lose every day to computers. This is another example of everything coming down to relationships between people. If we simply treat each other transactionally, maintain a professional distance, and keep one another at arm's length, aren't we bound to lose a throughput race to computers that are so much better at transactions?

When dealing with unknown unknowns, humans combine their ideas, guesses, fears, and arguments with their emotions and reactions to one another in conversations. It may not seem very efficient when we relate with one another through the genuine openness and trust of personal relationships, yet the ability to test an idea against alternatives in our gut-reactions or collective instincts turns assimilation into synergy because we arrive at an answer as well as an emotional commitment to it.

This message is especially important for consultants. We move beyond transactional relationships when we respond to each other's reactions to our inputs. It's not the input A or B of a transaction, it is "Do I understand how you feel about A or B? Do I understand how the transaction might affect you?" Dealing with recurring unknown unknowns requires head and gut, or brain and heart. Whether or not we need to be efficient depends on the scope of the problem. At any rate, we are compelled to be both affective and effective with each other if we want to continue to adapt and learn.

I suppose it's a good thing Ed won't be here to see the day computers replicate the social synergy I'm hinting at here. Nevertheless, in his last days, he remained quite concerned about humans letting technical obsessions obscure our social talents and obligations to one another.

Consulting Tip

Build every client relationship with genuine openness and trust, testing solutions and ideas against alternatives. In doing so, you will identify a solution that has the emotional commitment required for a successful implementation.

Spend More Time Observing Than Predicting

There are two things going on in this note. First, it draws directly from our experience with Bob Johansen at the Institute for the Future and our shared affinity for William Gibson's idea that "the future is already here—it's just unevenly distributed." Ed's family-first paraphrase is that we can anticipate much about the future if we just take the time and effort to observe (rather than judge) what the younger generations are up to. And it's not just referring to kids and grandkids; we all have plenty of younger colleagues or acquaintances we can observe as well. Ed and I added this idea to our nested model of the practice of culture in organizations—our *technical culture* (strategy, tactics, infrastructure, and design) is enveloped by our *social culture* (how we relate to each other), which is in turn a reflection of the *macro culture* (occupational, national and regional, and political-economic context) in which we live and work.

> *Don't predict the future; observe it in your kids and grandkids.*

These three nested dimensions of cultural practice are in motion whenever trends (what Ed and I call "metaculture") come and go, norms change, leaders rise and fall, technologies win and lose, and so on. It's all out there; the question is whether we take the time to observe and interpret it in the spirit of Clifford Geertz (1974), a founding father of cultural interpretation. "The trick," Geertz said, "is to figure out what the devil they think they are up to." This is tricky because the interpreter must be close enough to the subject to understand what they think.

It's easy to make a judgment about something you think might be important in the future. What matters, however, is what the youngest influencers of cultural directions choose to focus on. Perhaps Ed was suggesting we take the pressure off trying so hard to predict the future. It's a lot more meaningful and probably more fun to spend time in open and present observation, with eyes and ears, of what younger relatives or teammates do and say about what they are up to.

Consultants should spend time with a broad spectrum of their client's employees. Interview employees at every level, from every department, at all stages of their careers, and from every generation to ensure you have the data you require. *Observing* is a social process and a discipline that requires a sustained commitment to drive a sustained meaning. Understanding the metaculture requires continuous observation and active interpretation. But remember, this process of observing and interpreting does not diminish older cohorts' agency over the future—rather it frees us to hear new voices and new inputs so that our satisfaction comes not as much from predicting but from feeling like we are not surprised.

The second chord of significance in this note is the importance of inquiry. Here, Ed does not just refer to the biological parent, he means any person in a teaching, training, or mentoring role. He was well aware of how much his kids and grandkids looked up to him, but he would be quick to note that this had little to do with his status or seniority in the family. Instead, it was because of the effort and time he devoted to developing open and trusting relationships with each of his seven grandkids, individually, over the course of three decades. As the family patriarch, Ed could have directed his grandkids in ways that he valued, yet he would only offer up his values in response to what he sensed they valued. This is what *helping* meant to Ed. And getting to that level of helping took time—he had to draw them out and get them to share their hopes and fears before he could help his grandkids see for themselves what would work best for them.

> **Consulting Tip**
>
> Consulting requires that you learn what each client values. It is not about imposing the right answer on them.

Summary

I want to close with this final thought for *helpers* (also known as consultants). Ed would always disclaim that he was an expert on very few things because he believed that *expert* was a status or role with bounded value to add. Yet, Ed did have routines that were just as critical as any expert's axioms.

"Everything is an intervention," and the success of interventions depends upon developing openness and trust (level 2) with the people you are trying to help. It does not matter what you think they need to improve. What matters is how they begin to understand how they need to improve. In other words, your value-add, your help, is how well your clients learn to help themselves. And this is achieved through humble inquiry, which is a process not a lesson. If everything is an intervention and every situation is different, you may be wondering how it's even possible to scale. However, whenever I told Ed, "Easy for you to say. You're a well-known professor who's been doing this for 50 years," his response would be, "OK, but I learned this as a young professor on my first major consulting gig with Digital Equipment Corporation."

Go forward as a helper. From your very first engagement, be confident that you are learning to help by helping them to learn.

Actions You Can Take Now

- **Explore the consulting knowns and unknowns.** Draw a two-by-two matrix with "known" and "unknown" down the vertical and across the horizontal axes. Then, complete the grid based on your relationship with your most recent client.
- **Create quality questions.** Develop a list of interview questions to help you get to know potential clients as well as the problem they are trying to solve. Your starter list might include 20 to 30 questions in categories such as teamwork, quality, customer focus, or communication. This serves as a starting point prior to each new client interview. Then, add any new questions you come up with after each potential-client meeting. You will find that your list will grow to 100 quickly.

About the Author

Peter A. Schein is co-founder of the Organizational Culture and Leadership Institute (OCLI), which is dedicated to advancing organization development and design through a deeper understanding of organizational culture and leadership theory. Peter's expertise draws on many years of industry experience in marketing and strategy at technology pioneers including Apple, Sun Microsystems (Oracle), and numerous startups. He co-authored six books with Ed Schein, including *Organizational Culture and Leadership, Humble Leadership, Humble Inquiry, and Career Anchors Reimagined*. Peter has a bachelor's degree from Stanford University and an MBA from Northwestern's Kellogg School of Management. Learn more about Peter's work at OCLI.org.

The Soul of an Entrepreneur
Doing Consulting Your Way

CHRISTIE WARD

Many consultants don't immediately go into consulting—instead, they join the workforce and gain years, maybe decades, of lived experiences, ups-and-downs, successes, and setbacks that can and will inform who they'll be as a consultant. Remember, there are as many ways to consult as there are entrepreneurs. I encourage you to tap into your experiences, extract lessons, and apply them to whatever stage you are in your consulting journey. Create your own legacy—don't try to copy someone else.

My consulting journey has been a great one. My life is filled with stories that have given me wisdom and allowed me to become who I am and to do consulting my way. In this chapter, I'll share some of these stories and how I was able to translate the lessons learned into successful consulting experiences.

No Matter Your Path, Embrace Where It Leads You

When I was eight years old, my father sat across from me reading the newspaper and overheard a phone conversation I was having with a classmate. She was having trouble understanding our math homework and called me for help. When I hung up the phone, Dad put his paper down, looked at me, and said, "Christie, if you don't become a teacher, you will be doing the world a disservice. You can teach anything you can learn." That day he planted the seed that became a lifelong journey as a teacher, facilitator, and keynote speaker.

My father was a self-made man with the soul of an entrepreneur. To earn the money for law school tuition, he moved to Alaska to work in the oil fields. Once he became a lawyer, some of his trials set precedents for important laws. He never let me doubt that I could do

CHAPTER 30

anything as long as I had determination and perseverance; the only barrier to achievement was not trying.

In my pursuit to become a teacher, and with my BA in hand, I found an inner-city teaching job at a junior high school. I didn't last long in that job, but I found my niche later that year. I was fluent in Spanish thanks to a year living in Spain, so I began teaching English as a second language (ESL) at a private, adult language school in Washington, DC. I loved the students, and they loved me. Teaching was fun and it was rewarding to help people from outside the US adapt to their new country and acquire language skills they needed to succeed. I wasn't making much money, but that wasn't the driver for me. It was through this experience that I learned how much I loved teaching adults.

Network and Listen for Needs

Networking was a great pathway for my career advancement. My next teaching position was at an adult learning center in a public school district. I continued to teach adults while building my reputation and developing my expertise. Eventually, I took on the responsibility of managing the center, making curriculum decisions, and choosing textbooks. My students were from many countries outside the US and had many education levels. I learned how to flex my facilitation skills—tailoring content and delivery to each student's specific needs. Although I had never heard of *learner-centered learning*, that's exactly what I was doing.

When a family opportunity took me to Portland, Oregon, I looked to my networks again to find my next position. I talked to the ESL program director at Portland Community College, and she hired me on the spot. I was teaching adults once again, but this time, my students were earning credit in the community college system. I loved the semester system because of its definite beginning and end. With each new semester, I had new students, and the cycle began again. While teaching at Portland Community College, I was also able to work on a master's degree in adult education at Portland State University.

Consulting Tip

Continuing education is critical for a consultant. We need to be lifelong learners. Seek out higher education, certification, or more informal learning sources.

Be Willing to Reinvent Yourself

When a health issue put me in a hiatus, my classes were reassigned, and I had to make some decisions. I found out that the college's vocational education program had a grant opening for someone to work with students in its diesel program, focusing on basic skills like reading a micrometer and studying for college-level classes. The instructor didn't need to be a mechanic, so I applied and got the job.

My father's words quickly came back to me about being able to teach anything I could learn. Teaching diesel mechanics was a learning curve, but it was rather fun once I dove into it. I sat in on lectures about the electrical systems in a diesel engine and took notes on overhead projector transparency film, which I then used to teach students how to organize material and take notes.

To determine each student's proficiency in reading and math, I created an entry-level assessment that was based on diesel content. I interviewed faculty to find the gaps and found resources to fill them. I didn't wait to be told what to do. Instead, I sought out the issues and figured out how to address them.

Opportunity knocked again when we moved to Durango, Colorado. "Starting over" barely describes that transition. I had a new child and was in a fairly rural environment without a community college. There were few if any professional adult education employment options available. By this point, I had learned to assess the business landscape and then get to work. My circumstances were going to require some innovation on my part, but I would soon find that this would open an entirely new entrepreneurial path for me.

I began attending La Leche League meetings in Durango with other young, nursing mothers and realized a need in the community: There were no clothes for sale locally for nursing mothers. From this entirely coincidental and unlikely realization emerged a business concept: selling custom clothes for nursing mothers. So, I pivoted.

I began designing and making dresses, blouses, and nightgowns. I learned what was involved in starting a business, obtained a business license, and launched Mom and Me. I opened a shop in town. Word got around and the orders started coming in. The business grew quickly, and when I wasn't able to keep up with the demand, I hired women to sew for me. I got to learn about trade shows—I went to La Leche League conferences, set up a booth, and sold out in hours. The demand was quickly outpacing my production capacity. Then, Sears & Roebuck and Montgomery Ward started carrying nursing wear in their catalogs. It might have been a coincidence, but their clothing resembled my designs. (Did I mention that I hadn't applied for any patents for my designs?) I chalked it up to experience, and besides, I was ready to do something other than sit behind a sewing machine.

With this set of skills, I was ready when a surprising career opportunity emerged.

Teaching—and Consulting—Can Take Many Forms

Weight management often becomes a daunting challenge for new parents who are dealing with round-the-clock childcare responsibilities. This was no exception for me. After having my two beautiful daughters, I walked into a Weight Watchers (WW) meeting to begin my weight loss journey. Two years later, I had lost the weight, felt healthier, and found a new opportunity: a part-time job as a WW leader. I was back in the classroom, leading 30- to 45-minute sessions helping groups of people learn the skills that I had learned. I loved those sessions and the people. WW members are truly motivated learners who want answers and are willing to pay for them.

Although you can help most potential clients, others need more or different options than you can offer. When this happens, accept that realization and suggest how they can get the help they need. We can't be all things to all people, nor all things to all clients. Know your strengths and your limitations. Consulting is about solutions.

Lots of lessons emerged from leading WW meetings. Our members wanted a little entertainment along with practical tips, follow-up, and a peer mentor who would encourage them to achieve their weight loss and lifestyle goals. Perhaps even more, they wanted to voice their frustrations and challenges without judgment. I had to be both a role model and a facilitator. It was very fulfilling to help hundreds of people lose hundreds of pounds.

At one point, I had a client who weighed more than the scale could measure. The behavior changes he had to make were enormous, but with my guidance and his intention, he was able to lose more than 200 pounds. He disappeared for a while, and when he returned, he had regained 100 pounds. Rather than judging him, I suggested he reach out to a medical program counselor who was trained in chronic obesity and could work with him for more than a few minutes a week. I helped him find a program at a local hospital that provided the special attention he needed. Our connection brought him back to WW, but he needed a deeper intervention than I could offer. I hoped he would find a counselor in this new program who could connect with him too. Because consulting is about solutions, your job is finding the right solution for each client or company you serve. And it's OK if that solution isn't yours.

Consulting Tip

Identify a habit that you know you need to change. Make a commitment to start today, not tomorrow—today after reading this chapter.

Trust Your Gut—and Know When to Walk Away

One facet of strength is recognizing your own weaknesses and working to change them over time. Perhaps this process is also about forgiveness and grace. Sometimes philosophical differences arise with a client that are insurmountable or contrary to your values. At that point, you might need to leave.

After being promoted from WW leader to coordinator, I had to give up most of my meetings so I could travel throughout my region training leaders and staff. I loved training leaders as much as I loved being in the meeting room. Leaders and their decisions affect many people. However, companies and jobs change.

Toward the end of my time with WW, the company started a food program called Personal Cuisine, which members had to pay for in addition to the meeting fees. At variance with this approach, I believed that members should learn how to make their own meals. While I understood that some people preferred to purchase prepared food, I was concerned about the long-term sustainability of weight loss with such an approach. From a business standpoint, I recognized the corporate decision, but I didn't agree and struggled teaching it. I knew the time had come for another career change.

Seize Opportunities in Front of You—but Maintain Your Ethics

Not long after leaving WW, I replied to a newspaper ad for a job as a recruiter at Career-Track Seminars. I interviewed and got a job in Boulder, Colorado, at the largest public seminar company in the US. CareerTrack was founded by two entrepreneurs and operated like a startup. Although it was a corporation, it lacked the bureaucracy of an institution and instead mirrored the hearts and minds of its founders. The experience with CareerTrack put me through my paces and accelerated my career. As the recruiter for the international training corps, I watched application videos from aspiring trainers and either accepted or denied their employment.

Seeing and seizing opportunities is a core skill for any professional, and it's particularly important for your success as a consultant. Early on in my time at CareerTrack, I saw a need to provide training for new trainers, as well as professional feedback for trainers already on the road. Consistency is critical for public seminars. When people pay to see a product, they expect to see the same content and context, whether they're in Denver, Colorado, or London, England. Monitoring the seminar content and training delivery ensured consistency among our training corps.

Like many timely entrepreneurial ventures, growth at CareerTrack skyrocketed. They hired good people for both internal and external positions and had the most ironclad contracts I had ever seen. The external positions were filled with contract trainers who thought like entrepreneurs, and despite those contractual agreements, some were prone to tossing aside any facade of ethical standards and working directly with CareerTrack clients. As I advanced to managing the trainer corps, one of my functions was to enforce the contracts and hold trainers to their ethical responsibilities. I watched some trainers fail and then be shunned by the corporate community. Word gets around if you bend your ethics to get ahead. Clients talk. Consultants talk. Honoring your contracts is critical to your long-term success. Never cross the line and work with a client who belongs to someone else.

Have integrity, particularly with your competition. Ethical competitors often make referrals and extend invitations to work together on projects. When I work with my competitors, it not only enriches my business, but we're able learn from one another. Just remember, if you decide to partner with a competitor, make sure they are ethical.

Consulting Tip

The most important thing consultants have is their reputation. Never do anything that even hints of unethical behavior, or you'll endanger your reputation.

Ethical consultants also don't let the positive can-do approach overshadow the pragmatic. Seriously consider opportunities before you agree to take them on, especially if they involve what others will do.

By the time I was named director of training at CareerTrack, I was dealing with other department heads. One of them told me about a project involving a partner company and asked if I could commit some resources to the project. While I thought it was feasible, I didn't feel confident about the opportunity because it meant agreeing to work assignments that others would be doing. When I started checking for resources, everyone I contacted turned me down—they didn't have the bandwidth to take on the work, and I couldn't do it alone. The department head was furious, and she had a right to be. I had promised something I couldn't deliver. It was a painful lesson. My takeaway was to never say I could take on something if I couldn't secure the necessary resources or deliver them myself. This is one of the reasons I ultimately chose a single trainer business model instead of creating a larger training firm after leaving CareerTrack.

Volunteer Your Time and Learn From the Experience

Volunteering lets you participate in a cause and discover what an organization is really like. You can learn about the employees' values and which people will do what they say they will do. You can also practice your leadership and management skills.

While at CareerTrack, an associate introduced me to two professional associations that gave me perspective about networking and lifelong friends and associates. In the National Speakers Association (NSA), I learned the craft of speaking, storytelling, and business acumen. And I discovered the subtleties of training, facilitation, and curriculum design from the American Society for Training & Development (later renamed the Association for Talent Development). I refined my leadership skills by volunteering on the local boards for both associations. I also served on national committees and the national board for ATD, which put me in the company of many corporate and nonprofit leaders. For someone who was working out of her home office, it was not only an opportunity, but an honor and a privilege.

Lean Into Your Strengths and Limitations

As years passed, CareerTrack's large public seminar model became somewhat of a dinosaur. I had created my own career path from recruiter to trainer development manager to director of training. I even switched directions and worked as a sales manager in the sales department for a while; there I acquired skills I cherished once I started my own firm.

In 1999, I decided to incorporate and start my own training enterprise. I had one retainer with a startup company to provide recruiting and onboarding for new staff. I threw myself into my professional associations, nurtured and cultivated professional relationships, and kept my ears open for opportunities. I created a one-sheet of my offerings and sent it to the human resource directors for cities in my area. I kept in touch with the trainers and salespeople I worked with at CareerTrack. Several of the trainers went to other seminar companies.

I also heard from many of my training colleagues who said they'd work for me if I started a training company. I knew I could probably create something fairly substantial if I took them up on the idea, but I didn't want to manage trainers. I wanted to do the training. I still do.

It took me about three years to grow a profitable, self-sustaining training consultancy. You work like crazy to get it off the ground, and there may not be much money in the beginning, but stick with it. Follow your strengths. Mine is creating relationships. I'd frequently get to know new people at ATD meetings, and then, later on, they would introduce me to someone who could hire me. I'd connect with a colleague at an NSA board meeting, and they would ask me to join a team of trainers and speakers for a client. Both of those things happened 20 years ago, and I am still working for both clients.

However, not all clients will be a good fit. You must interview them, send them a proposal, and follow up until you think you're being a pest. If they don't hire you, ask them, "What could I have done to win your business?" Accept their feedback graciously. I no longer write long, protracted proposals. Instead, I find out what clients need—which is often a combination of what they want and what will solve their business problem—and then offer what I can do. I use a very simple model and give them three options:

- Option 1 is the most basic—it has the lowest cost and minimal amenities.
- Option 2 is still basic, but has more amenities and a higher cost.
- Option 3 includes everything in option 2 plus an extended plan or maybe a retainer for continued services. It has the highest cost and the most amenities.

Clients usually say they want option 3 but don't have the money. If that happens to you, don't lower your price. Instead, tell them what you can do for the budget they have. You might see how often they can find the money once they see what's possible. Occasionally, I'll barter with a client if they can't match my fee. For example, I might ask them to record the program and give me the master recording so I can use it for other purposes. On other occasions, I've asked for introductions to influential leaders in the same or other organizations.

Summary

My career has been a great ride and I don't regret a moment of it. One of the best decisions I made was hiring an office manager after realizing I shouldn't be doing all the tasks inherent to running a business. And who do you suppose I chose? She's one of the colleagues I volunteered with on a national committee for ATD. I noticed her when I watched people who were performing volunteer work. Because she was working for no pay, I came to understand her work ethic. She is with me to this day and is my right hand.

Embrace the journey and let it be a proud part of your legacy. There are as many ways to consult as there are entrepreneurs. Don't copy someone else. Enjoy your business and do it your way.

Actions You Can Take Now

- **Discover your consulting soul.** Pull out a family album or scroll through the pictures on your phone. Think about some of those times. What lessons did you learn during that period of your life? How can you translate those lessons into doing what you love and living what you know?
- **Consult your way.** Although this chapter is the story of how I did it my way, it contains dozens of one-liners about consulting. Review the chapter again and underline the pieces of advice that resonate with you. How can you consult *your* way?

About the Author

Christie Ward, CSP, founder of the Impact Institute, believes we can all amplify our talents and share our gifts. She teaches leaders to collaborate, doctors to empathize, and underprivileged children to use their voice. Teaching the next generation of learning professionals is one of her great joys. Whether you find her walking barefoot in Southeast Asia for her nonprofit or speaking on the international stage, Christie is a leader on and off the platform. She lives in Denver, Colorado, with her husband and giant schnauzer. Contact her at christie@christieward.com.

CHAPTER 31

How to Avoid the 10 Most Common Mistakes Consultants Make

STEPHEN L. COHEN

Chris sat at her desk with yet another vacancy to fill for her business. She'd left her corporate L&D job a few years ago after feeling stifled and unable to create transformative programming that made a difference. Now, three years later, her practice was thriving.

However, not all things were rosy. Chris had planned to be a solopreneur, but her consulting practice had grown too quickly by accident. She'd even had to hire a few full-time employees and several freelance contractors. She never had a plan in place. Even now, she still needed more office space and some additional staff. Chris wanted to expand her offer but was starting to feel a little overwhelmed. Indeed, some of the fun she derived from consulting was harder to come by. She loved working with clients and doing projects, but she was also responsible for managing a business and ensuring other people's livelihoods. In addition, she not only didn't like the managing part, but wasn't sure she was very good at it.

It was time to figure out what she really wanted to do, what she needed, and how big she wanted the business to get. While there was nothing wrong with staying small, Chris also didn't think that seemed very exciting. But if she wanted to keep growing, what should she do? Should she hire more people, and if so, what kind? Consultants? Administrators? Project managers? And what impact would all this potential growth have on her personal life? These were big questions that she needed to answer now.

In my 50 years as a consultant to other consultants, boards, and learning supplier companies, I've witnessed almost every mistake a consultant can make—including the ones Chris made and the subsequent angst she experienced. Did she, for example, establish a strategic plan and stick with it? Did she clearly define her purpose? All consultants will, at some time or another, face problems as they try to build and grow their businesses. But those who have succeeded don't make as many mistakes as those who haven't, or at worst, they learn more quickly from the mistakes they've made.

It doesn't have to be this way. This chapter identifies the most common, and perhaps most influential, mistakes I've made or observed others make and offers strategies for avoiding them. I've organized these top 10 mistakes into three categories:

- Mistakes made early in starting your consulting business
- Mistakes made when you should be improving your consulting business
- Mistakes made when growing your consulting business

Starting Your Consulting Business

While the mistakes I cover later in this chapter can have massive consequences for your business's success and growth potential, it's the mistakes you make when starting your business that can set you on a path to frustration and might even entirely turn you off consulting. Fortunately, there are ways to avoid them. Let's take a look.

1. Trying to Be All Things to All People

Many years ago, a traditional and quite successful consulting practice bought my custom learning and development business, ostensibly to cross-sell our training programs to its consulting clients. It assumed its clients would buy these programs because it had such long and trusted relationships with them. However, it neglected to consider two problems:

- Its clients weren't in the business of purchasing training programs.
- The firm's consultants weren't interested in selling them.

Obviously, it didn't work out. Trying to be all things to all people by straying outside your area of expertise comes with considerable challenges because the overall business models and operations are often significantly different. Think about leadership skills training companies that try to move into sales training or vice-versa. It is a much larger transition than it seems at first, and few businesses in the field have been successful.

When you're starting out, there's a tendency to present your business as the be-all and end-all for everything talent development. Rather than carving out a niche and being one of the best in that specific area, you dabble here and there, failing to build a competitive brand identity. Given how crowded the industry is, it's vital to differentiate yourself by standing out in one or, at most, two areas of expertise. The objective is for your current and potential customers to immediately think of your firm as one of the top three suppliers to address their business challenges. You can't possibly achieve this stature by trying to be all things to all people.

Here are some potential strategic solutions:

- **Define your purpose.** Be clear about why you are in the business you are in. What is driving you to succeed? What exactly are you looking to achieve? Knowing the answers to these questions will help you focus on what you like and do best.
- **Develop your offer.** Putting together your offer—whether it's product focused, consulting oriented, or even a combination of both—is key to establishing your business. It also will define what you will provide to clients and, more importantly, the challenges you aim to help them address.

2. Pricing Inappropriately

Many consultants have trouble pricing their services appropriately. If they make $90,000 per year at their current full-time job, they think that salary will be adequate as a self-employed consultant. However, they're forgetting they now have to pay for a variety of previously handled costs, including insurance premiums, office space and expenses, computers and phones, employment taxes, and travel expenses. They also forget they will not have paid time off, nor income when they take off. Typically, consultants must make an estimated 2.5 to 3 times the salary they desire to cover the additional overhead they will incur. So, what does this have to do with pricing? Everything!

The only way to cover your costs plus your salary, is to appropriately price your offer. If you don't do this successfully, it won't be long before you're out of business. Fortunately, you can figure out pricing if you understand your business costs and the margin you need to cover those and be profitable.

Unfortunately, most consultants, especially when starting out, either price themselves way out of the market or undervalue their contributions. One reason consultants undercharge is because they're nervous about charging a day rate that would surpass their current salary. While $1,000 a day might equal $365,000 a year, you likely aren't going to work 365 days straight, and you still have to absorb all those other costs. So, you can end up inadvertently undercharging for what you really need.

> ### Consulting Tip
>
> Determine your ideal salary. Multiply it by 2.5. Next, determine how many actual days you will be able to work. Remember to remove weekends, holidays, vacation, time to market and develop your skills, and downtime that simply doesn't match your client's availability. If you plan to charge by the day, divide the first number by the number of days you will likely work. The answer will be the minimum you need to charge per day.

There's also the issue of undervaluing your potential contribution if you underestimate what you think a client would likely pay. For example, years ago, my business proposed a project with a major Fortune 50 company. We thought we were asking for more than what they would be willing to pay, so you can imagine our surprise when they told us to double the price because the initial ask wasn't enough to cover our proposal. We were lucky because we had worked with them before and had a very strong and successful relationship. But even so, we undervalued our potential contribution.

You'll always be faced with others offering cheaper versions of what you're providing, so you have to clearly communicate the differentiated value you offer over your competitors. And, while there are risks to premium pricing, it can be very profitable in the long run.

Here are some potential strategic solutions:

- **Create a business plan.** Every business plan should have an annual operating budget that itemizes the specific revenue sources and expenses you will incur. You should also be able to predict a monthly profit and loss amount. If you have an accountant, they can help you identify the income and expenses categories.
- **Develop your offer.** Consider doing some research on your offer. Who else provides the services and products you will provide? How much do they charge? How much time will it take you to deliver what you plan to offer? It's essential that you can clearly state how you are different from and better than your competitors, and that you can professionally communicate it to your prospects and clients.

3. Dreaming Too Small

We dream too small because we fear failure, don't have confidence in our abilities, or simply can't see a bigger and better future. Dreaming too small can rob you of achieving greater heights than you thought imaginable, keep you from reaching your true potential, and prevent you from thriving. To avoid stagnating, start with the vision of what you want to be and do with your business. While this vision has to be realistic, it also has to be a set of goals pushing you to a new level.

Too many entrepreneurs don't give themselves enough credit or believe enough in themselves to boldly strike. Later, they regret not thinking bigger. Don't shortchange yourself by failing to put the necessary structure in place to allow for your rapid growth.

Here are some potential strategic solutions:

- **Figure out what you want and need.** Knowing what you are trying to establish before you can put it all together will translate into the dreams you have for your business. Recognize that dreaming small or big is not necessarily determined by the size of the business you want to build, but rather by the life you want to lead. Think boldy, create a vision of your future that requires stretch goals, and never regret not dreaming big enough.
- **Establish your growth plan.** It's never too early to establish a plan for growing your business. There are many ways to do this, and you are in total control. Begin by thinking about the role in which you see yourself. Are you the CEO of a company with many consultants, or do you have a partner or two to share the business with? Do you see yourself having a sales force to help promote your business? Your growth plan will, in many ways, operationally define your dreams. When putting it together, don't hesitate to push yourself to achieve more than you could imagine.

Improving Your Consulting Business

Unfortunately, once you've got your consulting business up and running, you're far from being out of the woods. There are countless possible missteps you can make when managing the day-to-day operations of your business, and they often relate to what you choose to focus your attention on. Let's take a closer look at some operational mistakes.

4. Failing to Professionalize the Business

Antiquated back-office systems—whether financial systems, project management processes, inventory control management, or human resource policies—can ultimately stifle growth. Failure to incorporate professional practices into the flow and dynamics of the business will likely be reflected in interactions with customers who find dealing with your business at best clumsy and at worst burdensome. Unfortunately, most consultants would rather think of big ideas and where they are going to take the business than spend time setting up systems, processes, and procedures. So, you must either hire people to help you build this infrastructure or outsource it (both viable options).

The very first person I hired when I started out on my own, with plans to build a full-scale business, was an accounting temp. Back then, I didn't have the typical software programs available today, so I knew I would need help with bookkeeping. She was a previous colleague of mine, so I trusted her to use a proper chart of accounts and systems to manage everything. As my company grew, we hired a full-time bookkeeper and then a CFO.

Financial management is just one way to professionalize your business. The same applies to human resource systems. If your company is too small to support a full-time HR employee, you can contract out these services until you're large enough to bring it in house. Putting these systems in place not only helps you run the business more smoothly, but it demonstrates to your clients you are serious about building a business and plan to be around for a long time to serve them.

Here are some potential strategic solutions:

- **Establish a strategic plan.** While the best laid plans don't always materialize the way you expect, they still offer a pathway to an end state, allowing you to monitor your progress toward various milestones along the way, make corrections as needed, and revise your goals as appropriate. With a plan in place, you will be able to project the kind of growth you expect to achieve, as well as what internal and external resources will be necessary to support it.

- **Develop your operating system.** Before you can put these systems and processes in place, you need to fully understand how your business operates, the levers that need to be adjusted to continue operating at an efficient pace, and how these contribute to both your top and bottom line financial success. A viable and dependable operating system will allow you to scale the business so you can do more for less and ultimately grow profitably.

5. Working *in* the Business Rather Than *on* It

At some point, to grow, you may need to get out of your own way and let others who are more skilled, experienced, and interested take over—this will allow you to do what you like most and do best. Rather than devoting too much time working in the business, your most valuable contribution should be working on it, largely by laying the foundation for its future, thinking long term, creating a vision, emphasizing your purpose, and establishing a strategic plan. By being engaged and focused, you can devote more time on value-added growth activities, such as sales, client interactions, and content development, all of which likely represent your true strengths.

I recall my experience with my dear friend, colleague, and mentor, Larry Wilson, founder of Wilson Learning. Larry was incredibly dynamic and one of the great all-time salespeople in the industry. His company's growth was meteoric in the early years but would often go off the rails, as Larry jumped from one idea to another having rarely completed the previous ones. It wasn't until he hired an experienced operations guy in Mat Juechter that the business really started to grow and become profitable. Mat had led Xerox Learning Systems and was the perfect partner to keep Larry and the business operationally focused and in line.

> **Consulting Tip**
>
> Think about what you like to do as a consultant. How can you spend most of your time doing that? How will you ensure everything else gets done?

Hiring Mat gave Larry the opportunity to think big and allowed him to execute his ideas. For example, Larry created the Pecos River Company outside Santa Fe, New Mexico, which brought experiential learning in the outdoors to reality for the industry. He created the Interactive Technology Group, which introduced highly interactive video and computer-based instruction of soft skills, namely leadership and sales, to the industry with the use of videodiscs. In this case, Larry worked on the business and Mat worked in it; by leaning into their interests and skill sets, they were able to become one of the most successful training suppliers ever.

Here are some potential strategic solutions:

- **Figure out what you want and need.** Growing profitably means first identifying what you are looking to do and become. Some people are perfectly satisfied with maintaining a small practice that doesn't require many employees or much infrastructure. Others are more interested and excited about building a bigger business that continually grows. Neither path is right or wrong nor better than the other. The critical thing is understanding exactly what fulfills your personal and professional needs before embarking on building any type of consulting enterprise.

- **Establish your growth plan.** Similarly, depending on where you want to go with your consultancy, you will need to build a plan that ensures you meet those goals. Unlike a strategic plan, which is typically limited to a finite time period, let's say three to five years, a growth plan identifies the longer-term vision for not only the specific pathways to growth but the timelines and resources needed to achieve that long-term success.

6. Getting Distracted From the Focus of the Business

Unfortunately, getting distracted is more common than you might think. It may include misalignment with the business vision, straying from its strategic plan, or just chasing one bright, shiny object after another. Of all the mistakes I've seen firms make, getting off focus is paramount. This doesn't mean experimentation is taboo, but there is a time and place for everything, including when to focus on what the business really is, whom it serves, and where it is going.

Remember Larry Wilson? He was notorious for chasing new and exciting projects. Fortunately, most of his ideas were way ahead of the industry (such as experiential learning and digital delivery). But, too often, entrepreneurs get entranced by some new thing and chase it without fully understanding what it will take to deliver, whether anyone really wants to buy it, or its impact on the rest of the business. There are just too many cases in which operating differently without clear guidelines has disastrous results.

Here are some potential strategic solutions:

- **Define your purpose.** One surefire way to stay focused is to be extraordinarily clear about why you are doing what you're doing. Being intentional gives you direction and a touchstone representing the core values you aspire to reach in every personal and professional endeavor. Your purpose keeps you grounded and serves as a constant barometer for whether you are actively living out your life's meaning. If you are truly intentional and aligned in how you think, act, and interact with others, you are more likely to stay focused and not get distracted in your business and personal pursuits.

- **Establish a strategic plan.** One way to operationalize your purpose is to bring it to life with an executable strategic plan. This will define your mission, purpose, and values in meaningful and actionable terms. Furthermore, it will provide timeframes, milestones, and action plans that are measurable at a moment's notice.

7. Putting Your Head in the Sand

You must stay alert when managing your consulting business. The last thing you want to do is ignore cues just because they don't line up with your current thinking or beliefs. Otherwise, you might end up rejecting something that is obvious and denying the truth. Examples in our industry include rejecting research contradicting your favorite practices or refusing to accept the technological changes taking place in the industry because they would require you to alter your delivery process. By refusing to acknowledge and react appropriately to the facts, you are setting yourself up to undermine your success over time, if not immediately. Furthermore, if this behavior keeps you from staying current and accepting advances in the industry, you'll likely be passed by your competition. Sticking with tried-and-true practices may seem like the safe approach—until it becomes tired and false.

Here are some potential strategic solutions:

- **Understand industry dynamics.** Among the most important strategies in building and growing any business in any industry is understanding how it operates. More specifically, this means recognizing what the competitive landscape looks like, who the buyers are, what performance challenges they are trying to address, and what solutions they tend to buy to solve those challenges. Without a clear understanding of how the industry operates, you are likely to flounder.

- **Recognize future trends.** Part of understanding the industry is also recognizing its trends, both retroactively and in the future. How has the industry evolved? What appears to be on the horizon? What have been and are likely to be the major drivers of industry success? How are you going to adapt to likely changes in the industry landscape that don't align with your current offer? How can you quickly pivot to be more aligned with the future of the industry? Answers to these questions are key to laying the foundation for your growth plans.

Growing Your Consulting Business

It's certainly possible to maintain a consulting business that remains relatively the same size throughout its life cycle. Without an eye to growth opportunities, however, you run the risk of becoming stale. You're also at the mercy of a small pool of clients who could, for any number of reasons, decide they don't need or can't use your services any longer. Growing your business thus becomes an imperative to remain solvent and successful. Let's look closer at some growth mistakes.

8. Keeping Bad Customers

If the customer is always right, how could they be bad? Truth is, while the customer is always the customer, they aren't necessarily always right. There are good customers who are relatively easy to deal with, supportive of your efforts, and think and act like partners for mutual benefit, but there are also customers who suck the life out of you, your business, and your employees. Hanging on to unproductive customers who create chaos with your business is very costly and disruptive. You need to fire them or, at a minimum, have a heart-to-heart discussion indicating why the relationship isn't working and what needs to change if you are going to move forward. Failure to get positive movement with your customers is grounds for severing the relationship—professionally, of course—and moving on to serve other customers more worthy of your offer.

How you define a so-called bad customer is entirely up to you. Some people are more lenient and have more patience than others, but it's important to identify the early signs that a customer is not worth engaging with, or at a minimum this is the first and last time you are willing to do so. So, what should you look out for? Consider an example involving a client who, regardless of what was delivered, continually said it did not meet their needs, even after specific feedback and itemized revisions were made to address the feedback. It was a continuous and repeatable process that cost my team significant time, money, and resources that could otherwise have been devoted to more partnership-oriented clients. In this case, we did grin and bear it until time ran out and the client had to finally accept our deliverables. At the time, we were working with many other divisions of the company and wanted to be sure we preserved our good reputation. However, we decided never to work with this particular client again, and respectfully declined when they offered us another project.

Certainly, there are more clear-cut cases of when to fire a customer, like when one exhibits questionable ethical behaviors, but those are easy to see and act upon. In any case, it's important to assess the situation objectively and act both quickly and professionally. And how you do it is just as important as taking action in the first place. In 2000, Carlene Reinhart and I wrote an article on 50 ways to (more or less) leave your client. While we offered some logical actions, the key message was if you have to sever a client relationship, be sure to offer options so the work and your reputation aren't left hanging.

Here are some potential strategic solutions:

- **Serve your customers.** This means satisfying, and even exceeding, their expectations. It seems simple to deliver a solution addressing the very challenges you were hired to help them solve. Unfortunately, not all customer interactions run as smoothly as we would like, sometimes due to our own inabilities to deliver what is needed, and other times due to the customer's inability to define what they really want. Your job is to get a clear picture of each project's specifications and requirements, preferably documented, which will serve as evidence for what is expected and the time and costs needed for delivery.
- **Market and sell your offer.** Whether you are a product-based or consulting services–based business, the solutions you provide represent what you stand for. In fact, they are your reputation. But, you must actively sell and market these solutions to stay in business. In your marketing messages, you are promising your prospects you can do what you say you will do both efficiently and effectively. Making false promises or hyping your offer just to get clients in the door, but not delivering on them, is an obviously short-term proposition. So, it is critical to ensure your business development engine, which includes your marketing communications and sales process and staff, is unwaveringly clear about the challenges you can help your clients address.

9. Failing to Scale

Probably the most important concept in building and growing a profitable business, regardless of industry, is scale. The basic underlying proposition of scaling a business seems relatively simple, but it's not always simple to achieve. You need to create replicable processes that take less time and labor to produce results, which brings in greater margins and more profitability. It also means getting more for less—more bang for your buck. It is all about leverage, whether referring to your labor, products, distribution, or customers. There are multiple ways to orchestrate leverage and scale by operational optimization, but failure to achieve it will significantly impede your opportunities for consistent growth. Although success is not necessarily defined by growth alone, you have to figure out how to scale if you want to grow.

The challenge is that the approaches are likely to be very different if your offer is products and programs or services. This is because the underlying operating principles around financial management, inventory control, costs, selling processes, and knowledge and skill demands are very different for these two types of offers. To scale consulting services involves managing how you staff your projects, package your offers, and replicate the process. To scale a product offer involves mass customizing the products, efficient inventory management, and distributing widely.

Here are some potential strategic solutions:

- **Create a business plan and structure.** Scaling a business doesn't just happen by accident. It requires a conscious and concerted effort to figure out how your business can return more for less. How you structure your business is one way to create an environment that not only supports but integrates scaling principles in everything you do to manage it. Creating a business plan and structure—which should include your overall strategy, assessment of your competitive landscape, sales and marketing plans, as well as implementation plans—is the first step in incorporating processes, procedures, and even policies that facilitate scaling your business.

- **Establish your growth plan.** Similarly, as you look ahead to your business growth, how will the aforementioned enable you to achieve even greater leverage in obtaining more for less? Your growth plan should address how scaling will support your business development engine, back-office systems, leadership, governance, and even culture.

10. Falling Behind

As talent development professionals, you'd think it would be part of the daily routine to stay abreast of what's taking place in the industry; that is, continuing to learn about the business of the business. After all, isn't this our main clients' need—developing talent through learning? Yet, I sometimes wonder how organizations in our industry emerge and exist without any interest in accounting for the larger environment in which they operate. Often, this is because of a tendency to focus on their own little corner of the world, believing that what they have to offer is far superior to what anyone can provide. They are more comfortable ignoring the rest of the world and avoiding any external noise that might interfere with their own plans.

This short-sightedness has been the doom for many businesses and not just those in our industry. The automotive industry is a prime example. Over the years, it has had to pivot many times to meet the needs of the consumer around the issues of gas availability, cost, and pollution. In each case, car companies had to pivot to remain competitive by creating more compact and fuel-efficient cars, including hybrid and electric vehicles. Any company that isn't acknowledging this change, and keeping up, will be out of business in short order.

This is also the case with the TD consulting world. Firms that are uninterested or unable to pivot to a more hybrid learning model combining face-to-face with self-directed digital learning paradigms in a variety of environments, or even convert their offer to entirely digital delivery, are not likely to be around in a few years. Staying on top of industry changes and anticipating future trends is the responsibility of every business leader—including you. And, perhaps more importantly, staying up to date is often what clients are depending on you to do for them so you can bring forth new tools, research, and methodologies that better serve them.

Here are some potential strategic solutions:

- **Understand industry dynamics.** Keeping up with our industry isn't a difficult task; it just requires persistent desire and action. We have widely available and accessible resources, including professional conferences, expos, journals, webinars, and blogs. Perhaps the only challenge is figuring out how to distill this enormous amount of information. One way is to identify the few but mighty outlets that appeal to your needs and you can readily access.
- **Recognize future trends.** Future trends are always signaled ahead in the sources noted here, but your clients and competitors are probably the best source of information about what the future holds. Your clients will help identify needs you don't currently meet—talk to them often about what they are seeing as the future of managing their talent development needs. Also, keep an eye on the competitive landscape, but don't limit this to just the corporate TD world. Take a broader perspective, including schools and technical institutes.

Summary

Most lessons are learned from the mistakes we experience by making wrong decisions rather than from the successes we achieve, and recovering from those mistakes can often lead to even greater successes. The mistakes identified in this chapter represent some of the most common ones that have the potential to have the greatest impact on the growth of your business. Those who learn from these will go on to great success. Those who don't and continue to incorporate dysfunctional practices rarely move forward and grow.

Growth can often be painful if we can't learn from and ultimately eradicate our repetitive mistakes. Consciously applying strategic solutions to your business can not only minimize the negative impact of critical mistakes, but also eliminate them completely. I hope this chapter will shed some light on the mistakes you have already made or might make in the future.

To help you reflect, you can refer to summary matrix table matching the strategic solutions with the 10 common mistakes on the handbook's website at td.org/handbook-for-consultants. You'll also find the complete list of strategies there.

Actions You Can Take Now

- **Start a list.** Understand why you are in the business you are in and what you need, want, and expect from it. Then make a list of all your thoughts.
- **Determine how you'll stand out.** Recognize where you can fit within the industry's competitive landscape, and determine how to differentiate your offer from everything that currently exists.
- **Plan to stay on top.** Create a plan to track the evolving nature of the talent development industry and how to stay current with the market. For example, consider how AI will affect your consulting practice and what you will do about it.

About the Author

Stephen L. Cohen has been a business founder, operator, leader, consultant, and investor in the education and training industry for nearly 50 years. Currently, he is the founder and principal of the Strategic Leadership Collaborative, a consulting practice focused on strategic growth planning, board and advisory services, and business coaching. He has demonstrated a proven track record for building equity by significantly growing top- and bottom-line performance for enterprises he has founded, led, or sold. He has served on 25 different advisory boards, preparing many of them for eventual sale or merger, and has facilitated strategic-growth planning projects for numerous others. Steve can be reached at 952.942.7291 or steve@strategicleadershipcollaborative.com.

A Guide for Looking Back and Planning Ahead

KEVIN MARSHALL

"Three to five years' experience required." I remember the conundrum of trying to land my first professional job after college—every job opening seemed to require years of experience that I didn't have. How can you gain experience if experience is a prerequisite to gaining it? You might relate to this challenge. And you will find that it is not confined solely to recent college graduates—it's something you may continue to face in consulting.

Dealing with this challenge early in my career began a pattern of behavior that continues to bias my attention and focus on the urgent and pressing issues that lie in front of me. I've mastered the habit of last-minute heroics with time-sensitive, professional deadlines. Now, more than 40 years later, I've often thought, "I wish I'd known *then*, what I know *now*."

What if we rephrase the question to create a different perspective? What if we instead ask, "What if I knew now, what I am going to know then?" How would that knowledge influence our current decisions, strategy, and focus? If you could have a conversation with your older self and learn from the wisdom and perspective that you'll inevitably gain from future years of experience, what questions would you ask?

This chapter provides some ideas for how to consider future perspectives, anticipate knowledge gained, and predict what you might know from a more experienced perspective. By using visionary thinking to remove the blinders of myopia, you can develop far-sighted abilities to forecast future perspectives and help inform your current decisions. Or, using the words of Marcel Proust: "The real voyage of discovery consists not in seeking new landscapes, but in having new eyes." You can learn how to improve your discovery by "having new eyes."

While time travel doesn't exist (at least not at the time of this writing), there are some practical steps you can take when considering what you might learn from your older, wiser self. This chapter can help you explore where you want to take your consulting business in the future.

Looking Back to Plan Ahead

When I was growing up, my family would pile into our 1971 Plymouth Suburban station wagon for an annual trip to see our relatives. There were six of us in our family—Mom, Dad, and four kids. If you're not familiar with station wagons of the 70s, they were huge. And some engineer was probably proud of the idea to include a stow away rear seat, that when raised, forced the passenger to sit facing backward.

I hated that back seat—not only because I was prone to motion sickness, but because it forced me to look back on the road we'd already traveled! For some reason, whenever I was in that seat, I felt like I was watching a rerun of a movie that the other forward-looking members of my family had already seen. I wanted to be one of the passengers who got to look forward as we rambled along our road trips. To this day, I prefer to look forward, not back.

Why? Perhaps, it is because I don't want to focus on my past mistakes or missed opportunities. Looking back seems to go against my innate desire as a leader and entrepreneur to tackle challenges, solve problems, and pioneer the way to new frontiers. But an important question to ask is, "What lessons or opportunities am I missing when I don't consider the perspective gained from looking back on the road traveled?" Furthermore, what if looking back could help us imagine and anticipate future perspectives we might have when we are older?

In our fast-paced world, I believe we've lost some of the art of introspection and personal reflection. We need to rediscover the benefits of looking back to plan ahead. But before we consider ideas, we should first review some key principles for planning.

Know the Difference Between Do and Done

Do you consider yourself to be a visionary person? Have you created a compelling picture of the future of your consulting practice? What does that vision look like? Use clear and precise wording to describe that vision. Before reading another word, stop and answer these important questions:

- What do you want your consulting practice to be in five, 10, or even 20 years? Be specific.
- How many people are in your practice?
- Who are your clients? Where are they located?
- What specific core practices do you use to provide value to your clients?
- How are your product and service offerings different than what your competitors offer?

Over the past few decades, I've posed these and other questions to many organizational leaders and found that the vast majority have not taken the time to clarify their vision for a desired future. Most will argue that they know where they want to be in the future, but few can articulate it well, and even fewer have it written down.

It's easier to plan *what to do* if we start with a clear picture of what it looks like *to be done*. Start with a clear picture of your expected outcomes, and then align your actions to achieve them. To do something requires action. For example, a good organizational mission is a call to action that should inspire and energize employees. Doing the mission should be the leader's battle cry. As Cynthia Montgomery describes in her book, *The Strategist: Be the Leader Your Business Needs*, an organizational mission should be ennobling and motivating and should bring the best energy out of employees. I can't overemphasize the importance of an excellent and compelling mission.

However, an even more important and often overlooked element is the ability to clearly describe what it looks like to finish the task or accomplish the thing you've set out to do. It requires visionary thinking and careful communication to describe what "done" looks like. The strategic terminology you adopt in your organization—such as mission, vision, purpose, or your why—doesn't matter if you can't recognize and clarify the difference between what you want done and what you're going to do to make it happen. Why? Because entrepreneurial people are not necessarily visionary people. Most of the ones I've encountered are doers— people of action who love to lead, solve problems, and rally the troops. However, a visionary has a clear picture of a desired future and can create a crystal-clear picture of that vision so that others know what it looks like to be done and participate in the actions designed to make it a reality.

Resist the urge to skip this section or minimize its importance. And don't simply reword your mission as an outcome. For example, if your call to action is to "climb the hill," the outcome shouldn't be that you've "successfully climbed the hill." While this may be true, it fails to address the real reason for climbing the hill. Clear outcomes describe why you're doing an action. A better way to state your desired outcome might be, that you are climbing the hill "to benefit from a higher perspective and leadership opportunity that only exists at the top of the hill."

Taking time to clarify a desired future may seem impractical when there are so many pressing and immediate tasks. That's why visionary thinking typically takes a back seat to more urgent and pressing issues that easily consume all available time and energy. It is so easy to put off visionary thinking until you have solved today's challenges. Unfortunately, each day presents a new set of urgent issues. If you are in—or aspire to be in—the practice of consulting, you must learn to overcome, as Charles E. Hummel described it, this "tyranny of the urgent" that makes it so difficult to pursue important visionary ideas.

Visionary thinking can produce anxiety that is rooted in the fear of making bad decisions, missing unforeseen opportunities, or failing to reach future goals. We may know intuitively that we should have a clear picture of where we are going. But high demands on our time, the busyness of work, and fears associated with an unknown future are easy excuses for avoiding introspection and reflection.

As consultants, we may even coach our clients on the need to clarify their vision. Perhaps it's time to take our own medicine. As Hippocrates, the father of medicine famously said, "cura te ipsum" (physician heal thyself). It is time to reflect on our intended consulting future with new eyes.

Elevating Your Value Proposition

What value have you created for your clients? Whether you've been in consulting for a few months or 20 years, this is a crucial question to answer. Don't make the mistake of thinking that your hard work always equates to value. As Peter Drucker (1985) wrote, "Quality in a product or service is not what the supplier puts in. It is what the customer gets out and is willing to pay for. A product is not quality because it is hard to make and costs a lot of money. . . . Customers pay only for what is of use to them and gives them value."

This is important. If you're not clear on your value proposition, you'll likely chase every opportunity that comes along, which obscures the focus of your consulting practice. A firm understanding of your core competencies, value proposition, and competitive differentiation is a crucial component of successful future thinking.

So, how do you create great value for your customers? Use the following three-step process to complete your value proposition chart:

1. **Identify your core competencies.** Core competencies are the attributes you've acquired or developed that your clients appreciate and value. They are typically hard for others to imitate and probably required a lot of time and effort to learn and develop. You don't need a long list of core competencies to be highly valuable to your clients. Identify your top three to five core competencies, and write them in the first column of the value proposition chart. This column represents what you bring to the client.

2. **Identify your value proposition for each identified core competency.** A value proposition describes why a specific competency is valued. Consider each of your core competencies from the perspective of your current or prospective clients. Why do they or would they value each competency? If you're not able to answer this question, you may need to reconsider whether that competency is important— it's safe to assume that if you don't know why it is valuable, your clients won't either. Write your answer in the second column of the chart next to each of the identified core competencies.

3. **Determine your competitive differentiation.** Now, it's time to identify how unique each core competency is to your clients. Are there other consulting practices that could provide similar value? Are those competitive consultants more convenient, higher quality, or available at a better price? You must research your market to find these answers. You may have a solid set of core competencies that collectively generate high value for your clients, but if your existing or prospective clients choose to work with a competitor, you may not achieve your vision for your consulting practice.

These three steps can help you complete your own value proposition chart. See Figure 32-1 for an example.

Figure 32-1. Value Proposition Chart

	Core Competency: What?	Value Proposition: Why?	Competitive Differentiation: How?
1	Breadth and depth of experience; management, industry, and technology.	Help clients discover best idea and solutions informed by a wide variety of industry and best practices; yield solutions and positive change.	We provide a unique combination of people and experience across a wide variety of organizations spanning many industries.
2	Coaching and facilitation that engages client participation; we practice a hands-on, highly relational approach.	Client teams become highly invested and take ownership in outcomes leading to desired improvement.	We commit significant energy to building ownership in the best ideas. We work with clients to ensure their confidence in the plan and ongoing participation in its execution.
3	Skilled analysis and synthesis of complex organizational issues; we bring focus and move teams toward unified thought, alignment, and commitment.	Tough issues are analyzed. We help teams negotiate difficult issues and conflict in a positive manner resulting in focused direction and team alignment.	We elucidate complex and often confusing scenarios to focus on the most critical factors of success and growth.
4	Deep thinking and applied knowledge; we are craftsmen who use our uniquely designed tools and methodology with expertise.	Knowledge and tools in collaboration with clients facilitate discovery of new ideas, new resources, and improved client confidence.	We invest in organizational learning and growth so we can always bring current and relevant content to every client engagement.
5	Every engagement provides a customized and specifically tailored product; we are not a cookie-cutter consulting firm.	Achieve highly valuable results at an appropriate cost.	We offer expert consulting services that are tailored to the specific challenges of each client.

Completing the value proposition chart helps you critically assess your potential value and competitive threats. Ultimately, your value is determined by the degree to which your clients accept, adopt, and apply the insights and advice you develop and deliver during a client engagement.

Consulting Tip

Select one or two of your valued clients or a trusted business partner. Set aside dedicated time to discuss your value proposition chart. You will gain great insights by obtaining an outside perspective.

Clarifying your core competencies, value proposition, and competitive differentiation has the added benefit of helping you communicate your value proposition to prospective clients, market your value, and improve your competitive position.

Practice Future Thinking

We've covered the importance of being visionary and having a clear picture of your desired future, as well as clarifying your value proposition by identifying core competencies and competitive differentiation. Now, imagine what it would be like to travel forward in time and talk with your future self. How would that conversation go? What questions would you ask? How would you respond? How much progress would you expect to see toward achieving your vision?

This exercise may seem silly at first, but before you dismiss it, find someone with more than 20 years of work experience, and ask them if they wish they'd thought more carefully about an issue earlier in their career or if they wish they could go back and change a decision or action in their past. I've not encountered a single thoughtful leader who couldn't identify at least a few situations when they would go back and change something about their past. A word of caution, however, this practice requires some deep reflection and introspection.

What will happen during the next five years? Ten years? Twenty years? Few could have imagined the impact of a global pandemic, but here we are. Many argue that because the pace of change is accelerating so rapidly, we can't begin to imagine what the future holds. How then can we envision future scenarios? In truth, some of what happens in the future will occur because of events that are beyond our control. Those things will happen to us. Other aspects of the future, however, will happen because of us.

An *event map* offers a practical and valuable method for anticipating and planning for a future that is beyond your immediate control (Figure 32-2). This tool is used to help identify and consider possible future events that may affect your business. Creating an event map involves three steps:

1. Identify as many potential future events as you can imagine. An event can be anything that happens as a result of external factors, such as:
   - Economic changes
   - Shifts in client or customer demands

- ○ Social or cultural changes
- ○ Federal or state laws and regulations
- ○ Political changes
- ○ Technology and innovation advances
- ○ New and different competition
- ○ Environmental factors
- ○ Global health factors

2. For each potential future event, determine if the expected impact on you or your business will be high or low.

3. For each potential future event, determine the probability (low or high) that the event will occur, and identify when you think it will happen.

Figure 32-2. Event Map

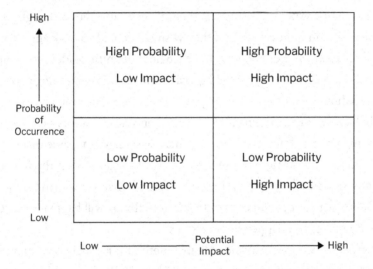

After you've identified the future events and determined their potential impact and probability, record them on a timeframe, like the chart in Figure 32-3. Use the first row of the chart to write down the events with the highest impact potential that you think are most likely to occur. Put each event under the year you anticipate it happening. Use the next row to record the events that are less likely but still have the potential for a high impact. The third row is for events that are highly likely but would have a lower impact. Finally, use the bottom row for events that are less likely and would have a lower impact. You can find a downloadable version of the Event Mapping tool at td.org/handbook-for-consultants.

Figure 32-3. Event Mapping Tool

	2025	2026	2027	2028	2029	2030	2031	2032	2033	2034	2035
Highly likely, High impact											
Less likely, High impact											
Highly likely, Low impact											
Less likely, Low impact											

After completing the event map, take time to reflect on the potential implications of this forecast. What challenges will you potentially encounter in your future? Do any of these high-impact events reveal opportunities that you can prepare for in advance?

The traditional event map focuses solely on external factors and influences that will potentially shape the future. It is important to note, however, that these factors and influences typically remain outside our control. So, the obvious question is, "What remains within my control?" The answer boils down to your decisions and your actions.

Creating an event map provides a canvas for future thinking. Take time to thoughtfully consider each potential event as if it has already happened. How would you react? What is your plan? How would you position your practice to thrive in the face of each event? Could you leverage it to your advantage? Next, consider how multiple events occurring simultaneously might affect your practice. Who would have envisioned a global health pandemic, coupled with an economic downturn, followed by a surge in behavioral health issues? Create an event map and make a plan.

> **Consulting Tip**
>
> Another more personal way to consider the event mapping activity is to think about future milestones or events in your personal life. This could include things like getting married, taking trips, returning to school, buying a home, or starting on your bucket list.

Consider Your Future Perspectives

As a final step in future thinking, imagine having conversations with a future version of yourself five, 10, and 20 years from now. For the sake of discussion, let's refer to the version of you in five years as "the pioneer." This may be the easiest future for you to envision. The pioneer is still creating new ideas, finding new clients, and boldly pursuing new consulting opportunities. The version of you in 10 years is "the conductor." At this point in your consulting business, you will have more appreciation for the greater results that come from getting others to participate in your work. Perhaps you hired staff or have contract workers, or maybe you have a partner. Like an orchestra conductor who found greater value from leading other musicians than trying to play every instrument, this future you will focus more on leading and motivating the team, rather than being the consultant on every project. How much longer do you plan to maintain your consulting business? Depending on your answer, the 20-year older you may see valuable history in the rear-view mirror. At this point, you may be considering your legacy and when or how you will retire or at least scale back. We will call this future you "the sage guru."

What do you think you could learn from the wisdom of the pioneer, the conductor, and the sage guru? How much experience do you think each might have from the additional five, 10, or 20 years? Consider three hypothetical conversations and write down your responses. Use the following considerations and questions to help guide each of the conversations. Feel free to add or modify any of these as you see fit to improve the process.

Conversation 1: The Pioneer

How old will you be in five years? What will your family life and friendships look like? How much energy will you have? What will be most important to you? What things that are important to you now might be less important in five years? Does your current vision still resonate? You've probably experienced some consequences from external events and decisions (planned and unplanned), some which helped your consulting practice, while others provided unique challenges. Assume that you've pioneered your way through and developed new clients, created or modified business processes, and grown the business.

Questions to ask the pioneer include:

- Assuming you have a multiyear strategic plan, how do you describe the impact of implementing that plan?
- Assuming your current vision is clear, what will you say about the organization's progress toward achieving that vision?
- What have been the biggest challenges in growing the business over five years?
- Why did you start consulting? Does that reason still inspire you five years later?

Conversation 2: The Conductor

How will your life be different in 10 years? What changes to your values and perspectives will occur in that time? Where will you find your greatest satisfaction and fulfillment in 10 years? How will your level of commitment and energy for work be different than today? What will be your most pressing business and career issues as the conductor?

Questions to ask the conductor include:

- How has your focus changed as you've matured from pioneer to conductor?
- What are your greatest challenges related to developing your team? Has it been difficult to delegate administrative responsibilities to others? What has been the biggest hurdle?
- What issues concern you most? Were those things less important in earlier years?
- What shifts have you seen in client demand? How do you anticipate clients' needs evolving over the next 10 years?

Conversation 3: The Sage Guru

Describe your life in 20 years. What are your most important priorities at work and in life? You may be giving some thought to retirement; are you actively planning your exit strategy? Will you sell your business? What legacy do you hope to leave? Who would that impact?

Questions to ask the sage guru include:

- How did your choice to become an independent consultant affect your family and other important relationships?

- What issues concern you most? Were those issues less important in earlier years?
- What are the most important nuggets of wisdom you can share with someone who is more than 20 years younger than you?
- What are your biggest business mistakes? How would you have done things differently?
- How important is work-life balance? Would you change any of the choices you made regarding your priorities in earlier years?

Summary

This chapter described several steps you can take to look back to plan ahead. Follow the recommendations in this chapter and practice reflection and introspection. Recognize that one day you will look back on your career with wisdom and experience you've not yet gained. Determine what you want to see done because of your consulting career. How will your core competencies evolve, and how will your value proposition improve your clients' success? Practice event mapping on a scheduled basis to prepare for future possibilities. And engage in the hypothetical conversations with the pioneer, the conductor, and the sage guru from time to time. Doing so will improve your focus and influence decisions you make as you grow your consulting business. If you make it your habit to follow these recommendations, you'll improve your decisions and actions, which will ultimately influence your future.

Actions You Can Take Now

- **Get clear.** Before you think about your future and next steps, clarify your mission and vision.
- **Read the future.** Select a futurist journal or online publication and start reading it regularly. (*The Futurist*, for example, is an online publication that reports on technological, societal, and public policy trends.) What is in the future that might affect you and your consulting business?

About the Author

Kevin Marshall is the founder of Marshall Advisory Group, a management consulting firm that specializes in helping organizations with strategic planning, business process improvement, structured innovation methodology, and developing high-performing teams. He is an engaging facilitator and trainer with 40 years of diversified experience from executive management roles in consumer and commercial manufacturing, technology, entertainment, and financial industries. His combination of corporate and consulting experience allows him to bring a balanced and innovative perspective to his clients. He is a team builder generating ownership and commitment with his clients, which lead to the execution of ideas and organizational change. Kevin believes a good strategy that is executed properly will always produce better results than a brilliant strategy that sits on the shelf.

5 Ways to Build Your Business

RUSTY SHIELDS

It was my second year as a consultant focusing on business development. I was working long days, some nights, and weekends for what felt like nothing in return. I was beginning to doubt my career choices and had even reached the point of updating my resume. One night, I decided to take a break to attend a networking event at a local brewery. I was sitting at a table by myself and enjoying a cocktail when a close friend walked up to me and said, "Rusty, you're too comfortable!"

I laughed it off, took another sip of my drink, and replied "Heck yes, I'm comfortable! It's been a long week!"

"I'm serious," she replied. Then, she sat down and proceeded to give me a slice of reality pie! She said she'd been keeping a close eye on my business and had noticed that I was not taking chances . . . not growing—I was too comfortable.

Caught up in my own ego, I reacted emotionally and left the event. How dare she tell me what I was not doing with my business. That night I couldn't sleep, so I decided to prove her wrong. I started running reports and looking at the data, and I discovered she was right. After the shock wore off, I took some time to reflect and come up with a new game plan. As an instructional designer, I like structure and models, so I created the VISIT model to help me better focus on business growth.

In this chapter, we will explore each step of the VISIT model, identify strategies for growing your business, and define some actionable steps to employ during each phase to set yourself up for success.

A Time for Reflection

Part of growing your business is gaining and sustaining credibility. To determine credibility, most people turn to others who know them or have done business with them to ask about their experience as a customer. Another way to do this is through the "What Story Is Your Business Telling?" exercise.

Here's how it works:

- Look in the proverbial mirror and ask yourself the following questions about your business:
  - Are you generating positive customer reviews and testimonials?
  - Can you find yourself on Google?
  - Are you dependable?
  - Do you deliver a quality product at a fair price?
  - Are customers able to reach you?
- Survey three to five of your customers and ask these questions:
  - Can you give a positive customer review or testimonial?
  - Can you find my business on Google?
  - Am I dependable?
  - Do I deliver a quality product at a fair price?
  - Are you able to reach me?
- Compare the results of the questions and see if the stories are the same. If not, then take some time to determine what story your business is telling.

This exercise provides a foundation for your plan to grow and sustain your business.

VISIT but Don't Get Comfortable

Why do we like being comfortable? Comfort makes us feel at ease and in control of our own environment. We want to stay and revel in the lack of stress that accompanies that beloved condition. Being comfortable allows us to operate in autopilot and conserve our limited time and energy resources to focus on what we find personally and professionally motivating.

I created the VISIT model as a way to get uncomfortable. These five strategies challenge you so you have room to grow:

- **V**isibility
- **I**nvest
- **S**acrifice
- **I**nvent
- **T**ransparency

You can access an action plan based on the VISIT model on the handbook's website td.org/handbook-for-consultants. I urge you to use it and reflect on what you've learned. Be vulnerable and take action to cultivate true change.

Let's now look closer at each step of the model.

Visibility

Visibility is the first step in the VISIT model because it is the first thing a potential client sees. At this phase, people need to know who you are and what you do. It might not take a rocket scientist to figure that out, but in my experience, this is the single most important business performance indicator that proves growth, yet it is also missed the most. So, what's the disconnect?

After struggling to grow for a few years, I was introduced to the VCP process by a friend and mentor. This process—created by Ivan Misner, founder of Business Network International (BNI)—defines a three-step formula for measuring a business's current state: visibility + credibility = profitability. If the business is getting referrals, that ultimately translates to growth. It's simple, yet effective.

Visibility is a byproduct of credibility. One of the easiest and cheapest ways to gain credibility is to take advantage of earned media, which is content (like reviews and social media posts) from people who have done business with you. What easier way to gain credibility and visibility than simply asking a customer to leave a review about their experience or sharing a Google review link with a customer in a follow-up email or survey. You'll gain instant credibility, increased visibility, and foundational trust.

Another way to gain credibility is consistency. Marketing efforts, whether through social media or other outlets, can't be sporadic. They require a consistent effort over a prolonged time. Your audience needs to get to know you and your work. If you only share a few blog posts or give out one or two business cards, you'll be forgotten in a flash, even by your most loyal customers. You must make a conscious effort to use multiple avenues, multiple times, for a long time to get the visibility you need for growth.

Consistency can be expressed in terms of your actual product, such as your quality, but also in how you deliver that product. Did the agreed upon solution deliver the desired impact? Did the learning event meet the organization's expectations? Did you show up on time for the appointment with your client? If yes, then your reviews will be very fruitful. But what happens to your credibility if the answer to those questions was no? I promise it's not good. So, spend that extra effort and pay attention to the details—it will make all the difference.

A final concern when it comes to visibility is *audience saturation*—the phase when your customers know your product so well that the available opportunities begin to slow down, and your business starts to plateau or take a dive. This situation takes a bit longer to unfold, but unless you stay ahead of it, it also takes the longest to come back from. Audience saturation can be caused by not knowing your audience or how your business is expressed or performing. The only way to learn about your audience is to ask them through reviews, surveys, focus groups, and industry research. Once you know more about the target audience, you'll be able to expand your reach, which in turn allows you to express your business in a new way. Growth will not happen until you know how to express your business.

Once you start looking at these challenges through the lens of your customers, you'll be able to see just how visible you are. As you continue learning more about the VISIT model, you'll find a recurring theme that points back to visibility over and over, so this is not the last time you will hear that word.

Consulting Tip

Go to a computer or pick up your phone and type the name of your business into an internet search browser. Look at the results. If your business does not appear on the first page, you are not visible.

Invest

Investing back into your business can be one of the hardest yet most important things to do to promote growth. It took me many years of falling down, getting back up, failing again, and reinjuring the same wound before I learned my lesson. I tried to skate by, taking the cheap way out. Although investing can take on many forms, both financial and human capital, I want to focus on investing your money.

During my first year in business, I didn't invest any money back into the business, and as a result, I took a 35 percent loss. Luckily, I had faithful clients. The next year, I invested a little (and by little, I mean less than 5 percent). In return, I took a smaller loss. At that point, my mentor sat me down and said, "Look young man, you have to start thinking long term, and not just about the now." When I asked for clarification, he smiled and said, "You'll figure it out."

That was when I finally realized my tunnel vision was preventing me from thinking about the future of my business. I was comfortable, but I wasn't growing—it was time to start investing my money.

The first thing I invested in was myself and my own development. That may sound selfish at first, but think about it—if you are not in a place to be the best you can be, then how can you provide the best product for your clients? I used ATD's Competency Model, now called the Talent Development Capability Model, to assess my current level of development in multiple functional areas and find where I had the highest need for development. I started attending conferences and workshops and getting certifications. These are tangible, credible ways to gain more visibility with your client base. Attending conferences in your field allows you to network and learn from industry leaders—you can't put a price on the opportunities these events provide. I remember being starstruck the first time I met Elaine Biech! I could not believe I was rubbing elbows with one of the top thought leaders in my field. I am so thankful for these relationships.

Workshops and certificate programs take your investment to a different level of benefits. They give you a chance to develop yourself, while also allowing you to network with and learn from your peers in the industry. Peer-to-peer learning is one of the most effective ways to learn. Additionally, you'll add more resources to your network who you can contact when you need feedback.

Other ways to invest in your business include outsourcing or hiring. Perhaps you don't have time to manage your own social media because of all the opportunities you have coming your way; in that case, hire a marketing firm to take over your social media marketing. In year three of my business, I started contracting out other consultants to assist with my workload. In hindsight, I'm so glad my mentor told me to think long term. Otherwise, I'd never have imagined I'd need someone else to help me because I never thought I would get this big.

Referral marketing is another option for investment. Business Network International (BNI), an international referral marketing program that has been in existence for 38 years, has locations in more than 80 countries. In this program, you invest in a "seat" in your area's local chapter, which then gives you the exclusive right to be the only person in your industry to sit in that seat in that chapter. My business grew 400 percent in the year after joining my local BNI chapter. Talk about a return on investment! Start looking for other local referral marketing programs to invest in—there are thousands out there.

Last, consider investing in your community or causes you support. When I first started graduate school, I needed to find a part-time job to support my expenses. So, I applied to be a direct service professional at an agency that takes care of individuals with physical and mental disabilities. The work was difficult but very rewarding. I also realized just how many deserving charities out there needed support. So, when I started investing in my business, I wanted to make sure that my money would make an impact. I decided to start sponsoring different events and causes for nonprofit organizations in my area. I was able to use sponsorship marketing to gain more visibility and credibility with potential and current clients, which led to more business.

Development efforts can be costly, but the initial investment will make up for itself as your business grows. Think about the value that certificates and experience bring to your business. Think of the time and energy you'll save when two people are working for your business, instead of just you.

Consulting Tip

Take a step back and think about ways to develop yourself and your business. Look for regional conferences and workshops to minimize travel expenses.

Sacrifice

I didn't have to wait long to experience sacrifice as an entrepreneur. After starting my business, I quickly found myself telling friends I could not go on our next vacation and family members I couldn't travel cross-country for the holidays. I also realized that I would have to sacrifice certain luxuries—I didn't drive a nice car, live in a three-bedroom house, or eat at fine-dining establishments. But these initial sacrifices helped prepare me for the different kinds of sacrifices that growing my business would require.

Time is one of the biggest sacrifices you have to make for your business to grow. From a professional standpoint, there are a few ways that sacrificing your time leads to great benefits to your business. For example, volunteering at local charities and nonprofits—such as food banks, afterschool programs, and community kitchens—increases your visibility to other organizations in your community and gives you more credibility with your customers. Depending on what you do while volunteering, you may also be able to learn more about your audience or discover more opportunities to sponsor deserving causes.

In my second year of being in business, I accidentally stumbled upon an opportunity that turned out to be one of the most fruitful things I have ever done. I went to lunch with a great friend of mine, who's also the membership development director of a local professional association. As she explained how work was going, she mentioned that she needed volunteers to serve as ambassadors for the association. The position would require about five hours of work a month, but it also came with the opportunity to attend networking events with more than 900 businesses in the community for free. Once I began volunteering, businesspeople started to recognize me, learn more about my business, and contact me for consultation. I also started noticing the sponsorship opportunities at these events. Well, thinking back to investing, sponsorships lead to more visibility. (Are you beginning to see how this model is coming together?)

After one networking event, I could not stop thinking about the fact that 450 businesspeople had just attended that night. I knew I wanted to sponsor an event, but I didn't yet have the financial means to do it. So, I started thinking—what could I trade with them to get that kind of visibility? What about me? I met with the person in charge of sponsorships the next day and offered to trade an all-day workshop on team building for their staff in exchange for a networking event sponsorship. And they said, "You got it!" It was that easy. Sometimes you have to sacrifice yourself and the product you offer in exchange for future growth. Because of that one sacrifice, I currently have enough income to sponsor events whenever I want.

Another sacrifice I made early on for the sake of growth was speaking at conferences for free. When I told my spouse that I was going to Atlanta, Georgia, to speak at a conference, the response was, "How much are you getting paid?" I said, "Nothing." We had a long discussion about it, and I said that I did not yet have the visibility or credibility to request a stipend. Fortunately, it wasn't long before I had generated enough industry clout that it was acceptable to ask to be paid for my speaking engagements. Sacrifice comes in many forms.

Finally, consultants must be willing to sacrifice their comfort. As entrepreneurs, we are out of our comfort zone every time we step out the door. Whether it is making a cold call, starting a conversation with a potential client at a networking event, or launching a new product, we have to get uncomfortable. This is the only way to experience sacrifice and become vulnerable, which inspires true growth not only for your business but within yourself. Celebrate those moments, for they will have a huge influence on your personal and professional life.

> **Consulting Tip**
>
> Examine your products and expertise for things you can exchange for more visibility around your community. I think you will be surprised by how many organizations are willing to scratch your back if you scratch theirs.

Invent

During the COVID-19 pandemic, we were forced to invent in many ways. We had to figure out new ways to go to the grocery store, how to work from home, and how to consult with clients and still get the desired results. How can we invent proactively with a growth mindset?

I remember this one time when my business was booming—I had all kinds of time to concentrate on growth, and I was excited. Then, my friend from the beginning of this chapter came along (you know, the "you look comfortable" one). This time, I started the conversation: "I am not comfortable!"

"I can tell," she replied.

A little frustrated, I said, "What do you mean, 'I can tell'?"

"When was the last time you launched a new product?" she asked.

I thought about it for a minute and began stumbling on my words. I got so mad I wanted to scream, and then I realized how lucky I was to have someone who cared so much. She was right—again. It had been almost two years since I'd launched a new product or something different. I may not have felt comfortable, but my business was, and my audience was saturated. My products were so well known that I was invisible. It was time to invent something new.

I decided to launch a new development program for local organizations. This required a lot of research and development to determine the state of the local industries and what they were struggling with. I soon found myself back in the first few steps of the VISIT model. I needed more visibility for this new program, so I invested in a new certification and extra guerilla marketing techniques. I then looked for some local organizations that I had partnered with during my sacrifice step and offered to trade my new program for some sponsorship opportunities. This allowed me to pilot the program and get feedback. Then, it was time to launch! My new program helped me keep current customers, thanks to the product updates, while also allowing me to upsell, next-sell, and cross-sell, which in turn led to new referrals and new customers. And this was all possible because I stepped out of my comfort zone and started inventing again.

I also realized during this invention phase that I needed to diversify my current products. As your business evolves, so does the world and its needs. If you do not take a step back and look at your current inventory, it won't be long before you become comfortable and your products get stale. Part of invention is also reinvention. This may take a little assistance from your clients, or more research on your part, but it all leads to continuous growth.

Finally, beyond inventing new products and services, we must also occasionally reinvent ourselves. When the COVID-19 pandemic forced us all to stay indoors, I found myself trying to figure out how to pass the time. I must tell you—I am not a homebody; I like to be out and about. So, I quickly realized that I would have to find a new hobby or rekindle an old one that I'd let fall by the wayside due to the hustle and bustle of life. My grandmother was a seamstress, and when I was growing up, I spent my entire summers at her house. She taught me to sew to keep me quiet and busy while she got her work done. So, in 2020, when I needed to rekindle an old hobby, I picked up sewing again. It made the biggest difference. Sewing provided a nice break while also filling me with a calmness fostered by memories of her. I found a way to generate a new sense of freshness daily, and my business grew because of it.

Sometimes, we have to reinvent ourselves and find that one thing again or invent something new by picking up a new hobby. I challenge you to invent in whatever way you can both professionally and personally.

Consulting Tip

Evaluate your current portfolio of products and services, looking for new opportunities to expand it. Think back to your development and how you can invest again to invent.

Transparency

Transparency strengthens your accountability, and accountability builds trust. The success of your business relies significantly on the trust of your clients. Research by *Forbes* shows that two thirds of consumers would pay a higher price and spend more if it meant buying from a transparent company (Craig 2018). A stunning 94 percent of consumers rank transparency as the greatest factor in brand loyalty.

As a child growing up in the Deep South, I knew no stranger. I could walk up to anyone and everyone and strike up a conversation. Let's just say I had the gift of gab. When I was about seven years old, we took a family trip to Walt Disney World in Orlando, Florida. No matter how many times we visited, it always felt like the first. As I walked along with my family, I reached up and grabbed my mother's hand; only it wasn't—it was a stranger's hand. The funny thing was neither of us realized at first, and when we did, neither of us cared! Talk about trust.

Unfortunately, I lost some of that ability to trust as I grew up. It's natural for adults to build walls and barriers around ourselves and our feelings in response to our life experiences. However, those barriers can prevent growth, both professionally and personally. It took being in business for a few years before I realized that without transparency, my business wouldn't grow.

One of the first things I realized was the importance of owning up to my mistakes. We all make them, but admitting our mistakes is hard. Failure offers a chance to get better as a person and as a business, whereas pride will hold you back and destroy a business. Owning up to your mistakes may initially break down the credibility and trust of your business, but it also creates respect. Having the respect of your clients is crucial. And if you continue providing consistent, quality products through a transparent lens, you'll be able to rebuild credibility and trust.

Communication is another way to create transparency for your business. As part of my investment in a marketing firm to manage my social media presence, I allowed them to shadow me (with the consent of my clients) to take pictures, film videos, and conduct interviews. The marketing firm used that content to create videos and posts for my social media accounts—opening the curtain and allowing everyone to see what goes on behind the scenes. This level of transparency allowed potential customers to see who we are and what we do.

Let's take communication a step further. When I work with clients, the word *communication* comes up 100 percent of the time. When you communicate with your clients and potential customers, you have to tell them what you know and what you don't know, but most importantly you have to tell them to ask questions for clarity. If they're missing any pieces of the puzzle, they will make something up to fill in the gaps, and you may not be able to come back from that disconnect.

You can also be transparent with your business documentation and strategy. For example, it's imperative that you provide a detailed contract that includes scope, a description of deliverables, timelines, and most importantly, pricing. Whether you're doing a contract or a consultation, your customers do not want to know an estimate of how much it will cost; they want to know exactly how much it will cost. If your pricing is complicated, they may think you're unprofessional or that you're going to take advantage of them. Always be honest and transparent.

The last thing I recommend is telling your story. Emotion controls everything we do, which means that our businesses should connect with people on an emotional level. We need to be vulnerable and transparent and tell our story. Customers want to work with businesses that share their core values. How can we, as business owners, grow if our core values can't be heard through our story.

It took me a long time to figure out what my business's core values were because I had to decide how I wanted my business to be viewed. Once I figured that out, however, I asked my marketing team to design an infographic around my core values, which I then launched on my social media accounts. Within days, I was getting new leads and opportunities. Trust me; work for your business, and your business will work for you.

Summary

If you only take away one thing from this model, I want you to have a plan. I designed the VISIT model to encourage you to take a step back and look for opportunities—not just opportunities to make money, but opportunities to grow. This requires that you look in the mirror, not just at the next stop sign. The model is also very iterative, with each step connecting to the one before it and the one after it. Once you begin to VISIT your business more, you will find that others visit your business too.

Actions You Can Take Now

- **Peek behind the curtain.** Look for opportunities to allow the public to see who you are and what you do. Ask friends, family, or local schools to shadow you for a day.
- **Evolve your communication strategy.** Look for ways to communicate differently by sharing what you know, what you don't know, and when they're going to know it. This may be as simple as giving clients a tiered rollout plan with dates.

- **Tell your story.** Add an About section to your website that shares your creation story. Include your core values and policies. This is the ultimate step in transparency and will lead to instant growth.

About the Author

Rusty Shields is the owner of and chief performance consultant at Develefy Consulting. His passion, energy, and excitement when facilitating business growth is palpable and contagious. As a facilitator and consultant in the learning and development field for the past 18 years, Rusty has worked with corporations and organizations of all sizes all around the world. He prides himself in his work with C-level executives, directors, managers, and high-potential employees. Rusty has experience designing and delivering customized leadership and business development programs, both virtually and in person. He also has many years of experience designing e-learning and other self-paced training programs in interactive and engaging ways. Reach out to him by emailing rusty@develefy.com or visiting Develefy.com.

CHAPTER 34

Consulting Is a Relationship Business

MIKE KENT

At one point in my career, I was a training manager for a small pharmaceutical company. I was in my element there, and I was given free rein to build an on-the-job training program from scratch for new manufacturing operators. I'd done this successfully a few times in the past, so I was confident that my efforts would once again create something amazing. I was collaborating with a colleague, Andy, a former teacher who had joined the company and became a lead operator at the plant. In between our working sessions, we chatted about our common passion for teaching and shared more than a few stories from our time as instructors. He always seemed to have a practical perspective and creative ideas that consistently improved our training content. When I asked questions, and really listened to Andy's answers, the rookie in our highly regulated environment was constantly teaching this old dog some new tricks.

Over the years, Andy and I lost touch, but one day, about a decade after we'd worked together, Andy sent me a message through LinkedIn. "I still remember the conversations we used to have about teaching and the great work we did back then," he said. "So, when it became clear we needed someone to help improve our operator performance, I immediately thought of you." I was blown away. A few months later, his firm hired me as a consultant. I couldn't wait to work with and learn from my old friend again. So yes, consulting is certainly a business of relationships.

In this chapter, I'll talk about building and maintaining those relationships by applying the concepts of curiosity, collaboration, humility, and servant leadership to your interactions with both current and potential clients.

Questions and Curiosity

First, before going further, let's take a moment to check in. What's your experience been like so far with this handbook? Think about it, I'll wait. . . . This is important. Which chapters and authors resonated with you the most? How did their ideas align with your objectives, your needs, and your reasons for investing time to flip through these pages? Did any strategies cause you to pause and examine how you could apply them to a specific situation or client? Did you highlight any paragraphs for future reference? You see, you've been constructing a relationship of sorts with this handbook and have likely already decided whether you'll refer to it in the future.

Your clients are constantly reading you too. They make value judgments based on what they think you might provide but more so about how you would provide it. Can they trust you? Do you connect with them where they're at, understanding them and providing what they need in this moment? It sounds eerily like going on a first date to me. . . . So, how do we make our relationships work? Specifically, how do we sustain the relationships we build as consultants?

A critical characteristic of good consulting relationships is authentic curiosity. Do you routinely convince yourself that you have all the answers and can cure what ails the client with little to no inquiry? After all, you're the expert, and they called you in to fix the issue. The most successful consultants don't assume they know everything. Instead they question everything to find out what's causing the issues.

Thankfully, L&D professionals have some unique tools to help diagnose problems. For example, the needs assessment is specifically designed to use a series of questions to uncover the root causes of a client's challenges. When used effectively, needs assessments can foster confidence, mutual trust, and an open collaborative spirit, which are also the characteristics of a good consulting relationship.

But what if the client doesn't think a needs assessment is worthwhile? I had such an experience shortly after returning from my very first ATD conference. My organization's vice president of quality handed me the business card of a pharmaceutical statistics expert and asked me to arrange a two-day training on statistics for our chemists and engineers. In response, I asked him and eight other stakeholders to attend a 90-minute meeting to identify the needs and specific outcomes for the course. On the day of the meeting, they sauntered into the conference room looking skeptical at best. I explained the intent of the needs assessment, nearly quoting the conference session presenter's justification word for word. I was petrified! Then, I began asking questions. Their responses were lukewarm, and after 20 minutes, the VP asked why I had summoned all these busy people to a meeting when I'd already been told what to do. It was my first real test as a training professional. I provided a rationale, he relented, and we got back to the questions. Ten minutes later, we discovered that the real reason people were having difficulty was because they were using unclear procedures and inadequate tools. The chemists and engineers knew how to perform statistical calculations—they simply lacked clear guidance on how and when to perform them and what data to gather for more meaningful conclusions.

L&D professionals know this tale all too well. However, the procedures weren't the only thing that doing the needs assessment changed. I also gained the trust of the organization's most influential people—and that proved invaluable. Future projects became true collaborations instead of being developed in a vacuum and thrown at the wall. To this day, some of those stakeholders remain dear friends and trusted colleagues. They recognize the value of this approach and they let others know it too.

Now, if a client balks at paying for a needs assessment, I facilitate it free of charge. I want them to know that I won't let a few hundred dollars get in the way of doing the right thing for the right reasons. This provides value to the client while building trust and demonstrating that I'm not out to nickel and dime them to death. Relationships always involve a bit of give and take, don't they?

Back to our central concept of curiosity. Part of being genuinely curious means listening to understand and resisting the well-intentioned but usually off-putting tendency to "pounce and pitch." This doesn't mean you shouldn't try to identify areas where you may be able to help, but it's a delicate dance that takes practice. Allowing that person to continue their train of thought may lead to a more fruitful or even different endpoint. With a better understanding of what is important to them and why, you can ask more relevant and probing questions. And they feel heard and appreciated.

Consulting Tip

Practice "pounce avoidance." During conversations with colleagues and friends, try to notice any strong desire to jump in with your thoughts, ideas, examples, or stories. Then, get curious about when and why you feel this urge to "pounce." Is the reason about you or about something else? If you must pounce, consider leading with curiosity rather than trying to prove yourself in that moment. Practicing in everyday situations will help you prepare for better conversations with clients.

I certainly struggle with the tendency to pounce and pitch, and I've learned it's a challenge for many consultants. After all, we're eager to be recognized as capable and to show we're ready and able to help. We're also driven by the desire to grow our business—you know, the livelihood that supports us and our families. I also recognize my ego can, and often does, get in the way. One thing that helps me control the urge is to imagine my prospect or client standing on a trampoline, and then I think of the phrase, "If you pounce, they'll bounce!" Have you ever tried to have a conversation with someone on a trampoline? It's not easy. When I choose to listen, summarize, and ask probing follow-up questions, I end up validating my understanding of the other person's key messages. This demonstrates respect, empathy, and a willingness to meet the client where they are for their reasons, not mine.

Facilitated Collaboration

This brings us to another characteristic of good consulting relationships—a concept I call "facilitated collaboration." Your goal could be described as jumping on the trampoline in sync with the other person, but before you get too excited about doing back flips together, let's get curious about this concept.

All good relationships rely on both parties being fully engaged, and consulting is no different. Your clients also have some accountability to make the relationship work. So, how can you help them be a good partner? Being what you need from them is a great place to start. Also, acknowledge that the relationship requires focus and effort from both of you, just as much as the work itself.

As a consultant, you can't assume that how you like to collaborate with clients will align with their preferences. This is where the "facilitated" part comes in. Have specific conversations about how you can and will work together successfully. Identify everyone's needs, as well as their biases, assumptions, and blind spots. Ask questions like, "What biases might be present? Is there anything we're not aware of that could influence the current situation or our new definition of success?" which may encourage people to dig a little deeper or widen or narrow their lens. Of course, you may need to work your way down to that question by starting with a simpler one like, "What haven't we considered, or may not have considered fully?" Don't immediately assume that there isn't anything if the room goes silent. As the saying goes, "You never find gold until you start digging." Facilitated collaboration means that you, as the consultant, have to take an active role in digging, coaching, guiding, and enabling the client to ask better, deeper, and more fruitful questions, rather than skimming the surface and hoping for the best.

Incorporating elements of guided discovery as part of facilitated collaboration can improve this curiosity-based approach to problem solving and keep the client engaged in performing their assigned tasks and responsibilities. More importantly, it enables the client to discover for themselves new ways of doing things through your facilitation and guidance. You know, the old "teach them to fish" analogy. This enhances the client's level of ownership for the ideas, which then improves the likelihood of finding and implementing a sustainable set of solutions.

Next, have an intentional exit strategy. I know this may seem counterintuitive—shouldn't we be aiming for repeat business? Getting that call from a client who says, "Hey, I still need you around for *X, Y,* or *Z*" can be a tremendous boost of confidence and validation, not to mention another paycheck. However, as a wise mentor of mine once told me, "If you're planning on making yourself indispensable, consider applying for full-time employment." Once the client can fish for themselves, it's time to move on. That's not to say you can't have a long-term consulting relationship with them. Many consultants do when it's mutually beneficial, always providing new and creative challenges to overcome. What distinguishes a good, solid, rewarding consultant-client relationship from the others is the motivation of the two parties. If you're intentionally holding back or drawing things out to keep the cash flowing, the client will see that, and it will likely cost you the relationship.

Humility

What might you miss if you're not willing to diligently prepare? Worse, what might the client miss out on?

Vin Scully, arguably the greatest sports broadcaster of all time, took the old training adage of "know your audience" to a whole other level. He consistently sought to understand and then deliver whatever the listener needed to feel like *they* could see the sky, smell the grass, and hear the crack of the bat *for themselves.* Scully was a storyteller, and some likened his broadcasts to poetry about batted balls around a meticulous sandlot of fresh-cut grass and brown dirt beneath a sky so blue it would make you cry just looking at it. Perhaps his greatest attribute, however, was that to Scully, it wasn't about him—it was about creating something special for others that enriched their lives, if only for a few hours at a time.

Scully prepared by methodically working his process, always engaging the humility of a rookie broadcasting for the first time. Even after 67 years behind the microphone, he spent hours before each broadcast going over his notes, warming up his voice, working through radio or TV production details, and having conversations with players and coaches. It didn't matter that these were all the basics and it would have been easy for him to think, "I've done this before. I know this. I got this."

When asked during a 2016 interview what contributed most to his Hall of Fame career, Scully said, "I would quote Laurence Olivier, because I've lived by his quote. Apparently, some young actor asked [Olivier] about his success, and he said, 'My success comes from a humility to prepare, and a confidence to bring it off'" (Dickerson 2016). I never met Vin Scully, but the relationship he created with me through the radio still has me hearing his voice every time I read that quote.

> **Consulting Tip**
>
> Consider each project and interaction as somehow unique and new. Then, prepare like you've never done it before . . . because you haven't.

Our humility to prepare infuses trust and sturdiness into our client relationships—not to mention the benefits of being able to perform when you're called on. Your confidence to bring it off, as Olivier seems to suggest, is a direct result of your preparation, which becomes the foundation for the client's confidence in you. When I focus on cultivating and improving relationships rather than simply landing my next client, I prepare intentionally and methodically and the work comes in waves. On the other hand, if I wing it because I think I know better or if I'm arrogant and focus on what I'll get out of the interaction instead of providing what the client needs for their reasons, things go south in a hurry.

Maintain the Spark

In my experience, and that experience has been both good and tragic, success comes down to exactly what you might think—effort and intention. And not unlike other relationships, people remember how you made them feel, as well as the little things that made you uniquely special and a good fit for that time in their life. For example, do you want to be viewed as the consultant that only calls when they need or want something? How do you feel when others treat you this way? What companies and people do you go back to and why? Which ones do you tell your friends to stay away from?

In most cases, it simply comes down to treating people like people first. You want to make sure they know that you see them as more than a meal ticket and that you're genuinely interested in their success for their reasons, not yours. It doesn't take much! Consider the people and who they are, what they enjoy, and what is important to them. Then, offer yourself in some meaningful way that aligns with those attributes. One suggestion I was given that has worked well for me is reaching out when I see something relevant to a client's situation or needs: "I saw this [*article, news story, new book, LinkedIn post, seminar, or conference session title*], and it made me think of you." These notes are most effective when you are not their subject. Why might that be?

Some consultants send gifts. This has always been tricky for me, especially during non-holiday seasons. I've had some clients really appreciate the gesture, while others either have not accepted or been unable to accept them due to corporate policies or their own comfort level. The last thing you want to do is unknowingly create a situation where the client feels like they owe you more business or special treatment, or worse, that you are sending it because you want or will expect that special treatment. When in doubt, ask if they are able to accept small tokens of appreciation. Regardless, they will appreciate the sentiment.

Here's an example of when sending a gift made just the right kind of impact. I noticed that one of my clients often mentioned looking forward to enjoying a cup of tea after our late afternoon check-ins. I like tea myself, so at year's end, I sent her a gift set from my favorite tea company. The sample of teas and a teacup were my way of thanking her for her continued trust and business. Even now, she tells me about how much she looks forward to being able to have tea in that mug after a long day. That $40 gesture may have reinforced my appreciation, but even more so, it expressed that I saw her as a person first and was grateful for the friendship we'd built while working together.

Don't Spam Your Clients With Email

Be very clear about your intention when sending anything, especially unsolicited communication. We all get too much email, and you don't want to end up getting filtered out by a junk-mail inbox rule. A strategy that works well for many consultants is to construct a calendar for networking and connecting with clients. If you get frustrated by networking or find it difficult to remember to connect with people, consider trying this approach.

Determine a time interval that is both manageable for you and based on how you think the individual will react. Schedule time to send a quick email based on that interval. Having email templates can really help, although people can often tell whether or not the message is original. In any case, make sure to check you've replaced all the *<client X name>* entries with *<client Y name>* if you're using a template. And before hitting send, ask yourself these questions: Why am I sending this message? Am I uncomfortable with a few months of silence from a potential or existing client? Am I trying to make myself look good, competent, or capable? Am I doing it because a consultant in a handbook told me it was a good idea? Above all else, be authentic when reaching out and honest about your motives. Also, respect the client and let their response inform the nature of your next steps. If they say they're busy, don't email them three days later with two more things you thought might interest them.

Try sending your message templates to a few consultants and trusted co-workers for feedback; just make sure you're open to whatever feedback you get. This attitude of trial and acceptance (as opposed to trial and error) can help cultivate a growth mindset that recognizes there is no such thing as failure, only data to examine in the context of determining what to do next. This will also help you practice responding rather than reacting to client feedback, where the stakes are higher.

Consulting Tip

Consider when, where, and how you want to connect with each of your clients. Capture these details in writing somewhere that you can—and will—refer to often.

Your Relationship Strategy

We create healthier client–consultant relationships through curiosity and authenticity—first seeking to understand and then practicing servant leadership to facilitate meeting their needs. In his landmark book *Servant Leadership: A Journey Into the Nature of Legitimate Power and Greatness*, Robert Greenleaf (1977) encouraged leaders to help those served become healthier, wiser, freer, and more autonomous through collaboration, trust, listening, and empowerment. This approach offers long-lasting change, not a temporary fix, which, oddly enough, aligns well with our goal as consultants. While that text has inspired hundreds of other works—including bestselling books, TED Talks, and leadership development programs—I see servant leadership as a cornerstone for leading clients on the path to self-sufficient "fishing."

One of our talents as L&D professionals is to create pathways toward *autonomous competency*—that is, enabling the person to be able to do what they need to do on their own. You might be thinking, "That's fine for a learner, but these are clients, and very knowledgeable ones at that," but stay with me.

Here's where applying concepts of adult learning theory to our consulting practice can help. We know that guided discovery enables individuals to create their own aha moments. We also know that people feel a strong sense of ownership for things they've created themselves. Knowledge, and the ability to apply that knowledge, is enhanced when using a more tactile, experiential learning approach. So, are there ways to blend guided discovery with experiential learning during our client projects? How might instilling a sense of curiosity, encouraging a bit of humility, and using facilitated collaboration create a space where better outcomes could occur, including ensuring those outcomes are sustainable? If one of our goals is client ownership of the results—and it absolutely should be—are there already tools in our toolkit that may be useful? I encourage you to explore where and how for yourself.

Consulting Tip

Do not do things for the client that they can do for themselves.

You Need People to Build Relationships

I'm lucky and grateful to have a group of people that I trust, who I can ask any sort of question or discuss any sort of challenge with and know that I will get real, honest, and direct answers in a way that is always in service to me and my higher purpose. I've known some of them for more than 35 years; others only 35 days. When we connect, we chat and talk about anything before the conversation inevitably turns to work. What then occasionally follows is something like this: "I had a conversation with so and so from a company that needs someone like you. I mentioned your name as someone they might be interested in getting to know." As a result, I'm also fortunate that I've never really needed to do any structured self-promotion or marketing to keep my business running and the lights on. This is a big deal because any introduction is always easier with that kind of referral. But the simple gestures don't always have to involve work.

A mutual friend introduced me to Joe. He's owned a consulting firm for a long time, and we've done some work together. Although we lived on opposite sides of the country, we'd occasionally have dinner together when he was visiting clients in my area. Once I made a casual comment about a client visit I was about to go on and the difficulty of finding a good place for dinner while traveling. Well, Joe pulls out his phone and shows me a map of the city I'm visiting—he's got a bunch of pinned restaurants on it. Joe asks what I might feel like eating, and then texts me a few options with notes about what to get and what to avoid ordering. Fast forward to my client visit. It had been a pretty rough day; I was exhausted and in no mood to roll the dice on dinner. Then, I remembered Joe's text message. Ten minutes later, I was enjoying a great meal while decompressing in preparation for day 2 of my trip. That restaurant list was not a huge thing until it became one in that moment. To Joe, it was just a little thing he did for me because he wanted to. I'm fortunate to have many otherwise-average Joe's in my life, and their friendships means more to me than any work we may do together or arrange for one another.

By the way, I hope you picked up on another of Joe's relationship-building strategies—go see people in person as often as you and they can make it happen. It makes a real difference to your interactions, and people appreciate when you make that level of sacrifice to better connect with them.

I hope these examples illustrate the power and necessity of having people in your sphere whom you have great relationships with—your community. The relationship with your support network, both personally and professionally, cannot be undervalued, and their influence on your success can never be overstated. These are the fun and mutually rewarding professional friendships that provide direct, honest feedback (so ask them often!), as well as opportunities to practice and fail safely, reflect honestly and openly, and be yourself. And speaking of that, who is the first name to appear on your list? It's yourself, of course. That's right. You!

Ever try to fill an empty cup from an empty pitcher? Among those who serve others, there is a tendency to forget to serve themselves. We've all experienced this, but are we intentionally finding opportunities to refill our pitchers? Put another way, and with apologies to the Buddha, this is perhaps another definition for the positive trait of "wise selfishness."

Begin Your Relationship-Building Journey

Consider beginning your journey by reflecting on your current relationships with the businesses and professional contacts you interact with. How do you appreciate being treated? Why do you think about that business or individual whenever the need arises or a friend or colleague asks for a recommendation? Your answers may provide insight on how you can enhance your relationships with others by mirroring what you value from those you interact with.

Use the Improving Your Relationship Skills assessment, which is available to download from the handbook's website at td.org/handbook-for-consultants, to gain clarity on where you are and how you can improve your proficiency with building trust, employing curiosity, and facilitating collaboration and servant leadership. Consider working through this tool once a quarter, and absolutely whenever you revisit your goals or objectives. It may also be useful to review your most recent entries both before and after connecting with a potential client. Keep the individual assessments in a binder, and look back every so often to see your progress.

Summary

Consulting is a tough business. Beyond the challenge of landing and keeping clients (until they can fish on their own), there's the reality that a lack of business can turn into a lack of security for you and those who depend on you. This fear can poison every source of water that might fill your pitcher—fear of missing out, fear of not having enough, fear of not being good enough, and so on. While some people are able to use these fears as motivators, we as L&D professionals know that fear is only a short-term motivator that often creates an unsustainable level of progress. So, what else is there? I invite you to shift your focus from "what" to "why." That is, shift from focusing on what the reasons are that you do what you do, and instead understand why you want to do those things and do them well. Make your why your North Star, and it will become your centering point—continuously calibrating your work, your decisions, and your actions. Your why will enable you to overcome your fear, serving as a constant companion you can trust for guidance, confidence, and purpose when the skies go dark.

I've come to view consulting as a partnership focused on improving how organizations do what they do by understanding the reasons why doing it is important. I've also recognized that collating a huge list of clients is not my business strategy. I feel a significant difference in my relationships with clients and my overall well-being when I focus on being a servant leader instead of the resident expert. When I'm clear on my motivations, and those of the client, we're able to discover and align to the best way to work together for our mutual advantage. Forming and maintaining your relationship then becomes less of a chore and more of a joy. And remember, dear friends, above all else, you can't spell *joy* without the *y*.

Actions You Can Take Now

- **Choose the people.** Compile a list of people you want to build good professional relationships with. Next to each name, write why they are important to you. If you put down "paycheck," that's OK. Just make sure you also list a second reason. Next, list a few words or a short phrase that describes their agenda and objectives. Finally, identify why their agenda and objectives are important to them. Reflect on this process, looking for any patterns in either your entries or how easy or challenging it was to arrive at them.
- **Use the tools.** We discussed investing time and effort, creating clarity around expectations and processes, and using the tools of active listening, facilitated collaboration, and guided discovery as ways to improve the quality of your consulting relationships. Evaluate how these tools may be useful and how you might incorporate them into your consulting practice.
- **Inquire within.** Examine how and when you employ curiosity, humility, and servant leadership in your relationships with clients and colleagues. Use the Consulting Relationships Improvement Assessment tool to identify your current and desired future states, along with specific actions to take in getting from one to the other.

About the Author

Mike Kent is an independent consultant driven to enable people to perform at their best. His passions for teaching and improving the quality of life for patients has sustained a multidecade career in the life sciences industry, including the launch of his own consulting firm, Catalyst Quality Partners. His work focuses primarily on improving human performance through more effective interactions with the processes, systems, tools, and environment that influence a person's work. Mike is an ocean-lover, sports fan, music and photography enthusiast, and an incredibly proud parent of his son, Rylan. Mike lives on the North Carolina coast with his canine better half, Chloe. Start a relationship with Mike at kentqpg@gmail.com.

How to Show Up and Stand Out as a Consultant

BEVERLY CROWELL

If you have the word *consultant* in your job title or description, chances are anyone outside the consulting business doesn't really know what you do. Worse yet, there are those who call themselves consultants who may not know either.

The mystery and misconceptions around my own consulting work were made apparent to me while shopping at a local retail store with my husband. He was scouring the aisle of wooden plaques with inspirational sayings and came across one that made him chuckle. It read, "I don't work here. I'm a consultant." After a moment of being slightly offended, I had to laugh too. Here, in the middle of a discount outlet store, was a visual (and mass produced) manifestation of the struggle consultants face every day.

If you've been a consultant, you know that we do work and we work hard. The harsh reality, however, is that our hard work may not always demonstrate our value. As Peter Block, author of *Flawless Consulting: A Guide to Getting Your Expertise Used*, says, "Stop being helpful and start being useful." Herein lies the problem. If we show up to help with the "customer is always right" mindset and deliver to our client's expectations, we might miss the mark because their expectations are far too low. In other words, consultants are simply being helpful if we give our clients what they think is right. It's only when we give them what they don't yet know they want (or need) that we become useful. It's a delicate but crucial shift in how we show up for our clients, but it's a shift that will ultimately develop trusting partnerships. Our goal should always be to work ourselves out of a job with a client because once they see how useful we can be, they often want us back.

You've read the words "show up" dozens of times in other chapters. In this chapter, I'll offer some best practices for how you can show up to stand out—how to start any consulting engagement the right way so you can shine and deliver the results your clients expect. Then, I'll wrap up with some lessons I've learned from my years of consulting.

It Starts on Day One

Being useful and being invited back is never a given, but there's a lot you can do to develop a collaborative relationship with your clients that invites trust and perhaps another project. It begins on day one—in how you show up in your earliest conversations with your clients. Almost at once, you start teaching your clients what it will be like to work with you based on what you are and aren't willing to do or accept. You should never try to wing it and see where the conversation takes you. Always plan the meeting to lay out the client's expectations and, just as importantly, the expectations you have of them. This is otherwise known as *contracting*.

In *Flawless Consulting*, Block calls contracting an "accurate predictor of how the project itself will proceed." Great contracting, great results. Bad contracting—well, you get the picture. It doesn't matter if you are an external consultant being hired by an organization or an internal consultant working inside the organization—contracting is the single most important predictor for how things will go, and it is consistently the one thing consultants, and clients, fail to do. Instead, consultants are lured into the promise of a problem to solve.

Most of us are naturally curious and can't wait to start asking questions, digging deeper, and getting to the heart of the problem so we can offer a solution. Not only does this fuel our curiosity, but there's a natural high that comes with offering our expertise and showing the client just how smart we are. At the same time, clients are ready for an answer; sometimes due to internal pressure or just plain old frustration, they will take any answer even if it's not the best answer. They want to jump straight to solution and implementation, believing that the sooner they start doing something, the sooner the pressure will cease. It almost always creates a messy ending of unmet expectations, disappointment, and lost or unimplemented recommendations. Clients may not realize how flawed this process of jumping ahead is, so it's up to consultants to show them a different way.

The Contracting Meeting

If contracting is a "predictor for how the project will proceed," how can you ensure the project proceeds in a way that both you and the client want? It turns out there is a logical sequence for reaching an agreement with your client, and it's outlined in *Flawless Consulting*.

First, do something that will help to increase the personal comfort level between you and your client. Make a personal statement on how you feel about working together and invite them to do the same. Find a way to connect before diving into the content. Next, ask questions and listen to understand why the client has brought you in. Once you have a picture of what you believe the client thinks is the problem, summarize it back to them. Don't try to solve the problem just yet. You don't have enough information, and you don't yet have an agreement.

Consulting Tip

Ask a friend to use a 10-point scale to rate how good you are at connecting with strangers. Be sure to ask why they gave you that rating.

Once you've connected, and after hearing an initial statement of what the client is concerned about, it's time to ask the client, "So, what do you want from me?" Block says, "The answer is the heart of the contracting process, and the question must be asked directly." This is the key qualifying question for determining whether and how you can succeed on this project. Then, share what you, the consultant, want from your client to make the project successful. This conversation should be a mutual exchange of what you want from each other and what you are willing to offer. It defines not only what you will be working on together, but how you will show up for each other. This is when you begin the business of building a collaborative relationship.

Asking for what you want is not always easy, but don't fall into the trap of offering elaborate explanations or vague ideas of what it will be like to work together—neither serves you or the client well. Instead, state what you want in simple, clear language. Let the want come first, and the justification can follow. The goal is to come to an agreement about what you are working on and, more importantly, how you will work together as authentically and transparently as possible.

Once you understand the importance of asking for what you want in a consulting agreement, you can begin developing a standard list of items to bring to every contracting conversation. Some should be technical (like access to data) while others will begin to lay out what it will be like to work together (such as providing feedback). For example, perhaps you want:

- To interview critical stakeholders in this project after you've given them a heads up on my involvement
- To meet weekly on the phone for 30 minutes to provide project updates and recontract on any new information or changes
- To be able to provide alternative solutions to the one you may already have in mind
- Adequate time to work on the project, which will start on [*include specific date*]
- To provide feedback about what's working well between us and any areas of concern
- A response to my emails or phone calls within 24 hours
- Access to certain documents, data, and records
- To be paid this amount on the third Monday of every month

These wants are never delivered in isolation. You will share them with your client as part of reaching an agreement for how you will move forward together. Ultimately, it must be a conversation—you may not get everything you want in the way you want it, and neither will the client. The important thing is that you ask, and you know why you are asking. Your clients want you to deliver a solution to their problem or issue as quickly as possible, so it's vital for you to show up to the conversation knowing what you can do to get them there faster. It's never about doing it your way; it's about doing it in a way that best serves the client and you.

After exchanging your wants with the client, you will either reach an agreement or get stuck. If you get stuck, step back and take time to understand why. Ask your client, "How do you feel about where we are heading and what we've agreed to?" Give them the opportunity to voice any concerns and talk about how to move forward, or not. It's OK to say no to opportunities at this point. If you can't do your very best work for your clients, you need to be willing to walk away gracefully and before you get too far along in the process. Surprisingly, the more I say no to some clients, the more they want my support. (Turns out, many people have a genuine appreciation for partnering with someone who is authentic and doesn't overpromise or sacrifice too much of themselves just to get the work.)

Once you've reached an agreement or even if you decide to walk away, give your support to the client. Make encouraging statements about what it's been like to work together, the challenges the client is facing, or even something they did in the meeting that you appreciated. For example, "You told me a lot about some of the challenges you and your organization are facing. Thank you for trusting me in that way." You want to end the meeting the way you began—with connection. Ultimately, consulting is about building relationships, and clients will remember how you made them feel as much as, if not more than, what you were able to do for them.

Last, agree on the next steps you both will take, and realize that while your initial contracting meeting has ended, it's never finished. Throughout the project, you will be recontracting with your client. No project moves forward without surprises or changes. Every one of these is an opportunity to recontract with your client to ensure you are still on the same page. This is why it's important to include "I want to be able to recontract with you anytime there is new information or changes in the project" during that initial meeting. Set the expectation with your client that consulting is a dynamic process that will require the two of you to have ongoing conversations.

Consulting Dos and Don'ts

I've been doing some version of consulting for the better part of my career. Because of that, I find myself coaching others on what it is, how to do it, and how to do it well enough to make a living. Aside from contracting, there are a few other dos and don'ts I'd like to share. Some words of wisdom if you will.

Never Ever Believe Your Own Hype

Once you start to believe you have all the answers, you're no longer a consultant. You're an expert. Being an expert isn't so bad—there is a lot of work out there helping leaders roll out new systems, implementing new processes, and fixing problems clients can't seem to fix themselves. However, the minute we start trying to fix the very issues we identify as the problem, we are no longer consulting. It's easy to fall into this trap because we have egos too. It feels good to fix something and be rewarded with the praise of doing so. But, if we are really trying to be consultative with our clients, we know that it's their win, not ours.

If you can't find satisfaction from giving them the win, it's time to reassess what role you really want to be playing with your clients.

Don't Run Scared

By the time a client reaches out to you for help, they've already tried working the problem without success. They may be under pressure from their management or simply overwhelmed by the whole process. The client's resulting stress often means you'll encounter some type of resistance, perhaps more than once. Although it may not feel like it, resistance is often the best gift a client can give a consultant. It's a flashing neon sign pointing to their fear, frustrations, and challenges. And while you should never allow yourself to be abused by a client's resistant behaviors, you should not run away from them. Instead, see the resistance for what it is. You are getting closer to their underlying issues or insecurities about what they have or haven't done. If not addressed, the resistance will become a roadblock. If explored, you and your client might get to the heart of the issue, where real change can happen.

Be Assertive Not Aggressive

A funny thing happens when you tell consultants it's OK to ask for what they want. They immediately equate asking for what they want with being too pushy or aggressive. However, when I press new consultants with the question of "What are you asking for?" they usually say something reasonable like, "responding to an email within 24 hours." I then ask, "Would you think it's unreasonable for your client to ask you to respond within 24 hours?" Their answer is almost always no.

Why then are we unwilling to ask for ourselves what we are so willing to give to others? Asking for what we want from our clients and hearing what they want from us is how we build collaborative relationships. Otherwise, we are just order takers. Certainly, you'll want to ask in a way that honors the other person, but an assertive consultant knows that the act of asking, then discussing, and negotiating is the only way the real work of relationships is done.

Know When to Walk Away

Great consultants build great relationships with their clients, and the clients may not always want those relationships to end. When you are working with someone to help overcome challenges and solve issues, it's ideal to form a collaborative partnership. Even so, it's important to remember that the consultant's role is meant to be temporary. You are not an employee or even a surrogate manager—you are a resource who can help lend your expertise to influence for change where you have no direct authority or control. If I find it hard to leave a client engagement or if a client finds it hard for me to leave, I can look back and see where I became a part of the solution.

I learned this lesson the hard way when consulting with an interior design company on their overall market strategy. Through our conversations, they quickly discovered I had a knack for operations, even though I knew very little about interior design. Over the course of our contract, my role continued to expand until I was no longer a consultant, but a de facto member of the team doing the work that the company's leaders were afraid to do. This ultimately created an unhealthy dependency and allowed management to say, "Well, Beverly said." Eventually, I reassessed the role I was playing in the solution and the new problem I had helped create. We contracted an exit strategy, and I once again took my place on the sidelines to champion their success, not mine. It's never fair for clients to become dependent on the consultant. Yes, we want our expertise used and appreciated, but we should always insist that implementation and sustainment is the role of the client and their organization. Let the client invite you back to partner on another opportunity because they already know how you will show up and how you can help.

Consulting Tip

When walking away from a situation is the right thing to do, it's a matter of ethics. Do it.

You Are Worth It

When I first started working as an independent consultant, I was scared. I knew that I had a lot to offer my potential clients, but I wasn't sure where to start. Today, in my coaching conversations with other emerging consultants, I hear a lot of the same fears. The question, "How much do I charge?" almost always comes up in conversation. It's not an easy question to answer. I've turned to the books *Consulting for Dummies* and *The New Business of Consulting* for ideas, and I've also talked with others in the field. What I learned then and believe even more now is that you are worth it—whatever you decide that worth may be. It took some time before I was comfortable asking for my desired fee, but once I did, I rarely experienced pushback and my clients still called. As consultants, our ability to be curious, ask questions, look at problems without bias, and challenge thinking is what our clients want. If they could do it on their own, they would have done so. So be fair, but don't sell yourself short. You are worth it.

Always Be Curious and Never Stop Learning

If you stop being curious about your clients and what's going on in their world, it's time to move on. If you stop being curious about learning and growing as a consultant, it's time to move on. Even with my 20 plus years in the field, I am still very inexperienced. Consultants who think they have it all figured out have, in many ways, become like the clients they are hired to help. So be curious, be humble, be authentic, and do the work.

I *do* the work. I'm a consultant.

Summary

You can guide your clients to the type of consultative relationship you want to have with them, but only if you contract, and contract early on. It really is that important. It is where you choose the role you want to play with your clients, and be assured that if you don't actively do so, your client will choose for you. Allow the client to choose and you will likely be implementing what they have already decided needs to be done. Instead, be collaborative and think about what your relationship will look like. Then, identify your wants with this kind of relationship in mind. What do you want from your client to ensure you are more than just a pair of hands implementing their solution or just an expert implementing a solution your clients may not have the courage to implement on their own?

You teach your clients what it will be like to work with you based on what you are and aren't willing to accept, so write down your wants and bring them to your contracting meeting. Then, be willing to talk about them authentically and do what you agree to. As Block says in *Flawless Consulting*, "Consultants are always functioning as models of how to solve problems. The message contained in the way consultants act is much more powerful than their words." So, be what you want to see in your clients, and ask them to do the same.

Actions You Can Take Now

- **Start your show-up list.** Create a list of wants around how you show up with your clients and how you want your collaboration to work. Share these with your client as part of your next contracting process. Remember to be clear, be specific, and negotiate. You may not always get what you want, but you always have the right to ask.
- **Review your contracts.** Assess your current consulting agreements and decide if you need to recontract around your work together. If so, schedule a time to meet to recalibrate what your working relationship will look like moving forward. Use the steps outlined in this chapter to help you plan for your conversation. You may also reference the Planning a Contracting Meeting tool referenced in chapter 1 and located on this handbook's website at td.org/handbook-for-consultants to help you plan for your conversation.

About the Author

Beverly Crowell is a managing partner at Designed Learning, a Peter Block Company, overseeing operations, sales, and marketing. She has consulted with many Fortune 500 clients, providing a range of organization development work including strategic talent management, employee engagement and retention, career development, executive coaching, business planning and marketing strategy, content and product development, and psychometric assessments. Beverly is a noted speaker and has presented at the Conference Board's Employee Engagement Conferences, the Talent Management Council, and numerous corporate leadership events. She is a contributing author to *The Talent Management Handbook* and *Coaching for Leadership: Writings on Leadership From the World's Greatest Coaches*. Learn more at designedlearning.com or contact her at bcrowell@designedlearning.com.

APPENDIX A

List of Tools

We are excited to present you with tools that align with the content you've read in the handbook. Contributors to *ATD's Handbook for Consulting* developed tools to help you implement the concepts you learned in each chapter. The tools are available for download at td.org/handbook-for-consultants. You are free to use these tools for your personal use or your consulting work, as long as you maintain the copyright information and the "used with permission" designation every time you use them.

Chapter 1. What Is Still True
Peter Block
- Tool 1-1. Planning a Contracting Meeting

Chapter 2. Essential Consulting Skills for Trainers
Rita Bailey
- Tool 2-1. Rate Your Current Consulting Skills

Chapter 3. From TD to Consulting: Transition Success
Sarah Cannistra
- Tool 3-1. A One-Page Transition Plan

Chapter 4. The Business Side of Consulting: What I Wish I Knew Before Starting Out
Maurine Kwende
- Tool 4-1. Reflection Questions for New Consultants

Chapter 5. Taking the Plunge: Making the Big Leap Into Consulting
Bill Treasurer
- Tool 5-1. A Career Risk Action Plan
- Tool 5-2. The 5 Ps of Risk-Taking

Chapter 6. Clarify Your Why

Cindy Huggett

- Tool 6-1. Clarify Your Why: An Introspective Interview

Chapter 7. The 5 Ps of Business Strategy: Possibilities, People, Payoff, Process, and Pivots

Ann Herrmann-Nehdi

- Tool 7-1. The 5 Ps Business Strategy Tool

Chapter 8. Consulting in a Large Company

Jacob Kuczmanski

- Tool 8-1. Responsibilities by Level at a Large Consulting Firm

Chapter 9. Is a Boutique Consulting Practice Right for You?

Sy Islam and Mike Chetta

- Tool 9-1. Boutique Consulting Self-Reflection Worksheet

Chapter 10. The Independent Consultant: What's Your Role?

Sharon Wingron

- Tool 10-1. Consultant's Role Tip Sheet

Chapter 11. Naming Your Business

Maureen Orey

- Tool 11-1. Business Naming Worksheet

Chapter 12. Establishing the 21st-Century Consultant's Office

Jonathan Halls

- Tool 12-1. Checklist for Setting Up and Running the 21st-Century Consultant's Office

Chapter 13. The Consultant as Entrepreneur

Brian Washburn

- Tool 13-1. The Entrepreneurial Readiness Matrix

Chapter 34. Consulting Is a Relationship Business
Mike Kent
- Tool 34-1. Improving Your Relationship Skills

Chapter 35. How to Show Up and Stand Out as a Consultant
Beverly Crowell
- Tool 35-1. Using Clarifying Questions in the Contracting Meeting

APPENDIX B

Recommended Resources

Most talent development professionals and consultants are voracious readers. Our authors have identified books and other resources that have helped them as they developed and built their consulting practices. Many of the books are tried and true; however, there are a number of resources that will help you think differently, which may be just what you need to be a successful consultant.

Consulting Resources

Books and Articles

Geoff Bellman, *The Consultant's Calling: Bringing Who You Are to What You Do* (New York: Jossey-Bass, 2001).

Elaine Biech, *The New Business of Consulting: The Basics and Beyond* (Hoboken, NJ: John Wiley & Sons, 2019).

Elaine Biech, *The New Consultant's Quick Start Guide: An Action Plan for Your First Year in Business* (Hoboken, NJ: John Wiley & Sons, 2019).

Peter Block, *Flawless Consulting: A Guide to Getting Your Expertise Used* (San Francisco: Pfeiffer, 2022).

Stephen Cohen, *The Complete Guide to Building and Growing a Talent Development Firm* (Alexandria, VA: ATD Press, 2017).

Stephen Cohen, *12 Winning Strategies for Building a Talent Development Firm: An Action Planning Guide* (Minneapolis, MN: SLC Press, 2022).

William Curry, *Government Contracting: Ethical Promises and Perils in Public Procurement*, 3rd ed. (New York: Routledge, 2023).

David Fields, "Should You Hire a Dedicated Salesperson for Your Consulting Firm?" David A. Fields Consulting Group, August 23, 2017, davidafields.com/should-you-hire-a-dedicated-sales-person-for-your-consulting-firm.

Carter McNamara, *Field Guide to Consulting and Organizational Development: A Collaborative and Systems Approach to Performance, Change, and Learning* (Robbinsdale, MN: Authenticity Consulting, 2006).

Jack Phillips, *How to Build a Successful Consulting Practice* (New York: McGraw-Hill, 2006).

Ethan Rasiel, *The McKinsey Way: Using the Techniques of the World's Top Strategic Consultants to Help You and Your Business* (New York: McGraw-Hill, 1999).

Edgar Schein, *Humble Consulting: How to Provide Real Help Faster* (Oakland: Berrett-Koehler Publishers, 2016).

Andrew Sobel, *It Starts With Clients: Your 100-Day Plan to Build Lifelong Relationships and Revenue* (Hoboken, NJ: John Wiley & Sons, 2020).

Andrew Sobel and Jerold Panas, *Power Questions: Build Relationships, Win New Business, and Influence Others* (Hoboken, NJ: John Wiley & Sons, 2012).

Michael Zipursky, *Consulting Success: The Proven Guide to Start, Run and Grow a Successful Consulting Business*

Other Resources

ATD's Consulting Skills Certificate (td.org/education-courses/consulting-skills-certificate)

Consultant Connection Coffee Chat Community, an online discussion group that meets twice each month (c5consultantconnection.com)

Consulting Success's blog (consultingsuccess.com/blog)

Harvard Business Review (hbr.org)

McKinsey Quarterly (mckinsey.com/quarterly/overview)

Entrepreneurial Resources

Books and Articles

Steve Chandler and Rich Litvin, *The Prosperous Coach: Increase Income and Impact for You and Your Clients* (Anna Maria, FL: Maurice Bassett, 2013).

Dorie Clark, *Stand Out: How to Find Your Breakthrough Idea and Build a Following Around It* (New York: Penguin Random House, 2015).

Paulo Coelho, *The Alchemist* (New York: HarperCollins, 2014).

Edward Del Goizo, Seleste Lunsford, and Mark Marone, *Secrets of Top Performing Salespeople* (New York: McGraw Hill, 2003).

Annie Franceschi, *Establish Yourself: Brand, Streamline, and Grow Your Greatest Business* (Durham, NC: Greatest Story Publishing, 2022).

Richard Freed, Joseph Romano, and Shervin Freed, *Writing Winning Business Proposals* (New York: McGraw Hill, 2010).

Michael Gerber, *The E-Myth Revisited: Why Most Small Businesses Don't Work and What to Do About It* (New York: Harper Business, 2004).

Marshall Goldsmith, *What Got You Here Won't Get You There: How Successful People Become Even More Successful* (New York: Hyperion, 2007).

Adam Grant, *Give and Take: Why Helping Others Drives Our Success* (New York: Penguin Random House, 2013).

Lisa Earle McLeod, *Selling With Noble Purpose: How to Drive Revenue and Do Work That Makes You Proud* (Hoboken, NJ: John Wiley & Sons, 2020).

Donald Miller, *Building a StoryBrand: Clarify Your Message So Customers Will Listen* (New York: HarperCollins, 2017).

Joe Pulizzi, *Content Inc.: Start a Content First Business, Build a Massive Audience and Become Radically Successful (With Little to No Money)* (New York: McGraw Hill, 2021).

Al Ries and Laura Ries, *The 22 Immutable Laws of Branding: How to Build a Product or Service Into a World-Class Brand* (New York: HarperCollins, 2002).

Katrina Sawa, *Jumpstart Your New Business Now: The Entrepreneur's Guide to Starting and Growing a Profitable Business Doing What You Love* (Orangevale, CA: K. Sawa Marketing, 2018).

Tom Spitale and Mary Abbazia, *The Accidental Marketer: Power Tools for People Who Find Themselves in Marketing Roles* (Hoboken, NJ: John Wiley & Sons, 2014).

Other Resources

Entrepreneur.com, an online resource and support for startups (entrepreneur.com)

Business and Leadership Resources

Books

Chris Anderson, *The Long Tail: Why the Future of Business Is Selling Less of More* (New York: Hachette, 2006).

Jim Collins and Jerry Porras, *Built to Last: Successful Habits of Visionary Companies* (New York: HarperCollins, 2002).

Kevin Cope, *Seeing the Big Picture: Business Acumen to Build Your Credibility* (Austin, TX: Greenleaf Book Group Press, 2012).

Ned Herrmann and Ann Herrmann-Nehdi, *The Whole Brain Business Book: Unlocking the Power of Whole Brain Thinking in Organizations, Teams, and Individuals*, 2nd ed. (New York: McGraw Hill, 2015).

Gary Keller and Jay Papasan, *The One Thing: The Surprisingly Simple Truth About Extraordinary Results* (Austin, TX: Bard Press, 2012).

Dolores Kuchina-Musina and Benjamin McMartin, *Public Procurement for Innovation: Research and Development at the US Federal Level* (New York: Routledge, 2024).

Pamela McLean, *Self as Coach, Self as Leader: Developing the Best in You to Develop the Best in Others* (Hoboken, NJ: John Wiley & Sons, 2019).

Donald Miller, *Business Made Simple: 60 Days to Master Leadership, Sales, Marketing, Execution, Management, Personal Productivity and More* (New York: HarperCollins Leadership, 2021).

Terrence O'Connor and Dave Clark, *Understanding Government Contract Law* (Oakland: Berrett-Koehler Publishers, 2018).

Jack Pitzer and Khi Thai, *Introduction to Public Procurement* (New York: NIGP, 2009).

Meagan Reitz and John Higgins, *Speak Up: Say What Needs to Be Said and Hear What Needs to Be Heard* (London: Pearson, 2019).

Edgar Schein and Peter Schein, *Organizational Culture and Leadership*, 5th ed. (Hoboken, NJ: John Wiley & Sons, 2017).

Edgar Schein and Peter Schein, *Humble Leadership: The Power of Relationships, Openness, and Trust*, 2nd ed. (Oakland: Berrett-Koehler Publishers, 2023).

Simon Sinek, *Start With Why: How Great Leaders Inspire Everyone to Take Action* (New York: Penguin Books, 2009).

Michael Stelzner, *Writing White Papers: How to Capture Readers and Keep Them Engaged* (Poway, CA: WhitePaperSource Publishing, 2007).

Bill Treasurer, *Leadership: Two Words at a Time* (Oakland: Berrett-Koehler Publishers, 2022).

Other Resources

PwC Talent Exchange, a marketplace where consultants can connect to projects and opportunities within PricewaterhouseCoopers (talentexchange.pwc.com)

SCORE, volunteer mentors supporting small business owners (score.org)

StoryBrand, an online resource to help businesses clarify their messages (StoryBrand.com)

The Project Management Institute (pmi.org)

Personal Improvement and Professional Growth

Andy Andrews, *The Bottom of the Pool: Thinking Beyond Your Boundaries to Achieve Extraordinary Results* (Nashville, TN: W Publishing Group, 2019).

Leo Babauto, *The Power of Less: The Fine Art of Limiting Yourself to the Essential . . . in Business and in Life* (New York: Hyperion, 2009).

Elaine Biech, *Skills for Career Success: Maximizing Your Potential at Work* (Oakland: Berrett-Koehler Publishers, 2021).

Brené Brown, *Daring Greatly: How the Courage to Be Vulnerable Transforms the Way We Live, Love, Parent, and Lead* (New York: Avery, 2012).

Brené Brown, *Atlas of the Heart: Mapping Meaningful Connection and the Language of Human Experience* (New York: Random House, 2021).

Julia Cameron, *The Artists Way: A Spiritual Path to Higher Creativity* (New York: Tarcher and Perigee, 2016).

James Clear, *Atomic Habits: An Easy and Proven Way to Build Good Habits and Break Bad Ones* (New York: Avery, 2018).

Stephen Covey, *The 7 Habits of Highly Effective People* (New York: Simon and Schuster, 2020).

Rob Cross, *Beyond Collaborative Overload: How to Work Smarter, Get Ahead, and Restore Your Well-Being* (Boston: HBR Press, 2021).

Amy Cuddy, *Presence: Bringing Your Boldest Self to Your Biggest Challenges* (New York: Little, Brown Spark, 2015).

Hector García and Francesc Miralles, *Ikigai: The Japanese Secret to a Long and Happy Life* (New York: Penguin Life, 2017).

Marshall Goldsmith and Mark Reiter, *The Earned Life: Lose Regret, Choose Fulfillment* (New York: Currency, 2022).

Daniel Kahneman, *Thinking, Fast and Slow* (New York: Farrar, Straus and Giroux, 2011).

Maurine Kwende, *Dream Big and Live Your Dreams Boldly: Taking Action to Fulfill Your Passion and Purpose* (2021).

John Maxwell, *Put Your Dream to the Test: 10 Questions That Will Help You See It and Seize It* (New York: HarperCollins Leadership, 2011).

John Maxwell, *The 15 Invaluable Laws of Growth: Live Them and Reach Your Potential* (New York: Hachette Book Group, 2012).

Gorick Ng, *The Unspoken Rules: Secrets to Starting Your Career Off Right* (Boston: HBR Press, 2021).

David Ramsey, *Financial Peace Revisited* (New York: Viking, 2002).

Katrina Sawa, *Love Yourself Successful: A Woman's Step-by-Step Guide to Finally Taking Charge of Your Life and Designing the Business of Your Dreams* (Orangevale, CA: K. Sawa Marketing, 2022).

Brian Tracy, *Eat That Frog: 21 Great Ways to Stop Procrastinating and Get More Done in Less Time* (Oakland: Berrett-Koehler Publishers, 2017).

Bill Treasurer, *Right Risk: Ten Powerful Principles for Taking Giant Leaps With Your Life* (Oakland: Berrett-Koehler Publishers, 2003).

Christopher Worley, Thomas Williams, and Ed Lawler, *The Agility Factor: Building Adaptable Organizations for Superior Performance* (San Francisco: Jossey-Bass, 2014).

Coaching and Training

David van Adelsberg and Edward Trolley, *Running Training Like a Business: Delivering Unmistakable Value* (Oakland: Berrett-Koehler Publishers, 1999).

Elaine Biech, *The Art and Science of Training* (Alexandria, VA: ATD Press, 2016).

Elaine Biech, ed., *ATD's Handbook for Training and Talent Development* (Alexandria, VA: ATD Press, 2022).

Michael Bungay Stanier, *The Coaching Habit: Say Less, Ask More, and Change the Way You Lead Forever* (Toronto: Box of Crayons Press, 2016).

Diana Howles, *Next Level Virtual Training: Advance Your Facilitation* (Alexandria, VA: ATD Press, 2022).

Cindy Huggett, *Virtual Training Tools and Templates: An Action Guide to Live Online Learning*, 2nd ed. (Alexandria, VA: ATD Press, 2024).

Patti Phillips, Jack Phillips, and Rebecca Ray, *Proving the Value of Soft Skills: Measuring Impact and Calculating ROI* (Alexandria, VA: ATD Press, 2020).

References

Babauta, L. 2009. *The Power of Less: The Fine Art of Limiting Yourself to the Essential . . . in Business and in Life*. New York: Hachette Books.

Biech, E. 2003. *Marketing Your Consulting Services*. San Francisco: Pfeiffer.

Biech, E. 2019a. *The New Consultant's Quick Start Guide*. New York: Wiley.

Biech, E. 2019b. *The New Business of Consulting*. New York: Wiley.

Black Bean Industrial Marketing. 2023. "What 'Spending Money to Make Money' Really Means." April 4. blackbeanmarketing.com/insights/what-spending-money-to-make-money-really-means.

Block, P. 2022. *Flawless Consulting*. San Francisco: Pfeiffer.

Bridges, W., and S. Bridges. 2019. *Transitions: Making Sense of Life's Changes*, 40th Anniversary Ed. New York: Da Capo Lifelong.

Cameron, J. 2016. *The Artist's Way*, 30th Anniversary Ed. New York: TarcherPerigee.

CBInsights. 2021. "The Top 12 Reasons Startups Fail." CBInsights, August 3. cbinsights.com/research/report/startup-failure-reasons-top.

CFI Team. 2022. "Transaction Costs." CFI. corporatefinanceinstitute.com/resources/economics/transaction-costs.

Cohen, S.L. 2017. *The Complete Guide to Building and Growing a Talent Development Firm*. Alexandria, VA: ATD Press.

Connaughton, B. 2023. "How to Write a Winning Sales Proposal in 2023." Qwilr, November 7. qwilr.com/blog/how-to-write-sales-proposals.

Craig, W. 2018. "10 Things Transparency Can Do for Your Company." *Forbes*, October 16. forbes.com/sites/williamcraig/2018/10/16/10-things-transparency-can-do-for-your-company.

Cummings, T.G., and C.G. Worley. 2015. *Organization Development and Change*, 10th ed. Stamford, CT: Cengage Learning.

Delfino, D. 2023. "The Percentage of Businesses That Fail—and How to Boost Your Chances of Success." LendingTree, May 8. lendingtree.com/business/small/failure-rate.

Dickerson, J. 2016. "Legendary Sportscaster Vin Scully: Don't Be Afraid to Dream." *Face the Nation*, November 27. youtube.com/watch?v=Ow5imT-cVYs.

Fields, D.A. 2017. "Should You Hire a Dedicated Salesperson for Your Consulting Firm?" David A. Fields Consulting Group, August 23. davidafields.com/should -you-hire-a-dedicated-sales-person-for-your-consulting-firm.

Fryer, B. 2006. "Sleep Deficit: The Performance Killer." *Harvard Business Review*, October. hbr.org/2006/10/sleep-deficit-the-performance-killer.

Galbraith, J.R. 2014. *Designing Organizations: Strategy, Structure, and Process at the Business Unit and Enterprise Levels.* Hoboken, NJ: Jossey-Bass.

Geertz, C. 1974. "'From the Native's Point of View': On the Nature of Anthropological Understanding." *Bulletin of the American Academy of Arts and Sciences* 28(1): 26-45.

Gilbert-Ouimet, M., H. Ma, R. Glazier, C. Brisson, C. Mustard, and P.M. Smith. 2018. "Adverse Effect of Long Work Hours on Incident Diabetes in 7065 Ontario Workers Followed for 12 Years." *BMJ Open Diabetes Research and Care* 6(1): e000496.

Greenleaf, R. 1977. *Servant Leadership: A Journey Into the Nature of Legitimate Power and Greatness.* New York: Paulist Press.

Greenleaf, R. 2002. *Servant Leadership: A Journey Into the Nature of Legitimate Power and Greatness,* 25th Anniversary Ed. New York: Paulist Press.

Gupta, D. 2022. "The 9-Box Grid: Benefits and Limitations in 2023." Whatfix, February 15. whatfix.com/blog/9-box-grid.

Harter, J. 2022. "US Employee Engagement Drops for First Year in a Decade." Gallup Workplace Blog, January 7. gallup.com/workplace/388481/employee-engagement -drops-first-year-decade.aspx.

Kahneman, D. 2011. *Thinking, Fast and Slow.* New York: Farrar, Straus and Giroux.

Kirkpatrick, J.D., and W.K. Kirkpatrick. 2016. *Kirkpatrick's Four Levels of Training Evaluation.* Alexandria, VA: ATD Press.

Love, S. 2016. "How To Conduct a Lightning-Fast Needs Assessment Clients Will Love." ATD blog, June 15. td.org/insights/how-to-conduct-a-lightning-fast-needs -assessment-clients-will-love.

Maxwell, J. 2022. *The 15 Invaluable Laws of Growth: Live Them and Reach Your Potential.* New York: Center Street.

McDonald, R., and R. Bremner. 2020. "When It's Time to Pivot, What's Your Story: How to Sell Stakeholders on a New Strategy." *Harvard Business Review*, September-October.

Montgomery, C.A. 2012. *The Strategist: Be the Leader Your Business Needs.* New York: HarperCollins.

Mullins, J. 2011. "Consulting Careers: A Profile of Three Occupations." *Occupational Outlook Quarterly* 55(1): 12–19.

Parker, K., J.M. Horowitz, and R. Minkin. 2022. "COVID-19 Pandemic Continues to Reshape Work in America." Pew Research Center, February 16. pewresearch .org/social-trends/2022/02/16/covid-19-pandemic-continues-to-reshape-work -in-america.

Pega, F., et. al. 2021. "Global, Regional, and National Burdens of Ischemic Heart Disease and Stroke Attributable to Exposure to Long Working Hours for 194 Countries, 2000-2016: A Systematic Analysis From the WHO/ILO Joint Estimates of the Work-Related Burden of Disease and Injury." *Environment International* 154: September.

Pulizzi, J. 2015. *Content Inc.: How Entrepreneurs Use Content to Build Massive Audiences and Create Radically Successful Businesses.* New York: McGraw Hill.

Ramsey, D. 2003. *Financial Peace Revisited.* New York: Viking.

Scharmer, O. 2016. *Theory U: Leading From the Future As It Emerges,* 2nd ed. San Francisco: Berrett-Koehler.

Schein, E.H. 2013. *Humble Inquiry: The Gentle Art of Asking Instead of Telling.* Oakland, CA: Berrett-Kohler.

Seibert, D. 2018. "Average Proposal Win Rate When Responding to RFPs." The Seibert Group, January. proposalbestpractices.com/2018/01/average-proposal-win -rate-responding-to-rfps.

Sinek, S. 2009. "Start With Why—How Great Leaders Inspire Action." TEDx Talks, September 28. youtube.com/watch?v=u4ZoJKF_VuA.

Sinek, S. 2010. "How to Listen." Re:Focus blog, June. sinekpartners.typepad.com/refocus /2010/06/there-is-a-difference-between-listening-and-waiting-for-your-turn -to---speak-just-because-someone-can-hear-doesnt-mean-t.html.

Society for Human Resource Management (SHRM). 2022. "Succession Planning: What Is a 9-Box Grid?" shrm.org/resourcesandtools/tools-and-samples/hr-qa/pages /whatsa9boxgridandhowcananhrdepartmentuseit.aspx.

Statisca. 2022. "Management Consulting Market Size in the United States From 2012 to 2022, With a Forecast for 2023." Statista. statista.com/statistics/1234739 /management-consulting-market-size-usa.

Stelter, S. 2022. "Want to Advance in Your Career? Build Your Own Board of Directors." *Harvard Business Review*, May 9. hbr.org/2022/05/want-to-advance-in-your-career -build-your-own-board-of-directors.

Stenger, M. 2016. "5 Big Reasons You Need A Business Proposal." Open Colleges, July 17. opencolleges.edu.au/careers/blog/5-biggest-reasons-you-need-business-proposal.

Sull, D., C. Sull, and B. Zweig. 2022. "Toxic Culture Is Driving the Great Resignation." *MIT Sloan Management Review* 63(2): 1–9.

Torres, M. 2022. "Here's What Happens to Your Brain and Body if You Work More Than 40 Hours a Week." *Huffington Post*, November 4. huffpost.com/entry/working-long -hours-body_l_6362d3c1e4b0ae77bc20e611.

Wagner, J. "Social Media Organic Reach 2021: Who Actually Sees Your Content." Ignite Social Media, April 7. ignitesocialmedia.com/social-media-strategy/social-media -organic-reach-2021-who-actually-sees-your-content.

Worley, C., T. Williams, and E. Lawler. 2014. *The Agility Factor*. San Francisco: Jossey-Bass.

Index

In this index, *f* denotes figure and *t* denotes table.

A

co-working spaces, 366
credibility, 24, 437
   See also visibility
credit card benefits, 149–150
CRM (client relationship management), 232*t*
Crowell, B., 463, 471
CTA (call to action), 330–331
culture in organizations, 393
   See also Star Model (Galbraith)
"culture of tell," 389–390
Cummings, T., 212
curse of knowledge, 338
"customer is always right" mindset, 416, 463
Customer Relationship Process (Amplify Growth), 315–320
customer relations management apps, 146, 147
customer reviews, 439, 440
customers, 416–417
   See also client entries
Cybersecurity Maturity Model Certification (CMMC) 2.0 program, 253

D

daily rate, for fee setting, 278
Dassat, H., 362
data collection and analysis, 188–191, 319–320
   See also assessments; client research; evaluation of results; market analysis; market research; Star Model (Galbraith)
data management, trainers and, 25–26
data presentation, 191
DCAA CAS. *See* Defense Contract Audit Agency (DCAA) CAS
DCMA (Defense Contract Management Agency), 257
debriefings. *See* feedback meetings and follow-up meetings; perspectives, collecting multiple
Dec, D., 139
Defense Contract Audit Agency (DCAA) CAS, 256, 257
Defense Contract Management Agency (DCMA), 257
defense federal acquisition regulations supplements (DFARS), 250, 251
define and agree phase, in consulting process, 186–188
DEI (diversity, equity, and inclusion) consulting, 221–222
deliverables section, for business proposals, 334
deliver and decide phase, in consulting process, 190–193
design and implement phase, in consulting process, 193–197

design thinking principles, 207–208
developmental evaluation, 208
DFARS. *See* defense federal acquisition regulations supplements (DFARS)
dialogic organizational development, 213
disadvantaged business status, 253
DiSC, 124, 129, 130, 241*t*, 351
discover and analyze phase, in consulting process, 188–190
disempowerment, factors leading to, 8
disengage and review phase, in consulting process, 197–199
diversity, equity, and inclusion (DEI) consulting, 221–222
domain availability, 136, 306
Douglas, R., 164, 269, 369, 380–381
Dream Big and Live Your Dreams Boldly (Kwende), 50
dreams, sharing, 50
Drucker, P., 426
Dweck, C., 3

E

ebb associates, 172, 185
Ecko, M., 298
efficiency versus effectiveness, 391–392
elevator speeches, 300, 310
email and client contact management tools, 309
email marketing, 304–305, 455–456
email marketing systems (EMS), 232*t*
emails. *See* communication systems
email templates, 456
empathy, 202, 203
employee performance measures. *See* human resources instruments and tools
EMS. *See* email marketing systems (EMS)
engagement and exit surveys, 236
entrepreneurial opportunities, 112, 425
   See also boutique consulting; solo practice consulting
Entrepreneur Readiness Matrix, 157–165, 166
entrepreneurs, consultants as, 153–167, 397–406
entry and contracting phase. *See* define and agree phase, in consulting process
entry strategies, 106
   See also transitioning to consulting
envelope process, 86
ethics. *See* compliance and ethics; integrity
evaluation of results, 197–198, 200, 239–240
   See also feedback and survey tools
evaluations, of passive income, 378–379

About the Editor

Elaine Biech, CPTD fellow, believes excellence isn't optional. Her passion is helping others achieve their passion. She specializes in maximizing individual, team, and organizational effectiveness using her expertise in OD, training, and consulting. Elaine has designed and delivered thousands of training courses and apps. Highlights of her career include designing and implementing the first process improvement programs for the Newport News Shipbuilding Company and McDonalds; the first creativity program for Hershey Chocolate; and one of the world's first virtual training sessions in 1985 for NASA.

Elaine's been called a titan of the training industry and has published 89 books, including *The Art & Science of Training*, which was a *Washington Post* number 1 bestseller. She has presented for 38 consecutive years at ATD's International Conference & EXPO, and has been featured in dozens of publications, including the *Wall Street Journal, Harvard Management Update*, the *Washington Post*, and *Fortune*.

Elaine has been active with ATD since 1982—she's served on the national board of directors, designed ATD's first training certificate program, was ATD's inaugural CPTD Fellow designee, and most recently was the principal author of ATD's *TDBoK Guide*. A talent development thought leader, Elaine was the recipient of ATD's 1992 Torch Award, 2004 Volunteer-Staff Partnership Award, 2006 Bliss Memorial Award, and the 2020 Distinguished Contribution to Talent Development Award. In addition, she was the recipient of ISA's 2001 Spirit Award, 2012 Outstanding Contributor Award, and 2022 Thought Leader Award. She was also the recipient of Wisconsin's Women's Mentor Award and sponsors several scholarship funds. Elaine currently serves on the board of directors for ISA, the Association of Learning Providers, and the board of governors for the Center for Creative Leadership.

Elaine stays busy mentoring new consultants, coaching individuals about publishing their first books, and searching for the next book she wants to write.

About ATD

atd The Association for Talent Development (ATD) is the world's largest association dedicated to those who develop talent in organizations. Serving a global community of members, customers, and international business partners in more than 100 countries, ATD champions the importance of learning and training by setting standards for the talent development profession.

Our customers and members work in public and private organizations in every industry sector. Since ATD was founded in 1943, the talent development field has expanded significantly to meet the needs of global businesses and emerging industries. Through the Talent Development Capability Model, education courses, certifications and credentials, memberships, industry-leading events, research, and publications, we help talent development professionals build their personal, professional, and organizational capabilities to meet new business demands with maximum impact and effectiveness.

One of the cornerstones of ATD's intellectual foundation, ATD Press offers insightful and practical information on talent development, training, and professional growth. ATD Press publications are written by industry thought leaders and offer anyone who works with adult learners the best practices, academic theory, and guidance necessary to move the profession forward.

We invite you to join our community. Learn more at td.org.